WORLD AND LIFE AS ONE

Cultural Memory
in
the
Present

Mieke Bal and Hent de Vries, Editors

WORLD AND LIFE AS ONE
Ethics and Ontology in Wittgenstein's Early Thought

Martin Stokhof

STANFORD UNIVERSITY PRESS

STANFORD, CALIFORNIA

Stanford University Press
Stanford, California

© 2002 by the Board of Trustees of the
Leland Stanford Junior University. All rights reserved.

Library of Congress Cataloging-in-Publication Data
Stokhof, M. J. B. (Martin J. B.)
　World and life as one : ethics and ontology in
Wittgenstein's early thought / Martin Stokhof.
　　p.　cm. — (Cultural memory in the present)
　Includes bibliographical references (p.　) and index.
　ISBN 0-8047-4221-9 (cloth) — ISBN 0-8047-4222-7 (paper)
　1. Wittgenstein, Ludwig, 1889–1951. Tractatus logico-
philosophicus.　2. Ontology.　3. Ethics.　I. Title.
II. Series.
B3376.W563 S76 2002
192—dc21   2002002460

Original printing 2002

Last figure below indicates year of this printing:
11　10　09　08　07　06　05　04　03　02

Typeset by BookMatters in 11/13.5 Adobe Garamond

For Clara

Contents

   Preface xv
   Note on Translations xvii

1 Backgrounds 1
   Introduction 1
   The Problem 4
   Logic 10
   Ethics 24

2 Main Themes 35
   Aims 35
      The Linguistic Turn 37
      The Ground-Plan of the 'Tractatus' 38
   Ontology 40
      Logical Atomism 40
      States of Affairs and Objects 44
      Structure and Form 49
   Picturing 52
      Pictures as Facts 52
      Pictorial Form and Pictorial Relation 53
      Logical Form 55
      Truth and Falsity 57
      Saying and Showing 58
      Thoughts as Pictures 60

x   Contents

    Language   63
      Sentences as Pictures   63
      Creativity and Compositionality   69
      Signs and Symbols   71
      The Realm of the Meaningful   75
        Elementary Sentences and Names   75
        Complex Sentences   80
    Logic   85
      Logic as Foundation   85
      Logic as Analysis   89
      Logic as System   91
    Nonlogical Necessity   97
      Mathematics   97
      Natural Science   99
      Conceptual Analysis   101
      The 'Tractatus'   102

3 Language and Ontology   104
    The Question of Realism   104
    Simplicity: The Argument from Language   110
      Determinateness of Meaning   111
      Semantic Ineffability   115
      Reconstructing the Argument   117
    The Nature of Objects   120
      Objects as a Logical Category   121
      Other Interpretations   126
      Conclusion   129
    Some Other Views   129
      Maslow: Instrumentalism   132
        Excursus I: Wittgenstein and Logical Empiricism   134
        Excursus II: Wittgenstein and the Vienna Circle   141
        Back to Maslow's Interpretation   144

   Stenius's Interpretation 153
   Ishiguro and McGuinness: Structuralism 154
   Malcolm: Physicalism 171
  The Realism of the *Tractatus* 180

4 Ethics 186
  Introduction 186
  The Will 191
   Individual and Metaphysical Subject 192
   Knowing Subject and Willing Subject 194
   Solipsism and Realism 196
   The Will and the Willing Subject 203
  The Nature of the Good 210
   Ineffability 210
   Will, Action, Value 212
   Good Will 214
   The Happy Life 216
   Living in the Present 220
  Ethics and Morality 225
   Compassion and the Other 225
   Moral Consequences 227
  "World and Life as One" 234
   The Linguistic Nature of Transcendence 235
   Ethical Experience 239
   The Proper Interpretation of Ontology 241
  Concluding Remarks 244

Notes 253
Works Cited 303
Index 313

Ein Gott vermags. Wie aber, sag mir, soll
ein Mann ihm folgen durch die schmale Leier?
Sein Sinn ist Zwiespalt. An der Kreuzung zweier
Herzwege steht kein Tempel für Apoll.

Gesang, wie du ihn lehrst, ist nicht Begehr,
nicht Werbung um ein endlich noch Erreichtes;
Gesang ist Dasein. Für den Gott ein Leichtes.
Wann aber *sind* wir? Und wann wendet *er*

an unser Sein die Erde und die Sterne?
Dies *ists* nicht, Jüngling, daß du liebst, wenn auch
die Stimme dann den Mund dir aufstößt,—lerne

vergessen, daß du aufsangst. Das verrinnt.
In Wahrheit singen, ist ein andrer Hauch.
Ein Hauch um nichts. Ein Wehn im Gott. Ein Wind.

—Rainer Maria Rilke, *Die Sonnette an Orpheus*

Preface

This book has been long in the making. Its main thesis, that Wittgenstein's ethical views provide an argument for a language-dependent interpretation of the ontology of the *Tractatus*, occurred to me back in 1988. The larger part of the book grew out of a series of courses for undergraduate philosophy students. This (partly) explains the book's character: it is not a monograph intended for Wittgenstein scholars; rather it is written for readers who have some familiarity with Wittgenstein's early thought but who have not studied in great detail either the *Tractatus* or the secondary literature on it. This work, therefore, contains a global overview of the main lines of thought of the *Tractatus* so far as these are important for the main argument of the book. It uses extensive quotations in order to be reasonably self-contained.

When I started studying the *Tractatus* and some of the secondary literature, I felt that most authors did not pay enough attention to the ethical part of the work. I was startled, for example, to observe that the index of David Pears's first volume of *The False Prison*, a thorough, serious, and in all other respects highly admirable work, did not contain an entry "ethics." Although no contemporary scholar will dare not quote the letter to Ficker, in which Wittgenstein mentions the "ethical point" of the *Tractatus*, it is still common to present just a short, and in most cases rather unsatisfactory, sketch of what Wittgenstein's views on the matter are taken to be. No attempt is made to link in a systematic way those views to the rest of the work. This book is meant to provide a counterpoint by discussing extensively the relation between two central aspects of the *Tractatus*: ontology and ethics.

I would like to thank collectively the students who attended my courses for the clarifications they insisted on and the objections they raised.

They forced me to try to formulate my ideas in a way that I hope is slightly less impressionistic than they occurred to me. I thank Johan van Benthem, Jaap van der Does, Jelle Gerbrandy, Arnaud Glaudemans, and Harry Stein, who read (parts of) the manuscript and provided valuable feedback. I owe special thanks to Göran Sundholm, who among other things, suggested to me the book's title.

MARTIN STOKHOF
ILLC/Department of Philosophy
Universiteit van Amsterdam
May 2002

Note on Translations

Throughout this work all translations from primary sources—that is, from the *Tractatus*, the *Notebooks*, and other works by Wittgenstein, as well as passages from works by Frege, Schopenhauer, Eckehart, and others—are my own. I have not used the standard translation of the *Tractatus* by Pears and McGuinness and that of the *Notebooks* by Anscombe for the following reasons. The Pears and McGuinness translation of the *Tractatus* and Anscombe's translation of the *Notebooks* make certain, unfortunate choices. One example is the uniform translation of the German *Satz* as "proposition," where the German term has a variety of meanings, including "sentence," "theorem," and, indeed, "proposition." In some cases this choice leads to translations that hamper a correct understanding (for example, in *Tractatus* 4.025, where Wittgenstein talks about translation and obviously means a relation between sentences, not propositions). Another example concerns the pair of expressions *Sinn* and *Bedeutung*. Pears and McGuinness translate these as "sense" and "meaning," respectively, which sometimes leads to akward results (for example, "sense of the world" as a translation of "Sinn der Welt," and "a name means an object" as a translation of "der Name bedeutet den Gegenstand"). I have chosen to use the more familiar "meaning" and "reference." Furthermore, while reading these standard translations, I was struck by the fact that they often do not do justice to Wittgenstein's stylistic persona. At times Wittgenstein's German is quite extraordinary. Pears and McGuinness and Anscombe have a tendency to "overtranslate" by producing more polished English than the original German justifies. I have tried to retain the tone of Wittgenstein's German as much as possible.

1

Backgrounds

INTRODUCTION

This book concerns itself with the relation between ontology and ethics in Wittgenstein's *Tractatus* and defends a particular interpretation of Wittgenstein's ontological views, arguing that such an interpretation is required by his views on ethics and their consequences for everyday moral behavior. If we regard the *Tractatus* as a coherent whole, that is, as a work whose component parts are systematically related, then a proper interpretation of the ethical part forces us to consider this interpretation of its ontology.

This book's argument is part of a broader investigation concerned with the question of realism in Wittgenstein's work. In what sense and to what extent is Wittgenstein a realist? How do the early and the later works compare in this respect? We want to defend the following position: both Wittgenstein's early works (the *Notebooks* and the *Tractatus*) as well as his later writings (the *Philosophical Investigations*, the *Remarks of the Foundations of Mathematics*, and *On Certainty*) are uniquely characterized by a commitment to what is essentially human in the subjects they address. Ultimately, the content and role of various key notions, such as meaning and rule but also world and value, depend on what we are: on our nature as human beings as well as on our physical and social surroundings, and on the ways in which these interact. Our experience as humans, both of the world and of ourselves, is the starting and end point of almost all of Wittgenstein's investigations. And he primarily concerns himself with the role various notions play in our human experience.

This argument positions Wittgenstein's early and late work differently than is commonly assumed with respect to the issue of realism. According to prevailing opinion the *Tractatus* can be regarded as a prototypical realistic theory. By contrast, the *Philosophical Investigations* are widely considered to be one of the sources of modern antirealist thinking. The problem with this received view is that it fails to take into account the characteristics of both the early and the later work. This is not to deny that there are substantial differences between the early and the later work. One of the most important differences is that whereas the early work is monistic and absolutistic, the later work is pluralistic and, to some extent, relativistic. The *Tractatus* is an enterprise that seeks to unravel one, unvarying, necessary, common core in all of language. In the later work this goal is abandoned, and description of "the motley of language" takes its place. But it is important to notice also that despite this fundamental difference in outlook there is a subtle "undercurrent" common to all of Wittgenstein's work: it maintains an emphasis—at some points more and at others less explicitly—on what is decisively human in many of the topics that it addresses.

The challenge, then, is to show that such an undercurrent does indeed exist. This book addresses itself to this challenge, aiming to show that for various reasons, one of which is provided by a proper interpretation of the ethical part, the ontology of the *Tractatus* has to be read in a distinctly nonrealistic way. The ontology is not intended as a theory of the fundamental components and structures of reality per se, but rather as a description of the structure of reality that is presupposed by language and thought. It does not characterize reality as it ultimately is, but rather how reality appears in the medium of human language and thought. To put it differently, the *Tractatus* deals with reality so far as it can be accessed by the discursive mind. Complementary to that, the ethics provides a model of the world as it bears on value, which is tied to human action. However abstract the analyses in the *Tractatus* may be, they are informed by concerns with what is human.

The basic tenet of the *Tractatus* is monism: there is only one way in which mind, language, and reality harmonize. In his later work Wittgenstein leaves room for more than one way of dealing with "reality," each particular way constituting within its own sphere a system of concepts, meanings, and rules not applicable outside. This transition from monism to pluralism certainly constitutes a major difference between Wittgenstein's early and later work. But it is important to notice that the later work is not radically relativistic. Wittgenstein stresses that external factors, notably nature in the two senses indicated above—our human nature and physical nature—place important restrictions on the systems of rules and concepts of which we can avail ourselves. Hence, in terms of a "realism-antirealism" opposition it seems that the earlier work cannot be classified as straightforwardly realistic while the later work cannot be said to be completely antirealistic either. The positions defended in each phase differ, but in more subtle ways than this dichotomy allows us to express.

With regard to Wittgenstein's views on ethics, it seems that a similar story can be told. However, it is more difficult to tell. For one thing, since he has not given any really systematic treatment of this topic, it is hard to establish the exact contents of Wittgenstein's views. In the earlier work remarks on ethics are relatively many, at least compared with the later work. Here we can draw on the *Tractatus* itself, the *Notebooks* and the "Lecture on Ethics," which dates from 1929. Other sources are the conversations with Engelmann (see Engelmann 1967) and with Schlick and Waismann, recorded by Waismann. As for Wittgenstein's later ideas, what we have at our disposal are the "Lectures on Religious Belief" and scattered remarks from various manuscripts and notebooks, a selection of which were published as *Culture and Value*. Apart from that we have to make do with indirect evidence, mainly to be drawn from the recollections of various people.[1] However, despite the fact that it is hard to get a comprehensive view on what Wittgenstein's thoughts on these matters are, it seems clear that here, too, there is much continuity between the earlier and the later work. This continuity derives from the same undercurrent pointed out above: Wittgenstein's interest in, we might almost say "devotion" to, what is human.

In short, there are both important resemblances and major differences between Wittgenstein's early thought and his later work. The differences are many and they have received a lot of attention in the literature. That is not to say that the resulting picture of "two Wittgensteins" has been universally

4   *Backgrounds*

adopted.[2] The resemblances are less, both in number and in perspicuity. The essentially language-dependent character of reality, traditionally a self-sufficient category, is one. The insight that our cognitive capacities are constrained by external factors, and yet do not exhaust our human nature, is another. One reason to think that the relationship between ethics and ontology constituted an ongoing concern for Wittgenstein lies in the objectivity of values he endorses. The most commonly held ontological positions—(metaphysical) realism and antirealism—both present a problem here. Realism seems to leave only reductionism and emotivism as options. Either values are facts, or they are mere expressions of noncognitive attitudes. In either case there is no room for an objective status of ethical values. Antirealism, by contrast, runs the risk of ethical relativism, certainly a position Wittgenstein does not take. If one wants to secure the objective nature of ethical values, then one needs to find an ontological position that is consistent with such a view. Both the *Tractatus*, as well as some elements of the later work, notably *On Certainty*, can (also) be viewed as attempts to come to terms with this problem. As a matter of fact, there seems to be continuity in Wittgenstein's thinking on this issue, his later thought gradually evolving from his earlier views, while keeping much of what stimulated and inspired them. And the differences in his views on ethics, such as they are, can be correlated with the different positions Wittgenstein takes toward language and its relation to reality.

A fully worked out defense of this broader thesis is beyond the scope of this book. Here we concentrate on one piece of the puzzle: the relationship between ontology and ethics in Wittgenstein's early work. Before proceeding with that, however, it may be helpful the sketch the background against which this question is to be answered.

THE PROBLEM

Our starting point is that the *Tractatus* is both a logical work as well as an ethical undertaking. The ontology is part of the logical theory, and we will study in detail the role it plays in the tractarian theory of language. That Wittgenstein intended the *Tractatus* to have ethical significance is nowadays a commonplace, but early readings of the *Tractatus*, for example, those in the tradition of logical empiricism, have been so occupied with bending its logical theory to their own needs that the ethical part was simply ignored, or brushed aside as a remainder from an earlier, immature period.[3] The (implicit) suggestion seems to be that Wittgenstein's views on ethics were, if not written, then at least conceived before he developed his logical insights and that hence the two are independent. Today, however, no one will want to deny that there are two sides to the *Tractatus*: the logical and the ethical. Many would even admit that so far as Wittgenstein's own intentions are concerned the latter is certainly no less important than the former.[4] However, that being so, many modern commentators still do not recognize any intrinsic relationship between these two sides of the *Tractatus*. To a certain extent this should come as no surprise. For what the *Tractatus* has to say about ethics is so condensed that it may very well appear to be little. It seems to characterize ethics only negatively, by indicating what ethics is not, but it does not seem to allow for a more positive interpretation, that is, for a reading in which what it says makes for practical moral consequences. Thus one may very well be tempted, *pace* Wittgenstein and all that this part of the *Tractatus* meant to him, to attach little value to it and to concentrate on the seemingly more rewarding study of the logical and semantical issues.[5]

However, such an approach does not do justice to the *Tractatus*: not to Wittgenstein's intentions in writing the book in the form he did, not to what he actually manages to convey in the few enigmatic phrases on ethics that it contains, and, most importantly, not to the internal coherence of the work. Despite appearances to the contrary the remarks on ethics in the *Tractatus* can be interpreted in a positive manner, that is, in such a way that at least the outlines of a substantial view on ethics can be traced and some connection with actual moral practices can be construed. Furthermore, this positive reading of the ethics has important consequences for the interpretation of other parts of the book, notably the part that deals with ontology. Some key features of the ontology can be understood only against the background of such a positive reading of the ethics.[6]

This way of viewing the *Tractatus* and its internal structure is in line with Wittgenstein's intentions as they are expressed for example in the following letter written to Ludwig Ficker in 1919:

> ... the point of the book is an ethical one. I once wanted to include in the preface a sentence that is now actually not there, but that I will write to you now since it

might be a key for you: I wanted to write that my work consists of two parts: of the one that is present here and of everything that I have *not* written. Precisely this second part is the important one. For the ethical is delimited as it were from the inside by my book; and I am convinced that *strictly* speaking it can ONLY be delimited in this way. In short I think: everything of which *many* nowadays are blethering, I have defined in my book by being silent about it.... I would recommend you to read the *preface* and the *conclusion* since these express the point most directly.[7]

This does not leave much room for doubt about Wittgenstein's concerns. It clearly indicates that whatever importance he attached to the logical theory he develops in the *Tractatus*, he considers the "point of the book" not to be a logical one, nor an ontological one for that matter. Rather, the logical part is subsidiary to the ethical goal. Now there may very well be some exaggeration in what Wittgenstein is saying here, but we must also not misunderstand him. What he says is not that the *Tractatus* is a book about ethics, in the sense that it develops an ethical theory. It is "the point" of the book that is described as ethical, not its contents or subject matter. Of course, the *Tractatus* is about meaning and truth tables and Russell's theory of types and identity and all that, not much of which is in any way intrinsically ethical in nature. Neither should we interpret Wittgenstein as saying that these logical matters are not of any interest as such. After all, he was not the kind of person to devote years of intensive study and excruciatingly hard work to matters that he considered futile and of no value. But what does come out clearly from the passage cited above is that he feels that what he has done in the sphere of logic and language has enabled him to solve an important problem, that of unambiguously and definitively assigning ethics its own territory. That is to say, the views on logic and meaning and on all that is subsidiary to that which the *Tractatus* contains have a direct bearing on what ethics is concerned with, a point indeed poignantly expressed in the conclusion of the book. From these considerations, it seems safe to conclude that at least according to its author there is an intrinsic relationship between the logical and the ethical part of the *Tractatus*: it is a coherent whole in which the various parts are tightly connected, not a loose collection of hard logical results and some aphorisms on mystical matters. Of course, authors may make mistakes when assessing their own work, but it seems reasonable to start from the assumption that here that is not the case, unless proof of the contrary is forthcoming. So we take it that the first premise of the present undertaking, that the *Tractatus* is a coherent whole, is not obviously wrong.

Let us then proceed to the second premise, that the ethical part can be given a positive interpretation. It seems that the *Tractatus* itself contains several remarks that indicate that according to Wittgenstein himself his outline of the ethical is indeed more substantial than a mere characterization *ex negativo*.[8] Compare the following two remarks:

The meaning of the world must lie outside of it. In the world everything is the way it is and everything happens the way it happens: *in* it there is no value. (6.41)

There must indeed be some kind of ethical reward and ethical punishment, but these must lie in the action itself. (6.422)[9]

What is important to note is that, although Wittgenstein emphatically denies that ethical value can be situated in the world, in the sense that some situations or events in the world are ethically more valuable than others, he does not deny that there is such a thing as ethical value, which is presumed to be connected with our actions. This may strike us as a blatant inconsistency and may hence entice us to dismiss this part of the *Tractatus* as "irredeemable nonsense," but the real challenge is, of course, to try to make sense of it.[10] Doing so will involve providing an interpretation of the notion of "world" that Wittgenstein is using here, which will show, on the one hand, why value is said not to be in the world, and, on the other hand, how value can be regarded as intrinsically connected with our actions, which, after all, are in the world.

Thus it appears that an interpretation of the ontology of the *Tractatus* is an essential ingredient of a proper analysis of its ethical part. This means that we will have to investigate in detail the various possible interpretations of the ontology and that we must examine to what extent each of them allows for a suitable interpretation of the ethical part. For the latter to be feasible, we must, of course, also closely study the contents of the positive interpretation of the ethical part.

It will become clear that the ontology of the *Tractatus* cannot be analyzed in isolation, without taking into account the parts dealing with logic and language. These three—language, logic, and ontology—are intimately connected and an investigation into one of them will automatically lead to a consideration of the others. This means that although we focus on the relationship between ontology and ethics, we will also have to pay some attention to the logical and grammatical aspects. Given that language and ontology turn out to be interwoven aspects of the tractarian system, an important subsidiary question arises: What is the relationship between language and ontology exactly? We know that the two are connected by means of the mechanism of picturing, but which component in this system is dominant? In effect, this question allows us to divide various interpretations of the ontology into two fundamentally different classes. First there are those that assume that the ontology is primary and that language takes on its fundamental features from reality. Second, we have interpretations that, to the contrary, hold that it is language, or logic, that takes precedence and that hence the ontology is not a theory of reality as it is, but only of reality as it appears in the medium of language. The first kind of interpretation can be called realist, in the commonsense or "naive" sense of the word. These interpretations differ among each other in what kind of reality (physical, phenomenal) they take the ontology of the *Tractatus* to describe. But they share the assumption that it is a theory of reality on its own terms. The second one is more aptly dubbed "critically realist," in a loosely Kantian sense. Here, too, there are substantial differences between the various analyses, but they have in common that they view language as the dominant element in the relation between language and reality.[11]

From what was said above, it will be clear that the analysis presented in this book falls within the second class. It differs from other interpretations by bringing into play yet a third component: ethics. As we will see, both on the level of reality as well as on that of language the *Tractatus* recognizes only contingencies. Reality consists of contingent situations, that is, situations that have both the possibility to be realized and the possibility not to be realized. In other words, there are no necessary situations, which obtain in every world, nor impossible ones, which do not obtain in any world. Analogously, every meaningful sentence is contingent: there is a world in which it is true and there is a world in which it is false. This follows immediately from the picture theory of meaning. Both ingredients of the tractarian system can be defended, although neither has been widely accepted. Here the important thing to notice is that this all-pervading contingency creates a problem. For apparently there are necessary truths, necessary properties and absolute, necessary ethical and aesthetical values. In other words, the question arises, in a world that consists only of contingencies, what is the status of logical and mathematical laws, conceptual relations, ethical and aesthetical values? Or, to phrase the same point in grammatical terms, if the contingent exhausts the meaningful, what status do logical and mathematical sentences have, and what are ethical and aesthetical sentences about?

A substantial part of the *Tractatus* is devoted to an exploration of these consequences. The bulk of this investigation is devoted to logic: Wittgenstein develops an original and ingenious theory of the nature of logical laws and logical symbolism, features of which survive in modern logical doctrine to a certain extent. Mathematics is treated in the same outspoken manner, but far less elaborately. Some intriguing remarks about physical laws are made, and finally Wittgenstein treats the status of ethics (and that of aesthetics, but not as a separate subject). Important for us at this juncture is what Wittgenstein says about the nature of ethics.[12]

A key feature is what might be called the "ethically contingent" character of the world. This is the result of two fundamental assumptions that underlie Wittgenstein's thinking in the *Tractatus*, namely that there is only logical necessity and that ethical values are not contingent. The first assumption holds that the only necessary relationships between situations are logical ones. All other apparently necessary connections between situations are in fact of a different nature: from a logical point of view they are accidental relations. The second point is not argued for, but simply assumed. In 6.41, part of which was quoted above, Wittgenstein says:

> If there is any value that has value, it must lie outside what happens and is the case. For everything that happens and is the case is accidental.
> What makes it nonaccidental cannot lie *in* the world; for if it did, then that in its turn would be accidental.
> It must lie outside the world. (6.41)

So whatever situations occur in the world, whatever is the result of our actions or the cause of them, they cannot be the locus of ethical values. But, this does not mean that Wittgenstein accepts some kind of moral nihilism, claiming that there are no ethical values to begin with. Values are real and exist in our acting. How this is to be interpreted will be the subject of further investigation. Here the important thing to note is that for a naive realist it is at first sight far more difficult to account for these features of the *Tractatus* than it is for the critical realist. For the former is unable to acknowledge an intrinsic connection between ontology and ethics. The position of the critical realist offers a better starting point here. It is in this sense that that a positive interpretation of the ethics constitutes an argument for a particular interpretation of the ontology.

10   *Backgrounds*

LOGIC

For a long time the *Tractatus* was read exclusively as a treatise on logic and language. To a large extent this was due to the adoption of the book by the logical empiricists of the Vienna Circle, who regarded it as a kind of manifesto of their logical revival of the older positivist ideas. Especially the alleged antimetaphysical trend of the *Tractatus* was, or so they thought, in perfect agreement with their own attitude toward traditional philosophy.[13] Wittgenstein had serious doubts about this association of his work with that of the logical empiricists; at the same time he did engage, albeit in his own way and on his own terms, in conversations with several of them, notably Schlick and Waismann. The atmosphere of the meetings that took place in Vienna and several other locations from 1927 to 1932 must have been a confusing mixture of recognition and deep misunderstanding.[14] Yet, although Wittgenstein later on tended to downplay the importance of his contacts with Schlick and Waismann, it must not be concluded that the logical empiricists were altogether wrong in their appropriation of the *Tractatus*. After all, it is a work that presents a new view on philosophy and that bases this on logic. As Wittgenstein says in 4.112: "The aim of philosophy is the logical clarification of thoughts."

Such claims can easily be misunderstood. What seems to be common to both Wittgenstein and the logical empiricists is the place they assign to logic in philosophy and the use that they want to make of it: the clarification of thought and therewith the elimination of traditional, speculative metaphysics. But what divides them is why they want logic to play this role. For the logical empiricists the enterprise of logical analysis was meant to contribute to the establishment of a "scientific worldview." For Wittgenstein the aim was altogether different: the safekeeping of the most important aspect of human affairs, ethics, from rationalizing thought. He has little sympathy for the notion of a scientific worldview. In 6.371 he claims that "the entire modern view of the world is based on an illusion, namely that the so-called laws of nature constitute explanations of natural phenomena." This makes perfectly clear, so clear that it is hard to see that someone might not understand it, that the logical empiricists and Wittgenstein differ radically in their conception of the goal logical analysis is to serve. But, and this surely must be kept in mind too, Wittgenstein did see an important role for logic in his enterprise and in this respect he did side with the logical empiricists.

This may explain also why many people outside the logical empiricist movement have always interpreted the *Tractatus* primarily as a logical enterprise. Early commentators such as Anscombe, Black, Maslow, Stenius, and Pitcher are all interested in the *Tractatus* mainly as a work that showed how logic could be applied as a tool in philosophical analysis. For Russell, too, the subject of the *Tractatus* is logic, as is evident from the introduction he wrote to the book. Wittgenstein's approach to ethics is briefly touched on, but not very favorably.[15] More recent introductions tend to stress the logical aspects also, most of them almost exclusively.[16] Only rarely does one find an author who displays a real affinity with the other, ethical part of the book and its relationship with the logical and ontological doctrines.[17]

However, this is not to suggest that the logical approach is wrong. Whatever it is besides that, the *Tractatus* is also a logical treatise and a proper understanding of the book as a whole cannot be gained without a proper understanding of the main lines of the logical doctrines it expounds. The work of Janik and Toulmin, along with the publication of other manuscripts of Wittgenstein that became available from the 1960s onward, did much to change the reception of the *Tractatus*. No longer could it be read as an analytical, let alone as a logical empiricist work, nor could its ethical side be neglected. However, although their book gives a thorough and illuminating description of the cultural and political climate that forms the background of Wittgenstein's youth and presumably of some of his motives for writing the *Tractatus*, it does not throw any real new light on its logical doctrines.[18] Such is of course not to be expected in the first place. For the technicalities of the *Tractatus* can be understood only against the backgrounds of the problems and theories in contemporary logic, that is, primarily against the background of the works of Russell and Frege.

So, it seems that we cannot neglect one side, either the logical or the ethical, of the *Tractatus* and concentrate on the other. We must view the *Tractatus* as a whole in order to gain a proper understanding of it. In this respect the book is remarkably like the man. Russell, in his autobiography, relates the following event, which took place somewhere around 1912.[19] Wittgenstein is visiting Russell in his rooms in Trinity and remains silent for more than two hours, pacing up and down. Russell finally asks him: "Wittgenstein, are you thinking about logic or contemplating your sins?" Wittgenstein answers: "Both." And this seems to be true: there is both a logical and ethical motivation behind the *Tractatus* and one cannot be understood without the other.

How Wittgenstein became interested in logic is a familiar story, which has been related in quite some detail by McGuinness (1988) and Monk (1990). In short, the story goes like this. Already as a child Wittgenstein was fascinated by machines and other technical matters. His education was intended to further these interests. Hence, after graduating from the Realschule in Linz, Wittgenstein went to study at the Technische Hochschule in Berlin, apparently destined to become an engineer. After two years, of which little is known, Wittgenstein went to Manchester to pursue his studies in the then evolving science of aeronautics. One project he was involved in concerned the construction of a certain type of jet-driven propeller. This construction posed some technical mathematical problems and this led him to devote himself to mathematics, more in particular to work on the foundations of mathematics. In the course of this he read Russell's *Principles of Mathematics* and later Frege's *Grundgesetze*. The combination of an interest in philosophical problems, which Wittgenstein had already developed when much younger, with fundamental problems in the philosophy of mathematics and logic turned out to be irresistible. After a few years Wittgenstein gave up on aeronautics and turned to the study of logic. He visited Frege, who advised him to go to Cambridge and study with Russell, which Wittgenstein did in 1912.

Under Russell, and after a short time with him, Wittgenstein worked on the current problems in logic as Russell saw them. It should be stressed, by the way, that the term "logic" as Wittgenstein, Russell, and many others at the time used it, covers a much wider territory than the modern formal logic that we may be inclined to associate with it. For Wittgenstein the term refers to an overall theory that covers not just logic in the narrower, technical sense, but also language and meaning, their role in philosophy, and so on. For Russell, knowledge, perception, and the like could be thrown in as well, but Wittgenstein had a remarkable tendency not to involve himself in epistemological problems, no doubt also because, not being trained as a philosopher, he did not know much about them, at least not in a systematic way. Wittgenstein's work of this period survives in the form of letters and postcards written to Russell, the "Notes on Logic" of 1913, the "Notes Dictated to Moore" of April 1914, and those of his surviving notebooks that cover the period 1914–16 (*Notebooks 1914–1916*).

What were the urgent problems in logic around that time? By the end of the nineteenth century logic had seen its first substantial progress since the Scholastics of the Middle Ages, through the works of Boole, Bolzano, Peirce, and Frege. Partly this renaissance of the subject was the result of more or less internal developments. The work of Boole, for example, with its emphasis in the mechanics of reasoning, can be seen as a continuation of that of Leibniz. But to a larger extent the invention of the "new logic" was stimulated by developments outside the field proper, mainly by what was going on in mathematics. After having been the paradigm of infallible knowledge for ages, mathematics, or at least mathematics as it was perceived in philosophy, had fallen into a crisis. The development of non-Euclidean geometries urged a reinvestigation of the very foundations of mathematics. One of the research programs arising from these concerns is that of logicism, which set out to ground basic parts of mathematics in logic.

For Frege, who was one of the founding fathers of the logicistic program, the search for a proper foundations of mathematics, however, was not the only source of inspiration. At least as important was his Kantian heritage.[20] In opposition to the naturalism and radical empiricism prevailing in German philosophy at the time, Frege wanted to show that the most fundamental part of mathematics, arithmetic, can be reduced to logic and thus has to be regarded as belonging to the realm of analytic a priori knowledge.[21] For this would show that induction, which is based on arithmetic and is a necessary ingredient of the acquisition of empirical knowledge, is analytic a priori, too.

In the course of the execution of this program Frege developed the first systematic theory of quantification and relations, in his *Begriffsschrift* (1879).[22] Having developed and sharpened his tools, Frege then set about his main task: the derivation of basic arithmetic from purely logical principles. First he gave a penetrating but informal analysis of the notion of number, in his *Die Grundlagen der Arithmetik* (1884). Then he proceeded toward the final step, that of founding arithmetic in logic in a formally rigorous way. The results appeared in the first volume of the *Grundgesetze der Arithmetik* (1895). Russell, when preparing his *Principles of Mathematics* (1903), studied Frege's work and discovered that a paradox can be derived from Frege's axioms. After some hesitation, Frege saw that Russell was right and added a postscript to the second volume of the *Grundgesetze*, which was already in press, in which he acknowledged Russell's discovery and presented a tentative solution (which, however, turned out not to work). By then Russell was underway to create his own solution to the problem. Whereas the discovery of the paradox seems to have been a fatal blow for Frege's interest in the program of logicism, Russell remained confident that it could be carried through. He developed his theory of types, which first appeared in the *Principles of Mathematics* (1903) and was given its definite form (which is known as "the ramified theory of types") in 1908 (see Russell 1908). The theory of types is also used in the *Principia Mathematica* of 1912–13.[23]

From the Frege-Russell line of research Wittgenstein inherited a great many problems, two of which we need to say something more about here, since they are directly relevant for a proper understanding of the main lines of thought developed in the *Tractatus*.

The first problem is that of the status of logical laws, that is, the nature of logical necessity.[24] This problem is inherently, but certainly not exclusively, a problem of logicism: if we reduce mathematics to logic, in order to safeguard its consistency and unassailability, we had better have a good insight into the nature of logic, into *its* unassailability. Whence does logic get its necessary character? Is there only one system of logic? Do we not run the risk of discovering the logical counterparts of non-Euclidean geometries?

Intimately connected with this problem is that of the choice of axioms in logic. The axiom of parallels had turned out to be the Achilles heel of Euclidean geometry: How could one be sure that the logical axioms that Frege and Russell had proposed did not contain a similar weak spot? Indeed, there was already a definite suspect: the axiom of infinity, which states that there are an infinite number of individuals and which is needed if we want to define the cardinal numbers in terms of sets of sets that have the same cardinality (see 5.35). A resort to the traditional approach of viewing axioms as immediately evident truths in this case is a dubious move, the axiom of infinity being extremely hard to adjust to that scheme.[25] And Wittgenstein indeed rejects this position in his characteristic apodictic way. According to him, "All logical sentences have equal rights: there is no essential distinction among them between basic laws and derived sentences" (6.127).[26] For Wittgenstein this is immediately obvious from the simple fact that instead of using a set of axioms one can make do with one, namely their conjunction. That such an axiom would not be self-evident he regards as irrelevant and he takes Frege to task for thinking so: "... it is strange that as rigorous a thinker as Frege has referred to the degree of self-evidence as a criterion for a logical sentence" (6.1271). Notice, however, that this constitutes not a rejection of the use of axiomatic methods per se, but rather of the idea that certain logical propositions have a privileged status, being axioms "by nature" as it were.[27]

The idea of a fundamental role for intuition, either in mathematics or in logic, is rejected by Wittgenstein already in the *Notebooks* in a discussion of the fundamental logical forms of judgments:

So we can ask ourselves: Does the subject-predicate form exist? Does the relational form exist? Do any of the forms exist that Russell and I were always talking about? (Russell would say: "Yes! That is evident." *Ha*!)

Then: if *everything* that needs to be shown is shown by the existence of subject-predicate SENTENCES and so on, the task of philosophy is different from what I originally supposed. But if that is not the case, then what is lacking would have to be shown through some kind of experience, and that I consider to be impossible. (3/9/14)[28]

Here we see Wittgenstein moving toward a position that seeks to answer these logical questions, neither through an appeal to some kind of intuitive self-evidence nor by reference to a special kind of experience, but rather by means of an analysis of language. Language has to be "alright," if, as we must, we are to reject an appeal to self-evidence and the like:

The "self-evidence" which Russell talked so much about can only become dispensable in logic if language itself prevents any logical mistake. And it is clear that that "self-evidence" is wholly deceptive and always has been. (8/9/14)

The assumption that language does indeed provide a key to these logical questions leads to a quite different conception of language and its place in logic and philosophy than Frege or Russell had espoused.

Also closely connected to the problem of logical necessity was that of logical constants, or, more in general, that of logical concepts. Do logical constants refer, and if so, what do they refer to? Are logical concepts such as generality real, do they have ontological counterparts? Logical necessity is intimately linked to the various logical concepts. Does this mean that it derives from properties of a special ontological category of logical objects? Again, Russell and Frege had proposed partial answers to these questions.

16   *Backgrounds*

Frege favored a platonic view on logical objects, placing them in a realm of their own, disjunct from both the sphere of empirical phenomena and that of mental objects. Both Russell and Wittgenstein shared Frege's antipsychologism, but Russell's empiricist alternative to Frege's platonism hardly suited Wittgenstein's taste. According to Russell logical objects had to be regarded as the most general traits of empirical reality.

Wittgenstein had original thoughts about all these questions, and a large part of the *Tractatus* is in fact devoted to expounding these and to criticizing, albeit mostly implicitly, the views of Russell and Frege. But before turning to a general characterization of Wittgenstein's position, let us first mention a second important problem that he inherited from Russell and Frege. It concerns the question of logical form. Ever since Frege's construction of his conceptual notation, a tension between what was traditionally viewed as the grammatical form of a sentence and its appropriate logical form was felt. In the Aristotelian tradition such a distinction did not play a role, since traditional syllogistic logic was limited to subject-predicate judgments, in which the grammatical form and the logical form coincide. Of course, much of the logical ingenuity of the scholastics was devoted to attempts to overcome this limitation and some awareness of a distinction had grown along the way. However, it was only with the invention of a formal language that radically differs in syntactic structure from natural languages that the issue could be clearly formulated and investigated. For Frege the distinction as such did not carry much philosophical weight, but for Russell, with his interest in an empiricist epistemology and ontology, it was crucial. His theory of descriptions sharpened the issue even more and was a major influence on Wittgenstein. However, on this topic, too, Wittgenstein takes an original stand.

These two problems—the choice of logical laws and the status of logical concepts—are fused in the formulation of a certain ideal for logic. It is important to remember that at the time one did not make the sharp distinction between semantical and syntactical approaches and definitions that we employ in logic today. More in particular, it would take another twenty years or so for our present-day distinction between the semantic, model-theoretic notion of entailment and the syntactic notion of derivability to fully mature.[29] And although Tarski's work on truth dates from the 1930s, it is not until the 1950s that we find it presented in the form that we are all now so familiar with, that of the Tarskian truth-definition.[30] If we had to give a characterization using modern terminology, we would have to say that at the time logic was syntactic: both Frege and Russell talk about logical systems in terms of axioms and derivation rules. The status of logical axioms and rules was not altogether clear. One way of trying to overcome these problems gives the notion of logical form a key role. It formulates the ideal of a logical language that will allow all the logical relationships between judgments to be evident from the form that these judgments can be assigned in that language. In other words, what seemed to be needed was a notation in which all logical relationships were completely surveyable, completely transparent in the form of the relevant judgments.

It is this ideal of a logically transparent notation that seems to motivate much of the *Tractatus*.[31] Wittgenstein wants to do away, not only with axioms but also with logical objects.[32] The idea that there are no logical objects, that logical constants do not refer, he calls the basic idea of the *Tractatus*: "My fundamental idea is that the 'logical constants' do not represent" (4.0312). If the logical constants do not refer, then there are no logical objects and a forteriori logical truths do not express properties of such objects, as Frege and Russell, each in their own way, would have it. Logical truths, according to Wittgenstein, show that they are what they are and reflect properties of logical space. It is important to notice that this does not represent a reduction of logic to ontology. Wittgenstein emphatically speaks of logical space and his fundamental dictum is that "Logic must take care of itself" (5.473). This claim occurs in the *Notebooks* (22/8/14) and is referred to as "an extremely profound and important insight" (2/9/14). It means that logic cannot be justified or grounded externally, nor does it need to be: "In a certain sense it must be impossible for us to be mistaken about logic" (2/9/14). The ideal of a transparent notation is the counterpart of this self-sufficiency of logic.

Thus Wittgenstein makes logic his rock-bottom.[33] On his absolutism with regard to logic and the concomitant idea of a logically transparent notation Wittgenstein also bases his out-of-hand rejection of Russell's theory of types, which the latter developed as a solution of paradoxes such as the one discovered in Frege's *Grundgesetze*. The theory of types involves a strict regimentation of the expressions of the formal language according to their type (expressions that refer to objects, predicates, predicates over predicates, and so on) and rules that restrict their application and thus rule out problematic expressions. Wittgenstein's position is that there can be no such thing as a theory of types: an adequate notation would simply show the relevant type-distinctions. If a certain notation would need the additional stipulations of the theory of types it would not be an adequate notation, and hence, in a sense, not a proper notation at all.

The reason that there cannot be a meaningful theory of symbolism is rooted in the picture theory of meaning and in the concomitant universality of language, a feature of Wittgenstein's thinking that will be discussed in more detail in Chapter 3. What the theory of types aims to say is something that can, in the end, only be shown. Here we encounter the distinction between saying and showing, one of the central concepts of the *Tractatus* and of Wittgenstein's philosophy of logic. It is closely connected with the distinction between the contingent and the necessary, and, like the latter, is a categorial one: what can be shown, cannot be said, and vice versa.

The saying-showing distinction is also related to another fundamental thesis of Wittgenstein's, which is that logical necessity is embedded in language. The necessity of a logical sentence, that is, its tautological or contradictory character, is an aspect of its form. Let us notice at the outset that this is not some kind of linguistic conventionalism, as was to become fashionable in logical empiricism later on.[34] For "language" here means every language; it refers to the common underlying logical form of every system of symbolic representation. So, Wittgenstein's view of logical necessity is a linguistic one, but he certainly does not subscribe to conventionalism or relativism. And neither does he follow Frege and Russell in their criticism of natural language. For Frege it was evident that natural languages, although suited for everyday purposes, were unfit to deal with mathematical and scientific reasoning. For example, the fact that natural language allows for names and descriptions that have meaning, but do not have a bearer, is a defect from the point of view of modeling formal reasoning in science and one that an adequate symbolic system should avoid. Russell shares this opinion and agrees that for certain purposes, notably reasoning in science, mathematics, and philosophy, our everyday natural languages must be superseded by formal languages.[35] As a matter of fact, Frege was rather subtle about the matter. In "Über Sinn und Bedeutung" (1892a) he compares natural language to the eye and formal languages to a microscope: when it comes to seeing minute details the latter is the more suitable instrument, but it cannot match the former when it comes to flexibility in seeing everyday objects.

For Russell the idea of a language reform also played a role in his philosophical system. Frege, already committed to a form of platonism with regard to mathematical entities, had no philosophical qualms about recognizing senses as an ontological category of their own and thus could deal with meaningful but nonreferring expressions in a straightforward way. Russell, however, at least in his empiricist period, aimed for a more parsimonious ontology and thus had to deal with such problems in a different, more indirect way. His solution is the famous description theory, according to which all referring expressions, including proper names, can be analyzed as descriptions that do not presuppose the existence of their referents but actually assert it.[36] Combined with his epistemological doctrine of sense-data and acquaintance, it provided him with a powerful tool that could be used to analyze various problems in epistemology, logic, and ontology. So, both Frege and Russell, for slightly different reasons and with different aims, were of the opinion that natural language, being somehow defective for certain purposes, needed to be analyzed, or reformed, or even partly replaced, by a more suitable logical language. Perhaps surprisingly, Wittgenstein does not agree, at least, not without viewing the entire problem from a different perspective. Wittgenstein takes seriously, very seriously indeed, the following problem: If natural language is indeed as incomplete, vague, and illogical as it is supposed to be, how can we explain that we can do with it what we do? For Wittgenstein it is axiomatic that the well-formed sentences of natural language have meaning and that this meaning is determinate. In this sense natural language does not stand in need of any reform, extension, or replacement. If an expression in natural language is well formed, then it has meaning; and if it has meaning, then there is no need to sharpen it or complete it. As a meaningful expression it simply expresses a meaning that is in itself complete and determinate. This is not to say that nothing can go wrong, but if something does go wrong this is not due to an inherent shortcoming of natural language itself. Again, this is a view expressed already in the *Notebooks* at an early stage:

Frege says: Every well-formed sentence must have meaning, and I say: Every possible sentence is well-formed, and if it does not have meaning that can only be because we have not *assigned* a reference to certain parts of it. Even if we believe that we have done so. (2/9/14)

Thus, according to Wittgenstein, the problem is not that there can be sentences that have no meaning due to some inherent defect of the language, but that there can be sentences that we have not given any meaning.

Consequently, Wittgenstein's notion of logical analysis is quite different from that of Frege and Russell. For him logical analysis is the bringing to light of that which is common to all languages, both natural and formal ones. In this spirit we must also understand Wittgenstein's quest for the "general form of the sentence" (see 4.5, 4.53): it is that which underlies the expressions of any meaningful symbolic system. This uncovering of its underlying logic has a therapeutic value. For it is the misunderstanding of this logic that leads to problems.

That this logic can be misunderstood and why this is almost inevitable, Wittgenstein explains as follows:

> Language dresses up thought, and in such a way that one cannot infer the form of the dressed-up thought from the outward form of the dress. For the outward form of the dress is shaped for completely different purposes than revealing the form of the body. (4.002)

At a first reading this might seem to echo Frege's and Russell's concerns. But Wittgenstein's claim that it is impossible to read off the logic from a natural language directly does not imply that it does not have such a logic, nor that it is deficient because of that. He observes that in general logical form and grammatical form differ, and this for good reasons, but he does not hold that there are grammatical forms that lack an adequate logical form. As 5.5563 says: "All the sentences of our everyday language are actually, the way they are, logically well-ordered." Any meaningful sentence as such determines its logical relationships with other sentences, all by itself and completely. Hence, about the logic of natural language there is nothing to add, or to make more precise, or to improve in some other respect.

This indicates the extent to which Wittgenstein follows Frege and Russell in their criticism of natural language. Anything that is a well-formed sentence of language has meaning, as the passage from the *Notebooks* cited above makes clear. This meaning being determinate, it leaves nothing to be desired: there is no vagueness that has to be made precise, no lack of rigor that underdetermines the logical relationships with other sentences. However, the expressions of natural language do fall short of an ideal in this sense that the logical relationships are not apparent from the surface grammatical form. That is to say, Wittgenstein agrees with Frege and Russell that the superficial grammatical form of a sentence may be misleading as to its intrinsic logical form. As 4.002 states, the grammatical form is determined by other needs than the logical form, and hence the logical properties of a sentence in general are not perspicuously displayed in the form in which it appears to us. This is how we must read Wittgenstein when he says in 4.0031 that "Russell's contribution is to have shown that the apparent logical form of a sentence need not be its real one." Wittgenstein acknowledges that this fact about natural language may be the source of (philosophical) confusion (see 3.323–3.324 and 4.003), and such confusion may even license the construction and use of formal languages (3.325). However, it seems that whereas Russell and Frege thought of this type of logical analysis as providing something that is not, or not completely, there, Wittgenstein thinks of it as uncovering something that is in fact there, but that for various reasons we somehow fail to see properly.[37]

This observation leads us back to the syntactic character of logic. From a logical point of view the ideal symbolism is one in which the logical properties of a sentence, such as its being a tautology or a contradiction, its logical relationships with other sentences, are shown by the sentence itself, in its form. Thus Wittgenstein claims that "Every tautology itself shows that it is a tautology" (6.127). And in the *Notebooks* we read:

In other words the sentence must be completely articulated. Everything that its meaning has in common with another meaning must be contained separately in the sentence. If generalizations occur, then the forms of the particular cases must be apparent. (17/6/15)

Analysis in Wittgenstein's book, then, is the uncovering of this completely perspicuous logical form, and hence primarily clarification, not reform.

In this connection another influence on Wittgenstein's thinking should be mentioned that comes to the fore precisely at this point, namely that of the physicists Hertz and Boltzmann who, together with Mach, were also a source of inspiration for the logical empiricists of the Vienna Circle. Wittgenstein became acquainted with their ideas through Hertz's *Principles of Mechanics* (1899) and Boltzmann's *Populäre Schriften* (1905) when he was still at the Realschule in Linz. There seem to have been plans for him to study with Boltzmann, who was professor of physics in Vienna. But Boltzmann died in 1906, the year in which Wittgenstein graduated, and he went to study in Berlin instead. Hertz's book influenced Wittgenstein profoundly, as the reference to it in 4.04 shows. In this book, Hertz develops the idea of a scientific theory as a model of reality. Viewed as such a model, a theory should meet three constraints: it should be consistent; it should have deductive consequences that can be confirmed by observational facts; and it should be stated in a simple, parsimonious, and perspicuous notation. Hertz described these models in mentalistic terms, something that Wittgenstein, in the wake of Frege's antipsychologism, was to reject. Nevertheless, it is clear that in particular the concept of a perspicuous notation, one in which the internal, logical structure of the sentences of a theory is completely transparent, caught on. The *Tractatus* may very well be viewed as the search for the universal principles underlying such a notation.

The above sketch gives only the rough outlines of the kind of logical and philosophical problems that form the background against which Wittgenstein develops his own ideas. But this much may suffice here, since in what follows we will not be concerned with the more subtle and technical logical issues that the *Tractatus* addresses.[38] There is one thing that we have not yet drawn attention to, however, and it is of some importance for our understanding of the relationship between ontology and ethics in the *Tractatus*. Wittgenstein's basic logical insights—that logical constants are not referring expressions and the concomitant view on logical necessity, and the distinction between saying and showing with its associated view on logical form—date from as early as 1913–14. Both theses already figure prominently in the "Notes on Logic," written in 1913, and in the "Notes Dictated to Moore," from 1914.[39] These insights, together with Wittgenstein's idea that meaning is determinate, lead to the view on natural language and logical analysis that we have sketched above. From that point Wittgenstein was led to the idea of the general form of the proposition, that is, to the position that there must be completely general principles that underlie any symbolic system. In the course of the search for these Wittgenstein develops the picture theory of meaning in 1914–15. So, the picture theory is to be regarded as a consequence of the earlier logical insights.

On 29/9/14 we find in the *Notebooks* the famous passage in which the basic idea of the picture theory appears for the first time:

The general concept of a sentence brings along a quite general concept of the co-ordination of sentence and state of affairs: the solution to all my questions must be *extremely* simple.

In a sentence a world is, as it were, put together as a try out. (As when in the law court in Paris a car accident is represented by means of dolls and so forth.) (29/9/14)

Notice that Wittgenstein quite explicitly says what he is after: a completely general theory of language and meaning. We will come back to the details of the picture theory later on. Here we just want to notice that it is only after the birth of the picture theory, which in its turn appears only after several fundamental logical insights have been gained, that we find remarks in the *Notebooks* that deal with ontological problems such as the relationship between simple and complex entities. The latter problems occupy Wittgenstein from the middle of 1915 onward.

From these observations we may draw the conclusion that the order in which the various components of the overall theory of the *Tractatus* make their appearance in the book itself is not a reflection of the order in which they were invented. In the *Tractatus* the ontology comes first. Then comes the picture theory in its general form, which is only subsequently applied to language. More technical logical issues are discussed after that. This order is perhaps dictated by systematic considerations; but we cannot be certain of this. In any case, it seems rash to derive any substantial conclusions from it as regards the conceptual relationships between the various components of the tractarian system, since the historical order of their invention is so radically different.

Finally, we note that it is not until the middle of 1916 that remarks about ethics begin to appear in the *Notebooks*. So far as their contents reoccur in the *Tractatus*, this shows that they cannot be brushed aside as the remnants of adolescent thought, a sin from youth, to be treated mildly, but not to be taken seriously.[40] In this form they appear only after Wittgenstein had developed all his (mature) insights in logic, language, meaning, and ontology. It should be noted that these remarks bear clear traces of the work of Arthur Schopenhauer, and it has been established that as a young man Wittgenstein read Schopenhauer.[41] However, we also know now that while engaged in the service of the Austrian-Hungarian army during the Great War Wittgenstein had gone through experiences that decisively changed his life and that no doubt provided him with the impetus to rethink whatever he had learned from Schopenhauer earlier on.[42]

This brings us to the background of the ethical part of the *Tractatus*, which is the subject of the next section.

ETHICS

Unlike the logical part of the *Tractatus*, the ethical part bears far less directly the traces of contemporary thought. As for the former, it is clear that the *Tractatus* expounds a systematic theory concerning problems that at the time were considered important and unsolved. And it does so against the background of opinions and debates that were prevailing at the time and that, although hardly discussed directly, clearly can be seen to have shaped its own doctrines. The ethical part, however, cannot be situated against a contemporary background in a similar way. The position the *Tractatus* undertakes to defend on the ethical plane is one that is in a sense so general that it can hardly be tied to contemporary issues and debates. It does not address a definite set of particular questions, nor does it discuss and defend anything that might be considered as answers to such questions. In that sense, it is the elusive part of the *Tractatus*, and there is every reason to believe that Wittgenstein intended it to be that way. In that sense, sketching the backdrop of the ethical views Wittgenstein propounds, is a difficult, if not altogether impossible, task. Wittgenstein evidently drew on a number of heterogeneous sources and personalized the insights he distilled from them in a unique way, only to come up with an ethics that from the point of view of modern moral philosophy hardly deserves that name. Literature, philosophy, and intensive reflection on his own personal experiences blend into an outlook on life that is at the same time uniquely personal and timelessly general. Still, some influences can be traced and in what follows the major ones are briefly indicated.

The cultural, political, and scientific developments in Vienna around the turn of the century definitely influenced Wittgenstein's outlook on life and its meaning. This has been amply illustrated by Janik and Toulmin in their *Wittgenstein's Vienna* (1973), a book that has played a major role in turning the attention of Wittgenstein scholarship from the more specific logical and linguistic aspects of the *Tractatus* to its more general philosophical and ethical outlook. But this influence can be made out only on a rather global level. Janik and Toulmin extensively describe the conservative, even reactionary and repressive character of the prevailing cultural and political powers. Austrian society at the time had its eyes turned to the past, rather than to its present and future, and it displayed all the signs of a fossilized culture. The discomfort resulted in what can be called an experimental counterculture in various fields: architecture (Loos), music (Mahler, Schoenberg), and literature (Kraus, Musil) are prominent examples. The Wittgenstein family being in the center of the cultural life of Vienna, Wittgenstein no doubt was aware of these revolutionary developments. But to what extent they actually influenced him is in fact hard to say. His taste in music and literature certainly does not reflect a great appreciation of these new developments. His musical and literary favorites (such as Beethoven, Schubert, and Brahms in music, and Goethe, Dostoevsky, Tolstoy, Mörike, Nestroy, and Grillparzer in literature) are not contemporaries, but well-established figures in their fields and can be called "classical" in more than one sense of the word.[43] Architecture was an exception, in a sense. Wittgenstein certainly admired what Loos tried to do, as is for example testified by his contributions to the house that Engelmann built for his sister.[44] But he also greatly admired the baroque architecture of Von Erlach, and it seems that in this field, too, his taste and ideas were shaped by tradition, rather than by contemporary developments.

One particular feature of the way in which people reacted to the political and cultural climate deserves more attention. Austrian society at the time has been characterized as a "culture of concealment." Nothing was ever to be said outright; everything had to be concealed in a language that was rhetorical through and through. For some this called for a "critique of language" [*Sprachkritik*] that was, however, not so much logically oriented but had a distinct ethical and political purpose. Here two authors in particular have to be mentioned, Karl Kraus and Fritz Mauthner.

Kraus devoted a lifetime to criticizing this aspect of Austrian society, as a satirist, essayist, and literary critic. His periodical *Die Fackel* constituted one prolonged attack on corruption, hypocrisy, nationalism, literary and philosophical fashions, and a host of other topics. One of the starting points of his many vehement assaults is a strict separation of facts and values. Politics, law, and art, according to Kraus, all too often mingle the two in an unacceptable way with devastating consequences. Another aspect that is relevant in the present context, is Kraus's identification of ethics and aesthetics and their relation to language. Art for Kraus is basically an ethical undertaking, and he is of the opinion that the moral and aesthetic qualities of a work of art are reflected in the language of the work itself. In that sense a critique of language always has a moral dimension. This is certainly a point on which Kraus and Wittgenstein agree. But the means and methods they bring to bear on the critical enterprise are quite divergent. The case of Mauthner is more complicated. Mauthner is one of the very few people who is mentioned in the *Tractatus* by name. According to Janik and Toulmin, Mauthner's critique of language, to which Wittgenstein alludes in 4.0031, constituted a major influence on Wittgenstein.[45] There are, however, reasons to doubt whether that is really the case. Drawing on classical scepticism, British empiricism, and Mach's positivism, Mauthner subscribes to an epistemology according to which knowledge is ultimately based on sensory experience and is located in the individual. Mauthner considers language to be basically a social phenomenon, an evolutionary successful invention that shapes our worldview and culture. (In this respect Mauthner continues the tradition established by Von Humboldt.) It is based on metaphor and hence, Mauthner concludes, unsuited as a means to convey any true knowledge. This leads him to adopt a basically sceptical attitude, as the following quotation makes clear:

Language is only a convention, like a rule of a game: the more participants, the more compelling it will be. However, it is neither going to grasp nor alter the real world.[46]

Mauthner's view on language, it appears, is that of conventionalism, where we should note that the social nature of language appears to consist in a certain equilibrium of individual usages. Thus Mauthner's rules have more the character of regularities than of prescriptive rules.[47] Although this suggests a kind of relativism, and with regard to knowledge and language Mauthner's position certainly must be classified as such, it is important to notice that in ethical matters Mauthner was far from a conventionalist or a relativist. It is language that leads us astray.[48] "When we try to say something really valuable, we must remain silent."[49] A philosophical critique of language should reveal this. In particular, it should expose the conventional political and ethical rhetoric that does not say, but merely conceals and obscures, for what it is: an instrument that confuses us, that is used to subjugate and to prevent us from seeing the important ethical issues clearly.

In 4.0031 Wittgenstein does refer to Mauthner's notion of a critique of language, but only to reject it: "All philosophy is 'critique of language' (though not in Mauthner's sense)." Does this mean that Wittgenstein was aware of his tribute to Mauthner but was reluctant to acknowledge it? The sentence that immediately follows suggests that the answer to this question is negative: "Russell's contribution is to have shown that the apparent logical form of a sentence need not be its real one" (4.0031). After all, pointing to the confusing, distorting role of language is, at least in modern philosophy, a stock item in the repertoire of philosophers of various denominations, and Mauthner's originality certainly does not lie here. Nor does Wittgenstein's, or Russell's, or Frege's, for that matter. But, unlike Mauthner, the latter did bring something new to the age-old philosopher's distrust of natural language: the idea that logic could serve as the basis for a philosophical critique and a fully developed and powerful logical machinery to back this up.[50] Inasmuch as Wittgenstein agrees with Russell and Frege on the way in which a critique of language is to be carried out, although perhaps not on the goal that such a critique is to serve, his outlook is fundamentally different from that of Mauthner. The latter regards natural language as based on conventions and sees no distinct role for an ideal, logical language. For Wittgenstein there can be no question of conventionalism with regard to the fundamental properties of language, precisely because he approaches the problem from the viewpoint of logic, with regard to which he takes an absolutistic stance. For much the same reason he does not share Mauthner's epistemological approach. So it seems that the influence of Mauthner on the technical aspects of Wittgenstein's ideas was after all rather superficial, Wittgenstein getting his main inspiration for his work on logic and language from Russell and Frege, and not from Mauthner.

But in one respect Wittgenstein's view on a critique of language definitely bears more affinities to that of Mauthner than to that of Frege and Russell. For the first two the philosophical enterprise of a critique of language has a distinct ethical dimension. Mauthner was one of the most outspoken critics of the social, political, and cultural climate at the time, and in this respect his influence on Wittgenstein is undeniable. Both called for a critique of language also, perhaps even mainly, for ethical reasons. Such a critique must enable us to do away with the lofty, intellectual, but also hypocritical discourse on ethical matters and expose it as mere empty talk. Their solutions differ, Mauthner holding a empiricist and conventionalist view on language, Wittgenstein trying to found it in logic, but their goals are the same: the safeguarding of ethics, which deals with absolute values, from the intrusion of both common and scientific discourse, resulting in a kind of "linguistic mysticism."

The main philosophical source for Wittgenstein on the ethical plane, however, is another philosopher, Arthur Schopenhauer, whose work by the way also attracted Mauthner. Schopenhauer's work constitutes a clear influence on Wittgenstein's early thinking, especially with respect to ethics. If we look at the *Notebooks*, we notice that not only the contents of the opinions expressed but also their very wording in many cases can be traced directly to Schopenhauer. As we shall see in Chapter 4, there is a great convergence in the main ideas on ethical matters and in the conceptual apparatus that both bring to bear on them. We will spell out these analogies in detail later on; here a short indication should suffice. The fundamental distinction for Schopenhauer is the one between phenomenon and noumenon, between the world as representation ("Die Welt als Vorstellung") and the world as will ("Die Welt als Wille"). It is in terms of the latter, the will, that Schopenhauer expresses and develops his insights into human morality and the ultimate spiritual goal. The individual, human will is a manifestation of the will as such, the driving force behind all that appears to us in perception and thought. Knowledge in the sense of knowledge of the world as phenomenon is secondary to acquaintance with its noumenal aspect. Schopenhauer distinguishes various ways of interacting with the phenomenal world and ranks them according to the measure in which they allow us to get in touch with the noumenon behind it. The recognition of the unifying nature of the one will should sprout compassion, which is the basis of all moral action. But Schopenhauer does not leave it at that. Entertaining a basically pessimistic view on the world we live in, regarding it as a continuous source of suffering and pain, Schopenhauer develops the idea of the renunciation of the Will as the ultimate spiritual goal.

Schopenhauer's ideas about compassion and the nature of absolute ethical value can also be found in Wittgenstein's writings, written "between the lines" in the *Tractatus* and more directly expressed in the *Notebooks*. Wittgenstein phrases his views in a typically Schopenhauerean vocabulary, speaking of the will as the bearer of good and evil (6.423), distinguishing between the individual, human will, and the absolute will, the Will of God.

But there are also some marked differences, which stem from the difference in their ontological and epistemological positions. Briefly, for Schopenhauer epistemology, in particular the opposition between the knowing subject and the known object, takes up the central position in his system of thought. In this respect he stays firmly rooted in the Kantian tradition. For Wittgenstein the ultimate point of reference is logic, which places him in the line started by Frege. These two different points of departure have consequences both on the ontological and on the epistemological level and the ensuing differences influence the ways in which Schopenhauer and Wittgenstein present their views on ethics as well.

Wittgenstein's attitude toward Schopenhauer is somewhat ambivalent. It is completely obvious that Schopenhauer exercised a major influence on Wittgenstein's thinking, first and foremost on his ethical opinions, but also on his more general philosophical outlook. To the extent that Wittgenstein can be said to be a Kantian philosopher, he is such no doubt also by having read Schopenhauer, for it appears that Wittgenstein never read much of Kant himself.[51] According to some, Wittgenstein's later work, too, bears traces of Schopenhauer.[52] A contrary opinion might result from what Wittgenstein later said about his relation to Schopenhauer. First of all, there is the story related by Von Wright in his biographical sketch, according to which Wittgenstein once remarked that in his early days he subscribed to a kind of Schopenhauerean idealism, which he then exchanged for a kind of conceptual realism under the influence of Frege.[53] However, it remains to be seen to what extent the *Tractatus* testifies to this. In particular we should investigate closely the discussion in the *Tractatus* concerning solipsism and realism. Another illustration of Wittgenstein's opinion of Schopenhauer is provided by the following quotation (from *Culture and Value*, 1939–40):

Schopenhauer, one might say, is really a *crude* mind. That is, he has refinement, but at a certain depth this suddenly stops and he is as crude as the crudest. Where real depth starts, his stops.

One might say of Schopenhauer: he never turns inward.[54]

This certainly does not bespeak a great appreciation on Wittgenstein's part of Schopenhauer. To what extent this may serve to downplay the influence of the latter, however, remains to be investigated. It is certainly true that Schopenhauer's work has a kind of schematic character, which makes it predictable and somewhat superficial at times, and it is equally true that Wittgenstein's own work in that respect is quite the opposite. But whether that is what Wittgenstein has in mind here is not obvious. He may also be referring to the difference in starting point indicated above. And another thing to bear in mind when assessing this quotation is the everlasting tension in Wittgenstein's own personality between what he calls his "vanity," and his at times low esteem of his own originality.[55]

All in all, it seems clear that Schopenhauer does constitute a major influence on Wittgenstein's early thinking, especially with regard to ethics. Our detailed investigation in Chapter 3 will provide ample illustration. But it must be added that Wittgenstein did absorb his Schopenhauer in his own manner.[56] Remarkable is that both authors in a sense suffered the same fate. Where the ethical part of the *Tractatus* for a long time was neglected, Schopenhauer encountered a similar problem. The great majority of those who subscribed to his doctrine of the will did not accept his view on the ultimate goal: that of the denial of that very same will.[57]

If we attempt to give more substance to the contents of Wittgenstein's general outlook on ethics and its relation to everyday life, however, it seems that we must assign at least as much weight to the influence of a variety of other authors, such as Saint Augustine, Böhme, Angelus Silesius, William James, Kierkegaard, Weininger, Dostoevsky, and Tolstoy.[58] These are not just philosophers but also novelists, mystics, psychologists, and theologians. The influences of Böhme, a visionary who lived in the sixteenth century and whom Hegel called the "first German philosopher," of Angelus Silesius, a seventeenth-century mystical writer, and of Dostoevsky and Tolstoy are global. There seem to be no specific doctrines or philosophical points that can be traced to them. Their influence is rather a matter of atmosphere and general spiritual attitude.[59] Of Tolstoy's *Comments on the Gospels*, which Wittgenstein came across during the war, he said that the book "had kept him alive."[60] All these authors stand in the Judeo-Christian tradition, and, even more than the philosophical system of Schopenhauer, it is the Christian tradition that provides Wittgenstein with the vocabulary within which he thinks and writes about ethical and spiritual matters.

Wittgenstein's relationship toward the Christian faith is complex, however. The Wittgenstein family was of Jewish origin, but converted to Christianity sometime around the middle of the nineteenth century. Wittgenstein was raised as a Catholic, but he certainly was not a believer in the ordinary, dogmatic sense of that word. His attitude was one of critical respect. It is remarkable that some of the pupils who were closest to him, such as Anscombe and Smythies, converted to the Catholic faith. Wittgenstein, though not afraid to use words like "God," "faith," and "sin," could not bring himself to accept any of the dogmas that the various Christian creeds connect with these.[61] Like Schopenhauer, who in the fundamental beliefs of early Christianity saw embodied the right ethical spirit of world-denial, Wittgenstein seems to have accepted the Christian faith in the same loose and at the same time fundamental sense, without attaching himself to any dogmatic creed.

Broadening and at the same time individualizing the search for elements that go into making up the background of Wittgenstein's ethics, we run into biographical facts. Before the onset of the war ethical concerns surely were not foreign to Wittgenstein, as the above-mentioned anecdote related by Russell illustrates. But his experiences during the war, in which he engaged voluntarily as an ordinary soldier in the Austrian-Hungarian army, seem to have provided him with a decisive impulse to change his entire way of life, along the lines of the views expressed by him in the *Tractatus*.[62] This may be clear from various facts, such as Wittgenstein's renouncement of his inheritance, his withdrawal from further philosophical research, his search for a useful way of leading his life, which led him to try his hands at being a teacher and an architect, among other things.

Another biographical fact that according to some, notably Bartley and Levi, must be taken into account in order to understand his ethical opinions is Wittgenstein's homosexuality.[63] This aspect of Wittgenstein's personal life has long been neglected, if not denied altogether, as for example Wittgenstein's official biographer McGuinness seems to do.[64] This attitude, also exemplified by the way in which Wittgenstein's literary heirs (Anscombe, Rhees, von Wright) have dealt with Wittgenstein's *Nachlass*, has spurted a great deal of speculation and hence exaggeration.[65] (For a more down-to-earth discussion, see Ray Monk's biography [1990, appendix]). Levi argues that Wittgenstein's ethics, with its characteristic trait of world-denial, in fact constitutes a kind of flight from his homosexuality, an attempt to shield himself from any moral indictments from others on this point. We will discuss this view later in somewhat more detail and argue that the biographical roots of Wittgenstein's views, though they certainly need not be denied, are not particularly interesting or revealing from a systematic point of view.

A similar conclusion must be reached when we consider the question whether his Jewishness is of relevance for Wittgenstein's ethical outlook. Wittgenstein's attitude here is somewhat confusing, certainly for a modern reader. Being Jewish, but not in a religious sense, Wittgenstein sometimes ventilates opinions, which for us, after the Second World War and the Holocaust, are hard to understand and even seem shocking. But such an attitude was not uncommon with intellectual and thoroughly assimilated Jews at the time. Another prominent example is Otto Weininger, whose main work, *Geschlecht und Character* (1903), for a while exerted a strong influence on Wittgenstein.[66] This was one of those books that are immensely popular during a certain period in time, only to be almost completely forgotten by the next generation. In his book Weininger comes up with a theory of sexuality that strikes a modern reader as definitely odd.[67] Weininger, too, was an assimilated Jew, who expressed strong and on some points quite negative opinions on the Jewish character. Within his theory about positive masculinity and negative femininity, Weininger associates Jewishness with the latter. Wittgenstein, during a certain period, makes remarks that are definitely influenced by Weininger. Consider the following quotation (from *Culture and Value*, 1931), in which Wittgenstein reflects on what he considers the essentially "reproductive" nature of Jewish thinkers:

> The Jewish "genius" is only a saint. The greatest Jewish thinker is just a talent. (Me for instance.)

> I believe there is some truth to it when I think that I am really only reproductive in my thinking. I believe I have never *invented* a way of thought, rather it was always given to me by someone else and I have just picked it up promptly and passionately for my work of clarification.

Given the immense influence that Wittgenstein has had on twentieth-century philosophy, we can only be baffled by this. At other times, Wittgenstein does show a keen awareness of the value and the unique character of his own work. This strange mixture of pride and (excessive) modesty threads through his whole life.

Homosexual, but not allowed, either by society or by himself, to realize it; of Jewish origin, but having been raised as a Catholic; from an essentially continental cultural tradition, but living in an Anglo-Saxon one—

these are oppositions that certainly must have left deep traces in Wittgenstein's personal life and in his personal view on how to live it.[68] In that sense these biographical facts are certainly relevant, but mainly for understanding Wittgenstein as a person. They explain, at least to a certain extent, why he held the views that he did. But they do not necessarily explain the contents of these views. After all, Wittgenstein's ideas about ethics and morality can be characterized quite independently of any specific biographical details and, moreover, they can be seen to be shared by people with altogether different backgrounds. Hence it seems that from a systematic point of view these specific biographical origins need not concern us too much.

There is one final point to be observed in this sketch of the backgrounds of the ethical part of the *Tractatus*, which concerns the "Eastern connection." As various authors have observed, there is an, admittedly rather global, connection between Wittgenstein's views on ethics and certain positions in Indian and Chinese philosophy, notably Buddhist and Taoist.[69] It is surely evident that there is no direct influence at work here. So far as we know, Wittgenstein never read any Buddhist or Taoist literature. However, that does not mean that from a systematic point of view the connection is merely coincidental. In fact, there may be two sources for it.

The first source is obvious: the work of Schopenhauer. The latter's reading of Indian philosophical literature, notably the *Upaniṣhads* and certain Buddhist texts from the *Pāli*-canon, not only helped to shape his views, but are also directly referred to in his main work; *Die Welt als Wille und Vorstellung* (The world as will and representation).[70] Wittgenstein was well acquainted with it, which is one way some of these ideas may have influenced him. In addition it must be pointed out that in 1913 Fritz Mauthner published several annotated translations from parts of early Buddhist literature.[71] It is well known that Wittgenstein was familiar with Mauthner's work, although we cannot be sure that he ever read these translations.

A second source is even more indirect. Where Schopenhauer and Wittgenstein draw on the Western, Christian tradition in thinking about ethics, they appear to subscribe to the views of early Christianity, with its characteristic attitude of renouncement of the world. In connection with that, it is worth pointing out that there is a historically traceable relation between certain Buddhist concepts, especially of the Mahāyāna tradition, and early Christianity. The strong gnostic tradition of the Christian thinking of the first to fourth centuries, which has survived as an undercurrent in Western Christianity and culture, and which has influenced, also indirectly, someone like Böhme, shows remarkable resemblances to certain ideas in *Mahāyāna* Buddhism. For example, the gnostic emphasis on *sophia* and *gnosis* parallels the *prajñāpāramitā* of the latter.[72] Although the parallels between Buddhism and Wittgenstein's thinking on these matters are only of a global nature, drawing certain parallels may at times serve illustrative purposes. It is this use that we will make of them in Chapter 4.

Having surveyed the main influences on Wittgenstein's early thinking on logic and ethics, we will turn to a more detailed study of his views on realism and values in Chapters 3 and 4. The exposition there will closely follow the text of the *Tractatus* and the *Notebooks*. It concentrates on the precise nature of Wittgenstein's ontology and its relationship with ethics. This discussion takes place within the overall framework of the *Tractatus*, and our exposition will presuppose some acquaintance with it. For readers lacking that, the following chapter provides an outline.

2

Main Themes

This chapter provides an overview of the main aspects of the *Tractatus* as a whole, with special reference to those elements that will be important for the detailed discussion of the relationship between language, ontology, and ethics that forms the main topic of Chapters 3 and 4. For readers with a working knowledge of the *Tractatus* it will not contain anything substantially new. The exposition that follows is not neutral with respect to the major interpretational controversies that arise in this area, but an explicit discussion of some of them is postponed to the following chapters. In this chapter our intention is rather to provide those readers who have only a superficial knowledge of what the *Tractatus* is all about with enough background to fruitfully study Chapters 3 and 4.[1]

AIMS

In Wittgenstein's letter to Ficker of 1919, he claims that the final aim of the *Tractatus* concerns ethics rather than logic: ". . . the point of the book is an ethical one. . . . The ethical is delimited as it were from the inside by my book." Perhaps this makes clear what Wittgenstein's ultimate aim in writing the *Tractatus* was, but in fact only a small portion of the book actually treats ethics, the larger part being devoted to logic, language, ontology, and a host of other subjects. So, apparently the ethical goal

Wittgenstein wanted to realize in the end could be reached only indirectly, through an extensive analysis of language and logic. For Wittgenstein such an enterprise was also valuable in its own right.

But how is it that determining the limits of the ethical involves an analysis of language and logic? In the same letter Wittgenstein says: "I'd recommend that you read the *foreword* and the *conclusion* since these express the point most directly." The conclusion, the (too) much quoted "About what one cannot speak, one must remain silent" (7), ends a discussion of the transcendental nature of ethics and the mystical in which the reality of that which is beyond language is explicitly affirmed: "The unsayable, however, does exist. This *shows* itself, it is the mystical" (6.522). In this context, 7 should be read as a poignant formulation of the ineffability of, among other things, ethics, and with its reference to what we cannot speak about, it expresses that a proper understanding of the limits of language is a requirement for gaining a proper understanding of where exactly the sphere of ethics begins and where it ends.[2] This point reappears in the preface, though this time without an explicit reference to ethics.

In the preface Wittgenstein speaks, not of determining the limits of ethics, but rather of drawing the limits of thinking: "[Thus] the book's goal is to draw a limit to thought." In this passage the critical tradition in philosophy resounds: philosophy is an undertaking that aims at determining the limits of our epistemological and ratiocinative powers, thus safeguarding us from trespassing into territory to which our ordinary discursive rationality gives us no reliable access.[3] However, Wittgenstein immediately notices a difficulty here: How can we draw the limits of thought in thought?

> . . . for in order to draw a limit to thought, we should have to be able to think both sides of this limit (that is, we should have to be able to think what cannot be thought). (preface, 2d para.)

The problem seems a genuine one: How can the thinking, discursive mind draw its own limits? Does this not presuppose that it is able to transcend those very limits? But then the enterprise seems doomed to fail. For what could thinking an unthinkable thought be like? Of course, Kant had an answer to this question, one we need not go into here, but evidently, it did not satisfy Wittgenstein. In line with Frege's critique and amendment of Kant's program he proposes to take a different, indirect route: we should not try to draw the limits of thought directly, in thought itself, but rather should aim to get hold of what constitutes the limits of "the *expression* of thought" (preface, 2d para., emphasis added), that is, language.

The Linguistic Turn

This transition from thought to language, presented in the *Tractatus* preface in an almost casual way, testifies to a momentous step in the history of philosophy. Here we see what has been called "the linguistic turn" actually being taken.[4] Of course, Wittgenstein is pressing Frege's footsteps here, for it is in the work of the latter that the change from thought and knowledge to logic and language as the key notions of philosophy first found systematic expression. But Wittgenstein carries this change of perspective much further than Frege ever did. Why does Wittgenstein think that the change from thought to language will bring the goal of determining the limits of thought, and thereby those of ethics, within closer reach? For does not a similar problem arise there—that we cannot say what cannot be said and that hence what can be said cannot be limited? The preface itself remains silent on this point, but from the way in which the *Tractatus* sets out to accomplish its task the following answer can be extracted. The limits of what can be said, of what is meaningful, can be drawn from the inside as it were because of the logical structure that underlies language. The totality of meaningful expressions is not an amorphous infinity that can only be approached in toto (which is obviously impossible); rather it is a structured whole. There are such things as smallest meaningful elements and ways of combining given meaningful elements into larger ones. And this structure of the meaningful can be explicated. The principles that determine what it is for something to have meaning and the rules for combining meaningful elements are essentially logical in nature and hence can be explicated in a suitably general logical theory. In this way the study of logic becomes the study of the foundations of language and thought.

This assumption of a logical structure underlying all meaningful symbolism will allow a strict determination of the limits of what can be meaningfully said. Given a further assumption—that what can be said and what can be thought are in essence one and the same (that they coincide structurally and extensionally)—such a determination will also draw the limits of thought and thus fulfill the critical goal. That Wittgenstein regarded thinking and saying, language and thought, as two sides of the same coin is stated as such in 4: "A thought is a meaningful sentence." Why this should be so, will become clear later.

That the realm of the ethical and that of the discursive (that is, of language and thought) are different is not argued for directly in the *Tractatus*. Rather it seems to function as a starting point that finds its justification outside the sphere of philosophy as such, in the experience of everyday life. But we do find some indication in terms of the characteristics that Wittgenstein attaches to meaningful language, on the one hand, and to ethics, on the other. The central opposition that is operative here is that between the contingent and the necessary: language and thought are concerned with what is contingent, ethics with what is necessary.

The Ground-Plan of the *Tractatus*

From the preface, the ground-plan of the *Tractatus* can be deduced. In order to reach the ultimate goal, the safeguarding of ethics, the limits of our discursive powers have to be drawn. This can be done through language, by determining the totality of the meaningful. For this a logical analysis is needed of what meaning is, of how it comes about and how it is structured. Wittgenstein's solution to the problem of meaning is the famous picture theory, which holds that a sentence is meaningful by virtue of it depicting a situation. The picture theory in its turn requires a theory of situations and their structure, that is, an ontological theory. It is with the latter that the *Tractatus* starts and from a systematic point of view this is quite natural. It should be kept in mind, however, that the motivation for the ontology is not intrinsic but extrinsic, which is reflected in the fact that in the development of Wittgenstein's thinking the ontology comes long after the main ideas on logic, language, and picturing have arisen.

The ontology, the general theory of picturing, its application in the analysis of meaning, and the uncovering of the basic logical structure of language form what we might call the "positive part" of the *Tractatus*. But there is more. The essence of meaning is contingency: meaningful sentences are pictures of contingent situations. This means that whatever discourse that claims to be concerned with the necessary is ruled out as meaningless. For example, the logical principles underlying language are, of course, necessary. Wittgenstein held firmly to the conviction that there is ultimately one logical system. In that sense he was an absolutist. Thus logic itself, that paradigm of necessity, falls outside the sphere of the meaningful, and a substantial part of the *Tractatus* is devoted to a discussion of the status of its necessary principles. But not only logic traditionally has claimed to be both necessary and meaningful; there are also mathematics, certain parts of the sciences, and philosophy. All come out meaningless, yet each is concerned with meaninglessness of a different kind. In the last parts of the *Tractatus* their status, too, is discussed. Finally, having come round full circle, the *Tractatus* shortly treats of the nature of ethics. Thus the book ends with a reference to what the preface also hints at, "the unwritten part." Having sketched the main claims of the book, Wittgenstein ends the preface with a startling evaluation of its worth. The book, we read, deals with all philosophical problems: "The book treats *the* problems of philosophy" (preface, 2d para., emphasis added) and claims to solve them. They rest on a misunderstanding of the logic of our language, and the *Tractatus*, it is stated, gives us the one right picture: ". . . the *truth* of the thoughts announced here seems to me unimpeachable and final. I therefore believe that essentially I have solved the problems once and for all" (preface, last para.). No minor achievement, one would think, but not so Wittgenstein:

And if I am not mistaken in this, then the value of this work consists [secondly] in that it shows how little has been done now that these problems have been solved. (preface, last para.)

Evidently, to Wittgenstein's mind the real problems lie elsewhere, not in philosophy or in logic or in science, not in any kind of inquiry or interaction with the world that is discursive. The hard problems, the problems of everyday life, have nothing to do with the questions we can meaningfully ask and the equally meaningful answers to them that we may obtain:

We feel that even when all *possible* scientific questions have been answered, the problems of our life have not even been touched upon. (6.52)

The real problems are not questions concerning the way the world is, and no amount of intellectual and empirical investigation of the world will answer them: "The solution of the problem of life one can tell by the vanishing of the problem" (6.521).

Indeed, "the point of the book is ethical," but it is a point that is made with the help of profound logical and philosophical insights.

ONTOLOGY

Logical Atomism

The ontology of the *Tractatus* is commonly described as "logical atomism," a description that for once is actually quite correct. But what is logical atomism? The first thing to notice about the ontology is that it is an ontology of facts, not of things: "The world is everything that is the case" (1), the opening passage of the *Tractatus* reads, and this is explained in the following remark: "The world is the totality of facts, not of things" (1.1). The ingredients of the world, then, are facts: entities that "are the case," that is, that obtain or, another phrase used by Wittgenstein, that exist. This feature sets the tractarian ontology apart from many traditional approaches that present the world as basically consisting of things (objects). The difference seems important because it seems to reflect two different views on what the world is, and how it changes.

Imagine that one is asked to describe a room. On the traditional view an adequate description might consist of an inventory of the objects that are in the room (a table, two chairs, a bed, a cupboard, two bookcases, 423 books, some clothes hanging on a nail in the door). On the tractarian view, however, this simple list of "ingredients" would not do. On this approach one needs to know more: Where is the desk located? What does the cupboard contain? How many of the books are in the bookcases? And so on. On the latter view, the room, or at least the way the room is, changes if one of the books is moved to another shelf, but on the traditional view no change takes place in this case, since the list of ingredients remains the same.

Is this a case of two opposing views on what the world is like? Although it may seem so at first sight, there is reason to doubt that the opposition in the end will hold much water. For notice that we may very well view the tractarian view as emerging from the traditional one by an increasing demand of explicitness and exhaustiveness. We may not be satisfied with a description of an object in the room that reads: "one bookcase, colonial style, teak with inlays of mahogany," but instead want to know more: How many books does it contain? What are its measurements? Where is it located in the room? If this information is added to our original description of the object, it will contain more and more sentences stating facts about objects and hence become increasingly like the tractarian description.

The difference between the two views in the end seems more gradual than it may have appeared at first sight. In part it depends on the context in which a description is asked, including the purpose for which it is to be used and the fine-grainedness that is required, whether we will get more of a "list-of-ingredients" type of answer or an explicit description stating various facts. But we also noticed that increasing the demand of explicitness increases the descriptive character. And that means that if we want a characterization of what it is that makes the world the way the world is, it is facts, not objects, which are fundamental. So given Wittgenstein's objective, an investigation into the way the world must be for language to be able to be about the world, his choice of starting point seems most apt.

Facts then are what the world consists of and it is only facts that make it up: "The world is determined by the facts and by their being *all* the facts" (1.11). On account of this the ontology of the *Tractatus* is called "atomistic." There is nothing over and above the facts obtaining in the world that enters into its makeup. With its facts the identity of the world is completely determined.[5] Since the facts are the parts of which the world consists ("The world decomposes into facts" [1.2]), the ensuing picture is one in which the whole, the world, is nothing more than the sum of its parts, the facts. Such an atomistic view is traditionally opposed to what are called "holistic" approaches, according to which the true identity of the world cannot be reduced to that of its components, but is something sui generis.

Again, traditionally atomistic and holistic views are sharply distinguished, and this certainly seems correct. Yet it is important to notice in this respect that the atomistic view with which the *Tractatus* starts out is balanced by another view, one that at least sounds much more holistic and that is presented near the end, when Wittgenstein discusses ethics. In 6.45, Wittgenstein says that "the view of the world sub specie aeterni is its view as a—limited—*whole*" (emphasis added). How these two apparently conflicting views, both apparently endorsed in the *Tractatus*, can be reconciled, will be one of the main topics of Chapter 4. The tractarian ontology is characterized as "logical" atomism in order to distinguish it from classical, material atomism. The distinctive feature is the nature of the atoms. The world consists of entities that "are the case," and the atoms are the smallest among them. They are called "states of affairs" [*Sachverhalte*]. In what sense are these states of affairs the smallest elements? In classical atomism, atoms are things: the smallest pieces of matter out of which larger, macroscopic objects are composed. They are atoms in the literal sense: indivisible, that is, not composed and hence without internal structure. The states of affairs are not structureless, yet they are properly called the atoms of the tractarian ontology. The key to understanding in what sense they are atoms lies in understanding what sense of composition is at stake. In the classical, thing-based view the ingredients of the world are things that are composed of other things, ultimately of atoms. Here composition is like gluing two or more things together to make a bigger one. In the tractarian conception the world consists of facts, entities that are the case. Most ordinary facts are composed of other, smaller facts. For example, the fact that you are now reading this book has several component facts, such as that of you having your eyes open, of the book being within a certain distance from your face, of particular lighting conditions, and so on. On this view composition is a logical process and hence an atom is logically the smallest entity that can be the case. Thus a state of affairs is something that can be the case, or not be the case, without this making any difference to the being the case, or the not being the case, of another state of affairs. If two facts depend on one another logically, at least one of them must be composite. This is expressed in 1.21: "One thing can be the case or not the case while everything else remains the same." In 2.061–2.062, this property of logical independence, that is, of logical atomicity, is explicitly attributed to states of affairs:

> States of affairs are independent of one another.
> From the existence or nonexistence of one state of affairs one cannot infer the existence or nonexistence of another. (2.061–2.062)

Thus we are presented with the following picture. The world consists of facts. These facts are "what is the case" in the world; they are what is realized and they determine the world completely. Facts are composite structures, being built from smaller facts. The smallest among these are states of affairs, which, being logically independent of each other, are the atoms out of which the world is constructed.

Before turning to a closer investigation of states of affairs, we must first clear up another point that has been left open, namely, what it means to say that a fact is something that is the case (obtains, is realized, exists).

Apparently, a fact is a special case of a more general category of entities: if there are entities that are the case, then there are also entities that are not the case. The very notion of an atom indeed requires this: states of affairs are logically independent, hence they can both have the property of being the case and lack it. It turns out that the general notion is that of a possible situation (which Wittgenstein often refers to as "situation" [*Sachlage*] [see 2.0122, 2.11]). Facts are situations that obtain: they are the situations that are realized and together make up the world. The atoms from which complex situations are composed are the states of affairs, which, like them, have both the possibility of obtaining and of not obtaining. Actual, that is, obtaining states of affairs can then be properly called "atomic facts."[6] The picture that arises as a result of this is that of a totality of complex possibilities, situations, built from atomic possibilities, states of affairs. Some of these possibilities obtain, and together they form the world.[7] This totality of possibilities makes up what Wittgenstein calls "logical space," and the world is a particular part of it. It is the part that is actually realized. Of course, the nonactual parts might have been realized, too, and hence they form what we may call "possible worlds." In fact, it seems that no further requirements are put on what forms a world, so any maximally consistent selection of possibilities, of situations, can be regarded as a possible world.[8]

The use of the term "space" here is metaphorical, of course. Situations are not to be thought of exclusively as characterizations of some spatial aspect of some possible world. They may be of various ontological demeanor: spatial, temporal, conceptual, mental, and so on. In fact any meaningful sentence depicts a situation, so the variety of types of situations is limited only by what can be expressed in language. But the metaphor is carefully chosen. It is meant to arouse in us associations that are in fact connected with what Wittgenstein himself considered one of the fundamental thoughts of the *Tractatus*—namely, that logical constants do not refer (see 4.0312). For the use of "space" suggests that the entities that are located in logical space are related to each other by that very fact, just like spatial relationships obtain between objects in ordinary space simply by virtue of their being objects situated in that space. In physical space each object occupies a definite position and thereby is spatially related to all other objects situated in the same space. An analogous association is suggested by talking of situations in logical space: they occupy some position and thereby bear intrinsic relationships, this time of a logical nature, to other situations. In other words, the logical relationships between situations are not to be found inside the situations themselves, as separate components thereof, nor are they separate situations or objects of some special logical type. Rather they arise from the very fact that situations are in logical space.[9]

States of Affairs and Objects

Let us now turn to a closer investigation of the states of affairs. Above we indicated why they are properly called the atoms of the tractarian ontology: they are the smallest independent elements from which the larger situations are composed. But, unlike their classical materialistic counterparts, they do not lack internal composition and structure. The states of affairs themselves are in their turn built from yet smaller elements, the objects (*Gegenstände*): "A state of affairs is a connection of objects (things)" (2.01). There are various reasons why in developing an ontology of situations, one would not want to stop at the level of atomic situations. One obvious commonsense reason is that the situations we encounter in everyday life are made up from material objects, people, mental objects, and the like. Another reason, clearly operative in the specific context of the *Tractatus*, is that if we want to use an ontology of situations to give an explication of meaning, we need access to the constituents of situations in order to provide for suitable semantic counterparts of subsentential expressions: if sentences are related to situations their constituents must have counterparts in situations as well.

These considerations clearly motivate a move beyond the level of states of affairs to that of its constituents. But those who expect to find ordinary objects at this level are in for a surprise. Far from being ordinary, the objects of the *Tractatus* have properties that make them a very mysterious, if not downright dubious, ontological category, and their exact nature is a subject of heated debate. This exegetical controversy will be one of the main subjects of Chapter 3; here we just note the most important characteristics the *Tractatus* ascribes to objects, without going too deeply into the question how these should be interpreted.

How do objects form a state of affairs? It is important to note that Wittgenstein locates the formative capacity entirely in the objects themselves. They are not combined by something else; they form combinations out of themselves:

The configuration of objects forms the state of affairs.
In a state of affairs the objects hang together like the links of a chain. (2.0272–2.03)

Just like a chain consists only of its links, with no other thing holding them together, the identity of a state of affairs is completely determined by the objects out of which it is composed. This capacity of objects to concatenate with one another into states of affairs is called their "form" [*Form*]: "The possibility to occur in states of affairs is the form of an object" (2.0141). This is the first passage where the notion of form makes its appearance. Form is one of the most central notions in the entire *Tractatus*. A general characterization of form would be something like "range of possibilities." The notion of form occurs with various types of entities. In the ontological sphere it is objects (2.014) and states of affairs (2.032–2.033) that have form, as does the world (2.022, 2.18, 4.121). With respect to language, form occurs in connection with expressions (3.31ff.), among which we must count both names and sentences. Form is also a key notion when it comes to logic: the most general form of the world, and hence of language, is its logical form (2.18–2.181). In every case the form of an entity of a certain kind (object, state of affairs, name, and so on) determines which of the totality of possibilities determined by its kind, the entity in question has.

Returning to objects, we note that their form, that is, their potential to occur in states of affairs, is claimed to constitute part of their identity conditions: "If I know an object I also know all its possibilities to occur in states of affairs" (2.0123). This seems to imply that not all objects have the same logical form: they are distinguished by the kinds of combinations they can enter into to form a state of affairs. In other words, objects come in different varieties, they are of different types, and the types can be identified with certain combinatorial properties.

This notion of the identity of an object, considered at the level of the variety or type of objects it belongs to, is intimately connected with the notion of an internal property: "To know an object, I indeed need not know its external properties—but I must know all its internal properties" (2.01231). An internal property is a property that constitutes a defining characteristic of the kind of entity to which it can be ascribed. Internal properties are, hence, necessary properties. The passage quoted in the previous paragraph (2.0123) continues as follows:

(Every one of these possibilities must reside in the nature of the object.) A new possibility cannot be discovered afterward. (2.0123)

Thus, the internal properties of an object are essential properties; they are inherent to the nature (*Natur*) of the object. Together they determine to what type an object belongs. And the nature, or essence, of objects is fixed. It follows directly from Wittgenstein's absolutism with respect to logic and necessity, that the internal properties of an object are necessary and do not change.

Opposed to its internal properties are the external properties of an object. These constitute its contingent features. Within the ontology of the *Tractatus*, ascribing an external property to an object is claiming that a certain state of affairs or situation in which it occurs is realized. Hence, the external properties are contingent, dependent on the world and do not determine the identity of an object. In view of this, it can be said that:

Disregarding their external properties—two objects of the same logical form are distinguished only by their being different. (2.0233)

The form of an object does not constitute the identity of the object itself since it may share its form with others. But besides the internal properties constituting its form, an object has only external properties, which are merely contingent features. With respect to the latter two objects of the same form may, of course, differ. However, at the level of identity conditions they are distinguished only by being not the same.[10]

It is important to bear in mind that objects in the tractarian sense are not atoms: they are the smallest entities but they are not independent. An object cannot occur on its own, but only as the constituent of one or more states of affairs:

A thing is independent inasmuch as it can occur in all *possible* situations, but this form of independence is a form of connection with the state of affairs, a form of dependence. (2.0122)

An object is not tied exclusively to a particular state of affairs; it may occur in several, depending on its form. And it follows from their logical independence that some of the states of affairs in which an object occurs may obtain, while others do not. But an object must occur in a state of affairs: that is an inherent property. This places a heavy constraint on the way in which we can interpret the nature of objects. For example, it strongly suggests that they cannot be conceived of as material atoms (elementary particles, or wave packets, or whatever), since for such objects the very possibility of an independent existence, however short-lived this may be, cannot be ruled out a priori. That is to say, even if some or all material atoms actually turned out never to occur on their own, but only in certain configurations, logically speaking they might nevertheless do so. The exclusion of this possibility would be physical, not logical. Hence, they cannot be objects in the tractarian sense. In a similar fashion one might argue that cannot be some kind of perceptual atoms, such as sense data. For such objects, too, it holds that no logical property prevents their independent occurrence, even if other properties would.[11]

We can conclude that objects inherit the logical nature of the entities that they constitute, that is, of the states of affairs. The latter are the smallest elements of a logical atomism: they are the entities that are logically independent. Thus the objects that make them up, too, have to be thought of as logical objects, not as material or perceptual entities.

The picture that emerges is something like this. Using a logical criterion—that of mutual independence—Wittgenstein isolates the atoms of the ontology, the states of affairs. In logical combinations they form situations. If these are to perform the function assigned to them—that of being what meaningful sentences describe—then the move from states of affairs up to situations and finally the world has to be balanced by a move in the other direction, directed at the constituents of states of affairs, which are to function as the counterparts of meaningful subsentential constituents. These constituents are the objects and they, too, form a logical category.

Objects and states of affairs are mutually dependent. The objects appear only as constituents of states of affairs, and conversely, the states of affairs are completely determined by their constituent objects.[12] The possibility of a certain state of affairs obtaining is completely determined by the combinatorial possibilities, the form, of the objects by which it is constituted.[13] Hence it can be said that: "If all objects are given, then thereby all *possible* states of affairs are also given" (2.0124). What is given are all possible states of affairs, of course, not just those that actually obtain. In this sense objects are the "substance of the world" (2.021); they are that which each world has in common with every other, however different (2.022). The objects determine the realm of all possibilities, that is, of all states of affairs, out of which each world "takes its pick," so to speak. Here we see that objects taken as substance and logical space considered as the totality of all possible states of affairs are in fact one and the same thing but viewed from a different angle. That is why Wittgenstein speaks of different worlds sharing a form (2.022), which form is immediately identified with the objects (2.023). This observation underscores the mutual dependence of the two notions of "object" and "state of affairs."

There is one other characteristic of objects that needs to be mentioned, although we shall only touch on it here and postpone a detailed discussion to Chapter 3. It concerns their simplicity. Objects, we are told, are simple (2.02), and the reason for their being simple is the role they play: "Objects form the substance of the world. Therefore they cannot be complex" (2.021). This may seem straightforward. Substance is that from which states of affairs are built. These states of affairs are complex; they have an internal structure. And they are contingent; they obtain in some worlds and fail to obtain in others. Suppose that objects, too, were complex, not simple. In that case their constitution would also be a contingent matter. For, as is axiomatic for Wittgenstein throughout the *Tractatus*, the only necessity there is, is logical necessity (6.3). The notion of a necessary complex is not ruled out ipso facto, but what would such a complexity amount to? If we say of some entity that it is complex, that is, that it has an internal structure, we mean that it has parts that make up the entity but that can in principle be identified separately. However, the concept of a logically necessary structure is at odds with this intuition and hence seems incoherent. Therefore, we may venture that if Wittgenstein speaks of complexity he means the contingent constitution of an entity. Evidently, if objects were complex in this sense, they could not form the substance of the world, that which all worlds have in common. For in some worlds a complex object might indeed "exist," that is, might indeed be constituted from its component parts, whereas in others the constitution might have "fallen apart," in which case the object would no longer be. That substance should not be viewed in this way is stated in 2.024: "Substance is what exists independently of what is the case." Contingent existence, that is, the kind of existence we would be likely to attribute to complex entities such as material objects, is a concept that does not apply to objects in the tractarian sense. And this seems to imply that objects are simple.

An argumentation like this fits in well with the tractarian framework. True, a straightforward formulation of one of its premises—that the existence of complex entities is contingent, not necessary—does not appear in the text, but it certainly does not seem alien to the spirit of the *Tractatus*. However, quite surprisingly, in the passages that deal with simplicity of objects (2.02–2.0212) Wittgenstein presents a completely different line of argument, one that appeals to features of language and description. After stating in 2.02 that objects are simple, Wittgenstein immediately goes on to notice that a statement about a complex entity can be analyzed in terms of sentences that describe the complex entity in question completely. Then follows 2.021, quoted above, in which the simplicity of objects is connected with their being the substance of the world. And this remark is followed by two more remarks (2.0211–2.0212) on language, which are obviously intended as an argument for the existence of substance. Basically, substance is presented there as a prerequisite for the meaningfulness of language. The argument itself, and its possible repercussions for a proper interpretation of the ontology, will be discussed in detail in Chapter 3.

In connection with the simplicity of objects another dependency between objects and states of affairs should be noted—namely, between the simplicity of the former and the logical independence of latter. The simplicity of objects and the atomicity of states of affairs are closely connected. Evidently, if objects were not simple but rather were complex, yet formed the ultimate constituents of states of affairs, the latter would not be logically independent. If a certain object were complex, its contingent existence would be a state of affairs or situation, one that might obtain or not obtain. And the possibility of realization of another state of affairs in which this object occurred would consequently be dependent on the realization of the first. This means that to investigate the nature of the objects is to investigate that of states of affairs. And it follows that reasons for objects being simple are at the same time reasons for states of affairs being logically independent.

Structure and Form

Finally, we note yet another relationship between objects and states of affairs. Objects have form, combinatorial possibilities. When certain objects of certain forms fit together, they constitute a state of affairs. The resulting state of affairs also has a form, which is directly determined by that of its constituent objects. Wittgenstein introduces the notion of form with respect to states of affairs indirectly through the notion of "structure": "The

50 *Main Themes*

way in which objects are connected in a state of affairs is the structure of the state of affairs" (2.032). A number of objects together make up a particular state of affairs. The objects do so by virtue of their form: they connect in a particular way, and this constitutes the structure of the state of affairs. In other words, a specification of the structure of a state of affairs is a specification of two things: of the particular objects out of which it is constituted and of the forms of these objects. If we leave out the first, what we get is the form of a state of affairs: "Form is the possibility of structure" (2.033). The point is this. In general there will be more than one object that has a certain form, but a given state of affairs will always be constituted by particular objects.[14] If we abstract away from the objects exemplifying the form, what we get is an abstract specification that represents a possibility: fill it with particular objects of the required forms and what you get is a concrete state of affairs. Fill it with different objects, of the same forms, and the result is a different state of affairs that has something in common with the first: its form.[15]

Consider the following abstract example. Suppose there are two types of objects, t_1 and t_2, which combine in the following way: an object of t_2 followed by one of t_1 and followed by one of t_2 again, constitutes a state of affairs. Let R be of type t_1, and let a and b be of type t_2. Then aRb is a state of affairs, and its structure can be pictorially illustrated by a tree-like diagram such as given in Figure 1.

Of course, this diagram is only an abstract illustration of some aspects of the structure of a state of affairs. Abstracting away from the concrete objects that constitute this state of affairs gives us its form, which can be specified as in Figure 2.

The diagram in Figure 2 no longer constitutes a picture of a state of affairs, but rather represents that which two states of affairs may have in common. So, despite appearances, form is not something that is to be found in a state affairs next to, or over and above, the objects constituting it. Suppose S is another object of type t_1, and c and d are objects of type t_2 different from a and b. Then the diagram in Figure 3 gives us another state of affairs that is of the same logical form as that in Figure 1.

The notion of form of states of affairs is extremely important for the whole theory of language, meaning, and logic that the *Tractatus* subsequently develops. By implication, it is extended from states of affairs to more complex structures: "The structure of a fact consists of the structures

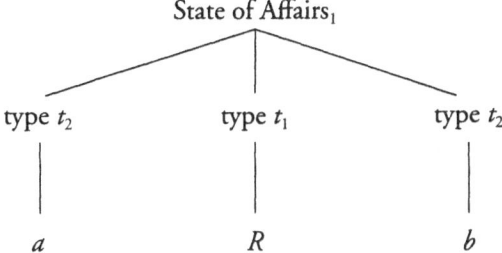

FIGURE 1. A State of Affairs

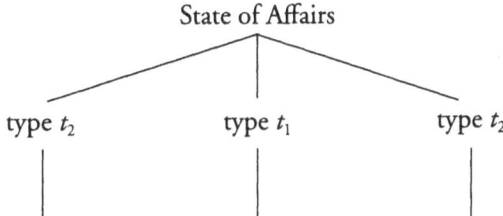

FIGURE 2. The Form of a State of Affairs

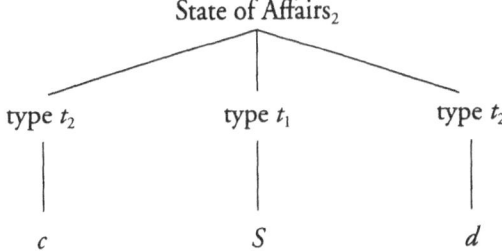

FIGURE 3. Another State of Affairs

of the states of affairs" (2.034). Not only states of affairs but also situations have a structure and hence a form, which means that situations, too, can share a form, be of the same form. Generalizing in the manner of 2.034, we arrive through the form of facts at the form of the world, and through the form of situations at the form of logical space.

With this general notion of form of situations, the basic concepts required for the picture theory of meaning are given and the stage is set for its unfolding, to which we now turn.

PICTURING

"We make ourselves pictures of the facts" (2.1): with that claim Wittgenstein starts his compact exposition of the general picture theory. Later on this general theory will be applied to language, but the exposition that Wittgenstein initially gives is meant to be complete and perfectly general. It is intended as a statement of the fundamental principles for anything to have meaning.

Pictures as Facts

In conjunction with the claim that "a picture is a fact" (2.141) the opening passage implies that one thing should be clear right from the start: pictures are facts and what they depict are facts, too, not things. (Thus, 2.1 and 2.141 echo 1.1.) How are we to understand this? For intuitively we are inclined to think of pictures as things, and in many cases what a picture depicts is intuitively taken to be a thing, too. For example, Vermeer's *View of Delft* is a thing, consisting of canvas, paint, and wood. What it depicts is the city of Delft: also a thing, but on a different scale and of a different nature. Or consider a map, say of the Dutch province of Friesland. It, too, is a thing, much folded, worn on the sides, with coffee stains and all. And, again, what the map refers to is also a thing in some sense of the word, but certainly not a fact. Or so it seems.

However, things may not be so simple if we ask ourselves how it is that a picture is able to tell us something. Take the example of the map. Sure, it is a material object, fabricated in certain ways from certain materials, spatio-temporally located in a certain position, and so on. But even the most exhaustive description of a map along these lines will not reveal that that is what it is: a map, something that refers to something outside itself and that tells us something about that to which it refers (correctly or incorrectly). If we want to explain to someone who has never used maps before what a map is, we will not refer to the various aspects of its material constitution or to other properties that are connected with it being a material object. Rather, we will speak of how it is used. We will explain that small black lines represent railways, and red ones motorways, that dots stand for cities, and that the bigger the dot is, the larger the city. We will point out that a light-green color means a clay soil, whereas purple refers to moors. Then we will show him or her how to use the map, say to find out how to travel from Leeuwarden to Dokkum. We will point out that the upper side of the map points to north. We will throw in a few remarks about scales and maybe even some about various chart projections. In doing all this we constantly make use of the structure of the map: of the way in which it is composed of its constituent elements. We identify the elements (lines, dots, colors) and explain their use (that is, their form). We also make use of the more abstract constituent parts, such as its two-dimensional spatial features. In other words, what we do is treat the map, not as a thing, but as something that has a certain structure, that is, as a situation, a fact. Likewise, what the map refers to, what it depicts is also not treated as some kind of thing, but rather as something that has a certain structure: the various elements have a distinct form that determines the relationships they bear to each other.

Pictorial Form and Pictorial Relation

These considerations bring out the point that is made by the two passages cited above. Both a picture and what it depicts have to be viewed, not as things, but as structured wholes, that is, as situations.[16] The point is crucial, since the pictorial relationship is defined in terms of the structures of the picture and the depicted, respectively. Structure has two aspects: form, and elements instantiating, or embodying, this form. Both play an essential role in defining when one situation depicts another. These aspects are characterized as follows:

That the elements of a picture are related to one another in a specific way represents that things are related to one another in that way.

54   *Main Themes*

> This connection of the elements of a picture will be called its structure and the possibility of this structure its pictorial form. (2.15)

This introduces the notion of "pictorial form" [*Form der Abbildung*], which is, of course, the same notion of form that was discussed above. The second aspect is introduced in the following passage:

> The pictorial relationship consists of the correlations between the elements of the picture and things. (2.1514)

The pictorial relationship (*die abbildende Beziehung*) is best thought of as a one-to-one mapping between the constituents of the picture and those of the depicted situation. Each element in the former represents an element in the latter and vice versa. This means that picture and depicted have the same number of elements.[17]

So, one situation picturing another depends on two things: that the constituent elements of the picture represent constituent elements of the situation depicted, and that the picture and the situation depicted have the same form.[18]

This can be illustrated by a very simple example. Suppose that when queried about the relative geographical positions of the cities of Amsterdam and Rotterdam, I want to picture the actual situation that Amsterdam lies (roughly) north of Rotterdam. I could do this in the following way. I take two coffee mugs and declare that the first one, say a red one, stands for Amsterdam and that the second one, let it be a white one, represents Rotterdam. This establishes a pictorial relationship between the respective mugs and the respective cities, but the result is not yet a picture. Now I identify the north, for example, by pointing in that direction and then I hold the red mug north of the white one. This spatial arrangement of the mugs then pictures the situation I have in mind: that Amsterdam is north of Rotterdam.

It is of crucial importance to realize that the picture in this case consists not just of the two coffee mugs, but also of these mugs being arranged in (physical) space in a certain way. What makes the arrangement a picture of the geographic fact in question is that the element representing Amsterdam itself bears a certain relation—namely, that of being located north of—the other element, which represents Rotterdam. So the spatial relation between the mugs is as much an element of the picture as the two mugs themselves.[19] The example also makes clear that the form of the pictorial elements is what makes a pictorial relationship possible: in the relevant aspect, that of being located in space, the mugs and the cities have the same form. The same situation can also be pictured in a more abstract way, for example, by using a map of the relevant area. When confronted with the same query, I could take a map, identify the cities on the map and trust that my audience is sufficiently familiar with the use of maps to figure out the answer. Note that by proceeding in this way a conventional element is introduced into the picture—namely, that of the upper side of the map representing the North.[20] In this case it is a spatial feature of the map that is part of the picture: on the map the dot representing Rotterdam is below that representing Amsterdam on a straight line.[21]

Yet another example, finally, is provided by linguistic expressions. Consider the sentence "Amsterdam lies north of Rotterdam." It, too, contains three elements: the proper names "Amsterdam" and "Rotterdam" and the relational expression "lies north of." An obvious pictorial relationship associates the names with the respective cities and the relational expression with the relevant geographical relation. But notice that as such that is not enough to get a picture of the situation. We need more than an association of expressions with elements of the situation to be depicted. There should also be identity of form. In the first case, that of the coffee mugs placed in an appropriate spatial relationship, picture and depicted shared a spatial form. In this case the form shared is more abstract. The cities are located in space, but the relevant form of the expressions is not their spatial arrangement but rather their grammatical relationship. It is by virtue of "Amsterdam" being the subject of the sentence in question and "Rotterdam" being the direct object, that the sentence depicts the situation in question. If we reverse these roles, what we get is also a picture, but of a different situation—that of Rotterdam lying to the north of Amsterdam. Notice that the fact that in English the subject and object roles are expressed in more or less spatial terms, namely, in terms of word order, is a rather superficial property. Other languages express the same distinction in terms of case marking, or by yet other means.

Logical Form

What do the grammatical form of the sentence and the spatial form of the situation have in common? At this point the distinction between pictorial form and logical form becomes relevant. The notion of pictorial form was introduced in 2.15 and is further explained in 2.151:

> The pictorial form is the possibility that things are related to one another in the same way as the elements of the picture. (2.151)

The picture is a situation, which means that it has a form: its elements are related to each other in a particular way, which, in its turn, depends on their combinatorial possibilities, their forms (see 2.032, 2.033). The elements of the picture are correlated with things in the situation that is depicted, via the pictorial relationship. Regarding the first situation as a picture of the second means that we view the way in which the elements of the picture are related as a representation of the way in which the corresponding things are connected. Pictorial form is described as a possibility, and this is in accordance with the way in which the notions of "form" and "structure" were introduced. Form is the possibility of structure; thus the form of the picture is the possibility of a certain structure, more in particular the possibility of the structure of the situation depicted. In the first instance, the requirement that picture and depicted share their form is stated in terms of pictorial form:

> What a picture must have in common with reality, in order to be able to depict it—correctly or incorrectly—in the way it does, is its pictorial form. (2.17)

Concrete aspects of a situation can be involved in making it a picture. In the case of the coffee mugs, their relative position in a spatial framework oriented toward the geographical north is an element of the picturing situation on which its being a picture of the fact that Amsterdam lies north of Rotterdam depends. In this case the pictorial form involves spatial form, and the picture and the situation depicted share this spatial form. This is expressed in 2.171: "A picture can depict any reality whose form it has. A spatial picture can depict anything spatial, a colored one anything colored, and so on."

However, that the sentence "Amsterdam lies north of Rotterdam" pictures the same fact shows that sharing a form need not always be sharing a particular, concrete formal aspect. For obviously, the spatial arrangement of the words is irrelevant for the sentence depicting the geographical situation in question. Evidently, we need to view both picture and situation depicted at a more abstract level in order to find a common form. This abstract form is what Wittgenstein calls "logical form":

> What any picture, of whatever form, must have in common with reality, in order to be able to depict it—correctly or incorrectly—at all, is the logical form, that is, the form of reality. (2.18)

Thus, logical form is what every picture shares with what it depicts: "A picture has the logical pictorial form in common with what it depicts" (2.2).[22]

Of course, picture and depicted may also share a nonlogical pictorial form, but in a certain sense that is not what constitutes the depicting relationship. For sharing a nonlogical form is a contingent feature, and what Wittgenstein seems to be getting at here is that it must always be possible to analyze picture and depicted in such a way and at such a basic level that no dependence on contingencies such as these remains. So although in fact the depicting relation between two situations may be based on a contingent-shared pictorial form, logically speaking this is not what makes one a picture of the other. Ultimately picturing requires sharing a logical form, a form that disregards the contingent features that picture and depicted also may have in common. Thus:

> Every picture is *also* a logical one. (However, not every picture is, for example, a spatial one.) (2.182)

This notion of logical form, the form of reality, or logical space, lies at the heart of the picture theory of meaning. It reveals the highly abstract, logical nature of that theory. Whatever a picture is, in the sense of whatever contingent features it may have, which may contingently enter into its picturing a situation, at bottom it is a logical picture. That is why every possible situation can in principle be depicted, no matter what its contingent features are: "A picture depicts a possible situation in logical space" (2.202). The only limitation set on picturing is that what is depicted is a situation, that is, something in logical space, no other properties being assumed to be present: "A picture contains the possibility of the situation that it depicts" (2.203).

Truth and Falsity

Picture and depicted are both situations, and not things; hence, it is natural to speak of true and false pictures. But since pictures depict possible situations and not just facts, their mere picturing does not establish their truth. In effect, all that is established by the observation that something is a picture is that it corresponds to a logically possible situation, one that may either obtain or not. In terms of this obtaining and not-obtaining of situations, Wittgenstein defines truth and falsity. A picture is true if the situation it depicts obtains; it is false if the situation does not obtain. In a nutshell this is the *Tractatus* theory of truth.

Notice that the intensional nature of states of affairs and situations is essential here. It is by availing himself of an ontology that acknowledges both existing and nonexisting states of affairs, and complexes thereof, that Wittgenstein manages to circumvent the age-old problem of true negative sentences. Of course, within a purely extensional framework this problem can be solved too, but only at a cost. The problem can be stated succinctly as follows. If what makes a sentence true is that it corresponds to a fact, what then is it that makes a negative sentence, one of the form *not-p* true? The answer to this question must meet certain requirements, one of them being that different negative sentences should be assigned different meanings. Within the extensional setup this means that they should be made true by different entities.

Depending on one's metaphysical inclinations one might prefer one answer over another. Russell, for example in his *The Philosophy of Logical Atomism* (1918–19), argues that there may be good reasons for postulating a category of "negative facts": according to him, just as there is an actual fact in the world of London being the capital of Great Britain, there may also be, in the same sense, an actual, negative fact of it not being the capital of France.[23] But others objected, mainly because of the ontological extravaganza that this solution seems to imply.[24]

Wittgenstein solves the problem in a different way. Instead of assuming that there is such a thing as the fact of "*not-p*," he observes that what makes *not-p* true is the same thing as what makes *p* false—namely, the not obtaining of *p*. So instead of postulating a separate fact "*not-p*" distinct from a fact "*p*," Wittgenstein makes do with just one entity. But it is no longer a fact, that is, something that is part of the actual world. By introducing possible states of affairs, that is, by allowing both obtaining and nonobtaining states of affairs, and pictures that depict such states of affairs Wittgenstein can explain what it is that makes a negative sentence of the form *not-p* true: that the state of affairs that is pictured by *p* does not obtain.[25]

Saying and Showing

So the notion of picturing is a broad one: any two situations that have the same logical form can be made to picture each other by setting up an appropriate pictorial relationship between their elements. But there is one thing that cannot be pictured—namely, pictorial form, and hence also logical form: "However, a picture cannot depict its pictorial form; it shows it" (2.172). Why should this be so? It is important to see what Wittgenstein is getting at here. Does this remark mean that the pictorial form of one picture can never be pictured by some other picture? Yes and no. Of course, various aspects of the pictorial form of a map can be described, that is, depicted. Likewise, the distribution in space of the coffee mugs can be pictured in all sorts of ways. But in that case what is depicted are contingent features. A picture can never itself depict its own pictorial form, that is, those of its formal aspects by virtue of which it is a picture.[26] Consequently, logical form cannot be depicted at all. For the logical form of situations is not a contingent feature, as other aspects of pictorial form may be, but rather a necessary one. Hence it can never be analyzed as a contingent situation that can be depicted.

Another way of arguing for the same result is the following. Given Wittgenstein's absolutism, there is at bottom only one way in which a picture can have meaning, one way in which something can be a picture of something else. The logical form that picture and depicted share can itself not be depicted, precisely because it forms the condition of possibility of any picture whatsoever. This impossibility of stepping out of the frame of reference is a recurrent theme in the *Tractatus*. In connection with sentences the point is formulated explicitly as follows:

> A sentence can depict all of reality, but it cannot depict what it must have in common with reality in order for it to be able to depict it—logical form.
>
> In order to be able to depict logical form, we would have to be able to position ourselves with sentences outside logic, that is to say, outside the world. (4.12)

The point is clear: in order to depict (describe, represent) logical form, which is the ultimate form of reality, we would have to be able to take up a position "outside." But that is impossible: for there would not be any means to represent anything from such a hypothetical, Archimedean point outside logical space. Identity of logical form is a requirement for any form of representation; hence it cannot be done away with.

Connected with the impossibility of picturing or describing logical form is the distinction between saying and showing. Although a picture does not depict what it has in common with what it depicts, it does show its pictorial form, as 2.172 puts it ("Es weist sie auf."). It lays it open to view, so to speak, but what it thus shows is not part of its content. Again the point returns in connection with sentences:

A sentence cannot depict logical form: logical form is mirrored in it. What mirrors itself in language, language cannot depict. What expresses *itself* in language, *we* cannot express by means of language.

A sentence *shows* the logical form of reality. It displays it. (4.121)

This notion of showing as opposed to saying is one of the earliest of Wittgenstein's contributions to the philosophy of logic.[27] It is closely connected with his emphasis on the absoluteness of logic and the universality of language. The saying–showing distinction represents a true dichotomy: "What *can* be shown, *cannot* be said" (4.1212). And the opposition between what can be said and what can be shown is a logical or linguistic reflection of the ontological opposition between the contingent and the necessary. They match perfectly: anything that can be said is contingent, and vice versa. Likewise, anything that is necessary can be shown, and vice versa. The distinction is a crucial element in Wittgenstein's characterization of the principles underlying any form of symbolic representation. For it allows him to account for these principles in a way that leads neither to a vicious circle nor to an infinite regress.

Let us take stock. Wittgenstein's theory of picturing is a general and highly abstract theory of what it takes for something to be a picture of something else. Both a picture and that which it depicts have to be thought of as situations, as structured wholes that instantiate a form. Ultimately the basic form is logical form. Picture and depicted share this logical form, and it is by virtue of this identity of form and of the existence of a pictorial relationship between their respective elements that one situation is a picture of the other. Logical form, being what makes picturing possible in the first place, can itself not be pictured.

Thoughts as Pictures

The picture theory plays an important role in the realization of the main aims of the *Tractatus*—the drawing of the limits of thought, and thereby the safeguarding of ethics. So how is the picture theory tied up with thought? Every picture is also a logical one. And logical pictures are called "thoughts": "The logical picture of the facts is a thought" (3). This places the notion of a thought at the center of the picture theory. All pictures are logical pictures, so all pictures are thoughts. This central position of thoughts in the tractarian system comes as no surprise given the way in which the aim of the book is described in the preface: "... to draw a limit to thought." But this does not mean that the *Tractatus* is an epistemological undertaking in the traditional sense of the word, for the sentence just quoted continues thus: "or rather—not to thought, but to the expression of thought." Traditional questions are given a new logical twist. The reasons behind this have already been discussed above. But it is important to bear this in mind, for it means that when the *Tractatus* mentions thoughts, we must be aware that what is meant is a very abstract notion.[28]

Being a logical picture, a thought needs no other similarity with the situation it depicts than identity of logical form. Hence a thought can picture any reality, however different from the actual world. So the limits of thinking are drawn quite liberally: anything that is logically possible can be thought: thinking and the world are perfect mirrors of each other. Since a picture depicts a situation in logical space (2.02), it follows that what thoughts are about is possible as well; hence thoughts are logically contingent:

> A thought contains the possibility of the situation that it thinks. What is thinkable is possible too. (3.02)

This means that there is no such thing as a contradictory or a tautological thought.[29] And since every picture is also a logical picture, that is, a thought, there can be no contradictory or tautological pictures of any kind, as likewise there can be no contradictory or tautological, yet meaningful sentences.

At first sight this may seem strange and in a certain sense it is merely a consequence of the way in which Wittgenstein defines his terms. But it is a consequence that does illustrate an important aspect of our intuitive grasp of these notions. For what do we mean if we say that a thought is contradictory or that someone believes a contradiction? Thoughts are pictures and as such they say something, they state a claim about how the world is. In this sense, believing a contradiction seems impossible: no one can claim, and hence believe, that the world satisfies both *p* and *not-p*. Of course, someone may very well have contradictory beliefs, that is, both believe *p* and believe *not-p*, but no one can positively believe that both *p* and *not-p*.[30] Therefore:

> We cannot think anything illogical, since if we did, we would have to think illogically. (3.03)

In other words, a contradictory thought cannot be consciously entertained as something that depicts, that is, as something that states a claim about what the world is like. In that sense any picture, hence any thought, is logically contingent. A picture stakes a claim to truth: it aims to describe some aspect of reality, be it actual or possible, in a truthful manner. In other words, if we decide to regard something as a picture this is not without consequences: it involves a relationship to reality—namely, the claim that reality is like the picture.[31] That is why there cannot be contradictory, that is, logically impossible, pictures. For the claim to truth that is an inherent feature of a picture derives from those properties by virtue of which it is a picture in the first place.

Picture and depicted share pictorial form and the most abstract pictorial form is logical form. This implies that picture and depicted must be contingent. An example may serve to illustrate this. A picture in three-dimensional Euclidean space can depict situations in this space, given a suitable pictorial relationship between the various elements, but not a situation that conflicts with the laws of Euclidean geometry.[32] The reason is simple: picture and depicted must share as their common pictorial form that of three-dimensional Euclidean space. Hence both must conform to its laws. But notice that we can depict a three-dimensional non-Euclidean situation using a two-dimensional Euclidean picture. The reason that the latter is possible whereas the former is not is the following. Such a two-dimensional Euclidean picture depicts a non-Euclidean situation by virtue of a common pictorial form that combines two elements—namely, the form of Euclidean two-dimensional space and logical form. The non-Euclidean aspect of the situation depicted resides in the third dimension, that of height (depth). This dimension is not part of the common pictorial form of picture and depicted, since it is neither part of two-dimensional space nor of logical form. Notice that such a picture, like any other picture, depicts something that is logically possible.

This suggests also why there cannot be logically impossible pictures. Since logical form is the ultimate, most abstract pictorial form, it is impossible for a picture to be in conflict with it, that is, to contradict the laws of logic. For if such were the case, the picture in question would have to use, in its picturing, a pictorial form that is even more abstract than logical form, which there is not. This means that if something is in conflict with the laws of logic it simply lacks anything that it could have

Main Themes 63

in common with a situation to be depicted and hence must fail to be a picture.[33]

Notice that Wittgenstein's absolutism with regard to logic plays a decisive role here. If one took into account other logical systems besides classical logic, such as minimal logic or intuitionistic logic, it might very well be the case that something would contradict the laws of classical logic and hence would not be a picture on that account, but at the same time would conform to the laws of intuitionistic logic, or those of minimal logic, and would count as picture in that sense. But given that Wittgenstein acknowledges only classical, two-valued logic, the impossibility of a logically impossible picture is absolute.[34]

Wittgenstein goes to quite some length to stress this point. And remarkably, again he formulates it in terms of language:

> It used to be said that God could create anything, but not something that would go against the laws of logic.—For we could not *say* of an "illogical" world what it would look like. (3.031)

The reason for the reference to language in this context is the intrinsic relation between language and thought. In 3.1 Wittgenstein says, "In the sentence the thought expresses itself so that it is perceptible by the senses." Sentences, then, are thoughts in a perceptible form.

Here we come to the next step in the unfolding of the tractarian system: the connection between thought and language. The goal of drawing the limits of thought, it was claimed in the preface, can be reached only indirectly, by drawing the limits of what can be said. And the reason for that lies in the intrinsically logical structure of the totality of the meaningful. Therefore, we now turn to the linguistic theory that the *Tractatus* offers.

LANGUAGE

Sentences as Pictures

The tractarian view on language is basically an implementation of the general theory of picturing. The most general type of picture is a logical picture, a thought. And thoughts find a perceptible expression in sentences. In this way any situation, be it actual or possible, can be communicated:

We use the sensorially perceptible sign of the sentence (auditory, written, and so on) as a projection of the possible situation.

The projection method is the thinking of the meaning of the sentence. (3.11)

In a sentence a connection is made between what is called a "sentential sign" [*Satzzeichen*] and a situation. The situation is the meaning of the sentence. Thus Wittgenstein analyzes a sentence at three different levels: that of the sentential sign, that of the sentence, and that of its meaning. The distinction between sentential sign and sentence is the following. The sentential sign is the sentence viewed as a sensory object, that is, as a string of marks or a complex of sounds. By itself it has no symbolic power; it does not represent or picture anything. It is merely what it is as a physical object and as such it is not perceived, or used, as an element of a system of symbolic representations. In order to get a feeling for what is meant here, think of an expression in an unknown language written down in an unknown script. If the script is sufficiently unfamiliar, we may not even recognize the expression as such, but mistake it for an ornament or for a doodle. Or think of the utterly strange way speech in an unknown language unrelated to our mother tongue may sound to our ear. It can be so strange that we have a real difficulty believing that the people uttering these sounds are really speaking and not just making funny noises. It is only when we recognize a sentential sign as belonging to a particular symbolic system that it becomes a sentence: "A sentence is a sentential sign in its projective relation to the world" (3.12). A sentence, then, is a thing, a physical object, viewed in a particular way, namely, as standing in a pictorial relationship to the world.[35] For the sentences of our own language it may be difficult to make the distinction between sentential sign and sentence, that is, to distinguish between the perceptible and the symbolic aspect. But the consideration of unfamiliar scripts and phonetic systems may help. Or think of the various examples of pictures we discussed above. Certainly, a particular spatial arrangement of two coffee mugs will strike us as a picture only after we have "added" the pictorial relationship. Without that, it is just what it is: two coffee mugs in physical space. Likewise, without the pictorial relationship a written or spoken sentence is just what it is: a string of marks or a complex of sounds.

Observe that in 3.11 Wittgenstein describes the connection between a sentence and the situation it depicts in terms of the process of thinking. This does not seem to square with his alleged antipsychologism, according

Main Themes   65

to which the traditional epistemological questions concerning thought and knowledge are not the most fundamental ones. But we also saw that thought and thinking have to be taken in a wide sense, so as to encompass all logically possible ways of picturing, which seems to deprive them of any intrinsic relation to human thinking that is of interest to epistemology as traditionally conceived. In the present context, that of an analysis of how a sentential sign, that is, a physical object, becomes a sentence, that is, an element of a symbolic system, the appeal to thinking can perhaps best be interpreted as follows.

First of all, it should be noted that a sentential sign is not intrinsically also a sentence, that is, a picture. It has to be viewed as such, since its pictorial character is not an inherent property, but rather something that has to be "read into it," so to speak. This means that it has to be regarded as something that has a certain structure, its elements standing in a projective relation to elements outside. This reading of a structure into something that by itself is merely a perceptible entity is done from the outside and "thinking" is simply Wittgenstein's general term for describing this process. Of course, once the sentential sign is viewed as a sentence, that is, as a picture, the pictorial relationship is an internal property, for the pictorial relationship "belongs to the picture" (2.1513).[36] Notice that the possibility of something to be a sentence (a picture, a symbol) is an inherent property of it, not one that we can attribute to it (through some convention). That would make meaning rest on a contingent basis. Of course, whether we actually use some concrete thing as a symbol is conventional and hence contingent. But that does not conflict with the inherent symbolic nature of things. Hence, it seems we must distinguish between taking a sentential sign as a sentence and attributing a meaning to it. The former depends on the recognition of an internal property, that is, a logical possibility. The latter depends on all kinds of conventional relations.

Furthermore, we may regard Wittgenstein's use of "thinking" in 3.11 as his way of dealing with the fact that in the case of actual languages or other symbolic systems the meaning-relation is essentially a conventional relation. Both natural and formal languages express the meanings they do by virtue of what is essentially a conventional assignment of meanings to their various expressions. Thus something extralinguistic has to assign the meanings to the expressions and Wittgenstein appeals to a long philosophical tradition in using the term "thinking" for this act of bestowing meaning, which he refers to as "the thinking of the meaning of the sentence."[37]

Of course, realizing that a sentential sign is a sentence, that it forms part of some language, is not the same as knowing its meaning. It means viewing it as something that has a meaning, but as such that falls short of actually knowing its meaning. Thus, there is a third aspect to discern with respect to a sentence: its meaning. A sentence can also be viewed as something that means *this*, as something that stands in a pictorial relationship to a particular situation. This is what is meant with the phrase "meaningful sentence" [*sinvolle Satz*].[38] These two aspects are distinguished in 3.13, where Wittgenstein states that "everything that is part of the projection is part of the sentence, but not that which is projected." The projection consists of form and pictorial relationship, but not of the projected situation. The latter is the meaning of a sentence, hence: ". . . its meaning is not yet included in the sentence, but the possibility to express it is" (3.13).

This "possibility to express its meaning" that is inherent in a sentence is its form. This means that a sentence is something that is articulate (3.141), which has a certain structure. In tractarian terms: "a sentential sign is a fact" (3.14). It is in view of this property that a sentence can be brought in a projective relationship to the world. Being a structured entity is a prerequisite for the possibility to express a meaning. For sentences, Wittgenstein notes, it may not be obvious that they meet this requirement:

> That the sentential sign is a fact is obscured by the usual form of expression of writing or printing.
> For in a printed sentence, for example, the sentential sign does not look essentially different from a word. (3.143)

The last point becomes more obvious when one considers a language like Latin, which does not use pronominal subjects and in which what looks like a single word, for example, *ambulo*, in fact is a sentence ("I walk"), which logically speaking has two separate components.[39]

Likewise, it is important to note that a sentence in which all elements of the depicted situation are associated with distinct expressions, is more than just the collection of those expressions. Essentially it is something that is of a certain form: "A sentence is not a jumble of words" (3.141).[40] And it has to have structure, that is, form, since "only facts can express a meaning, a set of names cannot" (3.142). This refers to an essential element of Wittgenstein's general theory of picturing, put to work in its application to language. Sentences are pictures; they have a pictorial form, which in most cases more or less coincides with their grammatical form. A consideration of the following two simple sentences will make clear what is at stake. Consider: "Amsterdam lies north of Rotterdam," and "Rotterdam lies north of Amsterdam." Both sentences are built from the same three main elements: the names "Amsterdam" and "Rotterdam" and the relational expression "lies north of."[41] This in itself is sufficient to show what 3.142 expresses—namely, that a mere set of expressions in itself does not form a sentence. Obviously, what is also important is the way in which the expressions are related in the sentence, which in the present case can be described in terms of the grammatical roles they play. In both sentences the relational expression forms the verbal part of the predicate. In the first sentence, the name "Amsterdam" functions as the subject and the name "Rotterdam" together with the relational expression forms the intransitive predicate. In the second sentence these roles are reversed. In either case a different sentence and a different assertion results. This shows, for a very simple example, what the pictorial form of a sentence can be like. It is the way in which the expressions are combined that is a crucial factor in establishing which situation is pictured. This, of course, depends on the inherent combinatorial possibilities of the expressions involved. For example, it is an internal property of the names "Amsterdam" and "Rotterdam" that they can perform the role of grammatical subject, a possibility that the relational expression "lies north of" does not have.

In this way the idea of regarding a sentence as a picture solves an age-old problem, that of "the unity of the proposition." In many traditional approaches, words were essentially viewed as names for entities of various kinds. Thus in "Paris loves Helen" the names "Paris" and "Helen" refer to two concrete individuals and "loves" is taken to denote the more abstract entity of Love. But, as we all know, merely throwing two people and Love together does not determine one particular situation. Frege's solution was to assume that the referent of a predicative expression is an "unsaturated" object, that is, a kind of entity that needs one or more other entities for its completion.[42] Wittgenstein's solution is similar, except that he does not make an explicit distinction between unsaturated concepts (Frege's "Begriffe"), the referents of predicates, and saturated individuals, the referents of names. In his abstract analysis every element of a picture, and hence every element of a sentence, refers to something that is unsaturated and indeed is itself unsaturated. For both the constituents of a picture and the elements in the depicted situation are entities that are characterized by their combinatorial possibilities, that is, by their internal relationships with objects of similar and other types.[43]

By now it should be clear what the application of the general picture theory to sentences demands: that we view a sentence as a structured whole, that is, that we regard the elements as standing in internal relationships to each other and as bearing a projective relationship to elements in the situation depicted. Thus a sentence functions as a "tableau vivant," presenting the situation that is its meaning:

> One name stands for one thing, another for another thing, and they are connected with one another. In this way the whole—like a tableau vivant—presents a state of affairs. (4.0311)

The two elements that make one situation a picture of another occur here almost literally. There must be a pictorial relationship, in this case a correspondence between names and entities, and identity of form: the way in which the names are related with one another in the sentence mirrors the way in which the corresponding objects are tied together in the depicted situation.

Identity of form and pictorial relationship are not depicted by the sentence itself, they do not belong to its assertoric content. Here Wittgenstein makes the distinction between what a sentence says and what it shows. The situation that a sentence depicts, is its meaning (see 2.21). And its meaning is what a sentence shows: "A sentence *shows* its meaning" (4.022). Understanding a sentence involves knowing its meaning, that is, knowing the possible situation it depicts: ". . . if I understand a sentence, I know the situation it represents" (4.021). But a sentence not only shows, it also asserts something:

> A sentence *shows* how things stand *if* it is true. And it *says that* things do so stand. (4.022)

A sentence not only determines a certain region in logical space, but it also asserts that this region is part of the actual world. Hence, for Wittgenstein a sentence is essentially an attempt at a (partial) determination of reality. Of course, a sentence may fail to determine the world as it is; it may be false. That is, although it has a pretense to truth, it may not live up to it. But by distinguishing the assertoric element and the meaning proper Wittgenstein avoids the problem of the meaningfulness of false sentences. Whether true or false, a sentence always has meaning, always determines some part of logical space. However, the assertoric force is an inherent feature of a sentence, as it is of pictures in general. This is why Wittgenstein describes the most general form of sentences as "This is how things stand" (4.5). The essence of a sentence, of language as such, is to reach out to reality, to describe. This feature, being necessary, again cannot be expressed in the sentence itself. The sentence does not say that it says something, it says what it says and shows that it says something.[44]

Creativity and Compositionality

Another aspect of the application of the picture theory to language concerns the issue of creativity. The structure of the picture theory provides an intuitive explanation for the fact that we are able to understand and to produce a potentially infinite number of sentences. The way in which a sentence determines its meaning and the truth-functional nature of all sentential operations are operative here. Wittgenstein discusses the point in connection with translation:

> The translation of one language into another does not proceed in such a way that one translates every sentence of the one into a sentence of the other, rather only the sentential elements are translated. (4.025)

At first sight this may appear rather naive. For translation to succeed, a dictionary alone will not do. We also need a correlation between the grammars of the respective languages. Recall, however, that expressions have form. This means that in the tractarian view a word comes with its logical grammar, that is, its combinatorial possibilities, and hence, with its potential for forming meaningful combinations with other words.

Whether the grammar of a natural language can indeed be entirely encoded in the forms of the lexical expressions, thus dispensing with a separate component of grammatical rules, is a moot point.[45] However, the point Wittgenstein makes is a sound one: although languages are infinite objects, a finite translation manual suffices.

What holds for translation, applies to understanding in general:

> The meanings of simple signs (words) must be explained to us if we are to understand them.
> With sentences, however, we communicate. (4.026)

Our ability to understand a language can be explained by our grasp of its vocabulary and its grammar, for that in effect determines what will count as a meaningful sentence. Once we understand the basic expressions, including their grammar, that is, their combinatorial possibilities, we can use the meanings of the sentences. No additional information is needed, since the meaning of a sentence is built up from the meanings of its constituent parts. This also explains that we can use and understand sentences that say something new. For Wittgenstein this is an essential feature of sentences: "It belongs to the essence of a sentence that it can communicate a *new* meaning to us" (4.027). New combinations of expressions result in new meaningful sentences that we understand on the basis of our understanding of their constituents. It is the picture theory that forms the core of Wittgenstein's explanation of this phenomenon:

> A sentence must communicate a new sense with old expressions. A sentence communicates a situation to us, and so it must be *essentially* connected with that situation.
> And the connection is precisely that it is its logical picture.
> A sentence says something only insofar as it is a picture. (4.03)

The compositional nature of reality and the compositional nature of language are essentially two sides of the same coin. And it is the picture theory that ties them together.

The application of the picture theory to language is worked out in various directions. To see which routes have to be followed and why, remember that the aim of the undertaking is to determine the limits of thinking by determining the limits of the expression of thought. Thoughts have been identified as logical pictures (3), the most general kind of pictures there are. And Wittgenstein has claimed that they find a perceptible expression in sentences (3.1). Hence sentences are logical pictures too. But this is only the first step toward achieving the goal. For the limits of the expression of thought—the limits of what can be said, the limits of the meaningful—can be drawn only from the inside: there is no way in which what is beyond those limits can be meaningfully expressed. Thus the *Tractatus* tries to reach its goal by making essential use of the logical structure of the meaningful. Hence, it is this structure that has to be identified and explored. This involves a movement in two directions: toward the identification of the smallest meaningful elements and toward the construction of larger ones. That is to say, we need to characterize the smallest meaningful elements and study how they acquire their meanings. And we need to uncover the general principles that determine how larger meaningful elements can be built from smaller ones. To these two tasks the larger part of the sections between 3.2 and 5.6, which make up more than half of the entire text of the *Tractatus*, are devoted. In the course of these investigations several other subjects are also treated, some in detail, others cursorily. Our exposition will be mainly restricted to what Wittgenstein says about the two issues just mentioned.

Signs and Symbols

Before turning to an examination of these issues, one other aspect of the tractarian approach has to be mentioned. Recall that what Wittgenstein is after is not an analysis of some particular language, or some class of languages. His stakes are higher: he wants to unravel the mystery of how any symbolic system has meaning, how it is able to express thoughts. This means that his analysis has to abstract away from any contingent aspect of a language that might factually play a role. Concrete sentences and sub-sentential expressions, being perceptible objects, obviously have all kinds of contingent features that are of no interest for the abstract analysis that the *Tractatus* pursues. Wittgenstein arrives at the required level of abstraction in two steps. First, he introduces the notion of an "expression" [*Ausdruck*] or "symbol":

> Every part of a sentence that characterizes its meaning I call an expression (a symbol). . . . Everything essential for the meaning of a sentence that sentences can have in common is an expression. (3.31)[46]

Symbols do not yet completely abstract away from the perceptible aspects of concrete linguistic expressions, but present a first step.

First of all, the introduction of the notion of a symbol directs our attention to the level of expressions as types instead of tokens, or occurrences. Two different sentences may contain an occurrence of the same symbol. Secondly, they disambiguate, by virtue of their being "characteristic for the meaning" of the sentences in which they occur. Thus, an ambiguous expression corresponds not to one symbol, but to more than one. For an ambiguous expression contributes to the meaning of a larger expression in which it occurs in more than one way (although not at the same time, of

72   *Main Themes*

course). Finally, one symbol may be expressed by two expressions in the case of synonyms.

Each of these three properties of symbols represents a move away from the concrete, perceptible aspects of expressions to more abstract, semantic ones. Concrete symbolic systems may differ from one another in instantiating a different relation between signs and symbols, that is, in employing different physical signs for the same symbols. Such differences are contingent and hence not of great interest for Wittgenstein's undertaking. The sign–symbol distinction enables him to abstract away from them.

Wittgenstein identifies the occurrence of homonyms and synonyms in actual languages as an important source of philosophical confusion. This is a traditional theme that Wittgenstein illustrates with, among others, the familiar observation that the verb "to be" functions in three logically quite different ways, namely, as copula, as identity relation, and as existence predicate. The remedy that Wittgenstein advises is also a familiar one: employ a logical language that avoids both homonyms and synonyms, that is, a language in which the relationship between sign and symbol, between expression and meaning, is one-to-one.

This aspect of the introduction of the notion of a symbol is interesting, not so much for the particular examples that Wittgenstein adduces, but because of the conclusions that he draws concerning the nature of a logical notation.[47] First of all, symbols are introduced as having both a content and a form (3.31). That a symbol has a content, that is, a meaning, follows from the way it is characterized—namely as that which contributes to the meaning of the larger expressions in which it occurs.[48] In view of the very general nature of this characterization, we may expect that not only ordinary expressions count as symbols. Indeed, when we look at formal languages, various devices that are used to disambiguate expressions, such as brackets, also turn out to be symbols. And in natural languages grammatical relationships are symbols too.

About the content of symbols Wittgenstein does not say very much, the more so he discusses their form. In this discussion the notions of a variable and of a logical syntax play an important role. The idea is that a symbol "presupposes the forms of all sentences in which it may occur" (3.311). This must be understood as follows. A symbol, being an expression, has a form, that is, certain possibilities to combine with other expressions to form larger ones and, in the end, sentences. By virtue of that, it partially characterizes these sentences. It is a common characteristic of a certain class of sentences that they may contain an occurrence of this particular type of expression.

A simple example. In the language of first-order predicate logic, an individual constant c may occur both as the argument of a one-place predicate as well as fill an arbitrary number of the argument places of an n-place predicate. We know this from its form, which, in the usual formulations of the syntax of this language, is coded in one (or more, depending on the particular format) of its syntactic rules. We may represent this aspect of a symbol by means of constants and variables. In 3.312 Wittgenstein says that the symbol "is presented by means of the general form of the sentences that it characterizes." In such a general form the symbol itself is represented by a constant and the remainder by variables (3.312). So, in our example such a form would be the sentence schema: $R^n x_1 \ldots c \ldots x_n$.

Perhaps a bit confusingly, Wittgenstein calls the representation as a whole also a variable. Its values are the sentences that contain the symbol (3.313). If there are only symbols and no variables, the result is a sentence, which Wittgenstein calls a constant (3.313).[49] Applied to our example this means that if we are concerned with the sentence Pc, there is nothing left to vary and the symbol is the constant, that is, the sentence Pc itself.

In terms of the interplay of variable and constant, Wittgenstein defines what he calls "a logical form" or "a logical proto-picture" (3.315). This is what we get when we turn all the constituents of a sentence into variables. Reverting to our example once more, what we end up with is: $Rnx_1 \ldots x_i \ldots x_n$. Such a logical form does not refer to the reference of any (sub)expression, but rather represents the pure "essence" of a certain class of sentences (3.315).

Here the idea of a logical syntax emerges. This is a set of rules for the use of signs (*Zeichen*) that are formulated in terms of expressions (*Ausdrücke*), that is, symbols. Thus logical syntax abstracts from the accidental properties of concrete signs, one of which is what they refer to: "In logical syntax the reference of a sign should never play a role" (3.33). Rather, it is concerned with the combinatorial properties of the symbols that they express: "It must be possible to formulate logical syntax without mentioning the *reference* of a sign: it may presuppose *only* the description of expressions" (3.33). What a sign refers to is accidental; hence it can never be characteristic of the essence of a symbolic system. Thus logical syntax is concerned with the form of the symbols, which is an inherent feature. And because it is formulated in terms of symbols, and not signs, the logical syntax of a symbolic system also avoids the confusions noticed earlier with respect to natural languages.

We see that the introduction of symbols is the first step away from expressions as perceptible entities, since it does away with the accidental features of linguistic expressions:

> A sentence possesses essential and accidental features. Accidental features are those that stem from the particular way in which a sentential sign is produced. Essential features are those that exclusively enable a sentence to express its meaning. (3.34)

These essential features characterize both a form and a content; they are what all sentences that have the same meaning have in common (3.341). This means that the symbol corresponding to a certain sentence is the equivalence class generated by it, with the relevant equivalence relation construed intensionally, that is, as that of expressing the same meaning.

In a similar manner Wittgenstein takes a second step away from the perceptible aspects of language, by concentrating on what is essential for symbols, on "what all symbols that can serve the same purpose have in common" (3.341). Here, it seems, an equivalence class of equivalence classes is constructed, taking together all those symbols that can fulfill the same purpose, that is, that can play the same role in combining with other symbols. This step does away with the particular contents of symbols and leaves us the pure logical form they embody. Such an essential symbol represents a formal possibility, stripped of particular content and of any particular perceptible features, analyzed in terms of the rules of a purely logical syntax:

> What signifies in a symbol is what is common to all those symbols by which it can be replaced according to the rules of logical syntax. (3.344)

Logical syntax at this level of essential symbols embodies the most fundamental principles of meaningful language, that is, the combinatorial possibilities underlying any particular way of expressing particular meanings.[50] That is why in the end, at the level of logical syntax for language as such, its rules do not, and in fact cannot, mention the meaning or reference of expressions: "The rules of logical syntax must be obvious from themselves" (3.334).[51] In the end form can only be shown, it cannot be said.[52]

The Realm of the Meaningful

It is at this most general level that Wittgenstein's analysis of the logical structure of the realm of meaning takes places. Abstracting away from any particular features regarding perceptible form or content, he focuses on the purely formal features. In this way, the particular features of concrete languages or symbolic systems are sidestepped, but at a cost: none of the formal features that thus come into view can be illustrated directly by referring to either a known language or to one that is constructed for this purpose. It is the fundamental orientation of Wittgenstein's enterprise, with its aim to uncover the principles underlying any means of symbolizing, that prevents it from being communicated in a direct way, by reference to a particular symbolic system.[53] We must keep this in mind when examining the way in which Wittgenstein works out the application of the picture theory to language.

The fundamental goal of the *Tractatus* and the way Wittgenstein sets out to accomplish it necessitate a closer investigation of the logical structure of meaningful discourse. This involves a movement in two directions: one that is directed toward the ultimate components of meaningful sentences and one that aims to explore the way in which the grand total of meaningful discourse is built up. Of course, the two are intimately related.

Elementary Sentences and Names

Let us start with the first investigation. If one views the totality of meaningful discourse as something that has a certain logical structure, that is, as a whole that is built up from smaller parts, then the natural question to ask is what are the smallest such parts from which the more complex sentences can be constructed.[54] As we have seen in our discussion of the ontology, this is in fact the question after atoms, logical atoms to be precise, since the structure in question is a logical structure. A logically atomic sentence is called an "elementary sentence" (4.21) and its logical independence means that it can be true or false independently of the truth or falsity of other such sentences (4.211). Language and ontology harmonize since:

> The simplest sentence, the elementary sentence, asserts the existence of a state of affairs. (4.21)

The meaning of an elementary sentence, a linguistic atom, is a state of affairs, an ontological atom. This follows straightforwardly from the use of the same criterion of atomicity in both cases and from the way in which sentences have meaning. It is the picture theory that provides the link. In view of the property of logical independence of elementary sentences it is evident that they should not be mistaken for grammatically simple sentences of some natural language. Unlike the former, the latter are not logically independent of each other, but, on the contrary, are caught in a web of mutual logical relationships. Even the grammatically simplest sentence is complex logically speaking. Grammatical simplicity and logical simplicity do not coincide, and elementary sentences, far from being the starting point, rather are the end point of a process of logical analysis of ordinary sentences. Or almost the end point, since their internal structure is also subjected to further investigation:

> An elementary sentence consists of names. It is a connection, a linking, of names. (4.22)

Names (*Namen*) have been introduced earlier on in the *Tractatus*, in 3.202, as the "simple signs" [*einfache Zeichen*] (3.201) of which a completely analyzed sentence consists. Recall that in 3.2 it was stated that a thought could be expressed in such a way that the elements of the sentence correspond to the objects of the thought. These elements are names and hence it is characteristic of names that they refer to objects: "A name refers to an object. The object is its reference" (3.203).

With names we have arrived at a category of linguistic expressions that is almost as mysterious as that of their ontological counterparts—namely, objects. Like objects, names are simple. This should be understood at the level of symbols. That a name is a simple sign does not mean that it is also as simple as a perceptible entity. For then it would have to be an object in the technical sense, but all perceptible entities are complex. Rather, this qualification must be interpreted as stating that a name does not have any relevant logical structure:

> A name cannot be analyzed further by means of a definition: it is a proto-sign. (3.26)

It follows that a name is a symbol that contributes to the meaning of the sentences in which it occurs, not by virtue of its descriptive meaning, which it lacks, but simply by what it refers to. This characteristic is connected with the simplicity of objects as follows:

I can only *name* objects. Signs represent them. I can only speak *about* them: *I cannot express them*. Sentences can only say how things are, not what they are. (3.221)

Why is it that objects can only be named by signs that represent them, but do not describe them? Recall that objects have both external and internal properties (see 2.0233–2.02331). The former are the contingent properties that an object has by virtue of being connected with others into some state of affairs or situation that happens to be realized. Such properties are ascribed to it by sentences, which, as the passage just quoted has it, says "how an object is."[55] But sentences cannot say "what an object is," they cannot express its internal properties, that is, its form, since these are necessary and hence cannot be depicted at all. Therefore, an expression that functions semantically as an indication of an object can only name it, represent it quite literally. It does not describe it, but goes proxy for it: "A name represents an object in a sentence" (3.22).

As was the case with objects, examples of names cannot be given. Like objects, names have to be viewed not as a category of entities that can actually be pointed out or discovered, but rather as a logical construction, the outcome of a process of logical abstraction. This being so, tractarian names nevertheless do behave like ordinary proper names in some ways. For example, the idea that names do not have descriptive content but serve merely as "tags," as labels attached to objects, resembles the rigid designator view on proper names, which goes back to Mill and which has been defended in modern semantics by Kripke, Donnellan, and others. A much debated issue is whether what names refer to, objects, are to be thought of as consisting of particulars only, or also comprise properties and relations.[56] The main argument in favor of the first, nominalistic, interpretation is thought to derive from the following passage:

Not: "The complex sign 'aRb' says that a stands to b in the relation R," but: *That* "a" stands to "b" in a certain relation says *that aRb*. (3.1432)[57]

It may seem that in this explanation of how aRb pictures the situation that a stands in the R-relation to b, the relation R itself is eliminated. However the crucial point is how the phrase "in a certain relation" is to be read here. If in a specification of this relation R reappears, this passage cannot be adduced as evidence for the nominalistic view that fully analyzed sentences consist only of names referring to particulars. As it happens, there is strong evidence that such a nominalistic interpretation of this passage is wrong. In the "Notes on Logic" we read: "What symbolizes in 'aRb' is that R occurs between a and b" (98). So the relation between a and b that 3.1432 speaks of is that of being to the left and to the right, respectively, of R. The context of this passage makes evident the point made here. It stresses that a sentence is not a complex referring expression but a structured whole. Hence, this passage cannot be used as an argument that names refer only to particulars; on the contrary. Various passages have been adduced in support of what is taken to be the alternative view, that objects include properties and relations and that, consequently, names refer to both.[58] In the *Notebooks*, in the entry for 16/6/15, we come across the following claim, which does not leave much room for debate: "Relations and properties, and so on are *objects* too." Also quite outspoken is an entry that dates from a few days later (21/6/15), in which Wittgenstein, discussing the applicability of logic to ordinary language, claims of "the thing Socrates" and "the property of mortality" that ". . . they just function as simple objects."[59] Other evidence comes from the "Notes Dictated to Moore," which date from 1914. But also in the *Tractatus* itself some, admittedly indirect, evidence can be found. For example, if objects consisted only of particulars, there would be little sense in talking of types, or kinds, of objects, as the text so often does.[60] Also, not just individuals are quantified over, but also relations and properties, for example, in 3.333 and 5.5261.[61]

Now do these passages indeed show that tractarian names refer both to objects as well as to properties and relations? Yes and no. They certainly do repudiate the nominalistic interpretation, that names stand just for particulars. But what is presented as the alternative view, that names refer both to particulars and universals, does not quite capture what the tractarian concepts of name and object are about. Actually, it seems that the entire debate is misguided from the start since it is quite obvious that the tractarian notion of an object cannot be understood properly against the background of the traditional object–property dichotomy. Hence the very question whether tractarian objects comprise also properties and relations or just objects starts from an altogether false premise.

There is one other aspect of the tractarian conception of names that needs to be mentioned. Names are stated to have reference only in the context of a sentence:

Only sentences have meaning; only in the connection of a sentence does a name have reference. (3.3)

This is the famous "context principle."[62] It is traditionally ascribed to Frege, who formulated it in his *Grundlagen der Arithmetik* as follows: "It is sufficient if the sentence as a whole has a meaning; through that also its parts have their contents" (section 60). This conclusion is reached by Frege in the course of his investigation of the reference of numerical expressions. Various candidates, such as ideas and objects, are considered and rejected, which seems to leave us without any reference for them at all. This, Frege concludes, is because we ask the wrong question. Inquiring after the reference of a numeral as such, that is, in isolation, can only suggest solutions that do not work (for independent reasons, which need not concern us here). Hence, we seem forced to conclude that there is no reference, that numbers do not exist. But that is not the conclusion Frege draws. Rather, he says, our investigation starts off on the wrong track. We are misled by the traditional paradigm of name and object, presupposing that for every type of expression an independent referent should be forthcoming. But this, Frege argues, is asking for the wrong thing: "The independence which I claim for numbers should not mean that a numeral refers to something outside the connection of a sentence. I only want to exclude therewith their use as predicate or attribute, which changes their meaning somewhat" (section 60).

Usually, the context principle is interpreted as reflecting a holistic view on meaning.[63] For apparently it says that words, or generally subsentential expressions, do not have a meaning of their own, independently of the sentences in which they occur, but rather they get their meaning from them. Hence, sentence meaning seems primary to word meaning, the latter being derived from the former. The principle of compositionality, according to which the meaning of a composite expression is determined by the meanings of its parts, also plays a crucial role in the tractarian system. At first sight there is a certain tension between the compositional aspects of the linguistic and logical structures involved and the context principle. This may seem a rather awkward position to take for someone who subscribes to a form of logical atomism, but here we should observe immediately that the matter is not so simple. For it is states of affairs and elementary sentences that are identified as atoms and not their constituents, that is, objects and names. We will not pursue this matter any further here, but defer a discussion of the various ways in which this tension may be dealt with to Chapter 3.

By now we have followed Wittgenstein almost to the end: after having established in a general fashion what makes a sentence meaningful, we have seen what the atoms of this realm of meaningful expressions are and how they are internally structured. What is missing is an indication of how meaningful expressions combine to build larger ones.

Complex Sentences

It is a striking characteristic of the *Tractatus* that on the one hand Wittgenstein goes to great pains to define the combinatorial operations that are assumed to be at work in the composition of complex sentences, while on the other hand he says virtually nothing about the descriptive, empirical adequacy of the result. Let us start with the positive. Bluntly it is declared that all meaningful sentences are the result of truth-functional combinations of elementary sentences:

> A sentence is a truth-function of elementary sentences. (An elementary sentence is a truth-function of itself.) (5)

The limitations inherent in this declaration are severe. For it says that, despite the use of intensional notions such as possible states of affairs in the underlying ontology, the semantics of the tractarian system is extensional.[64] The only operations that it allows us to use in the construction of complex meaningful sentences are those that can be interpreted in terms of truth-functions. The modalities are ruled out, as are typically intensional connections between sentences such as appear in counterfactual conditionals, temporal constructions, sentences involving causality, and the like.[65] The repertoire is limited to the basic truth-functional connections, that is, conjunction, negation, disjunction, and the material conditional, and those operations and connections that can be defined in terms of them. Existential and universal quantification are assumed to be definable in this manner. The way in which Wittgenstein substantiates this claim is rather intricate and not completely successful.

After introducing various truth-functional connections using the by now familiar truth tables (see 4.31) and after discussing the status of tautologous and contradictory connections in some detail (about which more

TABLE 1. Joint Denial

φ	ψ	φ|ψ
T	T	F
T	F	F
F	T	F
F	F	T

below), it is claimed that all truth functions can be regarded as the result of the application of a particular operation on elementary sentences:

> Every truth-function is a result of successive applications to elementary sentences of the operation (-----T)(ξ,.....)
> This operation negates all the sentences in the righthand pair of brackets, and I call it the negation of those sentences. (5.5)

Here "(-----T)" denotes a sequence of truth values, one for each sentence in the sequence (ξ,....), where "-" stands for F, that is, falsity, and T denotes truth. In 5.502, Wittgenstein introduces the notation $N(\bar{\xi})$. The idea is this. All truth functions can be thought of as being constructed from one basic function. This is a familiar result: we know that there are two such functions, namely, Peirce's "joint denial" and Sheffer's "alternative denial." Wittgenstein uses the joint denial, which has the truth table given in Table 1.[66]

Joint denial is the two-place instantiation of the operation Wittgenstein defines in 5.5. If the variable ξ ranges over two sentences, p and q, the result, $N(p,q)$, has the truth table just given. In terms of this two-place connective all other truth-functional connectives—of arbitrary -arity—can be defined: joint denial is what is called "functionally complete." For example, it can easily be checked that ¬ φ can be defined as φ|φ, and φ∧ψ as (φ|φ)| (ψ|ψ).

This much is uncontroversial. However, this applies only to the propositional part of language. More specifically, it does not reveal how we are to derive quantified sentences as truth-functional combinations of elementary sentences. And indeed, the way in which Wittgenstein introduces quantificational expressions is problematic. That the universal and the existential quantifiers are related to the truth-functional connections of conjunction and disjunction has an intuitive appeal. For example, saying that every object has the property f might be regarded as saying that a has f, and b has f, and . . . , and so on. Likewise, the claim that something has the property f seems to come down to claiming that a has f, or b has f, or . . . , and so on.[67] But however intuitive, the relation is not straightforward, at least not in general. The problem lies in the "and so on." For any given finite domain we will know how to go on, that is, how to fill in the dots. But that does not provide us with a completely general definition.

The first problem is the assumed finiteness of the domain. Only for a finite domain can we actually form a conjunction of the form $fa_1 \land \ldots \land fa_n$ that asserts of every object in the domain that it has the property f.[68] The other problematic aspect concerns the assumed givenness of what constitutes the domain. If we are to define the quantifiers in terms of elementary sentences, we can do so only, or so it seems, on the assumption that all elements in the domain of quantification are the bearer of some name in the language.[69] Such an assumption comes dangerously close to saying that the domain must somehow be fixed in advance, before a definition of the quantifiers is possible.

From a modern point of view, the so-called substitution interpretation of first-order logic comes closest to a definition along these lines. It manages to avoid the first problem, that of the infinity of the defining conjunctions and disjunctions, by using the distinction between object language and metalanguage. Given that distinction, we do not need to assume that we can actually form infinite conjunctions and disjunctions in the object language to serve as the definiens of the quantified sentences. The infinity of substitution instances is simply circumvented by recourse to quantification in the metalanguage. Thus we define: $\forall x \phi$ is true if and only if $[c/x]\phi$ is true, for all c, which is adequate, but only given the assumption that for every object in the domain there is at least one individual constant c in the language that refers to that object.[70] However, the last proviso also indicates that the substitution interpretation does make the second assumption mentioned above—that the domain is given. For on an extensional approach, the meaning of an individual constant simply is the object it refers to. But then it follows that if we assume that a user knows the language, we in fact also assume that he knows what constitutes the domain of quantification. Of course, with respect to a formal language, the entire issue does not arise in the first place, since we are not wont to even consider the formal languages of logic as languages that are used in this sense of the

Main Themes   83

word. But the consideration does reveal a possible objection to an application of the substitution interpretation to quantificational expressions in natural language.[71]

Let us now resume our exposition of the way in which Wittgenstein tries to substantiate the far-reaching claim that all meaningful sentences are truth-functional combinations of elementary sentences. How does Wittgenstein's operation of simultaneous negation allow him to derive quantified sentences? Here Wittgenstein uses the notion of a sentential function, denoted as "fx." The values of fx are the elementary sentences that we get by instantiating the variable x: $fa, fb, \ldots$. If we apply the function of 5.5 to fx, that is, compute $N(\overline{fx})$, what we get is $N(fa, fb, \ldots)$, which is $\neg fa \wedge \neg fb \wedge \ldots$, which, as Wittgenstein claims in 5.52, is the same as $\neg \exists x\, fx$. This result can be subjected to the same operation again, and the result is an existential sentence: $N(N(\overline{fx})) = N(\neg \exists x\, fx) = \exists x\, fx$. The use of a sentential function resembles in certain respects the use of quantification in the metalanguage in the substitution interpretation. It circumvents the actual construction of a possibly infinite sequence of elementary sentences.

Existential quantification can thus be defined. The derivation of universally quantified sentences, however, presents a peculiar problem. Notice that even though the $N(\bar{\xi})$ operator allows us to express negation and existential quantification we cannot straightforwardly obtain a definition of $\forall x\, fx$. As we just saw, the definition that one would try first, $N(N(\overline{fx}))$, defines the existential quantifier, not the universal one. The problem is that we cannot use the equivalence $\forall x\, fx \leftrightarrow \neg \exists x\, \neg fx$, because we cannot construct $\neg fx$ as such. For $N(\overline{fx})$ is something quite different, namely, the joint denial of all the substitution instances of fx and not, as would be required in this case, a negated sentential function.

There seems to be only one way out in this case, and that is to assume that the domain is always finite. For in that case we can simply define $\forall x\, fx$ as $N(N(fa), N(fb), \ldots)$. But clearly this is not Wittgenstein's intention. Not only does he not exclude the infinity of quantificational domains (see, for example, 5.535), he also quite explicitly says that there are no important numbers in logic (5.453, 5.553). But obviously, the finite cardinal giving us the number of objects would be a very important one. Hence, it seems that we cannot ascribe this way out to Wittgenstein.[72]

It seems, then, that we must conclude that Wittgenstein's formal exposition of his analysis is flawed. Only if we make the assumption, unwarranted by the text, and explicitly rejected in a letter to Russell of 19/08/19 ("Of course no elementary propositions are negative" [*Notebooks*, appendix III, 131]) that the $N(\bar{\xi})$ operator can be applied directly to negated atomic sentences, can universally quantified sentences be derived in terms of it. In that case the definition of the universally quantified sentence $\forall x\, fx$ would read $N(\overline{\neg fx})$. This would amount to the infinite conjunction $\neg\neg fa \wedge \neg\neg fb \wedge \neg\neg fc \wedge \ldots$, which is equivalent to $\forall x\, fx$.[73]

However, the general idea behind Wittgenstein's formal analysis seems rather straightforward and uncontroversial. It is that quantified sentences (complex sentences), both universal and existential ones, are intrinsically related to atomic sentences (elementary sentences) and can be derived from these in a truth-functional way, using the obvious analogies with conjunction and disjunction. Although it seems that strictly speaking Wittgenstein was not right in claiming that we can make do with just the $N(\bar{\xi})$ operator, it is clear that this idea can be worked out, and it can indeed be found in most approaches to the meaning of logical sentences.[74]

One consequence of Wittgenstein's claim in 5—that every sentence is a truth-function of elementary sentences—is a strict form of extensionalism. Since only truth-functional operations are allowed in the derivation of complex sentences, an intensional account of the meaning of modal and tense operators and of propositional attitude verbs (that is, expressions such as *believe*, *know*, and the like) is ruled out.[75] On such an account these expressions are not truth-functional: the truth value of a sentence of the form $O\phi$, with O such an expression, is not determined just by the truth value of ϕ. Following Frege, who claimed that they were a mere expression of our (epistemic) attitudes toward the situation expressed by a sentence, Wittgenstein may have done away with modalities and perhaps in a similar fashion also with tenses. As for propositional attitude verbs, that they do not fit the extensional mould of the *Tractatus* is acknowledged by Wittgenstein explicitly in 5.541–5.542. Here Wittgenstein proposes an ingenious analysis, which roughly comes down to a kind of metalinguistic analysis, which involves the logical elimination of the subject and consequently also of the corresponding attitude. Because of its far-reaching consequences for the notion of a subject, we will return to these passages when we discuss this notion in Chapter 3.

The limitations of an extensionalist approach to meaning, at least as far as natural languages are concerned, are arguably too severe. Nowadays most semanticists would acknowledge that intensionality is an irreducible aspect of natural language meaning. This attitude is furthered, no doubt, by the availability of formal tools that allow one to deal with intensional expressions satisfactorily.[76] Moreover, the extensionalism that some, such as Davidson, uphold today, must not be confused with the extensionalism of the *Tractatus*. One of Davidson's motives for taking an extensional stance seems to be his distrust of the intensional ontology that comes with an intensional semantics.[77]

But such qualms Wittgenstein cannot have had.[78] After all, his ontology is intensional. By acknowledging possible situations as what is depicted by false pictures (that is, as the meanings of false sentences) Wittgenstein has committed himself to the existence, at least in a logical sense, of certain intensional entities. Neither can Wittgenstein be charged with epistemological reasons for wishing to remain extensional. For epistemological concerns are deemed irrelevant in the *Tractatus*.[79]

If they are neither ontological, nor epistemological, what then are Wittgenstein's reasons for his extensionalism with regard to language? It seems that the origins of the extensionalism of the *Tractatus* must be sought in logic. It is the nature of logic that dictates it, for logic is the basis of the picture theory, meaning, and language. And there is just one logic, which is classical, two-valued, extensional logic. At yet another point we thus reach the rock-bottom of the *Tractatus*.

LOGIC

Wittgenstein's view on the nature of logic not only plays a decisive role in his conception of meaning, language, and its relation to reality, but also has consequences for the place Wittgenstein assigns to philosophy. In this section we briefly go into these matters and also sketch some other aspects of the tractarian conception of logic.

Logic as Foundation

Let us start with repeating the observation that was made several times before, namely, that Wittgenstein subscribes to an absolutistic point of view with regard to logic, and that the one "true" system of logic that he acknowledges is a classical quantification theory. The logic of the *Tractatus* is classical in the sense that it is extensional and two-valued, that is, meets the principle of bivalence. And the system is like the one developed by Frege in the *Begriffsschrift*, in that there is no bias toward first-order quantification. As is apparent from various passages (for example, 3.333) Wittgenstein allows quantifiers to range over functions as well as over individuals.

The assumption that logic is absolute plays a role at several points in the development of the tractarian system. For example, the uniqueness of logical space, that is, the a priori character of all that is possible, depends on it. This is evident from 2.012, where Wittgenstein declares that "in logic nothing is accidental." Likewise, he says in 2.0121 that "something logical cannot be mere-possible. Logic deals with every possibility, and all possibilities are its facts." The message is clear: what is possible is so necessarily, and the necessity involved is that of logical necessity, which is the only necessity there is (see 6.37, "There is only a *logical* necessity"). Another example is the impossibility of picturing pictorial, logical, form. This also follows from the absoluteness of logic. For it is only in view of the latter that it can be said that "a picture cannot, however, position itself outside its pictorial form" (2.174). This follows only because pictorial form ultimately is logical form and because the latter is unique. For that implies that there is no other form by virtue of which such a would-be picture could depict logical form. It would have to use logical form and therefore cannot picture it. The point made in 3.032, that we cannot picture something that contradicts logic, is a corollary of this.[80]

The absolute status of logic plays a more indirect role at other points. For example, it seems that the postulate of objects and names as the ultimate ingredients of states of affairs and elementary sentences depends, at least in part, on this assumption. Their absolute simplicity again derives from the absoluteness of logic. In view of the latter there can be only one process of analysis, which has to end in one set of basic elements. Hence, we cannot speak of things being objects or names relative to some scheme of analysis (which by the way is the reason that no examples from real life can be given either). Of course, if there is basically only one system of logic, then it is a natural conclusion that such properties as simplicity, independence, and the like are absolute too, given that these properties are logical properties to begin with.

Curiously, this fundamental principle of the *Tractatus* is not discussed, let alone argued for, anywhere in the text. It seems that it is a starting point, in the literal sense of the word: something from which Wittgenstein's thinking started and that he never, at least not in this period, bothered to question. It gives logic a peculiar status, one that is worth pondering a little.

"Logic must take care of itself." This apodictic claim is the first we find in the *Notebooks* (22/8/14) and it is repeated in the *Tractatus* in 5.473. The contexts in which it appears are slightly different but make essentially the same point, which is that legitimacy of a symbol does not depend on external factors but is entirely an internal affair. Thus Wittgenstein says that "a *possible* sign must also be capable of referring" (5.473). In the same passage he also remarks that if a legitimate sign lacks meaning this must be because "we have not made an arbitrary determination" (5.473), that is, have not assigned a reference to it. At first sight this might seem to contradict the earlier claim. But the point Wittgenstein makes is subtle. What is claimed in the first passage is that if an entity is treated as part of a symbolic system it is meaningful ipso facto. Being part of a language means that a sign has a logical form and this means that its meaning is determined. Thus, the possibility of an expression signifying something is an internal and hence necessary property, which is independent of it actually signifying something. So if something goes wrong, for example, if a sentence lacks meaning because one of its component expressions does not refer, this must be because we have failed to assign it an actual reference.

So there are two sides to logical matters that must be clearly distinguished lest confusion arises. That a certain perceptible object is treated as a sign, that is, that it has been assigned a certain logical role and has been provided with an external significance, is accidental and by and large a matter of convention. However, once this has been done, other things follow and necessarily so. Given that an object is treated as a sign and as such has been assigned a certain role, it cannot but enter in certain meaningful configurations with certain expressions, and be unable to do so with others. That is why Wittgenstein says:

> It is true that there is something arbitrary in our notations, but *this* is not arbitrary: that *when* we have determined something arbitrarily, something else must be the case. (This depends on the *essence* of notation.) (3.342)

Thus in establishing a notation, a symbolic system, convention and necessity go hand in hand.[81] The conventions are ours, the necessity is that of logic and logic does not stand in need of any further foundation or motivation, being itself the foundation on which any symbolic system is erected.[82]

All this points toward a particular view, not on logic as such, but rather on its position within the wider field of philosophy and the sciences. Logic takes care of itself and by doing just that it is able to take care of a lot of other things as well. It provides the ultimate foundation of language, meaning, and thought. It thereby establishes the most fundamental traits of reality as it can be captured in language and thought. It delineates the sphere of what we can reason and discourse about—namely, all that is contingent and thereby safeguards all that we must remain silent about, in particular ethics. In the course of this, it establishes philosophy as a discipline without a subject of its own, but with a method.

Philosophy, it is concluded in 4.111, is not one of the sciences, but something that is "above or below, but not beside" them. The reason is that in philosophy there cannot be any theses since any meaningful thesis is a contingent sentence and philosophy deals with the noncontingent. Thus, since the contingent exhausts the meaningful, philosophy is left without a domain of its own. It does not have a subject matter that it can investigate and acquire knowledge about. Yet, this should by no means be interpreted as a dismissal of philosophy as such. Viewed in the proper way, there is room for philosophy, not as a discipline on a par with the sciences, but as an activity (4.112). Its purpose is "the logical clarification of thoughts," hence "a work of philosophy consists essentially of elucidations" (4.112).[83]

The tools that philosophy uses are basically derived from logic, and the proper method would be ". . . whenever someone else wanted to say something metaphysical, to demonstrate to him that he failed to assign a reference to certain signs in his sentences" (6.53) The function of this philosophical activity is both negative and positive. It is negative so far as it is directed against a common practice, that of speculative philosophy. But it is not just destructive, although this may seem so to one who is subjected to it ("This method would be unsatisfactory for the other person—he would not have the feeling that we were teaching him philosophy—" [6.53]). Its aim is also a positive one. For, as Wittgenstein expresses in 6.54, it is only when we come to see clearly what can be said and what cannot be expressed, that we "see the world aright." And this seeing the world in the right perspective is ultimately connected with the ethical aim Wittgenstein had with the *Tractatus*. For the right way of viewing the world means distinguishing between (at least) two ways of dealing with it: as a logically structured complex of situations, capable of being grasped in thought and language, and as a "limited whole" (6.45), ethically and morally significant. Logic is the foundation of the former, ethics that of the latter.

Logic as Analysis

Logic is thus not only the foundation of the world as it appears in language and thought; it is also an instrument, a means to get at the fundamental structure of reality, thought, and language, the common features that enable thought to be about the world and to become manifest in language. The process of uncovering this structure is that of logical analysis. For language does not bear its congruence with reality on its sleeve, nor is the logical composition of reality apparent from the way in which it occurs to us through the senses and in thought. While natural language derives its grammatical form from various functional requirements (4.002), expedient as it may be in serving these functions, it can also be misleading as to the underlying logical form it is required to share with the situations in reality it depicts. Hence language is not just a source of insight into this logical structure, but also a source of misunderstanding. Thus Wittgenstein is able to maintain both that "all the sentences of our everyday language are actually, the way they are, logically well-ordered" (5.5563), but also that because of the ambiguities, synonyms, and homonyms that are characteristic of natural language ". . . the most fundamental confusions easily arise (of which all of philosophy is full)" (3.324). Notice that Wittgenstein speaks emphatically of misunderstandings that arise in philosophy, that is, when we use language for a particular purpose.[84]

Analogously, logical analysis has two goals: the clearing up of misunderstandings and the uncovering of its underlying logical structure. The first, therapeutic activity is directed mainly, one might say, against the misuse of language, the misunderstandings that haunt our philosophical vocabularies, the defects that are sometimes spurred by unfortunate properties of natural language itself. The second kind of analysis is more constructive. It is to "delimit the thinkable and therewith the unthinkable" (4.114). Both activities go hand in hand. When transgressions of the rules that define the meaningful are noticed, these rules themselves are illuminated. And a definition of the rules clearly sets apart what is not in accord with them.

Wittgenstein holds that every meaningful sentence can be analyzed completely and that the result is unique (3.25). This means that the grammatical form of a sentence allows a decomposition into an underlying logical form that is completely perspicuous, that is, from which the logical relations of the sentence with others can be read off without any need for further interpretation. Although the possibility of this process of uncovering the underlying logical form is of central importance to the tractarian system, Wittgenstein has remarkably little to say about it. From the few remarks that he makes about it, it is clear that he views this process in more or less Russellian terms. Thus, we saw that he credits Russell in 4.0031 in connection with the distinction between the apparent and the real logical form of a sentence. And it is the latter's theory of descriptions that appears in the *Tractatus* as the only example of an analytical tool that can be used to forge a link between grammatical form and logical form:

> A sentence about a complex stands in an internal relation to a sentence that is about the latter's constituent.
> A complex can be given only by its description and this will be correct or not. A sentence that says something about a complex will not be nonsensical if the complex does not exist, but simply is false.
> . . .
> The summing up of a symbol for a complex into a simple symbol can be expressed by means of a definition. (3.24)

The ultimate analysis of a sentence is a truth-functional compound of elementary sentences consisting of names (3.2–3.201). Names denoting objects, this implies that a sentence that contains a term referring to a complex is not fully analyzed. In particular, the complex is not named by the term, but rather described by it. This descriptive character does not need to be explicit in the grammatical form of an expression: a syntactically simple symbol can yet be descriptive, and hence semantically complex. Such links between simple expressions and complex contents are established by definitions: "Every defined sign signifies *via* those signs in terms of which it was defined; and the definitions point the way" (3.261). As the opening sentence of 3.24 says, such relations are internal, that is, they belong to the sphere of logic. Thus the process of analyzing grammatical form into logical form is not an inquiry into the historical accidents of grammar, but a conceptual undertaking, which is, hence, best understood as involving symbols, not concrete signs. That in 3.24 Wittgenstein invokes a Russellian notion of description is apparent from the claim that failure of existence of the complex described results in falsity, not in meaninglessness. Thus the assertoric contents of descriptions, being meaningful, are held to be contingent, in keeping with the general tractarian view on meaning. The actual carrying out of such a "vertical" analysis, from surface, grammatical form to underlying, logical form, is not part of the *Tractatus*. Wittgenstein may not have had any ambition toward such a goal; in fact he may even have thought it to be infeasible: "It is not humanly possible to derive directly the logic of language from [everyday language]. . . . The tacit agreements for the understanding of everyday language are enormously complicated" (4.002). It is the principle, not the practice, that he is concerned with. Therefore, the larger parts of the *Tractatus* are dedicated to developing these principles and to setting up the framework in which such an analysis could be carried out in principle. Thus what we can find is an outline of a logical grammar, not a detailed specification. Part of this outline is Wittgenstein's sketch of the system of logic itself. Some aspects were already dealt with above; in the next section we fill in more details.

Logic as System

Wittgenstein holds that all meaningful sentences are truth-functional combinations of elementary sentences. Truth functions are generated by the $N(\bar{\xi})$ operation. In terms of this operation Wittgenstein defines the usual connectives of propositional logic and explains their semantics in terms of truth tables, albeit in what is for us an unfamiliar notation.

Elementary sentences are true or false, independently of the truth or falsity of other elementary sentences. A truth-functional combination is a specific combination of the possibilities for truth (and falsity) of elementary sentences. These can be specified in the familiar truth tables for compound sentences, as, for example, in Table 2, which defines the implication $p \to q$.

With a slight modification, Wittgenstein uses such truth tables in 4.31, noticing in 4.442 that we can leave out either T or F without loss of information, and that, if we keep the order of assigning truth values to the

TABLE 2. Material Implication

p	q	$p \rightarrow q$
T	T	T
T	F	F
F	T	T
F	F	T

elementary sentences fixed, we can even make do with just the last column, writing the implication as $(T-TT)(p,q)$.

This is of some importance for Wittgenstein as he is most anxious to avoid treating truth values as a special kind of object, as Frege did in his "Funktion und Begriff" (Frege 1891), where he called them "The True" and "The False" and regarded them as objects denoted by sentences. Such views Wittgenstein wants to dismiss, since according to him there are no logical objects to begin with. Not only does this do away with truth values as objects; as we saw Wittgenstein also denies that logical constants refer: "My fundamental idea is that the 'logical constants' do not represent" (4.0312). Thus he explicitly opposes an ontological interpretation of truth functions, too: "Truth functions are not material functions" (5.44). Implication, conjunction, negation, and the like are not to be thought of as objects in the world:

> It is clear that no object (or complex of objects) corresponds to the complex of the signs "F" and "T," just as there are none that correspond to the horizontal and vertical lines or to the brackets.—There are no "logical objects."
> Of course the same holds for all signs that express the same thing as the schemata of "T" and "F." (4.441)

Thus Wittgenstein views truth tables in an instrumental fashion.[85] He does so to such an extent that it does not seem fit to call his use of them semantic in the modern sense of the word.[86] The reason for Wittgenstein's opposition to the more common view seems to be that he is afraid that it will lead to a treatment of logic as if it were any other science, that is, that it will make logical facts too much like empirical facts. Thus both Frege's platonistic interpretation and Russell's empiricist view are rejected because they fail to attribute to logic the unique place it occupies in the scheme of things. Logic neither belongs to a realm of its own, nor is it concerned with the most valid within the empirical domain. On both views the subject of logic would be like any other subject:

> Any theory that lets a logical sentence appear contentful is false. One might think, for example, that the words "true" and "false" signify two properties among other properties, and then it would seem to be a curious fact that every sentence has one of these properties. Now that would seem all but obvious, just as, for example, the sentence "All roses are either yellow or red" would not sound obvious even if it were true. Indeed, the sentence in question now completely acquires the character of a sentence of natural science, and this is a sure sign that it has been conceived wrongly. (6.111)

What Wittgenstein here calls a "logical sentence" [*Satz der Logik*] is what we would call a logically valid sentence.[87] The example under discussion in this passage is the Law of Excluded Middle. The valid sentences of logic deal not with facts but with the foundations of all facts, the "scaffolding" (6.124) of the world. Consequently, they do not describe, but are *sensu strictu* meaningless. The valid sentences of logic are obvious in the sense that their truth can be established without any need for comparison with reality, just from the symbolic expressions themselves. Wittgenstein regards this as their "distinctive feature" (6.113) and says that this "contains the entire philosophy of logic" (6.113). By contrast, "the truth or falsity of non-logical sentences *cannot* be known just from the sentence" (6.113), precisely because they depict particular situations and, by virtue of that, are meaningful. The distinction between the empirical and the logical thus is the distinction between the contingent and the necessary, between the meaningful and the meaningless.

Logical sentences are meaningless (*sinnlos*) because they are true no matter what the world is like. They are tautologies (6.1), that is, valid sentences. Tautologies and their counterparts, contradictions, are introduced as the limiting case of meaningful expressions (4.46, 4.466). Being always true, a tautology makes no claim about the world and hence lacks descriptive content, that is, meaning. Analogously, contradictions are meaningless because no world can satisfy them. However, tautologies and contradictions are not nonsensical (*unsinnig*), since they do serve a purpose. They show the properties of logical space by showing that in certain combinations of meaningful signs meaning is "dissolved." A tautology, such as

94   Main Themes

$((p \to q) \land p) \to q$, is composed of meaningful, contingent expressions (in this case p, q, $p \to q$, $(p \to q) \land p$), in such a way that the whole becomes tautologous. Every part of the example in itself determines a definite part of logical space, embodying the claim that that part is realized. The sentence as a whole, however, loses this grip on the world and that very fact shows that these parts are logically related in a particular way (6.12).

Wittgenstein's claim that all logically valid sentences are tautologies must be understood with some care. With regard to the propositional fragment of his logical system it is unproblematic. However, when we consider the quantificational part, things are slightly different. Wittgenstein's intention is to regard quantified sentences, too, as the result of a successive application of the $N(\bar{\xi})$ operation to some base of elementary sentences. We also saw that this claim is problematic, inasmuch as it is not clear how certain quantified sentences (universally quantified sentences, sentences with mixed, dependent quantifier prefixes) are to be derived. Wittgenstein's quantificational calculus is not developed very much in the *Tractatus*. This is a weakness, at least from a logical point of view. For the propositional part it is clear what the claim that valid sentences are tautologies amounts to. This property can effectively be checked by means of truth tables or using the more idiosyncratic method Wittgenstein describes in 6.1203. However, as Wittgenstein himself seems to indicate in that passage, this method cannot be extended to the quantificational part of the system.[88] But that leaves his claim that all valid sentences are tautologies a bit in the dark. Whereas Frege and Russell had given axiomatic treatments of the quantificational calculus, Wittgenstein explicitly refrained from doing so, for reasons we outlined earlier. However, no explicit semantic treatment in the modern, model theoretic sense of the word is given either, which leaves this part of the *Tractatus* in an unsatisfactory state, at least from the point of view of the working logician.

Two other aspects of Wittgenstein's treatment of quantification need to be considered briefly. The first is that, like in the case of Frege's *Begriffsschrift*, the quantificational logic of the *Tractatus* seems not to be limited to first-order quantification. Passages such as 3.333 and 5.5261 make clear that Wittgenstein was prepared to consider higher-order quantification, that is, quantification over properties, propositional functions, and the like. This matter is related to the question of what exactly objects are, more precisely whether Wittgenstein counted not just individuals but also other types of entities among them. This question has already been answered in the affirmative above.

The other aspect is Wittgenstein's treatment of identity. Identity, or rather the identity sign, is dismissed as not essential for a proper logical language (5.533). How does Wittgenstein propose to do without? First of all, he claims that identity is not a relation between objects, between what signs refer to, but rather a (misleading) way to say something about signs. That identity does not relate objects is argued for by Wittgenstein by pointing out that, thus conceived, identity sentences are either nonsensical, when they concern two different objects, or without content, when they deal with one and the same object (5.5303).[89] In both cases they are meaningless. Being about signs, identity sentences are misguided attempts to state what in a perspicuous notation would be shown—namely, that two expressions may be interchanged for each other (6.23). Hence Wittgenstein proposes to express (non)identity by using variables and names in such a way that different signs stand for different objects (5.53). Given this assumption, x and y stand for different objects and then $\exists x \exists y\, f(x,y)$ expresses that two different objects satisfy f (5.532). In the more usual fashion this is expressed by $\exists x \exists y\, (x \neq y \wedge f(x,y))$. And the common interpretation of $\exists x \exists y\, f(x,y)$ is expressed in Wittgenstein's notation by $\exists x\, f(x,x) \vee \exists x \exists y\, f(x,y)$. Together with the adoption of a similar convention for names, this, Wittgenstein claims, allows him to do without overt reference to identity. Notice that $\exists x \exists y\, f(x,y)$, read in this way, does not say that there are two distinct objects, but shows this (4.1272). Hence Wittgenstein can claim that it is nonsense to talk about the number of objects (4.1272) and that therefore Russell's axiom of infinity, which is intended to say that there are an infinite number of them, must be rejected (5.535).

Here we recognize once more Wittgenstein's conviction that logic can only be shown, in the rules for notation, that is, in the logical form of the expressions. There can be no meaningful sentences about logic, no theory, and this is basically also why Wittgenstein dismissed Russell's theory of types. The theory of types was Russell's way of dealing with the paradoxes of self-reference, as they occur for example in naive set theory when we ask the question whether the set of all entities that are not a member of themselves: $R =_{\text{def}} \{X | X \notin X\}$, is a member of itself: $(R \in R)$? Russell's solution was to type expressions referring to sets and their members and to lay down the restriction that the sign for the set membership relation be applied only to expressions of adjacent types. Thus $R \in R$ is ruled out as a well-formed expression and hence the paradox does not come off the ground. Wittgenstein regards this as an attempt to say what cannot be expressed but only shown. It is worthwhile to probe a little deeper into Wittgenstein's considerations at this point.

In a letter to Russell of 19/8/19 Wittgenstein reacts as follows to a suggestion of the former regarding the status of the theory of types (the sentence quoted is Russell's):

"The theory of types, in my view, is a theory of correct symbolism: a simple symbol must not be used to express anything complex: more generally, a symbol must have the same structure as its meaning." That's exactly what one can't say. You cannot prescribe to a symbol what it *may* be used to express. All that a symbol *can* express, it *may* express. This is a short answer, but it is true! (*Notebooks*, appendix III)

One may be inclined to think that Wittgenstein would agree with Russell: after all, what Russell says about the relation between the structure of a symbol and that of its meaning at first sight is in complete accordance with Wittgenstein's position in the *Tractatus* when he speaks of the requirement that a sentence have the same "logical (mathematical) multiplicity" as the situation it depicts (which is its meaning): "In a sentence exactly as much must be distinguishable as in the situation it depicts" (4.04).

The point is not that Wittgenstein disagrees with Russell about the requirement as such. What they do differ on is the question whether this requirement can be expressed, that is, whether it can be meaningfully formulated in a theory of correct symbolism. That is what Wittgenstein emphatically denies in the *Notebooks* passage just quoted. And in the *Tractatus* he states why this should be so:

Of course, this mathematical multiplicity itself one cannot depict in its turn. One cannot step outside it when depicting. (4.041)

So how does Wittgenstein propose to deal with Russell's paradox? Recognition of the saying–showing distinction does away with it, Wittgenstein claims:

A function cannot be its own argument because the function sign already contains the protopicture of its argument and cannot contain itself. (3.333)

What is of crucial importance in this passage is the distinction between function and function sign. The latter is said to contain the "protopicture" of its argument, and this must be understood as saying that a specification of the logical form of a function sign includes a specification of that of its argument(s).[90] While one might hold that a function can be applied to itself, it does seem quite impossible to imagine that a concrete sign contains itself.[91] According to Wittgenstein this is impossible, which given the perfect match of logical properties of language and reality shows that functions cannot be applied to themselves either.

With these last remarks we end our overview of the main ingredients of the tractarian system: the picture of meaning, the concomitant ontological theory, and theory of language and the logical system. In the last section of this chapter we take a brief look at the consequences of Wittgenstein's views on language, thought, and reality for other domains.

NONLOGICAL NECESSITY

The last parts of the *Tractatus* are devoted to an exploration of the consequences of the system for various disciplines that all, in one way or another, deal with necessity: mathematics, natural science, conceptual analysis, ethics and aesthetics, philosophy, the sentences of which it consists. This investigation is needed since Wittgenstein acknowledges only logical necessity (6.37), yet these disciplines do claim to produce meaningful but noncontingent sentences about their various domains. The strict dichotomy that the *Tractatus* posits between logical necessity and contingent meaning leaves no room for such sentences, however. Hence, unless they are to be discarded in one fell swoop as being mere gibberish, which is certainly not Wittgenstein's intention, the sentences of these various disciplines have to be classified in some other manner.

Mathematics

Logical necessity is shown by logical sentences and to a certain extent also by ordinary contingent sentences, so far as they show the logical form they share with the situations they depict. Mathematical sentences, too, are said to show the logical properties of the world:

The logic of the world, which the sentences of logic show in tautologies, mathematics shows in equations. (6.22)

Thus, logic and mathematics are much alike in this respect. However, this remark should not be taken amiss: it does not show that Wittgenstein subscribes to the program of logicism, promoted by Frege and Russell, according to which basic parts of mathematics can be reduced to logic. For that would imply that mathematical sentences are logical sentences, that is, tautologies, too. But Wittgenstein characterizes mathematical sentences as "equations": "The sentences of mathematics are equations, that is, pseudo-sentences" (6.2). Like the tautologies of logic, the equations of mathematics are without content: "A mathematical sentence does not express a thought" (6.21). Of course, this follows immediately from the theory of meaning that the *Tractatus* endorses. But mathematical sentences differ from logical ones in an important respect, which Wittgenstein describes in terms of use:

> For in real life we never need a mathematical sentence, but we use a mathematical sentence *only* to derive from sentences that do not belong to mathematics, other sentences that likewise do not belong to mathematics. (6.211)

The idea seems to be this. We do not use mathematical sentences as such, as descriptions of some mathematical reality, but put them to use only in the context of nonmathematical discourse, for example, when drawing conclusions involving certain numerical identities. Thus from "John owns one dog" and "Mary owns one cat" we infer, using the equation $1 + 1 = 2$, "John and Mary together own two pets." The mathematical equation is not about anything in the world, such as numbers, but merely serves as a tool that can be used to derive contingent sentences from other such sentences.[92] Mathematical equations are in this sense like identity sentences: they are concerned with expressions and serve to indicate that two expressions can be interchanged.[93] But whereas in a proper logical grammar we can make do without identity as such, mathematics essentially involves equations. It shows how we can generate equivalent expressions involving quantities. The *Tractatus* does not contain much more about the status of mathematical sentences besides what was related above.[94] How Wittgenstein's overall position must be evaluated is not altogether clear. Some of what he says has a formalist ring to it, especially where he emphasizes that what determines the nature of mathematical sentences is what we do with them (as in 6.211, just quoted; see also 6.2341). Yet, he also recognizes that mathematical expressions refer, and what would they refer to if not mathematical objects? An extensive investigation of these matters is, however, beyond the scope of the present general overview.[95]

Natural Science

Wittgenstein's insistence that there is only logical necessity seems perhaps most implausible when we consider natural laws, such as the fundamental laws of physics. The impression that Wittgenstein's position is a queer one, is reinforced by his claims about causality, which certainly will strike many of us as patently false. Thus we read:

> We *cannot* infer the events of the future from those of the present. Belief in a causal nexus is *superstition*. (5.1361)

This seems to say that belief in causal relationships between events is never justified, always a mere superstition. But that is patently absurd, for we do know very well that such causal connections exist and may lead to reliable predictions. Our lives in fact depend on them, and we could not imagine what a world without them would be like. And the sciences are devoted to discovering and systematizing such causal connections. So what is it that Wittgenstein means to say here?

As is so often the case, the wider context in which the passage occurs provides a clue. In 5.133 it is claimed that all deduction is a priori, that is, drawing inferences does not involve any knowledge of contingent facts. The counterpart of this claim is that the (non)existence of two disjoint situations is unrelated and that hence no inference relation can exist between sentences describing them (5.135). A simple example from propositional logic may serve as an illustration. Given that p, q, r, and s are elementary sentences no logical relations between them obtain. But this holds also for some (not all) complex sentences that may be formed from them. For example, whereas $p \wedge q$ and $p \vee r$ are logically related, $p \wedge q$ and $r \wedge s$ are not. We may think of two such sentences as describing two events that take place at distinct moments in time. Whatever the relation between such events might be, it cannot be a logical relation. It is the existence of a causal connection that would provide such an internal (5.1362), that is, necessary, relation, that Wittgenstein denies: "A causal nexus that justifies such an inference does not exist" (5.136). "*Such* an inference," not: any inference at all. Hence Wittgenstein's remarks on causality should not be interpreted as claiming there is no such thing as a causal relation in the first place. What

100 *Main Themes*

is denied is that causality is an internal relation between situations. In no way is it implied that there cannot be causal relations of a nonlogical kind. So, causality as a concept of physics, for example, or of everyday reasoning, is not discarded.

Given his view on causal connections Wittgenstein holds that relations between distinct empirical facts and the laws covering such relations have no claim to necessity in the logical sense of the word. Within the contents of a specific theory some such laws may be claimed to be "necessary," but that is necessity in another sense of the word. It means they hold in a limited set of worlds or circumstances, namely, those that satisfy certain laws or constraints, not in all logically possible ones. From a purely logical point of view they are contingent.

On this analysis of causality Wittgenstein bases his view of the freedom of the will, which, he says in 5.1362, consists in this, that we cannot know how we will act in the future. For the relation between knowing that p and p is an internal, that is, necessary, one: p logically follows from "x knows that p." However, my knowing now that I will do such-and-such tomorrow and my doing such-and-such tomorrow are typically two disjoint events, which are not logically related. Hence, I can never be said to know a future event.[96] The relation between my conviction (or my intention) that I will do such-and-such and my actually doing it (or not) is logically contingent. Notice that the point Wittgenstein makes is a logical one: it is not due to a lack of evidence that we do not know our future actions; we cannot know them in principle. But if our future actions cannot be known in advance, this must be because they are not determined in advance. Hence, at the moment it is performed, the action is "free," in the sense of not determined. This observation is not solely a logical one; it also has ethical repercussions. In fact, the contingent character of causal connections also plays a role in the ethical part of the *Tractatus* at another point, in Wittgenstein's conception of the relation between the will and the world. (This point will be discussed in more detail in Chapter 4.) Causality is not the only point at which necessity plays a role in scientific inquiry. In the natural sciences some principles are commonly attributed a status different from that of empirical generalizations. For example, the principle of induction and the principle of sufficient reason are regarded as noncontingent principles, expressing necessary features of reality. Within the tractarian scheme there is no place for such necessary principles since physical reality is contingent. According to Wittgenstein some of these principles, for example, the principle of induction, are in fact contingent truths (6.31). Others are assigned a different status. As was the case with mathematical sentences Wittgenstein takes his lead from the way in which such principles, such as that of sufficient ground, causality, and so forth, function. They are, he says, not laws themselves, but they characterize the form of natural laws (6.32, 6.34). They express, in a somewhat misleading way, an insight, not in the nature of reality, but in the way in which it can be described. Thus the principle of sufficient ground expresses that any satisfactory description of reality will have a certain form, formulating relations between events in terms of cause and effect. As Wittgenstein notes, such a principle in itself does not say anything about reality; it is not a contingent sentence. It does not distinguish one world, or class of worlds, from another and hence is not capable of verification or falsification. However, that a concrete description of reality that conforms to this principle is possible: that is a significant fact (6.342). But this is a significance that does not pertain to any world in particular. These insights are called "a priori" (6.33, 6.34) and that places them outside the empirical domain. Thus such principles are distinguished from mere empirical generalizations, and the status they are assigned comes close to that of logical principles. They are considered to be rules of grammar, not of language, but of theories. Hence, strictly speaking they are meaningless: what they try to express cannot be said, but shows itself in the form that actual theories about reality take (6.36).

Conceptual Analysis

Another source of apparent necessity comes from conceptual analysis: some relations between the concepts we use are analytic and hence are traditionally considered necessary. A traditional example is that of the relation of coextension between the concept of "material object" and that of "having (spatial) extension." Again, the tractarian scheme does not allow for this kind of necessity and Wittgenstein somehow has to explain it away. There is one passage in which this problem is discussed, in terms of color exclusion. That the same spot in our visual field cannot be simultaneously (all) green and (all) red, for example, is excluded. Evidently, this exclusion is inherent in the color concepts as we use them. According to Wittgenstein the exclusion is at bottom of a logical nature, since it is due to what he calls "the logical structure of color" (6.3751).

Thus Wittgenstein saddles himself with the task of showing that such conceptual ties can be analyzed in purely logical terms.[97] It is useful to point out that it is precisely at this point that he was later to find out that the tractarian scheme failed. The logic of color determination could not be described in the required atomistic terms and the reduction fails to work. This failure, reported in his "Some Remarks on Logical Forms," led Wittgenstein to abandon the strict atomism of the *Tractatus*, opening the way toward his later philosophy of language games.[98]

The *Tractatus*

At the very end the *Tractatus* treats ethics (and aesthetics) and returns to philosophy, in particular to its own sentences. The status of ethical sentences and their purported contents will be the main concern of Chapter 4, so here we will be satisfied with just a brief indication of what Wittgenstein's position with regard to them is. It is clear that Wittgenstein assumes that ethics deals with "facts" that are not contingent. Ethical values are absolute (6.41); hence sentences that are meant to express them must have a noncontingent character (6.42, 6.421). Ethics, like logic (6.13), is declared transcendental (6.421). Both are concerned with what constitutes the essence of the world, but in a different fashion.

As for philosophy, above we have seen that it is regarded as a discipline without a field of its own, that it is to be regarded as an activity— namely, that of logical clarification. This holds also for the *Tractatus* itself. In the penultimate remark Wittgenstein indicates that the sentences of the *Tractatus* are not meaningful, yet may serve a purpose:

> My sentences elucidate in this way that he who understands me sees in the end that they are nonsensical, when through them—on them—he has climbed up beyond them. (He must, so to speak, throw away the ladder after he has climbed upward on it.)
>
> He must surmount these sentences, then he will see the world aright. (6.54)[99]

The aim of the *Tractatus* is to determine the limits of the meaningful, limits that are a priori, and hence necessary. Hence its sentences do not deal with the contingent, and consequently are meaningless, nonsensical. This follows from these very sentences themselves, so anyone with a correct understanding of them, will come to regard them as such. The process of gaining this insight is not like that of learning facts, of being given information: it is one of being "enlightened": that is the function of the sentences of the *Tractatus*.[100] Once more we see that just as in the case of mathematics and principles of natural science, Wittgenstein takes his lead from the function of these sentences and not from their content. In other words he starts from the function they actually have in the case of mathematics and of natural science and from the function he wants them to have in the case of the *Tractatus*. When one starts out, one might be tempted to consider them as constituting a "theory." But once one grasps them, one sees that they cannot be regarded as such. It is in that sense that they have to be done away with.[101]

Of course, the question that comes to mind is: How do the sentences of the *Tractatus* manage to do this? They do not have meaning, so how can one learn something from them? Here, it seems, the doctrine of showing once again is of vital importance. The notion of an elucidation (*Erläuterung*) makes its appearance also elsewhere in the *Tractatus*. At one point it is adduced in the context of explaining the way in which names function (3.263). It seems that as the notion is used there, it is best viewed as that of a sentence that shows characteristic, internal properties of names.[102] Analogously, the sentences of the *Tractatus* themselves do not describe, but show: they show the logical properties of the world, of language and thought, by being consciously misguided attempts to say these things. It is for this reason that 4.112 states that "a work of philosophy consists essentially of elucidations." It is by absorbing rather than accepting them that one allows them to do their "enlightening" work. And if they have done so, one "sees the world aright." No need to say that the ultimate connotations of this phrase are ethical through and through.

3

Language and Ontology

THE QUESTION OF REALISM

The overview of the main themes of the *Tractatus* given in the preceding chapter at certain points already touched on the central question to be discussed in what follows, namely, whether its ontology is an instance of realism. The entire topic of realism is a notoriously difficult one. One particularly controversial issue concerns the criteria that should be used in assessing whether a particular view of ontology is an instance of realism. Let us take as a starting point for our discussion the way in which Michael Dummett has sought to sharpen this issue.

In various places, Dummett has proposed a way to come to grips with the question of realism that closely links it to certain aspects of meaning.[1] Traditional ways of trying to decide these issues fail, he states, among others things because they presuppose some thought and language independent access to reality and because they view the question of realism as an absolute one. His criterion for labeling a theory about a certain domain "realistic" is the use of a classical two-valued logic as the basis for the semantics of sentences about that domain.[2] The relevant principles of classical two-valued logic are those of bivalence and double negation. If the meaning of ϕ obeys bivalence, this means that either ϕ or its negation, $\neg \phi$, is true. And double negation guarantees that from $\neg\neg\, \phi$ we may conclude that ϕ, which means that "reductio ad absurdum" is a valid inference strategy. Together, Dummett holds, these principles reflect that the truth value of a sentence is determined by reality and is independent of our means to verify or falsify it. And that, he suggests, is the hallmark of realism—that truth is verification transcendent.

The advantages of this way of approaching the question of realism, Dummett says, are twofold. First of all, realism becomes less of a "yes-or-no" matter. One may take a realistic stance with regard to some domain, for example, that of perceptible objects and their properties, or that of events in the past, without necessarily treating other domains, such as that of mathematics, in a like fashion. The second advantage, Dummett argues, is that by phrasing the criterion in terms of the logical principles underlying a theory of meaning the issue becomes more readily assessable. For unlike ontological or metaphysical doctrines, a theory of meaning is surveyable, since it is "embodied," so to speak, in the very language that is used in actual linguistic practices, philosophical and nonphilosophical. This would mean that by using semantic, nonmetaphysical criteria, which moreover can be applied to all kinds of sentences, the metaphysical question of realism could be answered.

Dummett's approach has inspired a lot of discussion in the literature, much of which has centered around the opposition between realism and antirealism that Dummett also has brought into play and the associated issue of relativism. For our present purposes, however, we need not go into that discussion.[3] What interests us here is whether the ontology of the *Tractatus* must be thought of as an instance of metaphysical realism or should be given another interpretation. And the question to be answered presently is whether this issue can be resolved using Dummett's semantic criterion.

Taking our lead from the short characterization just given, it suffices to observe the following. Classical, two-valued logic is at the very heart of the *Tractatus*. It is the logic that Wittgenstein defines and uses in his analyses and that forms the foundation on which the entire tractarian structure rests. Language, thought, and reality have one and the same logical form and this is the form of classical, two-valued logic. Also there is no doubt that for Wittgenstein this logic is absolute, that it has no alternatives or rivals. All this surely means that he regards classical, two-valued logic as the basis of all discourse. So, it seems that by Dummett's criterion the *Tractatus* must be regarded as an instance of realism. However, things may not be that simple.

Dummett's criterion refers to the logic underlying the semantics of a language. Of course, the *Tractatus* does contain a theory of meaning, which defines the semantics of a language. In fact one of its aims is to define how any language can have meaning, to characterize the necessary and sufficient conditions of any kind of meaningful symbolism. And the underlying logic is indeed classical and two-valued. However, what we should bear in mind here is that it is the very essence of the tractarian notion of meaning that meaningful language is descriptive, contingent language. That within the tractarian conception any such language has a classical two-valued logic by Dummett's criterion only shows that according to the *Tractatus* such a language presupposes a realistic conception of reality. But do note that this does not imply that the ontology that the *Tractatus* itself expounds has to be viewed in the same manner. For the language of the *Tractatus* itself has a quite different status. Its sentences, including those on ontology, are not part of the kind of language for which the *Tractatus* defines a semantics. So Dummett's criterion does not really help us out here.

It follows from the very nature of the theory of meaning of the *Tractatus* that meaningful sentences are not about the ontology. In fact they cannot be. No meaningful sentence can describe the categories and other formal features of the ontology, since the very essence of meaningfulness is contingency and the formal properties of the tractarian ontology are not contingent. Hence the fact that the tractarian semantics of contingent language is a classical, two-valued one merely shows that it presupposes a realistic view on what can be described by means of such a language. But that which makes these descriptions possible—the ontology, picturing, logic—itself cannot be described and hence is beyond this assumption of realism. In other words, language as the *Tractatus* analyzes it, presupposes a realist ontology. But from that it does not follow that the *Tractatus* itself, as a theory about ontology, meaning, and logic, is itself also a realistic theory. Of course, the opposite—that the tractarian ontology is not realistic—does not follow either. It is clear, however, that a realistic stance on the part of the author of the *Tractatus* cannot be deduced simply from the fact that the theory of meaning contained in it rests on a classical, two-valued one. That must be argued for, if it can be argued for at all, in other terms and on other grounds.

For it is quite obvious that the sentences of the *Tractatus* itself, which do treat explicitly and directly of the formal features of the ontology, do not belong to the very language that it aims to characterize. Its sentences are not contingent and hence, by its own standards, are not meaningful. Of course, Wittgenstein was very well aware of this, as his remarks at the end of the *Tractatus*, in particular 6.54, show.[4] But Wittgenstein also indicates how despite their meaninglessness these sentences may yet contribute to the goal he has set himself in writing the *Tractatus*. The insight that its sentences are meaningless is presented as a mark of true understanding of the work. And this is more than a right view on the nature of meaning, its possibilities and limitations. Wittgenstein also hints at another "elucidation." For it is no coincidence that Wittgenstein discusses the status of the sentences of the *Tractatus* at the very end, right after the section on ethics.

So the question of the realism of the *Tractatus* is more complicated than it may have appeared to be at first sight. One way of analyzing the situation is by making use of the distinction that is sometimes made between "metaphysics" (including ontology) and "natural language metaphysics." This distinction comes to the fore when one wants to discriminate between the ontology some speaker subscribes to per se and the ontology his language presupposes. The two may coincide, but then they also may be distinct. That there is at least a possible gap between the two is obvious. For example, it seems that natural languages such as English presuppose a rather rich ontology, one that acknowledges not just material objects but also abstract objects, such as events, properties, propositions, intentions, beliefs, desires, and so on. Now someone might very well be of an ontologically more parsimonious inclination and still use English. He might even use English with its rich ontology to argue for a more nominalistic position and in doing so make use of the very kinds of entities that English presupposes and he wants to do away with.[5]

It is this distinction that we must keep in mind when we try to answer the question to what extent the *Tractatus* contains a realist ontology. And then we see why Dummett's criterion will not provide a straightforward answer: language and reality come into play at two different levels. The *Tractatus* provides a theory of meaning for descriptive language that is not tied to any specific domain of inquiry at all, but only presupposes very basic and fundamental features of the kind of reality such language can be about. And it provides a theory of reality itself, in order to be able to state this theory of meaning. Of course, these two aspects of the tractarian enterprise, that is, these two levels at which the relevant notions are being considered, are related but they are not identical, as was argued above. Hence, it seems we must conclude that we cannot really answer the question whether the *Tractatus* contains a realist ontology before we have decided what exactly it is that the *Tractatus* is all about. Is it about language and ontology as two separate domains of inquiry and about the relationship between these two? Or is it primarily a theory about language and does the ontology come in only relative to the language? If Wittgenstein's undertaking concerns the first, then Dummett's criterion will tell us that, yes, the *Tractatus* is a full-blooded realistic theory. But if the second interpretation is correct, then the very same criterion only tells us something about Wittgenstein's views on what meaningful language presupposes: a realist ontology. So if we want to answer the question about realism, we are forced to dig deeper into the relationship between language and ontology.

The focus of our investigation then should be the status of the ontology per se within the tractarian enterprise, in particular in relation to language. As for language, although more could be said about that than we have done so far, its status seems to be clear. The *Tractatus* aims to give an account of the logical basis of any kind of symbolic representation and at the very heart of this account is the idea of meaning as picturing. Now this account is not unproblematic, to say the least, but here Wittgenstein is quite clear. Any symbolic system, including natural language, starts from a core of logically independent atomic sentences from which more complex sentences are formed through truth-functional combinations. All sentences have meaning by depicting a situation and this depicting relation rests on two principles, that of the representation of objects by names and that of the identity of the logical forms of sentences and of situations. Any symbolic system, that is, any system of meaningful signs, can be understood in this way, although this need not be apparent from its surface grammatical appearance. Especially in the case of natural languages, it can be observed that they do not carry this basic structure on their sleeves, yet, inasmuch as their expressions have a clear and definite meaning, it can be analyzed along these lines. As for the ontology, however, although the basic outlines are again reasonably clear, it is not likewise obvious what it is that Wittgenstein wants it to be. Is it a theory of the basic structure of reality in its own right? Or is it essentially a derivative of the analysis of language that the *Tractatus* gives? It is this question concerning the status of the tractarian ontology, as opposed to its contents, that we will be concerned with in what follows.

Of course, the various answers that one may give to this question have repercussions for one's views of other aspects of the *Tractatus*, such as the relationship between language and reality. But before trying to survey the possible answers to our central question and investigating the arguments that can be adduced for and against them, it is worthwhile to ask ourselves a preliminary question: What are the distinctive characteristics of the ontology of the *Tractatus* and how are they argued for by Wittgenstein?

The ontology of the *Tractatus* is characterized by the following features. First of all, it holds that the world is a collection of facts, not of things. Secondly, it views the facts that make up the world as being either complex or atomic. Thirdly, it assumes that the atomic facts, or more in general, the states of affairs, are logically independent of each other. By and large, the first two features are unproblematic, which does not mean to say that they are universally accepted but merely that within a certain approach they are reasonable assumptions to make. The third feature, however, is far more controversial, and it is this feature that we need to investigate more closely.

This means that our initial, general question reduces to a more specific one: Why are the states of affairs logically independent? What role does this feature of the ontology play in the tractarian framework and how does Wittgenstein argue for it? Given that a state of affairs is nothing but a configuration of objects the question after the logical independence of states of affairs is the same as that after the simplicity of objects. For the logical independence of states of affairs ultimately rests on the simplicity of objects. If certain objects making up some states of affairs were not simple the latter would not be independent, since their realization would depend on the contingent realization of the complex nature of the object. And the question after the simplicity of objects is an investigation into their very nature: To what kind of ontological category do objects that are supposed to be simple in the sense of the *Tractatus* belong? It is this conglomerate of questions and the answers to it that have been proposed that we will survey in what follows. We first take a look at what the *Tractatus* and the *Notebooks* have to say about this. After having done so, we will turn to an examination of some characteristic interpretations that can be found in the literature.

Language and Ontology

SIMPLICITY: THE ARGUMENT FROM LANGUAGE

We start our investigation with the argumentation the *Tractatus* offers for the simplicity of objects. The main argument is contained in 2.02–2.0212:

Objects are simple. (2.02)

Every statement about complexes can be decomposed into a statement about their constituents and into those sentences that describe the complexes completely. (2.0201)

The objects form the substance of the world. Therefore they cannot be complex. (2.021)

If the world had no substance, then whether a sentence had meaning would depend on whether another sentence was true. (2.0211)

Then it would be impossible to draw a picture of the world (true or false). (2.0212)

The argument presented in these consecutive passages has the structure of a *reductio* and seems to run as follows.[6] Objects have to be simple since they form the substance of the world. Substance is what all the ways the world can be, that is, all possible worlds, have in common: the fixed form that 2.022–2.023 and 2.026 refer to. The idea is that every world draws from one and the same source of objects in the following sense. The totality of objects, through the objects' logical form, determines the totality of states of affairs (2.0124). And a world is simply a certain choice of these.

Now why does this role of the objects demand their simplicity? Here, rather surprisingly, in the heart of his exposition of the ontology, Wittgenstein draws on an argument that essentially rests on language. In 2.0201 he notes that a statement about a complex entity can be analyzed in terms of sentences about its constituents and a statement about its constitution. In fact, this refers to the notion of analysis that is presented only further on in the *Tractatus*, in the sections dealing with the structure of language. This essentially linguistic premise is used in 2.0211 and 2.0212, where the simplicity of objects actually is derived from the possibility of describing the world. According to 2.0211, if objects were not simple, one sentence having meaning would depend on another being true. What seems to be meant here is something like the following. Suppose a sentence contains an expression that refers to a complex entity. The existence of this complex entity is contingent; it may exist and it may not exist.[7] This contingent existential condition can be the content of another sentence, on which the first then depends. It is important to note that it is the meaning and not just the truth of the sentence containing the reference to the complex that is said to depend on the truth of the sentence asserting the existence of the complex.

This paraphrase of the argument as it appears in the *Tractatus* may serve to draw attention to an aspect of Wittgenstein's exposition that was already noticed before, namely, that one of the crucial features of the ontology, the simplicity of objects, is supported by an argument that draws on language.[8] It is therefore crucial to try to reconstruct the argument in more detail.

Two assumptions can be seen to play a central role in the argument. The first one is that meaning is determinate. If a sentence has meaning at all, this meaning is determinate in this sense that in every possible state of the world it allows for the assignment of a truth value to the sentence. The second assumption is that meaning conditions are ineffable. The fundamental principles that determine which combinations of signs are meaningful sentences, themselves cannot be expressed in such sentences. Notice, again, that both assumptions concern properties of language. We will now discuss them in detail.

Determinateness of Meaning

The idea that meaning is determinate is referred to in several places in the *Tractatus* and the *Notebooks*. For instance, in 3.23 it is said that "the requirement that simple signs be possible is the requirement that meaning be determinate."[9] The "simple signs" are the names, which go proxy for objects. Evidently, the simplicity of names and that of objects are intimately related. It is because objects are simple that the expressions referring to them, names, have to be simple as well. Objects being simple, they cannot be described, so the names that represent them cannot have descriptive content; they are simple signs, which only refer. So, indirectly, determinateness of meaning is tied in this passage to simplicity of objects. The same point is expressed in the *Notebooks* repeatedly and emphatically. For instance:

Every sentence that has a meaning has a COMPLETE meaning, and it is a picture of reality in such a way that what is not yet said in it simply cannot belong to its meaning. (16/6/15)

When I say, "The book is lying on the table," does this really have a completely clear meaning? (An EXTREMELY significant question.) But the meaning must be clear, for we do mean *something* by the sentence, and as much as we *certainly* mean must surely be clear. (20/6/15)

It seems clear that what we MEAN must always be "sharp." Our expression of what we mean can also only be right or wrong. And then the words may have been applied consistently or inconsistently. There does not seems to be another possibility. (20/6/15)

Determinateness of meaning must not be confused with completeness. That a sentence has a determinate meaning does not imply that it leaves nothing open, that it decides everything. Hence the completeness or incompleteness of the picture that a sentence is, is relative to a situation. In some situations a sentence may fail to picture completely, but as a picture it is always a complete picture of some situation:

> (A sentence may of course be an incomplete picture of a certain situation, but it is always *a* complete picture.) (5.156)

More in particular, a sentence may describe a certain situation only partially, leaving many of its features undecided, but those aspects of the situation that it does describe, it determines in a such way that it is possible to decide whether what it says is true or false:

> If a sentence tells us something, then it must be a picture of reality as it stands and a complete one at that.—Of course, there will also be something that it does *not* say—but *what* it says it says completely and it must be possible to delineate that SHARPLY. (16/6/15)

This passage occurs immediately before the one quoted above, which occurs in the *Tractatus* in 5.156.[10] So it seems that for Wittgenstein meaningfulness and bivalence are intrinsically connected. A sentence is meaningful only if it has a truth value in every situation, that is, if its meaning is determinate in the sense that the claim it makes on how the world is, is either correct or incorrect.[11]

Determinateness of meaning, then, says that if a sentence has meaning at all, the entire meaning is expressed by the sentence. Nothing is left out; nothing can be added later on. This means that all logical relationships with other sentences are also determined "in advance," so to speak. Hence, the process of analysis does not add to a sentence's meaning, nor does it sharpen it in some way nor does it make it more definite:

Analysis makes a sentence more complex than it was; but it cannot and may not make it more complex than its meaning originally was. (9/5/15)[12]

All that the logical analysis of a sentence does is make explicit what implicitly is already there, though perhaps hidden behind distracting and mystifying veils (see 4.002). Analysis is not a process in which we construct the meaning of a sentence, but one in which we explicate its logical form. In analyzing a sentence we make it as complex, in the sense of logical multiplicity, as the situation that it depicts, that is, as its meaning:

> In a sentence exactly as much must be distinguishable as in the situation it depicts.
> Both must have the same logical (mathematical) multiplicity. (4.04)

It is not the meaning but the sentence itself, as a syntactic object, that is analyzed, with the meaning pointing the way. This process of analysis explicates within the form of the sentence more and more of its meaning, that is, of the thought it expresses, which ultimately results in a complete harmony of the two. This possibility is what that 3.2 refers to:

> In a sentence a thought can be expressed in such a way that the elements of the sentential sign correspond to the objects of the thought. (3.2)

In 3.201 such a sentence is called "completely analyzed." It is important to notice that Wittgenstein only says that it is possible for a thought to be expressed by a completely analyzed sentence. He certainly does not present it as a necessary requirement. Obviously, also sentences that are not completely analyzed have meaning, that is, express thoughts.[13]

It is in view of the fact that sentences can have meaning, yet not be completely analyzed, that Wittgenstein speaks, in 4.002, of everyday language as "dressing up thought," while at the same time he holds that its sentences are "logically well ordered" (5.5563). The point is that the "dressing up" of thought is a matter of form, not of content. It is not that the sentences of our everyday language, if they have meaning, are meaningful only in a sloppy or imprecise or vague way. The meaning they have, if they have one, is determinate. Rather, the surface grammatical form of a sentence may fail to display completely the underlying logical structure of the meaning, since the grammatical form is not meant to do this, but rather is designed to meet other demands. But this is a matter of form, not of content. The form of a sentence may veil the form of the thought, but not the thought itself. Even an unanalyzed sentence expresses a thought, which we grasp when we understand its content. What we may fail to grasp completely is the logical form.

An important consequence of the thesis of the determinateness of meaning becomes apparent when we combine it with Wittgenstein's syntactic approach to logic. Wittgenstein's ideal is that of a logical language in which all logical relations are completely clear from the form of the sentences alone: the surveyability of logical relationships. There is no place for axioms; all sentences of logic "have equal rights" (6.127). In combination with the thesis of determinateness of meaning this implies that every meaningful sentence can be analyzed in such a way that its meaning is completely articulated formally. It is "spread out," so to speak, in a truth-functional combination of atomic sentences, which in their turn consist of names without any descriptive content in strictly formal combinations. Of course, this ideal end point of analysis is of a purely theoretical nature; we can be sure no actual process of analysis will ever take us there. But the very possibility of it (see 3.2 cited above) is at the heart of all meaningful discourse, of all symbolic representation. Thus, a complete analysis must show that the meaningfulness of expressions is a necessary feature and does not depend on the contingent realization of empirical conditions.[14] This is also evident from the following quotation from the *Philosophical Remarks*:

> An order is only then complete if it has meaning, whatever is the case. One could also say: then it is completely analyzed. (46)

The relationship with simplicity is evident. Witness the following:

> What I called "objects" at the time, the simple, is simply that which I can indicate without having to fear that it might not exist, that is, for which there is no existence or nonexistence, and that means that of which we can speak *whatever is the case*. (36)

The point at stake is expressed in the last sentence: if we can speak of something independently of whatever contingent conditions are realized, this means that it bears a noncontingent relationship to the meaningfulness of the expressions used. In other words, that of which I can speak independently of its being realized or not, is what can be expressed in a sentence of which the meaningfulness does not depend on the contingency of something existing. If the meaning of an expression, or even its meaningfulness as such, were to depend on the contingent truth of another expression, then meaning could not do what it is meant to, namely, to enable us to talk, not just about actual facts, but also about situations that do not obtain, or situations of which we do not know whether they obtain.[15]

Semantic Ineffability

Let us now turn to the second element of the argument for the simplicity of objects, namely, the ineffability of meaning conditions. This ineffability is a straightforward consequence of the way in which the picture theory of meaning is set up. The picture theory rests on two elements: the representation of objects in the situation depicted by elements of the picture by means of the pictorial relationship; and the identity of the pictorial form of the picture and of the situation. The most general case of pictorial form is logical form. Wittgenstein emphatically claims that logical form itself, and the identity of logical form, cannot be depicted. (For example, 2.172 and 2.174 express this in the context of the general picture theory; in 4.041, 4.12, and 4.121 the same point is made in the context of language.) This is an early insight of Wittgenstein's, one that anticipates the picture theory. In the notes that he dictated to Moore when the latter visited him in Norway in April 1914 we read:

In order that you should have a language that can express or *say* everything that *can* be said, this language must have certain properties; and when this is the case, *that* it has them can no longer be said in that language or *any* language. (108)[16]

The point that is made here is the same as the one about logical form, only formulated more generally. Whatever properties language has to have in order to be a system that can serve as a means to say things, cannot be expressed in language. Or to put it is the form of a slogan: "Meaning conditions cannot be expressed."[17] At first sight, this thesis seems obviously false, for is what semanticists are doing not exactly that, namely, expressing meaning conditions? In order to see what exactly Wittgenstein is getting at here, two things should be kept in mind.

First of all, we need to make a distinction between describing the meanings of the expressions of a language and describing the rules and principles by virtue of which these expressions have these meanings. The first task is definitely an empirical one, which consists in getting a certain set of contingent facts right. The second undertaking, however, is not so obviously empirical. It consists in laying bare the rules and principles that constitute the framework that makes these empirical relations between words and meanings possible in the first place. The study of this framework is arguably more of a theoretical, philosophical nature, and not a straightforwardly empirical enterprise.

Be that as it may, one might still object by pointing out that these theoretical aspects of meaning can be, and in fact are being, formulated. Here a second distinction becomes relevant, that between studying the meaning of a language and studying the meaning of language as such. Sure enough, we may come a long way in stating the semantic rules of one language using another language. But that is not what Wittgenstein is interested in. His stakes are higher; he aims at giving the requirements for any language, that is, for language as such, to be meaningful. And that, he states, cannot be done in language. For every way of expressing these requirements presupposes them and makes use of them, which means that in effect these requirements can not be explicated in toto and *ab initio*.

The point is perhaps more easily appreciated if we state it in terms of Wittgenstein's own picture theory, although that particular way of thinking about meaning is not presupposed by it. A fundamental aspect of the picture theory is the correlation of a name with an object. Suppose Fa is an elementary sentence, with F referring to $\bar{F}$ and a to $\bar{a}$. Part of an explication of the meaning of Fa might be to say that $\bar{a}$ occurs in the meaning of Fa, that is, in the situation that it depicts. It seems that any way in which we could formulate this, in its turn presupposes the very correlation of a with $\bar{a}$. In other words, this meaning condition is something that cannot be described from a position outside the language.[18] Of course, it could be said if we had an "outside" language that we could use. But in that case we would simply have traded our universalistic aim for a particularistic one: what would be characterized would be a condition for a particular language, not one that pertains to language as such.[19]

It seems that one either has to give up on the ideal of stating the necessary requirements for any language to be meaningful, or has to accept the ineffability of those meaning conditions. Obviously, Wittgenstein settled for the latter option, as the quotation from the "Notes Dictated to Moore" given above illustrates. Notice that he speaks there of a language "which can express or *say* everything that *can* be said." If meaning conditions were expressible they would be expressible in that language, which, for the reasons given, cannot be the case. Hence, the nature of language, that which is essential to any language or symbolic system, cannot be expressed in language. This does not mean, however, that it cannot be conveyed: meaning conditions show themselves in meaningful language. Almost immediately following the passage from the "Notes Dictated to Moore" quoted above, we read:

> Thus a language that *can* express everything *mirrors* certain properties of the world by these properties it must have; and logical so-called propositions shew *in a systematic way* those properties. (108)

Several prominent features of the *Tractatus* are already contained in this passage: the doctrine of showing versus saying; the idea of meaning as an isomorphism between language and the world; and the special status of logical sentences.

Reconstructing the Argument

The two assumptions—that meaning is determinate and that meaning conditions are inexpressible—play a crucial role in Wittgenstein's argument for the simplicity of objects, as it is presented in 2.02–2.0212. And both are essentially assumptions about language. Now that we have examined these assumptions in some detail, let us return to the argument itself.

Let S be a meaningful sentence. It follows from the assumption of determinateness of meaning that S can be completely analyzed. In its completely analyzed form S consists of a truth-functional combination of elementary sentences, which in their turn are concatenations of names. Names do not have descriptive meaning; they only have reference. Now suppose that S contains some name N that refers not to a simple object, but to a complex entity C. The existence of C is contingent, and hence the corresponding existential condition is expressible in some meaningful, contingent sentence T. Since T expresses the existential condition for C, and C by assumption is what N refers to, T in effect expresses a referential condition for N. However, since a name lacks meaning, its contribution to the meaning of the sentences in which it occurs is precisely its reference.[20] But that would mean that T expresses a meaning condition for S, which contradicts the assumption of the ineffability of meaning conditions. Hence it seems that whatever N refers to, it cannot be a complex entity that exists only contingently, but must be a simple object, that is, an entity that "exists independently of what is the case" (2.024).[21] It appears that this quasi-formal reconstruction of the argument in 2.02–2.0212 carries some force. Of course, it crucially draws on the two assumptions discussed above and these are far from obvious or unobjectionable. But it does seem to be what Wittgenstein had in mind and the important thing to note here is that this argument for the ontological thesis of the simplicity of objects firmly rests on logical, semantic assumptions concerning language and meaning.[22]

The argument can be given another form by rephrasing it in terms of the logical independence of states of affairs. This property of states of affairs, that the existence or nonexistence of a state of affairs carries no implications concerning the existence or nonexistence of others, is in fact no other property than that of the simplicity of objects. Since states of affairs are configurations of objects, it follows from the simplicity of objects that states of affairs are logically independent. Likewise, the logical independence of states of affairs implies that objects are simple. Now let S and T be two elementary sentences. Suppose that S and T are not logically independent; for example, suppose that S implies T. Then it follows that what T says is part of what S says, and hence T should be contained in S on the level of complete analysis. For determinateness of meaning implies, in conjunction with Wittgenstein's syntactic approach to logic, that all logical relationships between sentences are completely explicit and transparent at this level. They can be read off of their logical forms. But then S would be complex and not elementary, which contradicts our assumption. Hence it follows that if S and T are elementary sentences they are logically independent and hence consist of names that refer to simple objects.

This line of argumentation seems to be what is hinted at in the following passage from the *Notebooks*:

"There are no complex objects" then means for us: In the sentence it must be clear how the object is composed insofar as we can talk about its complexity at all.—The meaning of the sentence must appear in the sentence analyzed into its *simple* components—. And these parts are then really unanalyzable, since further analyzed ones just would not be THESE. In other words, the sentence then does not allow replacement by another one that has more components; rather any that has more components also does not have *this* meaning.

Whenever the meaning of a sentence is completely expressed in the sentence itself, the latter is analyzed into its simple components—a further analysis is impossible, and an apparent one is superfluous—and these are objects in the original sense. (17/6/15)

Notice again how the simplicity of objects is presented here as something that follows from essentially semantic considerations.

Yet another way to present essentially the same point is in terms of necessity. According to Wittgenstein, logical necessity is the only kind of necessity there is (6.3, 6.37), all other relationships between situations being contingent. This is the basis on which he rejects the view of causality as a necessary relationship: logical relationships between sentences are mirrored in the tautological nature of the corresponding sentences that show that such a relationship holds.[23] For example, that S logically implies T is shown by $S \rightarrow T$ being a tautology (see 6.1265, 6.127). This is one of Wittgenstein's first original insights in the field of logic (see 6.1). Again, determinateness of meaning, in conjunction with Wittgenstein's syntactic approach to logic, implies that the tautological character of logically valid sentences is a matter of form: it is their distinctive feature that their being true can be known "just from the symbol," that is, a priori (6.113). For any logically valid sentence is a special kind of truth-functional combination of elementary sentences, namely, one in which the possibilities for the parts to be false cancel each other out. The logical independence of elementary sentences and hence the simplicity of objects, then follows by a straightforward argument. Let S and T be two different elementary sentences. Suppose they are not logically independent, for example, suppose that S logically implies T. Then it follows that there is a necessary truth, namely, $S \rightarrow T$, which is not merely the tautologous result of truth functionally combining a number of contingent elementary sentences. For not every two different elementary sentences R and R' combined by implication into $R \rightarrow R'$ result in a tautology, which means that in order to recognize $S \rightarrow T$ as such, we would need to know more than their logical form, namely, their descriptive content. But that would contradict Wittgenstein's idea that there is only logical necessity that is to be accounted for solely in terms of truth-functional operations and that can be made completely surveyable in pure form.[24]

Wittgenstein's syntactic account of necessity seems to be related to his avowed monism and absolutism with regard to logic. An axiomatic treatment, such as Frege's or Russell's, leaves open the possibility of nonlogical axioms, with a concomitant notion of nonlogical necessity. Wittgenstein rejects the axiomatic approach flatly (see 6.127) and explicitly criticizes Russell on the second point (see 6.1232, 6.1233). That Wittgenstein wants to keep to his point that all necessity is logical necessity is especially clear from his remarks on color exclusion in 6.3751, which we already referred to above:

> For example, that two colors are simultaneously present at some spot in the visual field is impossible, in fact logically impossible, since it is excluded by the logical structure of color. (6.3751)

It was precisely this phenomenon of nonlogical necessity that led Wittgenstein to abandon his logical atomism in the early stages of his intermediate period. Closer study of the logic of color revealed a certain holistic structure that cannot be analyzed away by logical means and that he tried to capture in his notion of a "sentence system" [*Satzsystem*]. The idea of determinateness of meaning follows suit, in a later stage.

More important for our investigation in this stage is that Wittgenstein's position on the nature of validity—that all logically valid sentences are truth-functional tautologies—is of an early date: it precedes both the picture theory and the ontology. Above we noticed the essentially logical, semantical character of the assumptions of the determinateness of meaning and the ineffability of meaning conditions, which play a key role in the argument for the simplicity of objects. Here we note that the early doctrine of the tautological character of validity leads to one of the most central characteristics of the *Tractatus*—namely, the logical independence of elementary sentences and hence to the logical independence of states of affairs. All this seems to point in a certain direction: that the ontology, more in particular the notion of substance as the totality of simple objects, is postulated to provide a framework in which the earlier conceived views on validity and meaning can be formally explicated.

THE NATURE OF OBJECTS

We have sketched in some detail the role played by the assumptions of determinateness of meaning and ineffability of meaning conditions in Wittgenstein's argumentation for the simplicity of objects stated in the ontological sections of the *Tractatus*. We have done so because it is important to realize that this crucial feature of the ontology rests on essentially logical, semantical considerations. However, the question of what exactly the relationship between language and ontology is, seems not yet settled by these observations. Of course, it is quite evident that language and ontology as they are conceived in the *Tractatus* are intimately related. The foregoing discussion amply illustrates this. But that does not mean that we are already in a position to determine whether the ontology of the *Tractatus* is a metaphysical theory in its own right or whether it is an instance of what we have called "natural language metaphysics," a theory of the structure of the world as presupposed by language. Of course, the way in which the simplicity of objects is argued for strongly suggests the latter, but it does not show conclusively that the *Tractatus* must be interpreted in this way. Hence the question of what kind of realism it is that the *Tractatus* embodies still has not been answered, and it seems that we have to investigate the matter even more closely.

A plausible route to take is to inquire after the nature of the objects themselves. Up to now we have seen that they are assumed to be simple, and for essentially linguistic reasons. But that does not determine their nature completely. Additional information is required. The very nature of the tractarian objects has puzzled commentators and interpreters right from the start and a variety of opinions can be found in the literature. Our considerations will not prove one of them absolutely right. But they will provide additional reasons for thinking that the ontology of the *Tractatus* is best viewed as a theory of the nature of the world as presupposed by the fundamental features of language.

We can distinguish three main views on the nature of the tractarian objects. According to one, they are basically logical objects, that is, the outcome of a process of logical analysis. Another view regards them as material (physical) things. And according to a third interpretation objects are best viewed as perceptual objects, such as sense-data. At first sight, both the *Tractatus* itself and the *Notebooks* seem to provide evidence for all three positions. Proponents of all three views have pointed out various passages that they claim support their interpretations.[25]

Objects as a Logical Category

Let us start with the position that views the ontological category of objects as essentially a logical category, that is, as a category of entities of which the existence and properties are settled by logical means.[26] Clearly, this interpretation of what objects are is completely in accordance with the way we have reconstructed the argument for simplicity above. And in view of that, this very argument, as it is stated in 2.02–2.0212, can be adduced as the primary evidence to be found for this view on objects in the *Tractatus* itself. The *Notebooks*, too, contain various passages that seem to corroborate this interpretation.

The problem is, however, that the discussion of the problem of simplicity in the *Notebooks* is exactly that: a discussion, an ongoing attempt to unravel the problem, in which different positions are taken up, discussed with arguments pro and con, and in which a definitive conclusion is not easy to discern. Small wonder, then, that different views on what Wittgenstein means by simplicity can be substantiated with quotations from the *Notebooks*. However, we do feel that both the way in which the argument gets underway and the way in which it ends, suggests rather strongly that the view outlined above is the correct one.

For one thing, it is significant that the whole discussion of what a simple object is arises within the context of a question about names and their logical characteristics. Wittgenstein observes that names may stand for different forms and that the form is revealed by the syntactic use that can be made of the name (14/6/15). Then he raises the question: "Now what is the syntactical use of names of simple objects?" (14/6/15). This question after the syntactic use of names for simples, Wittgenstein notes, requires a better understanding of the concept of a simple: "What is my basic idea when I talk about simple objects?" (14/6/15). This introduces the problem of simplicity and the discussion of it takes up all entries of the next week or so.

Immediately after the introduction of the problem we find the following passage:

But one could also put the question as follows: it seems that the idea of the SIMPLE already is contained in that of the complex and in the idea of analysis, and in such a way that we arrive at this idea quite irrespective of any kind of example of simple objects or of sentences in which such are mentioned, and recognize the existence of the simple object, a priori, as a logical necessity.

Thus it looks as if the existence of the simple object is related to that of the complex as the meaning of $\neg p$ is to the meaning of p: the *simple* object would be *prejudged* in the complex. (14/6/15)

This passage construes the very notion of a simple object as one that is derived from that of a complex and from the idea that complexes can be analyzed. However, as such this does not establish the existence of simples. For what Wittgenstein is after is not a mere conceptual tie. The existence of simples is tied internally, that is, logically, to that of complexes, but in a subtle way. In an entry of the following day (15/6/15), immediately following the passage just quoted, Wittgenstein warns that this relation between a complex and a simple is not to be confused with that between a complex and its component parts. The latter is indeed a conceptual relationship: the concept of a complex carries with it that of a part, much in the sense that "being complex" means "having component parts." However, that is not the way complex and simple are related. For as Wittgenstein notes two days later (17/6/15): "And nothing seems to speak against infinite analyzability." That is, something could be complex, and thus a forteriori have component parts, without any of the latter being simple: the complexity might be all-pervading. Thus saying that there is a logical tie between complex and simple means something more; some other aspect than the conceptual relation between complex and component must be involved in making the connection.[27]

In the notes that follow the observation quoted above, Wittgenstein, not surprisingly, for this inspired the discussion in the first place, turns to meaning again:

All I want is just that *my meaning* be completely analyzed!! . . . For if in a sentence possibilities *are left open, exactly this* must be *determined*: *what* is left open. . . . What I do not know I do not know, but the sentence must show me *what* I know. And then is not this *determined* thing, which I *must* arrive at, just simple in the sense I always had in mind? It is, so to speak, what is hard.

"There are no complex objects" then means for us: In the sentence it must be clear how the object is composed insofar as we can talk about its complexity at all.—The meaning of the sentence must appear in the sentence analyzed into its *simple* components—. And these parts are then really unanalyzable, since further analyzed ones just would not be THESE. In other words, the sentence then does not allow replacement by another one that has more components; rather any that has more components also does not have *this* meaning.

Whenever the meaning of a sentence is completely expressed in the sentence itself, the latter is analyzed into its simple components—a further analysis is impossible, and an apparent one is superfluous—and these are objects in the original sense. (17/6/15)[28]

The first two paragraphs of this passage turn around themes that by now should be familiar—the notion of complete analysis (first para.) and its relation to the determinateness of meaning (". . . *exactly this* must be *determined*: *what* is left open" [second para.]). In the third paragraph these two themes are combined in the idea that simple objects are the terminus of the process of analysis. One might say that it is a defining feature of a sentence having a particular sense that its complete analysis resolves it into particular simple components (". . . any that has more components also does not have *this* meaning" [third para.]). Thus the notion of simple objects is intrinsically tied to that of analysis: they are what results when analysis is completed. An important remark is the one made in the final paragraph. What Wittgenstein points out here is that a sentence may have a definite meaning without this meaning being completely "laid out," so to speak, in the sentence itself. The goal of analysis is not to make definite what is vague or to make clear what is unclear, but to make surveyable what is already there, albeit in a nonperspicuous way. Once the meaning is spelled out completely, the process of analysis has come to an end: it has reached the objects. Note that this is essentially a linguistic criterion, not an ontological one: simplicity is not "out there" in the objects themselves, but is bestowed on them by the process of analysis, which starts from and receives its direction from the internal, logical structure of the meanings of sentences.

This linguistic character of the notion of simplicity is even more clearly expressed in the entry of the following day:

If the complexity of an object is characteristic of the meaning of a sentence, then it must be depicted in the sentence to the extent in which it determines its meaning, and insofar as the composition is *not* characteristic for *this* meaning, insofar as the objects of this sentence are *simple*. THEY *cannot* be further analyzed.—The requirement that things be simple is the requirement that meaning be determinate. (18/6/15)

What counts as simple, that is, as an object, depends on the meaning of the sentence. It is what is required by the determinateness of meaning and by the possibility of completely analyzing the meaning of a sentence in such a way that it becomes surveyable. Any further aspects of the actual constitution of objects (physical or otherwise) are deemed irrelevant.

It is interesting to note that the last paragraph occurs slightly differently formulated in the *Tractatus*. In 3.23, which was already quoted above, it says: "The requirement that simple signs be possible is the requirement that sense be determinate." That Wittgenstein switches from objects to names is significant and underscores the essentially linguistic nature of simplicity and, hence, of objects as simples. This linguistic perspective, however, can be developed in different directions, and we will discuss some possibilities later on.

In conclusion, it seems that these quotations from the *Notebooks* provide us with ample evidence in favor of an interpretation of objects as constituting a basically logical, linguistic category of entities. Both the impetus to inquire after the nature of simple objects in the first place and the way in which Wittgenstein proceeds in his investigations derive from what is essentially a logical, or semantical question: How is meaning possible? This strongly suggests that the resulting ontology is an attempt to provide foundations for what is initially and finally a semantic undertaking. The ontology is nothing more (and nothing less, of course) than a characterization of what the world must be like for it to be able to appear in language and thought at all.

It should be noted that, in addition to these clear and unambiguous passages, several remarks on the nature and terminus of the process of analysis corroborate this interpretation. Objects and the process of analysis are intimately related: the objects are what analysis results in. Hence, if Wittgenstein describes this process as a logical, linguistic one, this implies that the objects also are of a logical, linguistic nature. One example of a passage in which he talks about the process of analysis in precisely such terms is the remark of 14/6/15, discussed earlier, in which Wittgenstein discusses the idea of the simple being contained in the idea of analysis.[29]

Yet another relevant passage is the following:

But my difficulty still consists in this: In all the sentences that I encounter, names occur, which, however, must disappear again on further analysis. I know that such further analysis is possible, but I am unable to carry it out completely. Yet apparently I know that if the analysis were carried out completely, its result would have to be a sentence that once again contains names, relations, and so on. In short: it seems as if in this way I knew only a form without being acquainted with a single example.

I see: the analysis can be continued, and I am unable to imagine, so to speak, that it will lead to anything else but to the types of sentences with which I am familiar. (16/6/15)

To avoid misunderstanding it is important to notice that Wittgenstein is not using the term "name" here in the technical, tractarian sense, but rather in the more customary sense of "referring term." Names in that sense are analyzable, as is clear from the opening sentence in this passage.

It is clear that the question Wittgenstein is wrestling with is prompted by the fact that this process of analysis is not one of a familiar kind. That is to say that it is not a kind of reductionistic analysis of referring terms, such as Russell's analysis in terms of sense-data or a physicalistic one that would proceed in terms of material objects. Its essence, it seems, is that it is a grammatical, logical process, and what Wittgenstein seems to be finding out here is that the terminus of such a process cannot be *discovered*. What constitutes the end point of such an analysis is not an empirical matter. And neither is it determined by epistemological or ontological considerations. The discussion of simplicity is carried on in the *Notebooks* until 22/6/15. The number of remarks entered between 14/6/15 and 22/6/15 is quite large: evidently, Wittgenstein was deeply concerned with the problem. Throughout, it seems, the logical interpretation is sustained. For the most part Wittgenstein is occupied with the problem of the apparent vagueness of natural language and with the concomitant question whether, and if so how, logic can be applied to it. Some of the more central passages of this discussion have already been analyzed earlier on. Of course, simplicity plays a key role in these considerations. However, although Wittgenstein seems uncertain at points about how the notion of simplicity can be tied to natural language, it is quite clear that the position as he develops it in the beginning of the discussion, which we reconstructed above, is not given up. Of course, we cannot really be sure, because after 22/6/15, there is a gap that lasts until 15/4/16, but the conjecture seems a plausible one, especially since it leads to a consistent interpretation of what is said on the matter in the *Tractatus*.

Other Interpretations

At this juncture it is only fair to point out that there are passages in both the *Notebooks* and the *Tractatus* that may suggest another interpretation of the status of the ontology. And indeed other interpretations have been put forward in the literature.[30] For example, some have argued that the tractarian objects are material objects, others that they are sense-data, and yet others that they are best viewed as phenomenal objects. There is little direct evidence for such claims to be found in either the *Tractatus* or the *Notebooks*, yet some passages may be adduced to support such views indirectly.

For example, in 2.01123–2.01232 Wittgenstein speaks of "knowing an object," and Malcolm takes this to imply that objects are in fact material objects, for those are the kind of ontological entities that we may plausibly be said to know.[31] According to Malcolm (1986) the following passage from the *Notebooks* also supports his interpretation:[32]

And again and again it forces itself upon us that there is something simple, unanalyzable, an element of being, in short, a thing.

To be sure it does not go against our feeling that *we* cannot analyze SENTENCES so far as to refer to them by name, but we feel that the WORLD must consist of elements. And it seems as if this were identical with the claim that the world must be what it is, must be determinate. . . .

The world has a firm structure. (17/6/15)

Of course, nothing in this passage identifies simple objects as material objects, although it does appear to place the locus of simplicity directly in the world. But if we are investigating how Wittgenstein's notion of "world" is to be interpreted, this in effect tells us nothing new. It only says that simplicity is a characteristic of the world, but not what the nature of the world is or of what kind of entities simplicity is a characteristic feature.[33] However, there are no other passages in which Wittgenstein speaks in this fashion, whereas passages in which simplicity is tied explicitly to language and logic abound. We will return to some other problems surrounding this type of interpretation later, when we discuss Malcolm's views in more detail.

Let us now give a few examples of passages that to some have suggested that Wittgenstein's objects are neither material nor logical objects but rather are perceptual ones, that is, sense-data or phenomenal objects.

There is one passage in the *Tractatus* that mentions such experiential objects explicitly:

A spot in the visual field, though it need not be red, must have a color: it has, so to speak, the space of colors around it. A note must have *some* pitch, an object of the sense of touch *some* hardness. (2.0131)

This remark seems to be intended as an illustration of a characteristic of objects in the technical tractarian sense—the intrinsic, necessary relation-

128 *Language and Ontology*

ship between objects and the states of affairs in which they can occur. From our present perspective, the important question is whether it is meant as an illustration in the sense of a comparison or in the sense of an instantiation. For example, are the tractarian objects like a tone in that they, too, have to have certain properties, or is a tone an example of an object? If one constructs this claim in the latter way, it seems to corroborate a perceptual interpretation of objects, for color, pitch, and hardness are typically phenomenal qualities of entities. But if one reads it in the former way, it does not.[34]

Another passage that one often finds quoted in this connection is the following from the *Notebooks*:

It seems to me perfectly possible that certain areas of our visual field are simple objects because we do not perceive any point of these areas separately; visual impressions of stars certainly seem to be like this. (18/6/15)

Two remarks are in order. First of all, it should be noted that Wittgenstein is talking about perception, about the way in which our perceptual apparatus deals with impressions. The conclusion that certain areas in our visual field can be regarded as simple objects with regard to perception. But, of course, this does not say that they are also simple in an extended epistemological sense. Furthermore, it is important to note how this passage continues:

To wit, if I say, for example, this watch is not in the drawer, then it absolutely does not need to FOLLOW LOGICALLY from that, that a wheel, which is in the watch, is not in the drawer, for *I might not have known* that the wheel was in the watch, hence could not have meant by "this watch" a complex in which the wheel occurs. (18/6/15)

Again, it seems that Wittgenstein's inquiry is not after the essence of simplicity, either ontological or epistemological. Rather his concern is with how the concept is used, how it functions in our dealing with language, and its relation to the world.[35]

Of course, these remarks do not show conclusively that an epistemological interpretation of objects is not feasible. However, they do indicate that really unambiguous and direct evidence from either the *Tractatus* or the *Notebooks* is hard to come by. We will return to this issue below.

Conclusion

It is time to take stock. We have seen that the simplicity of objects, or, equivalently, the logical independence of states of affairs, forms the key to a proper understanding of the ontology and of the relationship between language and reality. Whether, and if so to what extent, the *Tractatus* subscribes to some form of realism depends on how we interpret these characteristics of objects and states of affairs. We have also shown extensively that both in the *Notebooks* and in the *Tractatus* these pivotal features of the ontology are introduced in the context of the analysis of language and meaning and that they are supported by arguments drawn from that same field. This suggests very strongly that the notion of simplicity, and hence that of an object and of a state of affairs, is primarily conceived of as a logical, linguistic notion. And that implies that the entire ontology has to be thought of as a subsidiary of the tractarian conception of language, meaning, and logic. That being so, we must conclude that, although the *Tractatus* does propose a realistic conception of the relationship between language and the world, it presents this as a presupposition of its linguistic and logical doctrines, not as a realistic ontology on its own terms.

However, convincing though the evidence may be, it is rather indirect. And other views have been advocated in the literature. What we will do in the sequel is to try to strengthen our case by doing two things. First of all, we will discuss some examples of alternative conceptions and show why and where they lead to difficulties. The remainder of this chapter is devoted to this task. Secondly, we will adduce some more indirect evidence, from a quarter that, with very few exceptions, has not been brought to bear on this issue at all: the ethical part of the *Tractatus*. Here we will argue that if we want to interpret Wittgenstein's views on ethics as an integral part of the *Tractatus*, we must interpret its ontology as essentially language driven. This argument will be developed in Chapter 4.

SOME OTHER VIEWS

In Chapter 1 we briefly discussed the main types of interpretations of the tractarian ontology. Before we turn to a discussion of alternative views,

130   *Language and Ontology*

it is perhaps worthwhile to give a bit more detailed account of the search space in which these views can be located.

It seems that the relationship between language and the world can be viewed from two fundamentally different angles. First of all, we can conceive of the ontology as being constructed from within language, or at least on the basis of it. Alternatively we can regard the structure of language as being derived from that of the world as an independent given. All interpretations put forward in the literature fall within one of these two broad classes. That within one class one may also find interpretations that differ in other respects is another issue and does not diminish the importance of this distinction as forming a kind of watershed between theories.

On the first view, the ontology with which the *Tractatus* starts out is a theory of reality as it can be grasped in and by means of language. That is to say that the basic characteristics of the various ontological categories—objects, states of affairs, situations—are not features of some independently existing ontological realm. Rather, they are simply those properties that the world and its constituents must have in order for language to be able to be about it. Also, in the *Tractatus* language and thought are more or less identified (see "A thought is a meaningful sentence" [4]); every meaningful sentence expresses a thought and every thought can be expressed in language. As a result this view places the *Tractatus* firmly in the critical, Kantian tradition. To what extent the *Tractatus* can indeed be interpreted as "the Kantian enterprise with a linguistic twist" is a moot point. Some have almost casually placed Wittgenstein in the Kantian tradition, as if this categorization is so obvious as to need no further arguments. Others have emphatically denied that the *Tractatus* can be thus interpreted.[36] The answer seems to rely more than just a bit on how strictly one wants to tie the use of the qualification "Kantian" to the work of Kant himself. For our present purposes it may suffice to note that if we use "Kantian" to characterize an approach that seeks to uncover the conditions of possibility of a certain field of phenomena (without requiring in addition the use of more specific elements of Kant's conceptual apparatus), then it seems that the *Tractatus* certainly has Kantian features. The ontology, with its particular categories and structure, then is to be viewed as constituting a condition of possibility of meaningful language.

The second view interprets the *Tractatus* as stating a theory of reality as it is, in and of itself. Here it is the structure of reality that accounts for that of language, and not the other way around. Because reality is the way it is, that is, because it has particular categories of entities, each with their particular features, language has to have a particular structure that matches that of reality. For example, on this view there are unanalyzable names in language because there are simple objects in the world. And elementary sentences are logically independent because states of affairs are, and not the other way around. In other words, the extralinguistic nature of reality is taken at face value. It is assumed that it is evident that our ordinary language is about an ordinary, extralinguistic reality. And since the process of analysis is taken to be meaning-preserving, it is concluded that at the level of complete analysis, too, reality is essentially language independent. So the avowed realism of this second view usually is of the commonsense type.

Theories that start from this second view, which is not critical in the philosophical sense of the term, are more likely to give an interpretation of the ontology along traditional lines, in terms of familiar epistemological or ontological notions. The interpretation of tractarian objects as sense-data is one example; the view that says that these objects are material things is another. This shows by the way that this view of the relationship between language and the world leaves room for quite different interpretations of the *Tractatus*.

The first view, too, underdetermines a particular analysis. Roughly, it seems that the following positions can be discerned (and actually have been defended). First of all, one may hold that "linguistic reality," by which is meant reality as it is accessible for language and thought, is not the "real" reality; that is, in terms of Kantian terminology, it is phenomenon, not noumenon. This might be considered as a linguistic form of critical realism. Another possible position is to hold that linguistic reality indeed is the only reality there is. This position can be further subdivided, since one can take either a relativistic or an absolutistic stance here. One may want to say that there is in the end only one such reality, or one may uphold that there are as many different realities as there are different languages. Finally, an extreme view of the language-dependent character of reality is that "reality" is not an ontological term at all, but denotes what is essentially a semantic concept. On this view the ontology of the *Tractatus* is no ontology at all, but a metaphor, which uses terms from the ontological vocabulary to describe the various semantical roles that expressions in language play.

In the following sections we will take a critical look at some interpretations of the relationship between language and ontology in the *Tractatus* that have been proposed in the literature. The analyses were chosen also with an eye to the various types of analyses distinguished above. Malcolm's interpretation represents the second type, which interprets the *Tractatus* as holding reality primary with respect to language. Maslow's interpretation and that of Ishiguro and McGuinness provide examples of the first approach, which assumes that in the *Tractatus* it is language that is the starting point.

Maslow: Instrumentalism

Maslow's book, *A Study in Wittgenstein's 'Tractatus,'* was first published in 1961, but it dates from 1933. This makes the book interesting for at least two reasons.

First of all, it is a good example of an interpretation of the *Tractatus* by someone who at the time considered himself to be a logical empiricist. Maslow clearly indicates this, both in his preface to the published version of 1961, in which he sketches his own philosophical position at the time of writing, and in the 1933 introduction to the book, which also gives an interesting account of the role of Schlick, who regularly visited UC Berkeley in the 1930s. The first to recognize the *Tractatus* as a work of major importance were the logical empiricists of Schlick's Vienna Circle. However, the way in which they hailed it as the manifesto of their movement did not meet with Wittgenstein's approval, since much of the ethical point of the work seemed to him to be lost on them. As far as certain members of the Vienna Circle were concerned this seems indeed to have been the case. But the work of Maslow shows that this is not necessary, perhaps. Although he certainly reads the *Tractatus* almost exclusively as a logical investigation, some sensitivity to what Wittgenstein wanted with the book from an ethical perspective is not lacking. This may be (partly) due to Schlick, who was genuinely interested in ethics and wrote a book about the subject that he himself considered to be his best piece of philosophical work.

A second reason why Maslow's interpretation is of interest is that it presents the view of someone who, besides Wittgenstein's 1929 paper on logical form ("Some Remarks on Logical Form"), has read only the *Tractatus* itself. Maslow did not have the *Notebooks* at his disposal (which were published only in 1961); most of the later work still had to be written and nothing of what Wittgenstein produced up to 1933 was published at the time.[37] Therefore Maslow's interpretation is one of someone for whom the issue of the continuity or discontinuity in Wittgenstein's work simply does not arise and hence does not influence his interpretation of the *Tractatus*. For almost all contemporary authors this question of how much continuity there is in Wittgenstein's work is at least in the background, if not a major factor in how they interpret the *Tractatus*. (We will see examples later on, and the present work provides another one, of course.) Maslow's interpretation of the *Tractatus* clearly bears the marks of the work of a logical empiricist.[38] Roughly speaking, logical empiricism can be characterized as a mixture of classical (Locke, Berkeley, Hume) and nineteenth-century (Mach) empiricism, and positivism (Comte), but with a linguistic, logical twist (hence the epithet "logical"). In one of its purest forms it holds that reality is the totality of all sensory experience structured by language. Maslow completely agrees and states that "we cannot separate the world from the perspective of the language by means of which we organize it."[39]

Another illustrative passage is the following:

> We are merely drawing attention to the tautological requirement for any sensible language: we can give sense to our propositions only within *our* experience, and therefore according to the rules of *our* language. Thus the discussion of the formal characteristics of the world, of *our* world, is nonmetaphysical.[40]

These quotations clearly show that Maslow shares the fundamental assumptions of logical empiricism. First of all, Maslow's ontology is that of an empiricist. The world is the totality of experiential facts; it is given in experience and not in some other way (by intuition, or by reason, or by revelation). What causes these experiences is not on the same ontological plane and in fact tends to drop out of consideration altogether. Secondly, and this is what distinguishes logical empiricism from its predecessors, language is taken to play a decisive role in forming the world of experiential facts. There is no experience as such, no "raw experience," or if there is, it is not accessible to us. Only structured experience is real, and it makes up the world. And the structure is provided by language, or by logic. (Logical empiricists and positivists tend to use "language" in such a narrow sense and "logic" in such a wide sense that the two become virtually interchangeable.) So in all there are three layers to be distinguished: the causes, whatever they are, of our experiences; our raw experiences; and our structured experiences. Only the latter kind are considered to be real and it is they that constitute the world. The structure being provided by language, Maslow is able to say: "The world is the universe of reference of our significant discourse."[41] In other words, what is real is what we can talk about; it is what the meaningful expressions of our language refer to.

It is also interesting to note that Maslow brings a kind of Kantian perspective to bear on the constitutive role of language with respect to the world. At least that is how he conceives it himself and at some point he also explicitly compares Wittgenstein to Kant: "Wittgenstein's view on language is a version of Kant's Copernican revolution in philosophy." Elsewhere Maslow says that Kant's problem as he formulates it in the introduction of the *Critique of Pure Reason* is like that of Wittgenstein, the difference being the "linguistic turn" in the latter.[42] The preface of the *Tractatus* certainly has a Kantian ring, as have such remarks as 4.113–4.116.

Two other characteristics of logical empiricism that Maslow's book shares with it are the primarily epistemological viewpoint and the antimetaphysical attitude. It is clear that the appropriation of the *Tractatus* by the logical empiricists, in which Maslow's study partakes, is based on the idea that Wittgenstein agrees on these points, and it is therefore interesting to investigate to what extent the *Tractatus* indeed shares these characteristics.

Excursus I: Wittgenstein and Logical Empiricism

Let us start with epistemology. It is clear that, notwithstanding the fundamental role it assigns to language, the basic outlook of logical empiricism is epistemological. In that sense it remains firmly rooted in the traditions of modern philosophy. The primary task of philosophical analysis is to investigate the foundations of knowledge, so as to enable us to distinguish sound, scientific knowledge from mere everyday belief and unwarranted, philosophical speculation. The linguistic turn that logical empiricism gives to the classical variety does not reside in changing the fundamental tasks or the starting points, but rather in providing a new tool, namely, logical analysis of language.

Wittgenstein's relation to the traditional epistemological concerns is altogether different. At the time of his stay in Cambridge with Russell, the latter was intensively concerned with epistemological questions. The suggestion has been made that there was to be some kind of division of labor between the two.[43] Russell concerned himself with the epistemology, leaving the logic to Wittgenstein.[44] Perhaps this was how Russell saw the situation, and Wittgenstein certainly showed an interest in Russell's work at the time. But it seems to have been an interest that was based on the conviction that Russell was on the wrong track. Wittgenstein's criticisms proved to be devastating to Russell's enterprise. Russell broke off work on the book that he was writing, called *Theory of Knowledge*, because Wittgenstein convinced him that there was a fundamental error in his approach, which he acknowledged but could not repair.[45] Although Wittgenstein evidently knew of Russell's epistemological concerns, neither the *Notebooks* nor the *Tractatus* bears any trace of a similar interest on his part. The only passages that could be interpreted as being concerned with epistemology in the traditional sense are *Tractatus* 5.6–5.641, which discuss the relation between solipsism and realism. However, as will be argued in Chapter 4, these remarks have to be interpreted differently and are not primarily epistemological. Furthermore, when Wittgenstein explicitly mentions epistemology (in 4.1121) it is only to brush it aside as irrelevant for philosophy, properly conceived. The task of philosophy is to provide logical clarifications, not epistemological foundations. But this needs some clarification itself. After all, Wittgenstein does identify language and thought (in the preface and in 4; see also 4.114–4.115), and thus it seems that what the *Tractatus* explicitly says about the former, it implicitly also claims about the latter. And in effect Wittgenstein accepts this consequence. In a letter to Russell, dating from 19/8/19 and written while in a camp for prisoners of war in Monte Cassino, Wittgenstein, answering various queries of Russell's about the *Tractatus* manuscript, writes (the quoted sentences are Russell's):

(2) ". . . But a Gedanke is a Tatsache: What are its constituents and components, and what is their relation to those of the pictured Tatsache?" I don't know *what* the constituents of thought are, but I know *that* it must have such constituents that correspond to the words of Language. Again the kind of relation of the constituents of the thought and of the pictured fact is irrelevant. It would be a matter of psychology to find out.

. . .

(4) "Does a Gedanke consist of words?" No! But of psychical constituents that have the same sort of relation to reality as words. What those constituents are I don't know. (*Notebooks*, appendix III, 130)

Wittgenstein acknowledges that language and thought are highly similar, in fact isomorphic. This follows from the relationship between thought and language: recall that the linguistic sign becomes meaningful by "the thinking of the meaning of the sentence" (3.11).[46] And this similarity of the two is what the approach of the *Tractatus* assumes in the first place: according to his preface Wittgenstein wants to draw the limits of thought through language. So why is the *Tractatus* not an epistemological enterprise? Why does Wittgenstein on the one hand identify language and thought, while on the other hand dismiss epistemology as irrelevant? At first sight, the position may seem rather weak, but the following should be kept in mind. First of all, we note that traditional epistemology is concerned with the limits of knowledge, whereas the *Tractatus* is devoted to establishing the structure of all logically possible thoughts. Arguably, these are different undertakings. Epistemology sets out to delimit within the totality of all thoughts a specific subset: those that constitute justified, reliable knowledge. An investigation into the logical structure of thoughts is much broader: it aims at discovering how anything can be thought at all. Epistemology is concerned with specific relations between specific thoughts: those of justification and foundation. The logical enterprise of the *Tractatus*, however, deals with the most general relations that thoughts can bear to each other: those of implication and contradiction. And even if all knowledge had a strictly deductive structure, the two would still be different, since deductive validity falls short of characterizing knowledge: we need in addition a characterization of the premises from which we may start. This is not to say that the logical analysis of thought and traditional epistemology have nothing in common. *Pace* Wittgenstein, one might say that both are concerned with the problem of establishing limits. But, to be sure, whereas epistemology is concerned with the limits of human knowledge, the *Tractatus* is devoted to establishing limits in a much wider sense. Secondly, the historical context is important here. The antipsychologism that Wittgenstein inherited from Frege, which the latter developed partly as a reaction against the idealistic turn that the Kantian tradition had taken in German philosophy, plays a major role in the *Tractatus*, as is evident from the way in which the passage denouncing epistemology continues:

> Does not my study of the language of signs correspond to the study of thought processes that philosophers have considered to be so essential for the philosophy of logic? But they mostly got themselves caught up in irrelevant psychological investigations and an analogous danger exists with my method too. (4.1121)[47]

From the point of view of the *Tractatus* an investigation of the way in which we actually think cannot be of any interest, at least not for the goal it has set for itself. For how we think surely is a contingent matter. We may not be able to imagine another way, but that does not mean that no other way is logically possible. Analogously, the way we actually speak, the ordinary language that we use, is not the primary target of the tractarian investigation either. Again, the contingency of natural language, whatever interest it has in its own right, makes it unimportant from a fundamental, logical point of view. Wittgenstein is interested in the structure and limits of all language, all thought, not merely in that of human speaking and thinking. That is why logic is prior to both language and thought, why logic provides the foundations of speaking and thinking, and not the other way around. For only logic is necessary and absolute.

Let us now turn to the antimetaphysical attitude of logical empiricism, which is supposedly to be found in the *Tractatus* as well. The "renunciation of metaphysics" is, of course, not a declared goal that distinguishes logical empiricism from other currents in Western philosophy. For one thing, the term "metaphysics" is conveniently vague and hence quite different schools of thought might agree on the necessity of abandoning it. Classical empiricism certainly can be said to be antimetaphysical at least in some of its manifestations, yet as a view on the world and our knowledge of it, it also embodies some claims that others would classify as metaphysical.[48] One of Kant's main motives was to put an end to speculative metaphysics and to provide the foundations of "a metaphysics that could function as a science." However, Kant's very own system of principles and concepts to the likes of others would clearly count as speculative and metaphysical.

So, its antimetaphysical stance as such is not a distinctive feature of logical empiricism. It becomes much more characteristic if we take into account its ancestry and its methods. Logical empiricism is a (declared) heir both to the classical (British) empiricism and to classical (continental) positivism. Characteristic of the positivism of Comte and Saint-Simon is the weight it attaches to the scientific method in the attainment of knowledge. The facts and methods of the positive sciences (mainly, the natural sciences) are what constitute our legitimate claims to knowledge. Hence, philosophy is left without a domain of its own and consequently should follow the lead of science, rather than pretending to be the queen of the sciences of old.

138   *Language and Ontology*

To what extent do such views emerge from the *Tractatus*, too? That philosophy is not an autonomous discipline on a par with the sciences is emphasized in 4.111–4.112.[49] However, that does not mean that Wittgenstein ranks the sciences as high as the positivists do. His attitude toward them is subtle. On the one hand, he grants that whatever there is to know falls within the domain of science. In this he surely agrees with the positivists. No other disciplines can stake a claim to knowledge. But that does not mean that science provides something like an ultimate, comprehensive understanding of the world.

Earlier it was already noted that in 6.371 Wittgenstein remarks that the idea "that the so-called laws of nature constitute explanations of natural phenomena" is "an illusion." One might well wonder what Wittgenstein means here. Why do not the laws of nature provide an explanation of the phenomena they govern? What more could there be to an explanation of the world than a correct description of the principles underlying empirical phenomena? An answer is suggested by the passage immediately following this remarkable claim, in which Wittgenstein, referring to people who subscribe to the "modern view of the world," says:

> Thus they stop at the laws of nature as if these were inviolable, the way people in the past stopped at God and Fate.
>
> And both are right, and wrong. Though people in the past are more clear in this sense that they acknowledge a clear end, while in the new system it is supposed to look as if *everything* were explained. (6.372)

Logical empiricism takes the laws of nature as discovered by science as the ultimate explanation of the world, one that leaves nothing out. Science explains the world in terms of itself, one might say. In this respect the modern view differs from the old one, which, inasmuch as it refers to God or Fate, places the ultimate explanation of the world outside of it: God and Fate are in a different realm. Clearly Wittgenstein's sympathy is with the latter. This suggests that for him, too, a real explanation of the world must go beyond it, must point toward a realm or dimension that is essentially different from that of the factual. This is borne out by the observation that the passages just quoted open up a treatment of the ethical, in which Wittgenstein introduces another way of looking at the world, one that enables us to transcend the factual.

Thus Wittgenstein's view on science is balanced. On the one hand, he acknowledges the legitimacy of its claims to knowledge within the domain of the contingent and even grants it exclusive rights there. On the other hand, he strongly opposes its transcending its own limits. Science explains a contingent world in a contingent fashion. Once it tries to go beyond that and pretends to furnish ultimate explanations, it must fail. And this is deplorable also because there being no formal difference between legitimate, contingent explanations and illegitimate, ultimate ones, confusion is bound to arise.

What connects Wittgenstein and the positivist, and what divides them can also be expressed in terms of the distinction between facts and values. Both draw a sharp, categorial distinction between these two domains. But whereas the positivist tends to downplay the importance of values and is inclined to view them as subjective, Wittgenstein attaches great importance to them and regards them as objective.

Two other distinctive features of logical empiricism need to be mentioned. The first is its empirical outlook on the sciences. For the logical empiricist science is basically empirical science and this empiricism is reflected in his epistemology. The empirical view on science is prominent in the *Tractatus* as well. All knowledge being empirical, it is clear that the natural sciences are also essentially empirical, not somehow dependent on the mathematical sciences. In this respect the *Tractatus* stands firmly rooted in the empiricist tradition. Epistemology is not a central concern of the *Tractatus* and there is no reason to classify it as empiricist in this respect. Thus the convergence between Wittgenstein and logical empiricism on this point is accidental, not one that is based on a shared conviction.

The last mark of logical empiricism is its use of logic as an analytical tool, both in the sciences and in philosophy. It was the development of modern formal logic, dating back to the work of Boole, Bolzano, Peirce, and Frege, that inspired in the logical empiricist movement the idea that finally the tools were available that would enable a radical and definitive dismissal of speculative philosophy. The aims of metaphysics would be shown to be unattainable, not by an analysis of its contents or methods, but by means of a thorough analysis of its language. On the role of logical analysis, Wittgenstein and the logical empiricist seem to agree. But with respect to the criterion of meaningfulness involved this is not so obvious.

According to the logical empiricists, metaphysical claims are not simply unscientific, but actually meaningless. The assumption underlying this idea is twofold: that there is an absolute criterion of meaningfulness, which the claims of metaphysics fail to meet, and that this criterion can be explicated and applied using the tools of logical analysis. On the one hand, the criterion has to link meaning to empirical reality if it is to distinguish between empirical science and speculative metaphysics. On the other hand, it has to be a logical criterion. So it cannot simply explicate meaningfulness in terms of some contingent property of sentences. It has to locate it in a noncontingent aspect of language that is amenable to logical analysis. It took some time for people to realize that there is a tension between these two demands.[50] Whether the logical empiricists thought the *Tractatus* contained the required criterion for meaningfulness is doubtful. Of course, the *Tractatus* does state when a sentence has meaning: if it depicts a situation in logical space. Situations being contingent, meaningfulness comes down to contingency. A sentence is meaningful if and only if it makes a contingent claim about the way the world is. However, this criterion does not completely satisfy the needs of the logical empiricists. It does part of the job, no doubt, for it excludes metaphysics and other branches of speculative philosophy. But whether it is of much use in providing the foundations of knowledge in the empirical sciences is doubtful, and that is what they were after. Hence, they sought to sharpen the issue by emphasizing verifiability as the hallmark of truly empirical sentences. For Wittgenstein in the *Tractatus*-period this issue simply did not arise.[51]

One question that needs to be asked at this point is, of course, to what extent the criterion of meaningfulness that the *Tractatus* provides is an instance of the same philosophical arrogance we observed above with respect to logical empiricism. The answer seems straightforward: obviously, the sentence "A sentence is meaningful if and only if it depicts a situation in logical space" itself does not depict a situation in logical space, and hence is not meaningful. But matters may be more subtle here. The point is that the *Tractatus* tries to play a double play: a meaningful sentence has two ways in which it tells us something. Through its meaning it informs us about the way the world actually is (if it is true). But that is not all. It has meaning by virtue of its (logical) form, and this shows us something about the world: not what the world is like in the empirical sense, but what its logical form is. In other words: a meaningful sentence says (correctly or incorrectly) what is actual, by virtue of its content, and shows what is possible, by virtue of its form. The point is that sentences that are not meaningful may yet fulfill the second role, though not the first. Thus the sentences of logic show the logical properties of the world, as do the equations of mathematics. The question is whether the sentences of the *Tractatus* themselves can be assigned a similar role. A passage such as 6.54 suggests that this is indeed what Wittgenstein intended—that he is of the opinion that the sentences of the *Tractatus*, though not meaningful, do carry information. In some sense, what Wittgenstein says in the *Tractatus* can be understood and understanding it means learning something about the essential features of language and the world. It seems that, like tautologies and equations, philosophical sentences also show something, display certain necessary traits of reality. Another way of expressing this is saying that in such philosophical sentences as the *Tractatus* consists of, the transition from the contingent to the necessary, which rests on the absolute character of logic, is formulated.[52]

It is thus, by employing the ambivalence between saying and showing, that the *Tractatus* tries to escape the charge of self-destruction that can be brought against its criterion of meaningfulness. In effect what the *Tractatus* does is assume that meaning in the technical sense of the word is not all there is to understanding language. Meaning exists by virtue of something else, namely, logical form, and understanding a meaningful sentence is *eo ipso* grasping this form. But this line of defense, if it can be made to work, opens up possibilities that for the hard-core logical empiricist should remain barred—namely, that nonempirical claims can be made about the logical structure of language and the world. For this seems to open up the possibility of speculative metaphysics, and thus to deprive the criterion of meaningfulness of its use. It is precisely this kind of objection that Maslow, in the tradition of logical empiricism, brings forth against certain aspects of the tractarian system. His reanalysis tries to overcome what he considers to be its defects. Whether it will stand as a faithful interpretation of the *Tractatus* itself remains to be seen.

Excursus II: Wittgenstein and the Vienna Circle

The conclusion seems warranted that the relationship between Wittgenstein and logical empiricism is ambivalent. There are certainly affinities, both in goals and in methods, but there are also obvious differences. A similar ambivalence is apparent in the contacts between Wittgenstein and members of Schlick's Vienna Circle. After having read the *Tractatus*, Schlick tried to contact its author, who at the time was no longer occupied with philosophy, but engaged in teaching at the elementary school in Otterthal.[53] It took Schlick some time and effort to persuade Wittgenstein to discuss his work with him and other members of the Circle. And the meetings that did take place were a mixed success. After having met a few times with the full Circle, which included beside Schlick also Waismann, Feigl, and Carnap, Wittgenstein decided that he did not want to discuss his work with others than Schlick and Waismann.[54] The problem seems to have been basically a wide divergence in character and cultural outlook. The following recollection of Carnap is telling:

I sometimes had the impression that the deliberately rational and unemotional attitude of the scientist, and likewise any ideas that had the flavor of "enlightenment," were repugnant to Wittgenstein.

Earlier when reading Wittgenstein's book in the Circle, I had erroneously believed that his attitude toward metaphysics was similar to ours. I had not paid sufficient attention to the sentences in his book about the mystical because his feelings and thoughts in this area were too divergent from mine.[55]

The members of the Circle wanted to discuss technical, logical matters with Wittgenstein. And it was not because he had no interest in such issues that Wittgenstein often refused to take part in these discussions. For after all, he did talk a great deal about logical matters with Schlick and Waismann and, in a different setting, with Frank Ramsey and later on with Piero Sraffa.[56] It seems to be their views on the end toward which logic was a means that divided them, as Carnap's description indicates and as is illustrated by the following well-known anecdote.[57] Once when attending a meeting of the Circle Wittgenstein refused to answer questions about certain logical details of the *Tractatus* and instead insisted on reading poetry to the assembly, sitting with his back toward the audience. The poetry was by Rabindranath Tagore, the Indian poet and novelist, winner of the Nobel Prize for literature in 1913. Tagore's work is lofty and mystical, and it is exciting to speculate whether perhaps the following was one of the verses Wittgenstein read to Carnap and the others:

> A mind all logic is like a knife all blade:
> It makes the hand bleed that uses it.[58]

Although Wittgenstein did not approve of the Circle and its professed goals, he had a high esteem for some of the individual members. When the

Circle's "mission statement," the brochure *The Scientific Conception of the World* (Die wissenschaftlichen Weltauffassung), appeared, Wittgenstein's reaction was a characteristic one: scorn mixed with insight and admiration. He wrote:

> Precisely because Schlick is no ordinary man, he deserves that people are careful not to make him and the Vienna school which he leads, with good intentions, ridiculous by boasting. When I say "boasting" I mean every kind of complacent self-reflection. "No to metaphysics!" As if that were anything new. What the Vienna school achieves, it must *show*, not *say*. . . . The master should be praised by his *work*. (*Ludwig Wittgenstein and the Vienna Circle*, introduction, section III)

This reaction is interesting for a variety of reasons. It clearly testifies to the mixed feelings Wittgenstein apparently had about the Circle and its members. Of Schlick, it is evident, Wittgenstein's opinion is high. But the way in which the Circle presented itself and its goals he rejects in terms that have a highly personal tone. It is not just that Wittgenstein does not agree; apparently he takes offense, in much the same way in which one objects to a person's behavior. And note that this is not because Wittgenstein disagrees as such: the "No to metaphysics!" is not what he objects to, but what he takes to be the claim of the Circle, that it is original in stating this goal. And rightly so, of course. Was not speculative metaphysics what Kant tried to fight? And at the same time that the Circle published its manifesto, was not Heidegger in his own way engaged in a struggle to liberate philosophy from a metaphysical tradition that was in his view not radical enough and hence obscured the real problems? Of course, we do not need to assume that Wittgenstein was actually thinking of these examples, but that he was aware that the issue was an old one and, perhaps even despite his own efforts in the *Tractatus*, as yet unsettled, seems clear.

But there is also a certain positive feeling toward the work and ideas of the Circle that can be discerned in the above words. The "school" apparently had achieved something in Wittgenstein's eyes, but it had taken the wrong way of communicating these results. And it is telling that Wittgenstein formulates this point of criticism in familiar terms, those of saying and showing, and gives familiar reasons. The results of philosophy, if such there are, cannot be formulated and communicated in the same way as ordinary scientific results. They cannot be said: "The result of philosophy does not consist in 'philosophical sentences' but in sentences becoming clear" (4.112). It is the work of the philosopher, his attempts to clarify thoughts by means of logical analysis, that shows what is at stake. In fact, here we come upon the same point as above with respect to the criterion of meaningfulness. An essential difference, perhaps the most important one, between Wittgenstein and the logical empiricists seems to be that Wittgenstein acknowledges that there are things that cannot be said, yet can somehow be communicated, by being shown.[59]

Wittgenstein creates room here, room that the logical empiricists deny themselves. Consequently they continue to struggle with the precise status of linguistic and logical rules, tending toward some form of conventionalism. As a matter of fact, in the post *Tractatus*-period such a strain of thought may not be altogether foreign to Wittgenstein's thinking either, but at least in the *Tractatus* the difference is clear.

Back to Maslow's Interpretation

This excursus on the relationship between Wittgenstein, logical empiricism, and the Vienna Circle provides the necessary background for Maslow's interpretation of the *Tractatus*. For this interpretation clearly bears the stamp of Maslow's logical empiricist background. The primary interest is in epistemology; logic plays the role of a tool that is to provide a criterion of meaningfulness; and speculative metaphysics is to be banned from philosophy. We have discussed to what extent these characteristics can be retraced to the *Tractatus* and we have seen that this is a complicated matter. Beside obvious parallels, there are also important differences.

In view of this it should come as no surprise that Maslow's book is not just an interpretation of Wittgenstein's intentions but also an attempt to reconstruct elements of it in such a way that they fit into his logical empiricist background. Consider the following passage from Maslow's original (1931) introduction:

I have *chosen* to interpret the book as an inquiry into the formal aspects of knowledge, that is, into language or symbolism in general.[60]

In other words, what Maslow is after is a reconstruction of the *Tractatus* that results in a system that works, one that can be applied fruitfully for the purposes that he derives from his logical empiricist background. The way in which Maslow equates knowledge and language is illustrative in this respect: there is no evidence that Wittgenstein was interested in this connection in the same way.

Another feature in which the specific character of Maslow's interpretation manifests itself is its antimetaphysical attitude. At some points Maslow discerns the same attitude in the *Tractatus* and he takes it for granted that the elimination of metaphysics is one of the goals of the work. Quite correctly he also notes that the *Tractatus* does contain what looks like a straightforwardly metaphysical theory about reality. At this point he accuses Wittgenstein of relapsing into the vocabulary of old time. A theory about the structure of the world is old-fashioned metaphysics and should not appear in a work like the *Tractatus*. A theory about the necessary properties of symbolic systems, on the contrary, is what is required, and where the *Tractatus* is concerned with that, it meets with Maslow's approval. The point to note is, of course, that Maslow does not so much acknowledge a difference in opinion, but rather chooses to correct Wittgenstein, without asking the obvious question why Wittgenstein would want to use the old-fashioned vocabulary of traditional ontology in the first place.

By way of illustration we quote one passage in full, in which this particular feature of Maslow's work is quite evident. In an exposition of the nature of objects, discussing whether they are to be taken as sense-data or as things, Maslow makes the following remark:

So far my interpretation of "object" has been in the empirical and positivistic spirit, but there also seems to be in the *Tractatus* signs of a metaphysical trend; at least Wittgenstein's terminology sometimes smacks of metaphysics. There seem to be two tendencies in the *Tractatus*; the major one positivistic, the minor metaphysical. Avowedly Wittgenstein is opposed to metaphysics and considers all metaphysics nonsensical, but occasionally he succumbs to the temptation and talks metaphysical nonsense; his treatment of "object" is an example. It seems that at times he means by "object" the ultimate ontological simple entities out of which the real world "in itself" is made, something akin to Whitehead's "objects" and Santayana's "essences"; and, considering that Wittgenstein was influenced by Gottlob Frege, it may be that he is inclined towards a kind of Platonic realism. Thus Wittgenstein says, "Objects form the substance of the world . . . what exists independently of what is the case" (2.021, 2.024), and it is suggested that it may be that we have no direct acquaintance with them (4.2211). But, as this metaphysical strain of Wittgenstein is not in accord with the general tenor of my interpretation of him, I will not pursue it here and will consider it as merely an unfortunate holdover from traditional metaphysical terminology.[61]

Evidently, Maslow is well aware of the fact that the *Tractatus* contains something like a metaphysics, but he chooses to ignore it since it does not lead to a workable theory, at least, not for him. Whether his assessment of the tractarian metaphysics as a kind of classical, platonic realism is correct, is another matter. This does not seem to be the case. Rather, the realism of the *Tractatus* is of a logical nature. The point to bear in mind at this stage is that failure on Maslow's part to see why Wittgenstein needs this approach to the nonlinguistic counterpart of language stems from his logical empiricist's presuppositions and in the end leads to problems of its own that resist satisfactory solution.

The same issue returns several times in Maslow's discussion of the main aspects of the tractarian system. His interpretation of the text is guided by his concern to get a working system out of it. This is particularly clear in his discussion of simplicity. Here Maslow concludes that "we are left without criteria for simplicity, and thus without means of *applying in the world* the formal requirements of significant language."[62] Obviously, the property of being a constituent of a logically independent state of affairs does not count as a criterion in Maslow's eyes. The lack of such a criterion deprives the notion of its usefulness: "But then these requirements themselves become useless, and in application to our world meaningless." However, "some criterion is indispensable," from which Maslow concludes that "*any criterion or rule of simplicity whatsoever is to be arbitrarily assigned* by ourselves, and that there is nothing in reality to impose upon us any rule."[63] Notice that Maslow in effect claims two things: that the criterion of simplicity is not provided by an autonomous ontological feature of reality, and that we are the ones who set the rules, arbitrarily as far as reality is concerned, guided by practical considerations. Thus he makes two moves: toward the primacy of the linguistic over the ontological; and toward a conventionalistic interpretation of the linguistic. The second is one step too far—away from Wittgenstein's intentions, that is.

The first move Maslow regards as one away from traditional, speculative metaphysics. Viewed as an inquiry into the formal requirements of knowledge through an investigation of the formal properties of language, the *Tractatus* is not an empirical undertaking but neither is it a traditional metaphysical one. Any discussion of objects, facts, and the like can be conducted only from the perspective of language: "The discussion starts from and is limited by the language we actually use at the time of our philosophizing about the world."⁶⁴ Notice again the two strains in Maslow's interpretation we called attention to above: the starting point is language, but this is not language as such but the language "we actually use."

Let us now turn to a brief characterization of the contents of Maslow's interpretation of the *Tractatus*. We will discuss three aspects of it that stand out and that are related to its logical empiricist background.

The first aspect is Maslow's view on the relationship between language, experience, and reality, which is characteristic for his concerns with epistemological issues. Maslow's starting point is that there is no such thing as "raw," pure experience. Experience is always structured, and the structure is determined by language:

> Language is the activity in which we use some parts of our experience to stand for or signify certain other parts of our experience. And the result of such an activity is a world. . . . Until [so] interrelated and interpreted, our experience is not the world. All our experience and knowledge of the world is through language in this wide sense of the word; there can be no other world for us besides the one that is organized on our own terms, and thus there can be no world for us except as understood through language.⁶⁵

That he regards this as a correct interpretation of the *Tractatus* is shown by the fact that Maslow continues this passage by quoting 5.6: "*The limits of my language* mean the limits of my world," and 5.4711: "To give the essence of the sentence means to give the essence of all description, that is, the essence of the world."

This passage from Maslow illustrates several points clearly. One thing that is remarkable is the way Maslow talks about language. For him it is something that we actively use, something concrete, not an abstraction. The emphasis is on what we do with it, not on its supposedly immanent structure. The language that structures our experience is our device (". . . which we use . . . ," ". . . on our terms . . ."). Secondly, this quotation illustrates a feature that distinguishes logical empiricism from classical empiricism. There is no independent world that impresses itself on us through the senses and thus produces in us experience and knowledge of it. The world as we experience and know it is the result of our structuring activity, an activity that takes place through language. This is not to say that there actually exists a world that conforms to our language: "the formal requirements of symbolism cannot dictate the nature of reality." That is, it does not follow, a priori, from the properties of our language that there is a reality that has the corresponding characteristics and hence can be described by it: "... to state the necessary conditions of significant language is not equivalent to an assertion that there *is* a reality conforming to these conditions."[66] If there is such a thing, this must be determined in and through our experience; hence such a claim is a posteriori. This makes the position Maslow takes toward reality ambiguous in a certain sense. On the one hand, it seems he assumes something exists that causes us to have experiences of it.[67] On the other hand, he stresses that what experiences we have, as such are not determined by whatever causes us to have them, but become experience and knowledge only through the intermediary, structuring activity of language. Thus it seems that Maslow implicitly acknowledges three different layers: that which causes experience ("reality"); experience in itself, unstructured and not productive of knowledge; and experience structured by language, on which knowledge is based. The first falls outside the realm of knowledge, since it cannot be talked about.[68] What corresponds to the latter is called the world, which hence is not the same as reality in the first sense. Clearly then, Maslow does not subscribe to a dogmatic kind of realism: knowledge is dependent on experience that in its turn is structured by the a priori requirements of language.

In certain respects this interpretation of the *Tractatus* seems to square with the interpretation we have outlined earlier, which claims its ontology must be regarded as a logical construction, that is, as the result of a logical analysis of the way in which language is able to reach out toward something outside itself. However, in one respect it goes much further: it ties the linguistic basis of the ontology to actual language and thus gives rise to a relativistic, conventionalistic interpretation. This will become more clear if we investigate in more detail the role Maslow assigns to language in structuring our experience and knowledge of the world.

The general characteristics will be clear from the above: there is no such thing as the world, or experience of the world, and hence no knowledge of the world, except through the intermediary of language. Now how would one argue for such a position? The best way to go about it, it seems, and the most natural one from the logical empiricist point of view, is to start from knowledge and to argue that it is essentially language dependent. This general tenet of Maslow's interpretation of the *Tractatus* has already been illustrated above. It plays an important role in his interpreta-

Language and Ontology 149

tion of several particular aspects of the tractarian system. We will discuss some examples.

In his exposition of the nature and properties of objects, Maslow claims that this notion must be approached from a linguistic point of view. "Object" is not a term that denotes some specific kind of entity in reality, but it is "a variable pseudo-concept," which means that it must be looked on as "a linguistic device for speaking about various kinds of entities, in particular the elements of sense data, common-life things, and ontological substances, all of which would not even appear in a perfect language."[69] Thus, Maslow suggests, the search for what exactly objects are, what Wittgenstein intended to denote with this term, is misdirected from the start: "object" is not a denoting term but a catch-all phrase that goes proxy for various denoting terms, such as "sense-datum," "material object," and the like. Thus a sentence about objects, for example, that they are simple, is not a claim about the world, but one about the various ways in which we can describe it. It means that if we talk about the world in terms of, say, sense-data, then sense-data are objects and hence the simple constituents from which the world is built. If we use another language, with another denoting phrase, such as "thing," it is whatever this term denotes that forms the substance of the world. Notice again the two strains of thought we distinguished earlier in Maslow's interpretation: ontological notions are interpreted linguistically and in a relativistic fashion, that is, relative to a particular language.[70] This interpretation of Maslow seems to be corroborated by 4.1272, where Wittgenstein states that the concept of an object is a pseudoconcept, which is referred to by an (individual) variable, not by a predicate:

> Wherever the word "object" ("thing," and so on) is used correctly, it is expressed in the conceptual notation by a name-variable.
>
> . . .
>
> Wherever it is used differently, that is, as a real concept-term, nonsensical pseudosentences result. (4.1272)

An example of the proper use is as in $\exists x \exists y\, (fx \wedge fy)$, which represents "There are two objects with property f."[71] Pseudosentences occur when we construct a sentence like "There are things" analogously to "There are books." Sentences concerning the existence of objects, or their number, do not express contingent situations. Hence, ". . . it is nonsensical to speak of the *number of all objects*" (4.1272). Such a thing cannot be said, but only be shown.[72] This point about objects is reflected in a similar remark concerning names, in 5.55, where it is implied that the number of names cannot be specified. This impossibility is not, of course, due to limitations on our part, but is an inherent feature of the notion as such. The category of names, like that of objects, is a logical one and hence cannot be the subject of empirical investigation and contingent description.

Another illustration of Maslow's primarily linguistic view on the central concepts of the *Tractatus* is provided by his discussion of elementary sentences and names. The need for these is explicitly tied to what he calls the "formal requirements for determinateness of sense and meaning."[73] Maslow's argument is straightforward. Given that there are complex sentences that have a determinate meaning, there must be elementary sentences and names. This argument, Maslow notes, relies on a compositionality principle for meaning.[74] The simplicity of names, and of what they stand for, is derived in a like manner. If some name occurring in an elementary sentence were to have a complex meaning, the sentence would stand in some logical relationship with other sentences, thus violating the assumption of its being elementary. Two remarks are in order. First, this interpretation of the tractarian argument stays completely within language. Second, the notion of elementary sentence it appeals to, must be conceived of as a syntactic one, on pain of circularity.

As a last example, we draw attention to the status Maslow assigns to grammar: "grammar logically precedes application."[75] By "grammar" is understood the "formal requirements" mentioned earlier, that is, the internal, formal properties of symbolism. These requirements are of a nonempirical nature; they do not arise by abstraction or generalization from experience, such as an empirical investigation into the nature of various languages. Thus preceding application, grammar also precedes experience. It constitutes the totality of all possible experience; that is, it displays the formal properties of logical space. It must be noted that in this connection Maslow cites such passages as 2.01231, which are about the internal properties of objects. This is remarkable unless we accept a purely linguistic, logical interpretation of the notion of an object.[76] Given that, they can indeed be used to substantiate a purely linguistic interpretation of other notions, such as "possibility," "logical space," and the like. But, of course, they do not as such prove the point. From this constitutive interpretation of gram-

Language and Ontology 151

mar, Maslow derives a criticism of what he takes to be Wittgenstein's solution of the color-exclusion problem. According to Maslow, Wittgenstein assumes in 6.3751 that two color-ascriptions, such as "*a* is red" and "*a* is blue," exclude each other for nonlinguistic, physical, reasons.[77] For Maslow this is one of Wittgenstein's unfortunate lapses into the old metaphysics. If experience were the source of our insight here, then its necessary character would derive from what causes this experience, and postulating such a basis is a metaphysical move. But, Maslow continues, such a basis is also not necessary. It is the grammar of color-expressions that accounts for the exclusion. And that is sufficient. There is no need to postulate fixed objects; fixed rules of grammar will do. Experience and grammar in this case fit, but accidentally. Thus we see that Maslow interprets necessity, too, as a purely grammatical phenomenon: "There is no necessity in facts, necessity is necessity of rules."[78] Within the three-layers picture, in which the causes of experience, raw experience, and structured experience are distinguished, this locates necessity in the relationship between the latter two, leaving the first one out of reach.

This grammatical interpretation forms the basis of Maslow's relativism. Consider the color-exclusion problem again. Maslow claims that the exclusion is guaranteed by grammatical rules governing the use of color-expressions and that the fit between this grammatical "fact" and our experience is accidental. Our sensory experience simply happens to be in accord with our grammar here: if we see something as red, we do not see it as blue. But this fit, though perfect, is not necessary. Given a different perceptual apparatus we could have had experiences that might not have fitted our grammar. Of course, description of such experiences would have been beyond the capacity of the grammar we actually employ, but as such this implies nothing with regard to their ontological status: "Discussion of different visual experiences [is] meaningless . . . but [this] does not make the actual structure [of our visual experiences] necessary."[79] Thus the knife cuts both ways: both grammar and reality become more autonomous.

Another illustration is provided by Maslow's own view on the simplicity of objects. Maslow concludes that the *Tractatus* does not provide a material criterion for determining when an object may count as simple. However, he maintains, we do need such a criterion, for otherwise there is no way in which we can apply Wittgenstein's insights. Hence, he concludes that we have to supply the criterion for simplicity ourselves since "there is nothing in reality to impose upon us any rule."[80] Reality is of no help precisely because it appears to us only in the form of experience that is structured by grammar, and hence cannot by itself supply a criterion of simplicity. The arbitrary character of the choice is eagerly acknowledged:

> It becomes obvious now that in the view here expounded, it is logically perfectly arbitrary what we shall choose to consider as simple elements and atomic facts. The criterion of simplicity is to be established by ourselves, not found in the world.[81]

And the choice we make is inherent in our choice of a language, of a particular set of grammatical rules: "[Objects] are simple, we must stress this, relative to the language, through the determination of language. There is no sense in speaking of absolute simples."[82]

Loosening the tie between grammar and reality gives one room to move. Instead of the grammar we actually employ, we could have used another one. Each choice of a grammar determines a logical space, a totality of structured experience that our language applies to. Within that space actual experience determines the actual world, which is as much a grammatical construction as logical space itself. Raw experience as such comes into play only as the stuff that our actual structured experience is made of. And whatever causes our experiences in the first place drops out as being beyond the scope of the picture and hence of a purely speculative nature.

This view strongly relativizes the ontological and logical theories of the *Tractatus* to the choice of a grammar. It is important to notice that in doing so this interpretation of the *Tractatus* goes much further than the one presented earlier in this chapter. It is one thing to argue that the ontology has to be viewed from the perspective of language. It is quite another thing to claim that this perspective is not unique. According to Maslow different grammars may exist side by side, each with a different organization to impose on experience, the choice between them being guided by practical considerations concerning applications, among other things. To be sure, given the goals of the logical empiricists the difference may appear less substantial. For them logic is primarily an instrument of analysis put to work in the context of epistemological issues.[83] But for Wittgenstein, in the *Tractatus* at least, logic has a foundational character, providing a solid and unique basis for language, meaning and thought. In the uniqueness of this foundation resides Wittgenstein's absolutism. For him the diversity of language is a superficial phenomenon that merely hides a unique and absolute underlying logical foundation. This foundation, moreover, is ultimate and neither allows nor needs further explanation (5.473). And when Wittgenstein wants logic to reveal the underlying structure of language and thought, this applies to all language, all symbolism. It is only against the background of his absolutism that we can understand the extreme importance that Wittgenstein attaches throughout his early work to the distinction between saying and showing. That the logical properties of language cannot be said but only be shown, is worth repeating over and over again only if this is an absolute feature, not one that holds relative to some choice of framework or grammar.[84] Wittgenstein's position here is quite outspoken and that in itself shows where Maslow's interpretation goes astray. By trying to bend the notions and principles of the *Tractatus* too much toward practical applicability, Maslow misinterprets Wittgenstein on a very basic issue.

Stenius's Interpretation

A similar objection can be made to the treatment of Erik Stenius, who wrote one of the earliest systematic introductions to the *Tractatus* (Stenius 1960), an admirable and still useful exposition of its main lines of argument. In particular, Stenius was the first to give a thorough, rigorous, and at the same time down-to-earth analysis of the picture theory of meaning, stressing correctly that many features of the picture theory do not depend on the tractarian atomism. But, it is significant that Stenius calls his work "a critical exposition." His aim is not just to interpret and expose; he also generalizes and evaluates. What he wants is a general theory that works. And, as in the case of Maslow, this objective leaves its traces.

For example, when discussing the notions of logical form and of internal properties, Stenius remarks correctly that the *Tractatus* strongly suggests that these two concepts are basically coextensive. The logical form of an object or a name determines its internal properties and vice versa. Yet, Stenius declares, "I find it clearer to use the concepts in a way that makes possible the existence of internal qualities other than those contained in the logical form."[85] "Clearer," because Stenius feels that it allows him to give a consistent account of the *Tractatus* as a theory that can be applied. Like Maslow, Stenius interprets the *Tractatus* in a relativistic manner. Thus the ontology is interpreted as defining concepts and stating principles relative to a "framework," where a framework is expressed in a "key of interpretation."[86] Concomitantly, the concept of simplicity, and related notions such as that of substance, are also interpreted in a relativistic way. An object is simple within a certain framework; substance is what is common to all worlds relative to a framework. Stenius notes that the text of the *Tractatus* as such underdetermines what the right interpretation is, but he opts for the relativistic one mainly because it squares better with his ideas of what the application of the tractarian framework should amount to. Accordingly, he makes much of the sections 5.55–5.5571, where Wittgenstein discusses how we are to determine what, for example, elementary sentences are. This question cannot be answered a priori, Wittgenstein seems to suggest in 5.55, for that would require fixing the number of names in advance (a possibility that was already rejected earlier on in the *Tractatus*). But it also seems not to be a matter of a posteriori experience, for that would make it a contingent matter.[87] According to Stenius, Wittgenstein's way out of this dilemma is to let the application of logic decide: "The *application* of logic decides which elementary sentences there are" (5.557). What is an elementary sentence, what is a simple object, and so on, does not depend on contingent facts and in that sense is an a priori matter. However, it does depend on the choice of a framework, for it is only within a framework that we can decide these issues and in that sense they are a posteriori. And the choice of the framework is dictated by the application of the system that we envisage.

As stated, in several respects the interpretation of Stenius is remarkably like that of Maslow and we gather that it is clear that the objections made above to the latter's approach by and large apply to the former's as well, so there is no need to repeat them. Rather, we now want to turn to another line of interpretation, which also takes language as its starting point, but carries it to other extremes than the instrumentalistic and relativistic view that we have found embodied in the work of Maslow and Stenius.

Ishiguro and McGuinness: Structuralism

The work of Ishiguro and McGuinness can be viewed as another reaction to the observation that also prompted the views of Maslow and Stenius, namely, that the *Tractatus* does not contain an identity criterion for objects and consequently does not provide a criterion for simplicity.[88] Whereas Maslow and Stenius, eager to find an interpretation that would turn the *Tractatus* into a workable theory, conclude that these criteria in the end are to be supplied by the applications we want to make of logical systems, Ishiguro and McGuinness uphold that, appearances notwithstanding, such criteria are not needed. In this sense, they argue, the *Tractatus* does not contain an ontological theory at all.

This is a far-reaching claim, one that obviously has repercussions for the interpretation of other elements of the tractarian system as well. Therefore we will investigate the arguments that Ishiguro and McGuinness present in favor of this view in detail in what follows.

Before turning to their arguments, however, let us first try to get a little bit more clear about the contents of the claim that is being made here. One way to formulate it is as follows: the *Tractatus* does not embody realism in the ontological sense. Thus McGuinness claims: "It was not Wittgenstein's intention to base a metaphysics upon logic or the nature of our language."[89] And Ishiguro holds: "The simple objects whose existence was posited were not so much a kind of metaphysical entity conjured up to support a logical theory as something whose existence adds no extra content to the theory."[90] Evidently, these authors make a much stronger claim than the one we defended earlier on—namely, that the tractarian ontology is based on language. According to them, there is no ontology to be found in the *Tractatus* at all.

There is one way to misunderstand the position of Ishiguro and McGuinness and that is by construing it as a negative answer to the question of whether language in the tractarian system has extralinguistic significance. Does language on Wittgenstein's view reach out to extralinguistic entities? This question surely must be answered in the positive. The entire picture theory of meaning is based on exactly this feature of language. Hence the principle of names standing for objects plays a fundamental role: "The possibility of the sentence rests on the principle of signs representing objects" (4.0312). It is by virtue of their ability to represent objects that names have significance. And this is the foundation for all meaningful expressions. The view that language is essentially related to another, nonlinguistic realm is at the heart of the tractarian view. In view of that, we should not misinterpret the claim of Ishiguro and McGuinness as a denial of this fundamental feature.

What then is the question that their interpretation answers? Here we should notice that it is one thing to acknowledge that according to the tractarian view language is related to a nonlinguistic reality, but quite another to uphold that the *Tractatus* itself contains a theory about this reality.[91] Does the *Tractatus* as a philosophical system contain any claims about the nonlinguistic reality with which language is fundamentally related, either independently of language, or on the basis of what the structure of language implies about it? It is this question that the Ishiguro-McGuinness interpretation answers in the negative. The *Tractatus* does not propose a theory about the nature and structure of reality. The consequences of this claim are far-reaching. For one thing, objects are not real referents of real names, but must be interpreted in a nonontological way. Analogously, reference is not an ontological, but rather a semantic category. More on that later.

For now we note that according to McGuinness there is a different sense of "realistic" that does apply to the *Tractatus*, namely, the Dummettian "truth transcends verification" sense. For in the tractarian system sentences are true or false (that is, meaningful) independent of the knowledge or experience we have of the world. But this kind of realism is restricted. It applies to sentences and, according to McGuinness at least, does not have realistic repercussions to expressions on the subsentential level. Hence, the ontological consequences are limited as well. The *Tractatus* postulates a reality that makes sentences true or false independently of our epistemological access to it, but this feature underdetermines its structure and nature: "We cannot grasp anything other than a concatenation of objects."[92]

What reasons are given by Ishiguro and McGuinness to substantiate their radical interpretation of the *Tractatus*? Before turning to their arguments let us pause for a moment and consider their motives. For McGuinness an important aspect of his interpretation is that it is the minimal interpretation that allows him to stay close to the goal of the tractarian system that Wittgenstein himself formulates in the preface and that is to draw the limits of meaningful language. The characterization of meaningfulness proceeds through the characterization of the notions of truth and falsity. Notice that viewed in this way, the tractarian enterprise is concerned first and foremost with sentences and that subsentential expressions come in only indirectly. This suggests that their role is instrumental and derived, not sui generis and pivotal, a view that seems corroborated by Wittgenstein's explicit appeal to the context principle. When this minimalistic interpretation of the goal that Wittgenstein has set himself is combined with additional constraints, of which the abolishment of any nonlogical necessity is the most important one, it seems to follow that the characterization of meaningfulness that the *Tractatus* is after has to be given independently of the way the world is, and hence independently of the reference of subsentential expressions.

Whereas these considerations of McGuinness are internal to the *Tractatus*, Ishiguro's main motive, it seems, is connected with the question of the continuity, or lack thereof, in Wittgenstein's work. Her interpretation of the *Tractatus* is part of an argument that the difference between the picture theory of the early work and the meaning-as-use view of the later writings is not as deep and principled as some have made it appear. She concentrates on the relationship between "naming" and "using" and claims that for names in the tractarian sense, too, use is fundamental. Again, this point should not be misconstrued. The question that Ishiguro addresses is not whether a name, in order to refer to a specific object, has to be used in a specific way. The answer to that is an obvious "yes." Rather, what Ishiguro investigates is whether the reference of a name can be settled independently from its use. That question has immediate bearing on the issue of realism. For if it is answered in the affirmative, then the *Tractatus* is a realistic theory in the strong sense, presupposing an independent relation of reference between names and objects upon which meaning rests, with as a corollary the independent existence of the objects. According to Ishiguro, however, the answer is in fact "no." Already in the *Tractatus*, she claims, reference of names depends in a strict sense on their use: reference of names occurs only in the use of sentences containing them.

At the center of Ishiguro's argument is a strict interpretation of the context principle. The principle derives from Frege and is stated in the *Tractatus* in 3.3. "Only sentences have meaning; only in the connection of a sentence does a name have reference."[93] According to Ishiguro, Wittgenstein's appeal to the context principle means that the meaning of a sentence is prior to the references of the names occurring in it. But that implies that the reference of a name cannot be determined independently from its use in meaningful sentences. The intimate relationship between use and reference can be substantiated by pointing to, for example, 3.328: "If a sign is *not used*, then it does not refer." Given that expressions when used are used as constituents of complete sentences, this underscores the primacy of sentences vis-à-vis names, also in the determination of the latter's reference.

Consequently, the relation of referring between a name and an object cannot be regarded as an independent relation, as one that holds independently of and prior to the meanings of sentences in which names occur. Reference is established contextually.

That this is indeed the proper interpretation of the reference relation in the *Tractatus* is argued for, more or less, as follows.[94] There are, *grosso modo*, two ways of giving a noncontextual interpretation of reference, one in which it is a direct relationship between a name and an object and one in which the link between the two is mediated. On both accounts the name–object relation is independent, noncontextual, and hence assumes that there is an independent meaning or reference for names. Various accounts differ in what they take this meaning to consist in. It can be the object itself, or some third entity, different from both the linguistic expression and the nonlinguistic object, which mediates between the two.

A prominent example of the latter approach is the one developed by Frege in his later works, in which reference is treated as an indirect relation.[95] Frege assigns names both a meaning (*Sinn*) and a reference (*Bedeutung*), setting up the meaning as that which determines the reference.[96] Thus, Frege makes the relationship between a name and its bearer an indirect one. A name has a fixed meaning, which in different circumstances may pick out different references. The meaning of a name is described as "the way the reference is given." Thus, the meaning specifies the necessary and sufficient conditions for something to be the reference of the name. And the descriptive content of these conditions may be such that in different circumstances different objects qualify. This approach has several things going for it. For one thing, it accounts for the cognitive value of a name, for its contribution to the information conveyed by a sentence in which it occurs. Another important advantage is that the existence of a reference is not a necessary condition for a name to be meaningful: the meaning may be a partial function, which solves the problem of the meaningfulness of utterances that contain a nonreferring term.[97] Of course, Frege's approach also has empirical and theoretical shortcomings. On the empirical side, it must be mentioned, as Frege himself does, that different speakers will often associate different descriptions with one and the same name, which would mean that they do not speak (quite) the same language.[98] For Frege the problem is not acute. He is not interested in the actual workings of actual languages (despite the many careful and sensitive observations that he makes about them, especially in his later papers), and thus can brush this problem aside as one that "in a perfect language would not occur."[99] But from Wittgenstein's perspective it is a serious drawback, since he does not side with Frege and Russell against the alleged imperfections of natural language. The theoretical, philosophical price that Frege has to pay is that of a rich, some would even say excessive, ontology. Meanings as objective, but nonsensory, abstract entities are an essential ingredient of his account. Note also that the various features that meaning is assigned on this Fregean account appear to be at odds with a strong interpretation of the context principle. Rather Fregean "Sinn" seems to be intimately connected with the principle of compositionality. Where contextuality makes the parts subsidiary to the whole, compositionality presupposes their semantical primacy.[100]

Let us now turn to the other type of account, which goes for a direct relationship between names and the objects they stand for. From a systematic point of view one way to understand it is as a reaction against the ontological extravaganza of a Fregean account. It aims to analyze the descriptive content of referring expressions away in favor of a basic set of expressions that refer directly. Thus Russell's view on names, prominent at the time of the composition of the *Tractatus*, assumes that the meaning of an ordinary proper name is to be explicated in the form of a complex description, an analysis that takes place within the context of the sentence in which it occurs.[101] This process of analysis is founded on a rock-bottom of expressions that refer in a nondescriptive manner. These are the so-called logically proper names. These expressions do not have descriptive content. Rather they refer directly, and the objects they refer to constitute their meaning. Here the link between expression and object is forged not by an abstract entity such as a meaning, but by the intentional act of the one who uses the name, that is, by an act of inner ostension. Such use is in "inner speech": logically proper names are not used in a public language, to refer to ordinary, macroscopic objects, but in an inner language, in that they refer to sense-data and other elements of consciousness. On this account the problem of nonreferring names and that of the meaningfulness of sentences containing such names, is solved by two assumptions: that ordinary names are concealed descriptions and that logically proper names are directly linked to their bearers. The latter assumption secures the existence of a base of expressions that are guaranteed to be meaningful, while the former assures us that this base can in the end always be reached. It is precisely these assumptions that some consider to be objectionable features of the direct account. And the objections are again both empirical and theoretical. Empirically, it seems unjustified to regard all proper names as descriptions in disguise. Moreover, the problem that Frege encountered with respect to fixing the meaning reoccurs when it comes to fixing the description. Theoretically, the direct account does seem more parsimonious ontologically, but it is not at all philosophically innocent. On the contrary, at least in Russell's version the background is a quite distinctive set of epistemological and metaphysical assumptions. One important ingredient is the distinction between two kinds of knowledge: by description and by acquaintance. Ordinary objects are known to us in the former mode. Hence, we refer to them by means of (concealed) descriptions. Our knowledge of their existence and identity is liable to error and mistake. With the special objects (sense-data and the like) that are the references of logically proper names we are acquainted directly: about their existence and identity we cannot be mistaken.

Now that we have sketched these two accounts of the reference relation between name and object, let us return to the interpretation of Ishiguro and McGuinness, and investigate why they feel neither can act as a model for the tractarian view on this matter. Recall that what is at stake here is the strong interpretation of the context principle, which holds that reference is not an independent relation: names do not refer to objects independently of their meaningful use in sentences. Despite their differences, both accounts discussed above, Russell's as well as Frege's, assume that reference is in this sense independent (and foundational). So, why do Ishiguro and McGuinness think that neither view suits the *Tractatus*? After all, like Frege, Wittgenstein does make a distinction between meaning (*Sinn*) and reference (*Bedeutung*). And, like Russell, he does assume that names, in his technical sense, refer directly, without any intervening descriptive content.

The arguments are derived from what the *Tractatus* says about the nature of objects. What objects there are, and what objects are, that is, both their existence and their identity, is independent from what is actually and contingently the case. For objects are the substance from which any world is made; hence they cannot depend on any particular feature of any particular world. They are what is solid (2.027). But this means, Ishiguro argues, that they cannot be identified, either by ostension or by description. For both ostension and description are essentially contingent acts; they are identifications that must depend on contingent features of the entity to which they pertain. A descriptive or ostensive identification of an object will be in terms of its external properties and hence cannot serve to (re)identify it in different situations, since in some such situations it may lack some of these properties. The true identity of an object is a matter of its internal properties, but these cannot be expressed at all; they can only be shown (3.221). Objects do not occur on their own; they are always part of configurations. They never appear "purely," that is, without contingent features (2.0122).[102] In other words, in whatever sense we can be said to have knowledge of the identity of tractarian objects at all; it can be neither knowledge by description nor knowledge by acquaintance in Russell's sense. Thus McGuinness says that the "contact" we have with objects cannot be explicated in terms of experience of them (like the experience, sensory or otherwise, we have of ordinary objects), nor with descriptive knowledge about them. Interestingly, according to McGuinness this is all that the simplicity of objects amounts to. They are simple in that the ordinary epistemological categories do not apply to them.[103]

It is clear that these observations refute any straightforward identification of Wittgenstein's view on names and their reference with either Russell's or Frege's account. But do they also constitute an argument for ascribing to him the strict interpretation of contextuality, as Ishiguro and McGuinness seem to think? We will do well to postpone assessment of their claim until we have outlined some of its consequences. But at this stage it may be useful to draw attention to one point.

One question is what Wittgenstein actually means when he talks about "use" in such passages as 3.328. Let us compare the preceeding 3.327: "Only in conjunction with its logico-syntactical employment does a sign determine a logical form." The employment (*Verwendung*) that Wittgenstein refers to here seems to be not the actual use of a sign in concrete utterances, but rather its being assigned a well-defined position within the logical grammar of the language. What we need to know is how an expression can be used, not necessarily how it is actually used. This, we take it, is also what is at stake in 3.328. It is is not a lack of actual use that makes an expression meaningless, but its not having been given a definite grammatical identity. For otherwise the meaningfulness of an expression would become a contingent matter, which at least in the case of names seems not what Wittgenstein has in mind.[104] But in view of these considerations one might well ask to what extent there is a real continuity in Wittgenstein's thinking on these issues, as Ishiguro claims there is. The "logico-syntactical employment" that the *Tractatus* refers to seems a far cry from the actual, practical, day-to-day use that the *Philosophical Investigations* makes so much of.

So let us now turn to a brief investigation of the consequences that according to McGuinness and Ishiguro are connected with an adaptation of the strong version of the context principle. We will discuss three of them in some detail and only mention some others. The first consequence is that objects form a logical, not an ontological, category. The second is that the identity criteria for objects are contained in sentences that contain their names. And the third is that names are not real names, but rather a kind of variable.

Let us start with the first consequence, that being an object is not an ontological property, but a logical (grammatical) one. If an entity is classified as an object, no claim is being made about ontological properties. A claim to this effect is not part of an ontological classification that assigns various elements to various categories and deals with the relationships between these. Rather, calling an entity an object is nothing but saying that it plays the role of the reference of a name. In that sense, "being an object" is a grammatical predicate. More specifically, objects are used to express properties of names. For example, the name as a symbol is characterized using the concept of an object in the following way. Every name, as a sign, which in the same combinations delivers the same truth value, is the same name, as a symbol. Here the role of the concept "object" is that of an auxiliary notion. It is used in the specification of the truth potential of a sentence. In connection with this, it is relevant to note that the passages in which the notion of symbol is introduced (3.31ff.) immediately follow the canonical formulation of the context principle, in 3.3. If we combine the notion of a name as a symbol, that is, as an equivalence class of signs defined by the relation of "having the same reference," with the principle that the name–object relation is fixed, then it follows that objects and names, as symbols, stand in a fixed relation. So, at this fundamental level ontological and logical-grammatical entities are hardly distinguishable and could in fact be identified. It is this aspect of the tractarian view on names and objects that lead Ishiguro and McGuinness to conclude that the term "object" refers to a formal (that is, logical-grammatical) concept that characterizes an internal property of a particular category of linguistic expressions, those that function as names.[105] Hence, McGuinness concludes that completely analyzed sentences, in which only names occur, are neither about us, that is, about our minds, nor about language, nor about reality.[106] They deal with the logical form that these three domains have in common, since objects are nothing but (a partial specification of) the form that every kind of reality necessarily partakes in.

We now turn to the second consequence drawn from the strict view on contextuality, that the identity criteria of objects are given with sentences in which names occur. This is clearly in line with the view on objects just outlined. If the notion of an object is a grammatical one, we may expect to find the identity criteria for the entities falling under this concept in grammar as well. The central argument here is derived from the passage in which the notorious idea of an elucidation (*Erläuterung*) is introduced, and that immediately precedes 3.3:

> The reference of protosigns can be explained by means of elucidations. Elucidations are sentences that contain the protosigns. So they can be understood only if the references of these signs are already known. (3.263)

Names are called "proto-signs" in 3.26 because they cannot be analyzed. The passage 3.263, and concomitantly the notion of elucidation, is problematic both on a weak and on a strong interpretation of the context principle. If we assume that there is an independent relation of reference between names and objects and hence interpret contextuality weakly, the first sentence in 3.263 is hard to interpret.[107] What is there left to explain about the reference of names, if such is given independently? At best, one might say that sentences containing names enrich our understanding (knowledge) of the objects referred to, but an explanation in any fundamental sense is not needed, it seems. This problem, however, is minor compared with the one that the strong interpretation, which denies an independent relation of reference, encounters. In this case it is the last sentence that becomes mysterious. For in what sense can the reference of a name be known (*bekannt*) prior to these elucidations if, as strong contextuality would have it, it is these elucidations that determine the reference? This points toward a fundamental problem with the strong interpretation of contextuality: How do we come to understand the meaning of a sentence? Compositionality provides a natural answer to this question, and it seems quite unproblematic to attribute such an appeal to compositionality to Wittgenstein, for example, in view of the discussion in 4.026ff. So how does Ishiguro manage to turn vice into virtue here?

Crucial for her understanding of 3.263 is the interpretation of the concept of object as a formal concept, a point that she takes to be established independently. Given that, Ishiguro says, to know an object (in the sense of being "bekannt" with it that Wittgenstein means in 3.263) does not mean to be acquainted with it in a Russellian sense, nor does it mean to have any other kind of knowledge about it. It is not an epistemological notion but a grammatical one. It simply means to know what the sentence as a whole is about. Now in what sense can one know what a sentence is about if one does not know what its constituents refer to? Actually, natural language provides straightforward examples. Consider the following, simple question: "Which of you is Dr. Johnson?" That the actual reference of the name "Dr. Johnson" is not known is a condition for the proper use of the sentence as a whole and certainly no obstacle to understanding it. Then what does the condition of the reference of a name being known amount to? According to Ishiguro it is to know the grammatical role that the name plays and that the name refers to an object is one aspect of that role. The object that we are assumed to know is not an actual object but a formal object, a peg onto which the elucidations hang the properties they assign to the reference of the name.[108] The example Ishiguro gives is that of the Peano axioms for arithmetic, which elucidate, but do not define, the primitive entity o. So, the notion of use that is presupposed by that of reference (rather than the other way around) centers around a nonempty, consistent set of meaningful sentences.[109] These are the elucidations from which the reference of a name, conceived of as a symbol, can be grasped. But what is grasped is not an object in the ordinary sense, but a set of logical-grammatical rules for the use of the expression.

This interpretation of what the reference of a name is has far-reaching consequences for the understanding of other parts of the *Tractatus*. One illustrative example concerns the nature of identity sentences and the status of the corresponding substitution principle. Normally one would hold that if $a = b$ is true, then a and b can be substituted *salva veritate*. In other words, because the references of a and b are the same, they can be put to the same use. On the present approach, however, things work just the other way around: given that *a* and *b* can be used in the same way, which should be apparent from their having the same set of elucidations, we infer that *a* = *b* is true. Two conclusions can be drawn immediately. The first is the point already made above, that the elucidations indeed tell us something only about reference in the sense of the logical-grammatical category of signs, not about their reference in any extralinguistic sense. And the second is that identity, apparently, is a relation between signs, not between objects. Let us start with the latter point. As a matter of fact, that identity is to be conceived of in this way is explicitly stated in the *Tractatus*:

> When I use two signs to refer to the same thing, I express this by putting the sign "=" between them.
> So *a* = *b* means: the sign *a* can be replaced by the sign *b*. (4.241)

This fits the Ishiguro interpretation quite well. An identity sentence signals that two signs are used in the same way. Hence, Wittgenstein says, an identity sentence belongs to the realm of grammar and does not have extralinguistic significance:

> So expressions of the form *a* = *b* are just representational substitutes; they don't say anything about the reference of the signs *a*, *b*. (4.242)

An identity sentence is a grammatical device, which serves to indicate something about the use of certain signs. Notice that it is not an assertion about signs or their use, because as such it would be contingent, contrary to Wittgenstein's intentions. For the grammar of a sign is an internal property and hence a necessary feature. At most, one could say that identity sentences show something.[110]

So, Wittgenstein's position with regard to the problem of how contingent identities involving names are possible is clear: they are not.[111] Here Wittgenstein takes up the position that Frege adopted in the *Begriffsschrift*, but from which he later, in "Über Sinn und Bedeutung," withdrew—that identity is a relation between signs. But Frege's reasons for discarding this analysis do not seem to apply here. Frege thought that the position was untenable because, the relation between signs and objects being conventional, it did not provide a proper account for the cognitive significance of identities of the form *a* = *b*. Thus he concluded that identity is a relation on the object-level, explaining the meaningfulness and contingency of *a* = *b* through his meaning–reference (*Sinn–Bedeutung*) distinction. That Wittgenstein is able to hold on to the former view depends on the distinction he draws between expressions that have meaning (which include complex denoting expressions), and names that only have reference. It is at the level of names that an identity sentence is a grammatical device and not a contingent claim about the world.[112]

This seems to be the most reasonable interpretation of the various tractarian sentences about identity. But notice that for Ishiguro's interpretation there is a snag. It is clear that Wittgenstein uses the phrase "reference" [*Bedeutung*] in the first sentence of 4.241 and in the last sentence of 4.242 in a different sense. The first one fits the Ishiguro interpretation quite well. We could in fact paraphrase it as: "If I *use* two signs in the same way" (emphasis added). Clearly, "reference" is here tied to "use," that is, to logical grammatical form. However, the occurrence in 4.242 carries a totally different meaning. Here "reference" should be understood in the extralinguistic sense: "expressions of the form $a = b$ are just representational substitutes; they do not say anything about the *reference* of the signs a, b" (emphasis added). If we were to take both occurrences of Wittgenstein's term "Bedeutung" as referring to the references of signs in the same sense, the result would be a contradiction. For according to the first sentence $a = b$ would signify that the reference is the same, while the second sentence would claim that $a = b$ has nothing to say about the reference. Hence, the first sentence, although in line with Ishiguro's interpretation, does not support her conclusion that reference in the extralinguistic sense has no role to play in the *Tractatus*. For it seems that 4.242 explicitly mentions reference in that sense.[113] Ishiguro's view of the reference of names underscores her interpretation of the nature of the elucidations that according to Wittgenstein are our only source of explanation thereof (3.263). Evidently, in her view elucidations do not provide contingent information about references in the extralinguistic sense, that is, about real objects, whatever their nature may be. The only way in which elucidations carry information about the identity of objects is by showing their internal properties via those of names. An elucidation shows that such-and-such names in such-and-such a combination make up a meaningful sentence. So, if elucidations are to tell us anything about the identity of an object, their meaning has to be taken for granted. That is why Wittgenstein says that ". . . they can be understood only if the references of these signs are already known" (3.263).[114]

Let us now turn to the third consequence that Ishiguro connects with her interpretation of the context principle. It is that names in the technical, tractarian sense are not like the proper names of natural language, but are best likened to what she calls "dummy names," by which she means to refer to the particular use of terms in mathematical and logical reasoning. Here, terms are often introduced in the following way: "Let P be the intersection of the lines L_1 and L_2. . . ." Such a use of P fixes the identity of the object it refers to by stipulation. P becomes a kind of contextually rigid designator (where the context is the relevant part of the discourse), and the way in which it picks out its reference, and hence the identity of that reference, is fixed in this sense that more can be learned about it, but not that it does not have the properties by means of which it was introduced.[115]

This view on names is supported, Ishiguro claims, by what is said in the *Tractatus* about the identity of objects. Objects have internal and external properties. The former make up its logical form; the latter arise when the object combines with others to form states of affairs. It is the internal properties that constitute the identity of an object (2.01231). This squares with Ishiguro's interpretation of the status of elucidations. The identity criteria of objects are given with the grammatical properties of the corresponding names, which are shown in the various ways in which these names can be used in meaningful sentences. There is one consequence of this view that we need to draw attention to: the possibility of truth preserving uniform substitution. Given two names a and b of the same logical type, which hence share their internal properties, uniform substitution of a for b and vice versa is truth preserving. If Fa, Gb, Rab exhaust the relevant elementary sentences, then $Fa \wedge Gb \wedge \neg Rab$ is the same sentence as $Fb \wedge Ga \wedge \neg Rba$. For there is no other way to determine the properties of the objects referred to than by the logical type of the referring names. To put it differently, there is on this view no independent relation of reference that ties the two names to different objects and that may make, for example, Fa true and Fb false. It is important to note that this does not imply that the reference of a is the same as that of b. As is evident from 2.0233 Wittgenstein explicitly leaves open the possibility of different, that is, nonidentical objects that have the same logical form and share their internal properties. Identity of internal properties does not entail identity, period. But this does not hold for names. At the level of symbols any two expressions that have the same logical type are identified. Here we touch on a serious problem for Ishiguro's interpretation. If, as it seems she claims, objects are merely another way of speaking about names, the problem arises how this discrepancy is to be explained. For names, identity of form entails identity *simpliciter*, for that is precisely what an identity sentence expresses. But for objects, which are supposedly just a kind of metaphorical shadow of names, Wittgenstein explicitly denies this.

Ishiguro also notes and discusses some other consequences of her interpretation, which we pass over here, except for the following, which prima facie seems to corroborate it rather directly. Elementary sentences are defined in the *Tractatus* as concatenations of names (4.22). Yet, on Ishiguro's view of what names are, in particular given the claim that there is no independent relation of reference tying names to objects, it would follow that in effect anything that an elementary sentence consisting of names says can be said also by a purely general sentence.[116] For example, fa would say the same as $\exists x\, fx$.[117] This may come as a surprise, for ordinarily we say that fa is equivalent with $\exists x\,(fx \wedge x = a)$, which is stronger. But given the particular nature that Ishiguro's interpretation ascribes to names, the second conjunct $x = a$ does not, in fact, state a claim about the world. At best, it introduces another way of referring to the object associated with x. This follows, of course, from the fact that names do not refer in the ordinary sense: they do not identify a particular object. This remarkable feature of names seems to be mentioned in the *Tractatus* itself. In 5.47 Wittgenstein says: "For 'fa' says the same thing as "$\exists x\,(fx \wedge x = a)$'." And in 5.526 we read:

> One can describe the world completely by means of fully generalized sentences, that is, without first assigning to any name a particular object.
>
> In order to arrive at the usual way of expression, one should simply say following an expression "there is one and only one x such that . . .": and this x is a. (5.526)

In the light of the foregoing, this surely comes as a surprise. Is it really the case, as Ishiguro phrases it, that "within the framework of the logical atomism of the *Tractatus* it hardly makes any difference at all whether one claims that final analysis leads to elementary propositions or to existential sentences logically equivalent to them"?[118] Let us be careful when we examine this point. It might very well be that in fact a certain distinction that Wittgenstein makes in the *Tractatus* turns out to be unimportant, or uninteresting. Certainly, we are not to take his words as the gospel; his text may very well contain mistakes, inconsistencies, or irrelevant remarks. But what we want to find out here in the first instance is not whether Ishiguro's claim is correct as such, but whether it is the claim that Wittgenstein himself makes, for example, in 5.526. We will argue that it is not and then turn to Ishiguro's point and try to evaluate it on its own merits.

That 5.526 should be read differently, in a way that assigns a special position to elementary sentences, seems obvious, at least at first sight. For Wittgenstein defines an elementary sentence as a concatenation of names (4.22); he states that elementary sentences are the terminus of logical analysis (4.221); he claims that all meaningful sentences are truth functions of elementary sentences (5).[119] Also, in his illustration of the way in which the picture theory applies to language, Wittgenstein clearly thinks of elementary sentences as providing a foundation (3, 3.201). This surely indicates that elementary sentences have a distinct role to play, one that their fully generalized equivalents do not have. One could say that an elementary sentence such as fa and its fully generalized equivalent $\exists x\, fx$ are interchangeable in a sense, but not the same: fa has a foundational role that $\exists x\, fx$ lacks. Now in what sense are fa and $\exists x\, fx$ interchangeable? The crucial question to be answered is what Wittgenstein means when in 5.526 he talks about "describing the world completely." Does he mean the world in the sense of some concrete (actual or possible) world? Or does "the world" refer here, as it sometimes does, to the totality of all that is possible, that is, to logical space? That it cannot be the latter can be argued for as follows. Suppose $\exists x\, fx$ were part of a "description" of logical space.[120] Logical space being what it is, $\exists x\, fx$ would not be a meaningful, contingently true sentence, but a necessary one. For everything that holds of logical space holds necessarily. But then, $\exists x\, fx$ would be neither meaningful, nor elementary.[121] So it seems that what is meant in 5.526 is a description of the world in the sense of some particular world or other. Now what does it mean to say that in a description of a world in this latter sense fa and $\exists x\, fx$ are interchangeable? If we think of worlds in terms of models, then fa selects a smaller class than $\exists x\, fx$, given that the interpretation of a is part of the model. But if we look upon the referring relation as fixed independently of the models, the difference disappears. So, the referring relation between a name and an object is unlike that of the individual constants of ordinary logic. But it is also unlike the way ordinary names in everyday language function, whether we take the description view or the rigid designator approach. But what then is it? Or is Ishiguro right, and is the talk of reference with respect to names merely metaphorical? Only the latter option seems open to us, although it appears to go against many of the sentences and phrases of the *Tractatus* itself. In particular, the blurring of the distinction between elementary sentences as consisting of names and their generalized counterparts seems forced if we go by the textual evidence. But perhaps our way of thinking here is too much colored by our by-now standard semantic vocabulary, and a more syntactic point of view is called for. From resolution logic we are familiar with so-called *Skolemization*, the procedure by means of which we "dismantle" (certain) occurrences of existential quantifiers and replace them with individual constants.[122] The crucial point in that procedure is that each time we come across a new quantifier, we choose a new constant. That means that we do not rely on the availability of an independent relation between constants and entities. We simply use constants as another way to express what the quantifier expresses, a way that makes it possible to reduce the complexity of the formulae and that in the end leads to a formal (in the sense of syntactical) account of the logical properties of and relations between formulae. The reduction in resolution logic is to quantifier-free, elementary sentences and their negations.[123] Constants are used in this process as a kind of arbitrary name. However, the point is that they still are considered as referring expressions, at least in this sense that the various steps in the reduction process are considered to be sound, that is, interpretation preserving.[124]

So it seems that Ishiguro is right in stressing that names in the tractarian sense are quite unlike proper names. They lack descriptive content and do not refer outside the context of a sentence. However, the conclusion that reference does not take place at all seems one step too far. It does not square with Wittgenstein's terminology and it conflates distinctions that are very prominent in the text of the *Tractatus* itself, such as that between elementary sentences and generalized sentences. Moreover it obscures the foundational role that elementary sentences play and thus downplays a feature of Wittgenstein's treatment of logic that he obviously considered to be a very important one.

Let us finally briefly consider the positive interpretation that Ishiguro herself proposes to give of names and objects. She notices that objects cannot be identified with spatio-temporal entities or with sense-data. The former are not simple and the latter, being tied to a particular world, cannot form the substance that objects supposedly are. In her view objects should be regarded as instantiations of irreducible properties. Being instantiations they acquire an objectlike character, while the irreducibility accounts for the simplicity, and the intensionality is derived from their being properties. This interpretation, Ishiguro argues, is corroborated by Wittgenstein's discussion in *Philosophical Investigations* 46–48. After his criticism of the postulate of simples as a general foundation of language and reality, Wittgenstein gives an example of a language game for which this conception of simples does make sense. In this example, colored squares are denoted with predicate-like names ("Red," "Green," and so on). Several objections can be raised against this interpretation. For one thing, the evidence from the *Philosophical Investigations* seems questionable, since there Wittgenstein in no way suggests that tractarian objects can be considered in this fashion. It seems that this "evidence" presupposes what Ishiguro starts out to prove—that there is no essential difference in Wittgenstein's views on names in the *Tractatus* and in his later work. Furthermore, the interpretation seems contrived. It depends on the questionable premise that names do not refer to properties and relations. It is more complicated than necessary and, most importantly, it seems to evade the problem. For the question about the nature of objects is not settled in this way, but reappears as the question about the nature of these irreducible properties: What are they? Not space-time properties, since these are not logically independent; not properties of sense-data, since these are arguably not world independent; and so on. But this point is not discussed by Ishiguro at all.

Summing up, we conclude that the McGuinness-Ishiguro interpretation is correct in that it stresses the fundamentally logical nature of the key notions of the *Tractatus*, in particular that of various ontological categories. But it does seem to carry this view a bit too much to an extreme, by denying the ontological and semantic vocabulary of the *Tractatus* anything more than just a metaphorical meaning.

Malcolm: Physicalism

By way of contrast we now discuss a view of the *Tractatus*, in particular of its ontology, that is quite the opposite of that of Ishiguro and McGuinness, in that it is straightforwardly realistic. It is the interpretation of Norman Malcolm, as expounded in his book *Nothing Is Hidden* (1986). The intention behind Malcolm's discussion is clear from the subtitle of the book: *Wittgenstein's Criticism of His Early Thought*. Whereas Ishiguro stresses the continuity in Wittgenstein's thinking on some fundamental issues, Malcolm represents the opposite trend in Wittgenstein scholarship. According to him, Wittgenstein's later work, most prominently the *Philosophical Investigations*, constitutes "a massive attack on the principal ideas of the *Tractatus*."[125] Malcolm lists fifteen theses that he claims can be found in the *Tractatus* and are rejected in Wittgenstein's later work. The first three of these are relevant for our present discussion. They read as follows:

- That there is a fixed form of the world, an unchanging order of logical possibilities, which is independent of whatever is the case.
- That the fixed form of the world is constituted of things that are simple in an absolute sense.
- That the simple objects are the substrate of thought and language.[126]

These three theses lead Malcolm to postulate that substance, that is, the "fixed form of the world" that consists of the objects (see 2.021, 2.023), is a fundamental conception in the *Tractatus*, one that forms the basis on which other, notably the logical and linguistic, notions rest. So, according to Malcolm the ontology of the *Tractatus* is prior to its logical and linguistic insights: "What makes sense in language and thought is dependent on and derived from the nature of the objects."[127] This view on the relationship between the ontology and the theory of language and logic is the opposite from the one presented by the interpretations of Maslow, Stenius, McGuinness, and Ishiguro. Here it is the fundamental properties of the world, that is, the categories and relations that are exhibited in any possible or actual world, which determine the structure of language and thought. In fact, at some points Malcolm suggests that this is not just the proper systematic view, but also the historically correct one: "The conception that complex things and states of affairs are *composed* of objects was thought to *require* the theory of language and logical analysis of the *Tractatus*."[128] But, as we have seen above, the evidence from the *Notebooks* makes it quite clear that the tractarian ontology was shaped after the main logical and linguistic doctrines had been developed, so this line of argument can be safely ignored.

Malcolm's treatment of the tractarian ontology assigns it the status of a metaphysical theory with strong physical overtones. The way he words his views suggests that he is of the opinion that the basic ontological categories—those of objects and of states of affairs—allow for a physical interpretation. Change, for example, is described by Malcolm as consisting in "new combinations of the objects." This is strongly reminiscent of the picture of classical atomism.[129] But there is an obvious problem with reading that view into the *Tractatus*. Within a physical atomism, not all possible states of affairs of which an object is a part, can be realized at the same time, which obviously leads to a conflict with the requirement of logical independence.[130] From the realization of a certain state of affairs the nonrealization of certain others in which the object could occur would follow.[131] Nevertheless, Malcolm holds that "objects are . . . not conjured up to support a logical theory."[132] Wittgenstein, he states, regarded the ontology as "solid reality."[133] As direct evidence for that claim he refers to a conversation he had with Wittgenstein as a student (which we already referred to above), in which the latter, when asked whether he had ever thought of an example of a simple object at the time of writing the *Tractatus*, replied that he considered this to be a purely empirical matter, which, being a logician, did not regard him.[134] The crux is, of course, what "empirical" means here. Malcolm has no doubt that Wittgenstein intended that it would take a physical, or perhaps a physiological or psychological, investigation to determine what objects are. But others, such as Maslow or Stenius, could very well construe this remark of Wittgenstein's differently, claiming that what Wittgenstein meant was that simplicity depends on a context of application. Also, the very significance of such remarks, made years afterward and in a context that is hard to reconstruct, is not easy to establish.[135] But this kind of biographical detail is not the only kind of evidence that Malcolm adduces for his interpretation. His arguments can be classified in three categories: those that he derives from the *Tractatus* itself; arguments that he bases on his assumption that the later work criticizes the earlier work; and arguments that are intended to show that alternative interpretations do not work.

One kind of argument that Malcolm derives from the text of the *Tractatus* itself concerns the terminology that is used to express various aspects of the relationship between language and the world. For example, Wittgenstein talks about names and objects in terms of the former "representing" (or "going proxy for") the latter.[136] Malcolm is inclined to take this quite literally, and concludes that it follows that objects are primary and independent from names, the latter being dependent on the former and simply mirroring their properties. Likewise, the use of "showing," as in the claim that a sentence shows its meaning (4.001), and that of "determining," as in the claim that a sentence determines a location in logical space (3.42), Malcolm takes as evidence for the same point. Since Wittgenstein did not use an expression like "create," it follows, according to Malcolm, that language and thought are derivatives from an independently given, fixed form of the world.

This line of argumentation seems not altogether convincing. Certainly, the terminology Wittgenstein uses to phrase his views, has a realistic flavor. However, by itself this does not mean that he regards the various parts of his theory in a realistic way. If we keep in mind the distinction between the presuppositions of the semantics of a language and those of the theory describing this semantics, it will be clear that such observations as Malcolm makes, will not answer the relevant question, namely, whether the *Tractatus* itself, as opposed to the semantics it describes, is a realistic theory. And it is an answer to the latter question that we are after.

But there are other arguments that Malcolm derives from the *Tractatus* and that appear more substantive. One of them centers around the fact that Wittgenstein talks straightforwardly about knowledge of objects, in 2.0123 and 2.01231. It is clear that the kind of knowledge referred to here, is not ordinary, empirical knowledge, which would consist in our being aware of contingent features of objects. Rather, being concerned with internal properties, it is like some kind of direct, unmediated contact with them.[137] That is why, Malcolm suggests, in 2.0124 Wittgenstein speaks of objects "being given."[138] This kind of a priori experience, which is properly speaking not experience at all, according to Malcolm, is what is alluded to in 5.552:

> The experience that we need in order to understand logic is not experience that something is so and so, but rather that something *is*: that, however, is *no* experience.
>
> Logic is *prior* to every experience—that something is *so*. It is prior to the "how," not prior to the "what." (5.552)

Malcolm concludes that objects are independent of language, since an unmediated acquaintance with them, which is even prior to logic, language, and thought is presupposed.

Again, it is not quite clear whether such a conclusion follows. First of all, it may be questioned whether what 5.552 says is compatible with Malcolm's physical interpretation of the nature of objects, which seems to imply that we, as ordinary beings, can have knowledge of them. After all, obtaining or having such knowledge would be a kind of experience. But according to 5.634 no experience is a priori, whereas the kind of "experience" (and note that the scare quotes are Wittgenstein's) that 5.552 refers to is not a posteriori. Knowledge of objects in the sense alluded to in 2.0123–2.10231 cannot be ordinary knowledge that an ordinary subject may have concerning ordinary objects. For that kind of knowledge is always limited and contingent, whereas knowledge of tractarian objects is necessary and unlimited. If such knowledge can be ascribed to a subject at all, it must be the metaphysical subject referred to in 5.633ff., which is the limit of what is constituted by the objects—namely, logical space.[139] A further problem for Malcolm's argument here is that Wittgenstein quite often links knowledge of objects, or logical space, explicitly to knowledge of the grammar, or logical form, of expressions.

Similar objections can be raised against Malcolm's analysis of thinking and thoughts that he brings to bear on the issue. In his view, the use that Wittgenstein makes of these notions is tied strictly to actual thinking and thoughts. But this is surely at odds with the characterization of a thought as a "logical picture" (3). The tractarian notion of a thought is a purely logical one and hence so abstract that the issue of its intrinsic relation with a situation need not be raised with reference to the way in which we actually think.[140] On the whole, the central role that Malcolm assigns to the matter of thinking and thoughts does not seem to square with the fact that, except for a few remarks in the beginning of the *Tractatus*, Wittgenstein does not refer to thoughts at all. (And given the isomorphic structure of language, thought, and the world, there is no need to do so.)

Thus, it seems that the evidence Malcolm finds in the *Tractatus* itself mainly consists of a quite literal reading of certain passages, which lend themselves to other interpretations as well and which, on the intended reading, are not easily reconciled with certain other claims. In all, this part of Malcolm's argumentation is far from convincing.

The same holds for the second type of argument that Malcolm brings forward, that which is based on the idea of a strong opposition between Wittgenstein's early and his later work. Malcolm, being a pupil of Wittgenstein's in the late 1930s, is convinced that in particular the first part of the *Philosophical Investigations* is an outright "massive attack" on the basic principles of the tractarian system. Of course, the extent to which that is the case has been, and perhaps still is, a matter of debate. What is at stake here, however, is not so much who is right on this issue, but rather the way in which either position is used in the debate. The problem is that a circularity threatens to arise. For a certain view on the relationship (opposition versus continuity) between the early and the later work must rest, to a substantive degree, on an interpretation of the relevant texts. But then it is hard to see how such a view itself can be adduced as an argument either in favor of or against a certain interpretation of the texts themselves. Only to the extent that it is based on nontextual evidence, a particular view on the relation between early and later work can be used for this purpose. But such evidence seems scarce and rather inconclusive. From this perspective, the arguments that Malcolm, and Ishiguro too for that matter, derive from their respective views on this issue are certainly too weak to decide any fundamental interpretational controversies.

But perhaps Malcolm's arguments against rival interpretations provide some evidence for his own account? Malcolm discusses in some detail the views of Ishiguro, McGuinness, and Winch, and, more globally, a position that can be compared to that of Stenius and Maslow. We will not go into the details of the various considerations that Malcolm brings to bear on these issues, but rather concentrate on the particular pattern underlying them. Important features of Malcolm's critique are that he tends to take the various claims of the *Tractatus* quite literally, and that he attaches much importance to the linear development of the text. For example, that the outline of the ontology precedes the remarks on picturing and language is taken at face value and is not placed in the historical context of the actual development of Wittgenstein's views. Thus assuming, rather than making plausible, that the *Tractatus* contains an independent ontology, Malcolm holds it against other interpretations that they do not comply with this view. Of course, such an approach might turn out to be successful: the emerging view may allow for a (more) consistent and simple interpretation of the text. However, in Malcolm's case, he seems to run into some intriguing interpretational loopholes.

Consider the following example. Ishiguro subscribes to a strong interpretation of the context principle, taking it to imply that the reference

Language and Ontology 177

of a name cannot be established outside the context of meaningful sentences. Since it construes the dependence relation between language and the world in what he takes to be the wrong direction, Malcolm cannot agree. His counterargument, however, is not that Ishiguro's interpretation is inconsistent, or too complicated, or runs into other difficulties. Rather, he restates his own interpretation, in this case claiming that analysis does not start with language but with the world. It is not sentences that we analyze, hitting upon names of which the reference has to be determined. Rather the primary target of logical analysis is a situation described by a sentence. A situation is to be analyzed in terms of simple objects, which are after all given a priori to any linguistic or logical considerations. Names then come in as an expedient means for framing this analysis, deriving their properties from the objects that they are used to denote. This is quite remarkable, because it seems that this conception of analysis, which apparently Malcolm feels his interpretation calls for—namely, that of a process that in the first instance is directed at unmediated ontological structures—seems to be quite absent both from the *Tractatus* and the *Notebooks*. In almost all passages in which analysis is discussed, it is conceived of as essentially a linguistic or logical process.[141] Also, it seems difficult to reconcile Malcolm's view with the apparently intrinsic nature of the name–object correlation.

This pattern can be traced also in Malcolm's criticism of other aspects of the Ishiguro–Winch interpretation, such as the particular view on the relation between identity and use of names, and in his arguments against Stenius. Of course, the plausibility or attractiveness of Malcolm's own interpretation does not suffer from this, but it must be said that his critique of these rival views does not provide strong evidence in favor of it either.

Malcolm's own interpretation is realistic, in the sense that he takes the *Tractatus* to contain an independently motivated ontology, which he seems inclined to interpret as a more or less physicalistic framework. This ontology, it is claimed, provides the starting point for the linguistic and logical analyses that the *Tractatus* contains. But if we consider the way in which Malcolm himself describes Wittgenstein's arguments for the simplicity of objects, after all a core element in the ontological framework, we notice a remarkable discrepancy. In his outline Malcolm bluntly states that linguistic considerations play a distinctive role: "In both the *Notebooks* and the *Tractatus* the requirement that sense be definite provides a basis for postulating simple objects."[142] The question then rises how this observation can be squared with Malcolm's view that the ontology is primary.

Malcolm discusses various arguments for simplicity of objects, one that centers around a passage from the *Notebooks* and several others that he takes from the text of the *Tractatus* itself. The first argument concerns a passage from the *Notebooks* that we already quoted above, but that we repeat here for convenience sake:

And again and again it forces itself upon us that there is something simple, unanalyzable, an element of being, in short a thing.

To be sure it does not go against our feeling that *we* cannot analyze SENTENCES so far as to refer to them by name, but we feel that the WORLD must consist of elements. And it seems as if this were identical with the claim that the world must be what it is, must be determinate. (17/6/15)

The *Notebooks* certainly also contain passages that seem to indicate a more ontological approach to the problem of simplicity, besides a host of remarks that present a logical, linguistic point of view. Evidently, Wittgenstein's thinking in this particular period had not settled on a definite point of view on this issue, and the passage just cited considers it from an ontological angle. The interesting thing is not that this passage occurs in the *Notebooks*, but that, according to Malcolm, its argument can be traced in the *Tractatus* as well, not explicitly formulated, but as an assumption in the background. Malcolm's contention is that bivalence implies simplicity. In 4.023 it is claimed that "Reality must be fixed by a sentence on 'yes' or 'no'. For this to be so it must be described by it completely." According to Malcolm, this implies that reality itself is a "yes-or-no" affair. Further, he observes that 3.23 demands that the meaning of a sentence be determinate. But since the meaning of a sentence is nothing but the situation it depicts, it follows that situations must be determinate. This Malcolm ties to the Law of Excluded Middle, that is, to bivalence. This is surely correct, but the question is whether it suffices to establish the simplicity of objects. According to Malcolm it does: "The assumption that reality is composed of simple elements," he continues, "appears to be the only way of satisfying the requirement of Excluded Middle."[143] Then everything falls into place once we decide on an interpretation of Excluded Middle: "a Law of Reality or ... a Law of Propositions." According to Malcolm, Wittgenstein definitely regarded it as an ontological principle, and he refers to the passage from the *Notebooks* quoted above as evidence for this interpretation.

It seems that this argument has two weak spots: the proper interpretation of the *Notebooks* passage, and the step from bivalence to simplicity. As for the first point, although one must concede that Wittgenstein is taking an ontological view on the matter in this particular passage from the *Notebooks*, it is nevertheless quite unclear to what extent this can serve to read a similar view into the *Tractatus*. First of all, there are many more *Notebooks* passages in which the issue of simplicity is discussed from a primarily logical, linguistic point of view. And secondly, the fact that the relevant *Tractatus* passages, too, are all phrased in typically grammatical vocabulary certainly suggests a different interpretation than the ontological, and this must be accounted for somehow, if one wants to defend it nonetheless, as Malcolm does. But Malcolm gives no such explanation. The second weakness is also not to be taken lightly. It is quite evident that bivalence by itself does not force the assumption of simplicity on us. We can very well have an ontology without a level of logically independent states of affairs and still have bivalence. It is not the latter property, but the much stronger one of bipolarity that we need in order for the argument to go through. The principle of bipolarity states that every meaningful sentence is true in at least one world and false in at least one world, that is, that it is contingent. Whereas bivalence is compatible with their being necessary but meaningful sentences, bipolarity rules them out. It follows from determinateness of meaning and Wittgenstein's professed absolutism and monism with regard to logic. And even bipolarity by itself is not enough. It is only when we combine it with Wittgenstein's specific notion of logical form that simplicity really follows. For it is the notion of a pure, completely perspicuous logical form that is the terminus of the process of analysis, that provides us with names and objects. Now neither Wittgenstein's view with regard to the status of logic, nor his conception of logical form, can be said to be intrinsically ontological. So neither can one claim, it seems, that simplicity can be derived in this way as an ontological feature.

As was remarked above, Malcolm also discusses some passages from the *Tractatus*, which he claims provide evidence for his ontological, physicalistic view on objects. We will not go into the details of Malcolm's treatment here, since the main objections to his analysis will be clear from the above and apply in these instances as well. No really new insights are forthcoming. The main objections are that Malcolm ignores the overtly "grammatical" phraseology of the text, and when outlining his interpretation of the tractarian atomism, fails to notice that its physicalistic nature is fundamentally at odds with logical independence. All in all, it seems we must conclude that Malcolm's attempt to establish the primacy of the ontology in the *Tractatus*, and hence the inherent realism of the system as a whole, is not successful.

THE REALISM OF THE 'TRACTATUS'

The central question under discussion is whether the *Tractatus* provides us with an independent, realistic theory of reality as part of a theory of meaning that accounts for the relation between language and the world. In this chapter we have been looking mainly at internal, direct evidence, studying what the *Tractatus* and the *Notebooks* say about language and ontology, thereby concentrating on the issue of the simplicity of objects. In the next chapter we will try to answer the same question indirectly, approaching the matter from a quite different angle, that of the ethical part of the *Tractatus*.

We started this chapter with a detailed analysis of some crucial textual material from the *Notebooks* and the *Tractatus*, trying to reconstruct the argument for the simplicity of objects that these texts contain and assessing its nature. Then we turned to the secondary literature, distinguishing two main streams, each with its different varieties. Some authors clearly view the ontology as being constructed from the viewpoint of language. They relativize the various ontological categories and their properties to corresponding linguistic ones. Two typical examples of such an approach have been discussed in detail: those of Maslow (and Stenius), and of Ishiguro and McGuinness. Other authors construe the relationship differently: they discern an independent ontology in the *Tractatus* and view the structure of language as derived from that. An author that holds this view is Malcolm, whose arguments we have discussed in some detail. Other authors who can be classified in this second category are Pears, who defends a "basic uncritical realism" as the proper interpretation, and Hintikka and Hintikka, who espouse a form of sense data realism.[144] In the remainder of this chapter we will briefly assess the merits of the various approaches and summarize our findings.

The Maslow-Stenius approach is too much a reconstruction, a rational reinterpretation of what the *Tractatus* should or could have been for it to give an adequate picture of the tractarian point of view on this issue. This clearly holds for Maslow's interpretation of the text, perhaps less so for that of Stenius. To be sure, as such this does not constitute a criticism of these authors. Maslow intends his interpretation not as a faithful interpretation of Wittgenstein's intentions, but rather as a systematic exposition of ideas that fit into his own logical empiricist background, or can be made to do so. But if we are interested in finding out whether the resulting picture gives an adequate interpretation of the *Tractatus* itself, we must note some shortcomings as well as positive points. To start with the latter, it must be noted that Maslow and Stenius were the first to note the basically Kantian nature of the tractarian enterprise, thus contributing to a proper historical assessment of the text. Further, Stenius was the first to give a complete and systematic exposition of the theory of meaning that the *Tractatus* embodies. This exposition makes clear that important elements of the tractarian system survive in one form or another in modern semantic and logical theorizing. For example, important elements of the picture theory of meaning appear in the compositional interpretation process as defined in modern model theoretic semantics of natural and formal languages.[145] On the negative side, we have seen that the relativism defended by Maslow and Stenius does not stand up to closer scrutiny, at least not as a faithful interpretation of the *Tractatus* itself. Wittgenstein's absolutism with respect to logic and associated notions, such as necessity, logical form, and so on, is quite obvious from the text. The picture sketched by Maslow and Stenius deviates from this crucial aspect of Wittgenstein's theory and hence cannot be regarded as adequate in this respect. Of Maslow one might say that his own logical empiricist goals led him to formulate a much more pragmatic, conventionalistic view than can reasonably be ascribed to Wittgenstein.

Turning to the Ishiguro-McGuinness analysis, we note that this, too, brings out some important features of the tractarian system very clearly, but, at the same time, does not provide a really balanced interpretation. One aspect that is rightly stressed is the essential interrelatedness of the various layers of notions and the special position that semantics plays in this integrated whole. Thus the basic unity of the *Tractatus* is accounted for, in McGuinness's case including the ethical part. It seems, however, that the resulting interpretation takes the primacy of language one step too far. It will not do to argue against Ishiguro and McGuinness that the *Tractatus* ascribes to language extralinguistic significance and that hence their interpretation does not get the basic question regarding realism right.[146] That within the tractarian system language has extralinguistic significance is obvious and certainly not something that Ishiguro and McGuinness would deny. Rather, the issue at stake is whether the tractarian system itself contains a theory about this extralinguistic reality that is independent of the linguistic theory it provides. Here, it seems, the Ishiguro-McGuinness interpretation stretches a basically sound view beyond its limits. To say that the ontology is nothing but a semantical theory in disguise surely goes beyond the claim that whatever the *Tractatus* says about reality is conceived from the point of view of language. For it leaves unaccounted for the fact that the *Tractatus* does contain an ontology, one that, moreover, precedes the theory of meaning in the systematic presentation that the book offers. As we have remarked several times before, it is quite clear from the *Notebooks* that Wittgenstein's basic logical and semantical insights occurred before his ideas about various ontological issues were formulated. But that in itself does not mean that therefore the ontology is merely another way of phrasing these linguistic principles and logical insights. On the contrary, if that were the case, it would make no sense for Wittgenstein to wrestle with, for example, the matter of simplicity of objects as long and as hard as he did. And there would hardly be any point in presenting the results in the way they actually are presented in the final text. Also, we think that some of the problems that Ishiguro's analysis encounters, which we have discussed above, in fact arise from confusing the linguistic perspective on ontology, which is quite clearly present in the *Tractatus*, with a completely structuralistic, internal analysis that regards the various ontological claims as mere metaphors.[147]

That we do not regard the physicalistic realism that Malcolm discerns in the *Tractatus*, as a valid interpretation of what the book is about, will be fairly clear from our discussion of Malcolm's arguments above. What Malcolm presents is basically a completely linear and quite literal reading of the text. But this simply fails to do justice to the inherently linguistic nature of Wittgenstein's argumentation in matters ontological, something that Malcolm himself acknowledges, but does not offer a plausible account of. Also, the resulting interpretation faces many difficulties that are not dealt with adequately. To repeat just one, the physicalistic view on objects encounters severe problems with regard to simplicity and logical independence. Also, it leaves completely unaccounted for that many of the crucial remarks on the ontology are stated from the perspective of language. These problems, however, are not discussed by Malcolm adequately. Other more or less realistic interpretations basically face the same kind of problems and hence must be rejected for more or less the same reasons.[148]

What then is the right interpretation of the *Tractatus* in this respect? The main ingredients of what we feel is at least the most plausible way of interpreting what Wittgenstein says about ontology and language have been discussed before, but we will summarize them here. Before doing so, however, it must be pointed out that the question at hand has a presupposition that may fail to obtain—namely, that there is indeed one correct way of reading the *Tractatus*. It could be that the text itself is ambiguous, that it lends itself to more than one interpretation that is both internally consistent and covers the various claims that are made. Or perhaps Wittgenstein's own intentions simply underdetermined his views on certain points. However, keeping this possibility in mind, we do want to investigate to what extent a consistent and determinate interpretation of the text is possible, if only to find out how far the ideas expressed in it may take us. Given that, we think that such a plausible interpretation should account at least for the following aspects.

First of all, the absolute character of the various notions and distinctions that occur in the *Tractatus* should be acknowledged. This applies to logic, the picture theory, ethics, and a host of other notions. Logic is classical, two-valued logic and no alternatives are available. Ethical values are absolute and the distinction between the world of contingent facts and the sphere of necessary ethical values is unalterable and definite. Likewise, there is only one way for symbolic representations to have meaning and consequently the borderline between what can be said and what can only be shown is fixed once and for all as well. A second feature that we think is established by now quite firmly is that the ontological views are construed from a linguistic perspective. When Wittgenstein talks about objects, states of affairs, situations, logical space, about facts and the world that is built from them, he is not phrasing any insights into the ultimate constituents and the basic makeup of reality as it is. Rather, he is stating what the world looks like from the viewpoint of language, that is, any language. It is not how the world is, but how we must conceive of the world for language to be possible in the first place, that is accounted for in the opening sections of the *Tractatus*. Yet, and this is the third aspect, even though conceived from the linguistic point of view, the result is an ontological theory. That is to say, it does pretend to state some fundamental properties of reality, albeit only reality insofar as it can be described in language, accessed in thought. One should not make the mistake of denying an ontological status to this language-dependent reality. In this sense, we think, the *Tractatus* does contain an ontology, a metaphysics if you like. Finally, the basically Kantian spirit behind the tractarian enterprise should be kept in mind. The *Tractatus* is, after all, not an inquiry into any empirical issues concerning language and meaning, or ethics and the world. Rather, it sets out to determine, not any concrete, empirical contents (nor a concrete ethical theory, for that matter), but the basic principles and features of the phenomena in question that make it possible for them to occur the way they do in the first place. Given this much, we think the following picture can be sketched of the *Tractatus*'s basic setup.

Starting from an a priori fixed set of logical principles Wittgenstein undertakes a search for the conditions for any language to be possible: How is meaning, any meaning, available? Wittgenstein's starting point, then, is the meaningfulness of language, his aim a completely general characterization of its possibility. The picture theory of meaning is his answer, and this theory contains as one of its essential elements a theory about the logical structure of reality. The ultimate structures enabling meaning to come about are revealed by a process of logical analysis. Starting with meaningful sentences the terminus of this process consists of elementary sentences built from names. The reality corresponding to these is formed by states of affairs constructed from objects. Ordinary meaningful sentences picture ordinary everyday situations. Analogously, logically analyzed sentences are concerned with a logically analyzed reality. Substance, the totality of objects, is the limit of the logical analysis of sentences, that is, a logical construction that shows how meaning is possible. So, in whatever sense substance can be said to exist, it is in a different way than ordinary things and ordinary situations. That is why we neither have knowledge of objects, nor are able to state their identity criteria.[149] The result is a certain freedom. On the one hand, the absolutism with regard to logic leaves us with but one way in which language has meaning, one way in which it and the reality associated with it can be constructed. On the other hand, given that the perspective from which this analysis is carried out is essentially a linguistic one, the resulting ontology is not forced on us outside the realm from which it derives its essential characteristics. The world as it shows itself in language, in thinking, is exactly that: the world as it must show itself in language, in thinking. Thus, because the ontology is tied to language, the question of realism as such need not arise. But the crucial thing to observe is that precisely for that reason there is also room for reality to confront us in other ways, which are not amenable to linguistic expression but are nonetheless as real. It will be main goal of the next chapter to argue that not only is this a possibility, but that Wittgenstein actually needs this room for an alternative way of viewing reality in order to be able to assign ethics a place that allows it to have practical consequences. Thus, it will be argued that such an analysis of the ethical part of the *Tractatus* will provide another, independent argument for viewing the ontology the way we have done in this chapter—as essentially a linguistic, logical construction.

4

Ethics

INTRODUCTION

This chapter is devoted to a closer investigation of Wittgenstein's views on ethics in the *Tractatus* period. Unlike with logic, language, and ontology, the material at our disposal here is scant. The primary sources are the short passages in the *Tractatus* that treat of ethics and the related issues of the subject (mainly 5.541–5.5423, 5.6–5.641, and 6.37–7) and the entries in the *Notebooks* that deal with the same topics (in particular those between 11/6/16 and 10/1/17). Secondary sources, which are mostly of a later date, are the "Lecture on Ethics" of 1929 and the records of the conversations with Schlick, Waismann, and others, dating from the years 1929–32. Also biographical data and the personal recollections of people such as Engelmann, who were in close contact with Wittgenstein during this period of his life, are relevant here.

Providing the backdrop for our investigation is the question of what relationship there is between Wittgenstein's views on ethics and the ontological theory of the *Tractatus*. That is a question that Wittgenstein, too, posed himself at the time. In the *Notebooks* he says:

But now at last the connection between ethics and the world has to be made clear. (9/10/16)

This passage occurs in a period in which the entries in the *Notebooks* are almost exclusively devoted to a discussion of ethical matters. From a systematic point of view, too, this is indeed a central question, one that touches the core of the tractarian system. This becomes clear immediately once we realize that the ontological theory of the *Tractatus* implies that there can be no ethical values in the world. The world is what we might call "ethically contingent." This observation immediately raises the question of what the relation between ethics and our actions can be. Even if ethical values are not in the world, our actions surely are, so how can there be a connection? The problem that presents itself is whether a system that places ethical values outside the world can properly be called an ethics, that is, a system of values that has positive implications concerning the question of how we are to act.

Clearly, in asking this question our assumption is that ethics is connected with our acting in the world, in everyday life. An ethical system should guide us in our everyday life; it should help us in deciding how to act and how to interact with others and with ourselves. Any view that cuts the tie with everyday action results in something that is at best of limited, theoretical interest, but hardly worth the kind of dedicated effort that people put into it. Furthermore, we assume that this is indeed also Wittgenstein's view, and that hence we have to look for an interpretation of the *Tractatus* that solves this problem. That is to say, we take it that we must find a way to read the book that allows for a positive interpretation of Wittgenstein's views on ethical matters. We shall argue that such an interpretation is indeed possible and that moreover it has interesting consequences for our interpretation of the ontological part of the *Tractatus*.

There are various passages in the *Tractatus* that can be adduced in support of the claim that Wittgenstein views ethics in the way we just indicated. These will be treated in detail later on. For now it may suffice to simply point out some of the more obvious reasons to think that the above line of approach is a sensible one.

First of all there is Wittgenstein's letter to Ficker, which was already quoted in Chapter 1, in which he explicitly states that the *Tractatus* was (also) an ethical undertaking: "the point of the book is an ethical one." He also says what his aim in writing the *Tractatus* was, namely, to draw limits to the sphere of the ethical from the inside. What Wittgenstein wants is to secure a "safe haven" for ethics, to protect it from the intrusions of the discursive intellect. This would hardly constitute a task that one feels one should devote one's energy to, unless one considered the task worthwhile, that is, unless one felt that the ethical is worth safeguarding in the first place.[1]

Then there are, of course, the biographical data. It is clear that in his personal life Wittgenstein considered questions of ethics and morality of the greatest importance. Such concerns seem to have been constantly present in the way Wittgenstein shaped his life (and that of others). Of course, the particular way in which Wittgenstein conceived of this changed over the years. The Great War clearly marked a watershed. His experiences in the Austrian Army, first on the eastern, later on the southern front, proved to be a decisive influence. These years were an intense struggle, with his homosexuality, with the thought of suicide, with his composure in the face of mortal danger. At the same it was also a spiritual quest, a search for a "decent way of life."[2] The struggle transformed Wittgenstein's outlook on life. One thing that bears witness to this is Wittgenstein's attitude toward money. Whereas before the war he seems not to have been bothered by his wealth, after the war he decided to give up his share in the family fortune. Also in another respect he changed his life. He gave up philosophy and became a teacher at a primary school in a small Austrian mountain village. In his personal relationships, too, Wittgenstein attached enormous importance to moral values. In this respect he demanded the utmost, both of himself as well of others. That this made him a difficult person to live with is quite clear from the testimonies of various people who knew him intimately.[3]

Another interesting source of insight into Wittgenstein's views on ethics, especially from the perspective of the question that we want to address in this chapter, is the already mentioned "Lecture on Ethics," which Wittgenstein delivered in 1929. In this lecture he says that trying to formulate ethics in meaningful sentences is like running into the boundaries of language. It is a hopeless attempt to say what cannot be said, an attempt that is doomed to fail. As such this is a claim that need not imply that one thinks the attempt itself is of any value. But Wittgenstein continues:

It is a document of a tendency in the human mind that I personally cannot help respecting deeply, and I would not for my life ridicule it. ("Lecture on Ethics," 15)

Although one might sense a kind of distance in this formulation, it also reveals that for Wittgenstein ethical concerns are of great importance. Ethical considerations are not dismissed as futile; they are not mocked or deemed unimportant gibberish. What he claims is only that an attempt to cast them in language, to formulate them in meaningful sentences, is fundamentally misguided. In his personal life, too, Wittgenstein showed great respect for those who were religious believers, such as his later pupils Anscombe and Smythies.[4]

The evidence that the ethical part of the *Tractatus* is to be interpreted as an attempt of Wittgenstein to get his views on the contents of ethics across, is not merely circumstantial. In Chapter 1 we drew attention to the following passage from the *Tractatus*:

> When an ethical law of the form "Thou shalt . . ." is laid down, the first thought is: And what if I don't?
>
> . . .
>
> [For] after all something must be right about this line of questioning. There must indeed be some kind of ethical reward and ethical punishment, but these must lie in the action itself. (6.422)

This shows quite clearly that Wittgenstein acknowledges the reality of ethical values: in some sense ethical reward and ethical punishment exist. Values are not argued away or dismissed as illusory, but they are recognized as real. This passage also indicates in what the reality of value consists. Punishment and reward, which correspond to the ethically just and the ethically unjust, are intrinsically related with action; they must "lie in the action itself." So apparently it is the action itself that carries its value, both positive and negative. This relation between action and ethical value is a serious one; it is a matter of life and death. In the *Notebooks* Wittgenstein says:

> If suicide is allowed, then everything is allowed. If anything is not allowed, then suicide is not allowed. This throws a light on the essence of ethics. For suicide is, so to speak, the elementary sin. (10/1/17)[5]

This should be read in conjunction with the following passage from the *Tractatus*: "The facts are all just part of the problem, not of the solution" (6.4321). Evidently life itself, our everyday life and the way we live it, presents us with a task that is ethical through and through. It is a task that cannot be solved either by adopting a certain philosophical point of view or by refusing to take part in it. The ethical problem constituted by life as it confronts us, cannot be solved by declaring that some contingent situation, be it at a personal or a social level, constitutes its solution. But neither is it a task that can be refused: performing the very act of refusal is taking an ethical stance. Suicide is the ultimate form such a refusal may take. And the ethical stance it embodies is a negative one.

All this makes clear that there can be no doubt that Wittgenstein is convinced that ethics and our everyday life are intimately tied together. There are such things as good and bad actions; there is such a thing as ethical value. But we should also note that he emphatically claims both that ethical value cannot be expressed (see the quotation from the "Lecture on Ethics") and that it does not reside in the world (6.41). The point we try to make in this chapter is, of course, that this is no coincidence.

It was pointed out in Chapter 1 that at the time of its appearance, the *Tractatus* was read by some as claiming that there is no such thing as ethical value. Nowadays the extreme importance of ethical matters for Wittgenstein is widely recognized. Nevertheless, little attention is paid to the particular relationship between the various parts of Wittgenstein's early work that consequentially must obtain. But a clear recognition of this connection is necessary if we are to obtain an interpretation of the *Tractatus* that makes it a really integrated whole. It will not do to just acknowledge the importance of the ethical part of the *Tractatus* and not to investigate how it is related to the other parts, in particular to the ontology.

Our treatment of Wittgenstein's views on ethics will consist of a more detailed look at four aspects of the matter. First of all, we will need to look at the notion of the will, for it is in terms of this notion that Wittgenstein formulates certain central aspects of his views. In doing so, we will need to say something about the work of the philosopher who probably had the most direct influence on Wittgenstein in matters ethical and philosophical: Arthur Schopenhauer. After we have gained some insight into the role the will plays and its intimate connection with the ethical, we will take a closer look at the contents of the ethical, that is, the nature of the good. That will serve as a starting point for an investigation of the intersubjectivity of Wittgenstein's ethics. To what extent do his views commit us to a certain morally just behavior toward others? This is relevant since an ethics that does not guide us in this respect cannot be called by that name. Finally, we turn to the aspect that connects the present discussion with that of the foregoing chapter: the relation between ethics and ontology. We will argue that the very fact that Wittgenstein's ethics is indeed intimately tied to our everyday life constitutes a strong argument in favor of the interpretation of the ontology that we argued for along different lines in Chapter 3, namely, that of the ontology as a logical construction.

THE WILL

It is in the notion of the will and the role it plays in the *Tractatus* that the influence of Schopenhauer, and thereby indirectly that of Kant, on Wittgenstein is most clearly detectable and arguably most direct.[6]

That Schopenhauer has exercised a major influence on Wittgenstein is quite evident for anyone familiar with the works of these two authors. Yet, there are quite a number of books devoted to an exposition of Wittgenstein's early thought without any real discussion of the influence of Schopenhauer.[7] And some of the authors that do devote more than a scanty remark to the relationship between Schopenhauer and Wittgenstein misrepresent the former's ideas and, consequently, give a distorted picture of the influence they have had on the work of the latter.[8]

Schopenhauer's notion of the will is intimately related to his views on subject and object. Some of this is reflected in the *Tractatus* passages that deal with solipsism and realism, but on the whole the primarily epistemological approach of Schopenhauer is missing from the *Tractatus*.[9] The notion of a subject is a complicated one, and we can find traces of various aspects of Schopenhauer's views both in the *Notebooks* and in the *Tractatus*. The complexity is partly due to the fact that two pairs of distinctions are made. There is the distinction between the individual, or psychological, subject and the metaphysical subject. And in addition there is the contrast between the willing subject and the knowing subject. These distinctions are by and large orthogonal and this leaves us with four notions in all, or better, with four aspects of the one notion of a subject. Not all aspects are equally prominently present in the *Tractatus* and distinguishing them sharply might be misleading to a certain extent. However, if we are to gain a proper understanding of Wittgenstein's views on ethics in the context of the ontological theory of the *Tractatus*, we would do well to keep these distinctions in mind. Therefore, in what follows we will investigate systematically how and why these four aspects of the notion of a subject are treated in the *Tractatus* and the *Notebooks*. In order to do so, we need to go into the views of Schopenhauer in some detail since in this area Wittgenstein is clearly tracing Schopenhauer's footsteps.

Individual and Metaphysical Subject

The distinction between the individual (or empirical, or psychological) subject and the metaphysical subject can be extracted from the *Tractatus* if we compare 5.5421 with 5.641:

> This also shows that the soul—the subject and so on—as it is conceived in present-day superficial psychology is an absurdity.
> For a composite soul would not be a soul anymore. (5.5421)

> So there really is a sense in which we can talk about the I in philosophy in a nonpsychological way.
> The I enters into philosophy by the fact that "the world is my world."
> The philosophical I is not man, not the human body, or the human soul with which psychology is concerned, but the metaphysical subject, the limit—not a part of the world. (5.641)

The first quotation appears in the context of a discussion of the logical form of sentences of the form "*A* thinks that *p*" (5.541–5.5421).[10] Intuitively, we might be inclined to think that a sentence of this form states that a certain type of relation holds between an object and a sentence. This, however, Wittgenstein cannot accept, for it is at odds with his claim that a sentence contains other sentences only in extensional, truth-functional contexts (5.54, see 5). And "*A* thinks that—" is clearly not extensional. So the grammatical form of such sentences does not convey their real logical form in a perspicuous way. What then is their logical form? Wittgenstein suggests that we look at the logical form of this type of sentence as a structure of the form "'*p*' says *p*" (5.542). This suggestion, however wild it may seem at first sight, is in fact a rather natural one—that is, given two assumptions that Wittgenstein makes about thought and the mind. The first of these is that there is a strict isomorphism between thinking (and hence thoughts), language, and reality. That Wittgenstein makes this assumption is evident, not just from the relevant entries in the *Tractatus*, such as "A thought is a meaningful sentence" (4) and the remarks about thinking being the projection-method that links a sentence with the situation it depicts (3.1), but also from the correspondence with Russell. In Chapter 3 we quoted several passages from a letter Wittgenstein wrote to Russell in 1919. There he says: "I don't know *what* the constituents of thought are but I know *that* it must have such constituents which correspond to the words of Language.... [A thought consists of] psychical constituents that have the same sort of relation to reality as words." This means that a fully analyzed thought, just like a fully analyzed sentence, has the same logical form as the corresponding situation and that its constituents are in a one-to-one correspondence with the elements of the latter.

The second assumption is a kind of Humean approach to the subject. That such an assumption is operative is quite evident from 5.5421, cited above. Here the individual subject is described as a "composite soul" [*zusammengesetzte Seele*], that is, as a mere conglomerate of sensory impressions, thoughts, emotions, and so on without an underlying bearer. Over and above the "contents," which may be of various kinds, there is nothing in which the identity of a subject consists. There is no "container" that contains the contents but is yet distinct and independent from those contents.[11]

These two assumptions make the analysis referred to above more plausible. What Wittgenstein claims is that a sentence ascribing the entertaining of a thought to an individual can properly be considered as a sentence that does not refer to the individual as such, nor to the thought in question. The first part follows because in the end a subject does not consist of a separate entity over and above the gamut of thoughts, emotions, perceptions, and so forth that it contains. The thought it entertains is part of the subject; it partly constitutes the subject and, hence, cannot be separated from it. And the second part follows from the strict isomorphism of language and thought. The thought is the meaningful sentence. So, a sentence of the form "A thinks that p" contains no essential reference to the subject A, since being a composite soul the latter disappears in the final analysis. Nor does it require the reference to a thought: the sentence expressing the thought does the job.[12] Thus the expression A, which apparently refers to a subject that has the attitude in question and thus seems to carry the thought that forms its content, on closer analysis turns out to be merely a convenient label, without an independent, substantial reference.[13]

Wittgenstein's conception of the individual, psychological subject must be sharply distinguished from his idea of a "nonpsychological" notion of the "I," which is referred to in the second quotation (5.641) given above. This passage is concerned with a different notion of a subject altogether. It concerns the metaphysical subject, which is to be clearly distinguished from the psychological, individual subject. We will analyze Wittgenstein's ideas about the nature of the metaphysical subject below, where we will discuss the context in which it plays a role, namely, the remarks on solipsism and realism. Before we can do so fruitfully, however, we first have to introduce a second contrast that is of paramount importance for the present topic and that Wittgenstein also got from Schopenhauer: that between the knowing subject and the willing subject.

Knowing Subject and Willing Subject

The distinction between the knowing subject and the willing subject is the pivotal opposition around which Schopenhauer's main work, *Die Welt als Wille und Vorstellung* (The world as will and representation), turns.[14] According to Schopenhauer, the world is not an independent reality of material objects, but rather a world of experience, of representations (*Vorstellungen*) that conform to principles inherent in the subject. The most important of these principles is that of sufficient reason (the *Satz vom Grunde*), which says that everything that happens or occurs has a ground, a cause that makes it happen or occur the way it does.[15] From this principle Schopenhauer derives the familiar Kantian notions of causality, reason and truth, space and time, but also will and motivation.

It is important to note that Schopenhauer wants to distinguish his notion of the knowing subject from the idealist notion that, he claims, appears in the work of such philosophers as Fichte and Hegel. These authors, he argues, view the relation between subject and object as an essentially asymmetrical one, the former being in some sense primary with respect to the latter. According to Schopenhauer, however, the relationship between subject and object is one of mutual dependency. The following quotation illustrates this clearly:

The fundamental mistake of all systems is that they fail to appreciate this truth, that the intellect [that is, the subject, *m.s.*] and matter [that is, the object, *m.s.*] are correlates, that is, that one exists only for the other, that they stand and fall together, that one is just a reflex of the other, indeed that they are really one and the same but viewed from opposite directions; and this One—and here I anticipate— is the appearance of the will or the thing-in-itself; that consequently both are secondary and that therefore the origin of the world is to be found in neither.[16]

From this quotation it is quite clear that Schopenhauer wants to oppose what he considers to be two fundamentally wrong conceptions of the relationship between subject and object. One is the idealist conception, which views the subject as primary and the object, being somehow dependent on the subject, as secondary. The other mistaken view is that of materialism, which Schopenhauer presents as a kind of reductionistic metaphysical realism and that holds that the object, that is, material reality, is primary and that the subject, that is, mind or consciousness, is dependent on the object and hence secondary.

The quotation also introduces the second part of the opposition referred to above, the notion of the will. Both subject, the knower, and object, the known, are considered to be secondary in the sense of being two aspects of one and the same, more fundamental reality. This is the will, which is Schopenhauer's version of the Kantian thing-in-itself (*Ding-an-sich*). This notion of the will as the ultimate reality is introduced by Schopenhauer in the following fashion. He observes that we are acquainted with ourselves, with our actions and emotions, with our bodies and minds, not only from the outside—that is, in the same way as we are acquainted with others, with their actions and emotions, bodies and minds—but also from the inside. The external acquaintance is that of the knowing subject: here we appear to ourselves as objects, with properties known and unknown, in accordance with the principles that shape and characterize all perception and knowledge. In other words, externally we are confronted with ourselves as objects among other objects, as we are confronted with others. But we are also acquainted with ourselves in another way, "from the inside," so to speak, internally. Here we do not observe ourselves as an object, but experience ourselves as will, as a force, a drive that results in externally observable actions and events, but that cannot be equated with them. For example, if one consciously raises one's arm, there is a publicly observable, knowable event of one's arm moving in a certain way. However, it is only rarely that one observes this particular event in this way. Far more often, one's consciously raising one's arm is something that appears in an altogether different way: as a conscious act of willing and thereby performing a certain action. The "thereby" is used on purpose here, for it is important to note that this act of willing cannot be separated from the corresponding performance. The act of willing and the performance of the action are not distinct events, separated in time and only causally connected; rather they are in an important way one and the same. This should be obvious from the fact that time and causality are categories characteristic of the knowing subject, not of the willing subject.

Thus the subject and the will are related in two, categorically distinct ways. The subject can observe itself as a manifestation of the will, like the material objects, events, and also the other subjects that it encounters in the world. It then confronts itself as an object in space and time, that is, as a phenomenon, and hence as an object of knowledge. But the subject can also experience itself as manifesting the will directly. This experience is not in space and time; thus it is not a form of knowledge, and it is restricted to the subject itself.

From this confrontation with oneself as will, to be distinguished from that with oneself as an object, Schopenhauer extrapolates to the notion of one will, which manifests itself in others as well, both in animate subjects and in inanimate objects. From there it is, conceptually at least, but a small step to the notion of the World-as-will. It is in the latter sense that the will appears as Schopenhauer's noumenon, his version of the Kantian thing-in-itself.

Returning to the *Tractatus*, we observe that the contrast between the knowing subject and the willing subject appears there, too. The knowing subject figures in the famous solipsism–realism sections, 5.6–5.641. And the willing subject makes its appearance in the last sections, 6.37–7, which deal with ethics. Also in the *Notebooks* we find ample references to the notion of a willing subject (see the entries of 21/7/16 and 4/11/16) and it appears that Wittgenstein is using the terms in more or less the same way as Schopenhauer. But note that there is one essential difference: the world to which the subject is related is characterized in an altogether different manner. More on that below.

Solipsism and Realism

We first turn to the discussion in 5.6–5.641 of the role of the knowing subject and the relationship between solipsism and realism. It is important to note that this highly condensed exposition of these notoriously problematic philosophical notions follows a discussion that starts at 5.55 and that is concerned with the relationship between logic and experience. Logic, it is claimed in these sections, is prior to all experience of empirical, contingent situations, more or less in the same way that logic is prior to its application (5.557).[17] Logic is connected with another kind of experience, namely, the experience "that something *is*" (5.552). However, this kind of experience "is *no* experience" (5.552), since it is not connected with anything in the world, with an aspect of the world that distinguishes it from other worlds. This "logical experience" is not connected with something that is the case. It is experience of existence as such, not of experience of something particular, but a direct, unmediated confrontation with being.[18] Interestingly, a similar contrast, between how the world is and that the world is, occurs in the sections that deal with ethics. In 6.44, where this distinction is made, the fact that the world is, is described as "the mystical." In 6.45 another expression for the same concept is used, namely, "the view of the world sub specie aeterni," which is "its view as a—limited—whole." This raises the question whether the experience presupposed by logic is the same as what these ethical terms refer to. If so there would be an intimate connection between logic and ethics.

If we place 5.6–5.641 in the context provided by 5.55, this suggests an interpretation of what these passages are concerned with, namely, the question of what the limits of possible experience are. In 5.6 we immediately find the answer: the limits of my world, which we can equate with the limits of all that I possibly could experience, are identified with the limits of my language. Apart from the perhaps unexpected reference to the first person, this should come as no surprise. For we have already seen, and in effect this is also what 5.61, immediately following 5.6, says, that by virtue of the picture theory every possible configuration of objects, that is, every possible situation, can be depicted by a sentence in an idealized, logical language. So the fit between language and the world is perfect: everything that can be the case, can be expressed, and everything that can be expressed, can be the case. Given that experience is always experience of a situation, that is, of something being the case or of something not being the case, this means that the world, language, and the totality of all possible experience are intrinsically tied together. That Wittgenstein expresses this in the particular way he does, with an explicit reference to the first person, is explained in 5.62: the world, in the sense of the totality of all possible experience, is "*my* world," that is to say, it is also the totality of all my possible experience. For, as 5.634 states quite explicitly, no part of my experience is a priori: no experience is either a priori included in my experience or a priori excluded from it. My factual experiences are limited, no doubt, but what I could experience is unlimited, bound only by the limits of logic, that is, the limits of language. Hence, Wittgenstein can say in 5.62 that "the limits of *language* . . . mean the limits of *my* world." For just as the limitations of my actual experience are contingent, accidental, not a priori and necessary, so are the limitations of the actual language I speak. At the rockbottom of logic, whatever language I speak, insofar as it is a language that reaches out into the world and depicts the situations that make up the world, it is a logical language, that is, language as such. Hence the interjection in the passage just quoted: "(the language that alone I understand)."[19] Any actual language that can be used at all, when stripped from its actual but contingent deficiencies and idiosyncracies, is at bottom the same language. This is also quite clear from those passages, like 4.014, in which Wittgenstein emphasizes the translatability of various symbolic systems.[20]

This equation of the totality of all possible experience with the totality of all my possible experience depends, not just on my language being in essence identical with the one logical language, but also on a particular view on the individual subject. For an obvious rejoinder to the equation in question would be that surely it would be impossible for me to experience being you. At least that aspect of my experience must be a priori, it seems. However, here Wittgenstein's Humean view on the individual self, namely, that there is no such self over and above its experiences (taken in a broad sense), is essential. For this view implies that there is no such experience of being me (or you). The "me" and "you" are labels that conveniently distinguish one contingent bundle of experiences from another, but they do not refer to intrinsically different bearers that exist over and above the experiences contained in those bundles.[21]

The central point of the discussion in 5.6–5.641 is summarized in Wittgenstein's famous dictum "that solipsism, carried through strictly, coincides with pure realism" (5.64). How does Wittgenstein reach this conclusion? There are in fact two lines of argument that can be discerned in these passages. One is that since the totality of possible experience of an individual subject is identical with the totality of all possible experience, there is no question of one such subject occupying a special privileged position with regard to the others, as a rather trivial interpretation of solipsism would have it. There is however another interpretation of solipsism, and there Wittgenstein's second line of argument plays a role. For a solipsist might claim that it is not an empirical, individual subject that occupies this privileged position, but a metaphysical one. (The distinction between solipsism in this sense and certain forms of idealism becomes rather vague.) This is the position that Wittgenstein attacks in 5.631ff. The opening sentence of 5.631 reads: "The thinking, representing, subject does not exist." Notice that this does not refer to the individual subject, for obviously the individual thinking subject is real, though according to Wittgenstein not in the way we may be inclined to think. As the passages following 5.631 make clear, the notion of subject that Wittgenstein refers to here is that of the metaphysical subject. And in his discussion of the relationship between the metaphysical subject and the world, Wittgenstein is quite obviously indebted to Schopenhauer. In 5.631 it is argued that the metaphysical subject cannot be found in the world, that it is not an object among other objects. Rather, as 5.632 puts it, the metaphysical subject "is a limit of the world." This is completely in line with Schopenhauer's view of subject and object as mutually dependent notions, for the relation between the world and its limits is one of mutual dependence. In 5.633–5.6331 Wittgenstein illustrates this mutual dependence by means of a comparison: the subject is likened to an eye and the world to its visual field. This comparison, which can also be found in Schopenhauer, illustrates the two points made above. In the same way as the eye does not belong to the visual field, the subject does not belong to the world. And where there can be no visual field without an eye and no eye without a visual field, subject and world are mutually dependent as well. Now in what sense does this show that "what solipsism *means*, is completely correct" (5.62)? Obviously, this does not refer to the more common and trivial meaning of solipsism, the one that Schopenhauer curtly dismissed by saying that it is not a philosophical position that can be argued, but a mental illness that needs to be treated. The meaning that Wittgenstein refers to is the one that involves the metaphysical subject. The sense in which solipsism thus conceived is right then boils down to there being only one metaphysical subject. This is indeed straightforward given Wittgenstein's absolutistic and monistic view of logic. Since there is only one logic, there is only one world; hence there is only one limit of the world, and thus only one metaphysical subject. Thus, in the *Notebooks*, in an entry dated 23/5/15, Wittgenstein says that there is only one "world soul" and that this shows in what sense solipsism is right. In view of this, Wittgenstein can indeed claim that solipsism, properly conceived, coincides with realism. The victory of the solipsist is a Pyrrhic one, however.

There is only one metaphysical subject, but this subject is as dependent on the one "reality coordinated with it" (5.64) as reality is dependent on this subject.

Above it was claimed that Wittgenstein's line of argumentation here derives from Schopenhauer in a rather straightforward way. However, there is also an important difference between their positions. This difference has its roots in the different ways in which both authors view the world. For Schopenhauer the world is essentially an epistemological notion. His notions of subject and object are epistemological in a Kantian way. The object, that is, the world, is what appears for the subject in accordance with the epistemological categories and principles that are inherent in it. Wittgenstein, however, conceives of the world primarily in logical terms. In the *Tractatus*, the Kantian critical program takes the form of drawing a limit "not to thought, but to the expression of thought," as it is worded in the preface. Therefore 5.61 claims that "logic pervades the world; the limits of the world are also its limits." Obviously, this difference in perspective results in different conceptions of the world. For Schopenhauer the world as representation is given with the epistemological categories and principles of the metaphysical subject. Since he gives these categories and principles an essentially Kantian content, emphasizing in particular the principle of sufficient reason, Schopenhauer, like Kant, ends up in a Newtonian, deterministic position. For Wittgenstein the world as representation is the world as language. It is given with substance, which is essentially a logical category.[22] Following this logical perspective and holding on to his absolute stance with regard to logic and necessity, Wittgenstein rejects causality as a necessary relationship between situations and thus ends up in a position that is the mirror image of Schopenhauer's determinism. For Wittgenstein everything in the world is accidental, from a logical point of view, that is:

> There is no way in which one can conclude from the existence of some situation to the existence of another, completely different situation. (5.135)

Two situations are completely different, that is, disjointed, when no logical connections between them exist. The spatial metaphor of logical relationships makes this clear. Disjointedness of two regions in logical space means that no logical ties between them exist. One such situation may be realized without the other being realized as well. The point to bear in mind here is that what is at stake is the existence and nonexistence of logical connections. Thus we cannot conclude that Wittgenstein also rebuffs the existence of other kinds of connections between situations, in particular causal ones. It only implies that such causal connections are not necessary (5.136). Logical relationships are a priori ("All drawing of conclusions is a priori," 5.133), but causal relationships are not. They are empirical, and therefore contingent. Hence a merely causal relationship between two situations or events can never enable us to logically deduce the existence of the one from that of the other. This holds in particular for events separated in time (5.1361).

So, in Wittgenstein's logical approach Schopenhauer's epistemological categories are in a certain sense arbitrary.[23] It should be noted that both Wittgenstein's and Schopenhauer's positions, however different, lead to the same ethical problem: the moral responsibility of the individual. Evidently, both a completely deterministic worldview and one in which everything that happens is only contingently related to everything else, do not lend themselves easily to the idea of individual moral responsibility, with the concomitant presuppositions of free will, of the possibility of deliberate agency, and so on. At least, that is how it seems at first sight. But both systems provide a possible way out: the will. In the case of Schopenhauer, the determinism of the phenomenal world is balanced by the noumenal will, which is not similarly restricted. And in the case of Wittgenstein it is the will as the bearer of ethical values that escapes the logical contingency of the world of language and thought. This reading of sections 5.6–5.641 puts Wittgenstein optimally in the line of Kant and Schopenhauer and it implies that the originality of Wittgenstein's contribution is that he replaces the traditional epistemological perspective by a logical one. This linguistic turn started with Frege, and it is indeed on this score that Wittgenstein is deeply indebted to the latter.[24] But the *Tractatus* is more than just Schopenhauer from a Fregean perspective, for Wittgenstein carries Frege's insights much further than Frege ever did. One might say that also in his later work Frege never really thought out the consequences of his insights to their limits.

It must be remarked that the present interpretation differs from the more common one, according to which the sections 5.6–5.641 defend what is called "a Fregean conceptual realism" against "a Schopenhauerean idealism."[25] However, such an alternative interpretation faces some serious difficulties. For one thing, it is forced to interpret Schopenhauer as some kind of Fichtean idealist, which he emphatically is not. Schopenhauer never gets tired of opposing this "false view," which construes the subject–object relationship asymmetrically, and of emphasizing the mutual dependence of subject and object. The same mutual dependence is expressed in 5.6–5.641, so the only way to see a difference between Wittgenstein and Schopenhauer here is by misinterpreting the latter on this point. Another problem is that it is not at all clear in what sense the ontology of the *Tractatus* is a kind of Fregean conceptualist realism, of the kind expressed in Frege's later papers.[26] For example, the ontological distinction between the realm of platonic senses (Frege's "Third World") and that of sensory, material objects, which is the very foundation of Frege's brand of realism, appears to be lacking in the *Tractatus* altogether. Rather, the tractarian system seems to be realistic in a more Schopenhauerean sense.[27]

The interpretation outlined above, which presents Wittgenstein as giving a Fregean linguistic turn to basically Kantian and Schopenhauerean themes, does raise a question, namely, what is the relationship between the metaphysical subject, on the one hand, and logic and substance, on the other? Logic shows the scaffolding of the world (6.124), that is, the structural aspects of logical space. Likewise, substance is characterized as the form that any two worlds, however different, share (2.022–2.023). So logic and substance are, as it were, two sides of the same coin. Both determine and show the totality of all that is possible. In what sense does the metaphysical subject, being the limit of the world, perform the same function? The relevant passages do not provide a clear answer, but we should notice that here both logic and the metaphysical subject are described as a "limit of the world" (5.61 and 5.632, respectively). In that sense the two can be identified, which reinforces the strongly logical, semantical flavor that pervades Wittgenstein's discussion of these matters.

A final observation before we turn to a discussion of the willing subject and ethics. In view of the isomorphism between thinking, language, and the world the metaphysical subject may seem to perform an epistemological role after all. Since the world as the totality of all possibilities is the same as the totality of all that is thinkable, the metaphysical subject can also be regarded as the limit of what is thinkable. This seems to give the notion an epistemological flavor. However, Wittgenstein did not attach much value to epistemology (4.1121). And it should be noticed that since Wittgenstein interprets the world logically and not epistemologically, an epistemological role of the metaphysical subject is actually quite empty, at least from a traditional perspective. For Wittgenstein regards some of the traditional epistemological categories and principles of the thinking subject as accidental, contingent, generalizations and assigns a logical status to others. Again, this follows from his monistic view on necessity. There being only logical necessity, epistemological principles have to be treated as either contingent or logical.[28]

The Will and the Willing Subject

Let us now turn to the notion of the will and that of the willing subject. Schopenhauer claims that there is an intrinsic relationship between will and action. I am acquainted with and related to my actions, and in an extended sense to all phenomena of my consciousness, not just externally, from the outside, by means of sensory perception, but also internally, from the inside, when I experience them as will. Will and action are intrinsically related and can be regarded as two ways of conceiving of one and the same phenomenon.

In an extended sense the will occurs in Schopenhauer's philosophy as the noumenon, as the true thing-in-itself. This may be called the metaphysical willing subject. However, it should be kept in mind that this notion of subject does not depend on a corresponding notion of object. The will manifests itself in the world of phenomena, and it is only within the context of the latter that the epistemological opposition between subject and object is valid. The will as such remains outside the scope of these conceptual distinctions altogether. Viewed in this way, it has the following important characteristics. First of all, it is undifferentiated. It is neither one, nor many, but escapes all attempts of quantitative determination. It can also be described as limitless. This feature is familiar from all kinds of descriptions of mystical experiences that describe a kind of "unio mystica," in which all differentiation is uplifted. Secondly, the noumenon manifests itself in everyone and everything. This means that it cannot be characterized in a qualitative manner either, as all qualities that inhere in individual entities (of various types: things, properties, situations, worlds) imply differentiation between those entities to which the quality applies and those in which it is not realized. In itself this does not contradict the first characteristic, but it does imply a sharp, categorical distinction between the noumenon and its manifestations. Insofar as the will manifests itself in the world, it can be said to be the ground of the world as phenomenon, but not its cause. For causal relationships are internal to the world of phenomena and do not apply outside of that realm. Finally, although the will as noumenon is the origin of the world as phenomenon, it is independent of space and time. This follows directly from the fact that for Schopenhauer, as for Kant, space and time are the categories of the knowing subject and thus primary characteristics of the world as representation. But since knowledge is confined to the world as representation, the will as the noumenon is unknowable in principle.

The fact that the noumenon cannot be an object of knowledge does not mean that it goes unnoticed, that we do not experience it in some way. Contact with the will as noumenon is established primarily through the individual will. This is indeed the most direct way in which we may be subjected to the will as it makes itself manifest in us. Quite often the source of our willful actions is unknown to us. We cannot control them; they indeed sometimes seem to be forced on us from outside, originating in a source that is beyond ourselves and that expresses itself in and through us. Notice that this direct contact with the will is not knowledge of it, as an object among objects. It is an experience that transcends the realm of knowledge, its categories and forms, altogether. In a similar vein Schopenhauer conceives of the second way in which we can be acquainted with the noumenal will: through platonic forms (*Ideen*). These platonic forms play a double role in Schopenhauer's system. The phenomenal world is viewed as the outcome of the urge of the will to manifest itself. As we know it, it is not an arbitrary whole, but has a strong internal, systematic structure. The regularity and uniformity that we find across individual phenomena are accounted for by Schopenhauer by an appeal to platonic forms, of which the individual phenomena are concrete instantiations. The platonic forms are, as it were, the channels through which the noumenal will flows into the phenomenal world. And as such they provide the second way in which there can be contact between us and the noumenon. By contemplating the forms through their various manifestations we gain an impression of the noumenal will. According to Schopenhauer the various forms are hierarchically organized and consequently so are their manifestations. This hierarchy of "objectification of the will" runs from gross material objects to the most abstract aesthetic expression: music. The various branches of human cognitive activity, from natural science to the arts, are ordered accordingly. Art is placed above science, since whereas the latter deals with material manifestations, the former has human consciousness as its object. Of the arts the first place is occupied by music, it being the most abstract expression of the most general phenomena of consciousness. It is in the sciences and the arts that the knowing subject grasps the platonic forms and thereby, albeit indirectly, various aspects of the noumenal will. It must be kept in mind, however, that the platonic forms are not the noumenal will itself and that hence contemplation of them is not direct contemplation of the will. For, like their manifestations, the forms are differentiated, whereas the noumenon is undifferentiated and escapes all quantitative and qualitative characterization.[29]

The contact with the noumenon that is established either through the individual will or through the platonic forms is hence not knowledge of the will. It is, at best, a momentary state that enables us to temporarily transcend the limitations of our individual self and thus provide us with the kind of experience that will enable us to see through the false idea of a permanent ego and give us a proper view on subject and object, on the mutual dependence of the two, and on their secondary nature with regard to the noumenal will. For Schopenhauer this insight clearly also has a moral dimension. From our awareness of the relativity of our notion of an individual self and of the undividedness of the will should spring forth compassion for others, which is to form the basis of our interaction with them. Thus unity, not individuality, is the ground on which proper moral and spiritual conduct should be based.[30] In the end, it should also lead us to adopt what is the ultimate ethical and spiritual goal: the renunciation of the will. The manifestation of the will through the false idea of an individual ego and the concomitant continuous struggle for self-assertion are the sources of suffering. Awareness of the illusory nature of the self is thus a prerequisite for a proper moral and spiritual stance.

The ethical dimension of the world in relation to the noumenal will is important to bear in mind, not just in connection with Wittgenstein. It is probably no coincidence that this aspect of Schopenhauer's work has met with the same kind of negative and unsympathetic reaction as the ethical part of the *Tractatus*.[31] However, to neglect it would be to severely misrepresent Schopenhauer's intentions, as he is quite explicit about the matter himself. For example, in the *Parerga und Paralipomena* he says:

That the world has only a physical and not a moral significance is a fundamental error, one that is the greatest and most pernicious, the real perversity of the mind.[32]

Various aspects of these views of Schopenhauer can also be found in Wittgenstein's work, most prominently and directly expressed in the *Notebooks*. For example, the feeling of a unity behind the diversity and individuality of the phenomenal world is manifest in those passages in the *Notebooks* in which Wittgenstein speaks of "one world soul" and "the spirit." For example:

There really is just one world soul, which in particular I call *my* soul, and as which alone I grasp what I call the souls of others. (23/5/15)

This passage nicely reflects Schopenhauer's view that I am acquainted with the one noumenal will primarily through my own will and that it is by extrapolation that I postulate such a will also in others. The same thought is expressed elsewhere in the *Notebooks* as follows:

But remember that the spirit of the snake, of the lion, is *your* spirit. For it is only from yourself that you know the spirit at all. (15/10/16)

Wittgenstein, too, speaks of the will as something that does not belong to the sphere of experience: "The act of will is not an experience" (9/11/16). What is meant here is that we do not confront our will, which is the will, as an object, as a phenomenon, that is, as something within the sphere of knowledge and experience. It is something that bears an intrinsic relation to our actions. What that relation is and how the will differs from the deliberation and decision that precede an action are indicated in the following passages from the *Notebooks*:

It is clear: it is impossible to will without already performing the act of will.
The act of will is not the cause of the action but is the action itself.
One cannot will without doing.

. . .

For does not the willed movement of the body happen just like any unwilled one in the world except that it is accompanied by the will?
But it is not just accompanied by the *wish*! But by the will.

. . .

Wishing is not doing. But willing is doing.
(4/11/16)

At first sight it may look as if will and action are separate, for often we first decide to do something and only subsequently act accordingly. However, what precedes an action and constitutes (one of) its cause(s), is not the will but what Wittgenstein calls the "wish." The wish is distinct from the action, conceptually and temporally. The relationship between them is causal, that is, external and hence contingent. A wish to perform a certain action may fail to result in that action. The will is an altogether different aspect of action. Any action is internally and hence necessarily related to the will. It is a manifestation of it and as such cannot be separated from it. The will is the action itself and not its contingent cause. Like Schopenhauer, Wittgenstein describes the will as that which constitutes the ethical dimension of our actions and thereby of the world at large: "I will call 'will' first and foremost the bearer of good and evil" (21/7/16). In the *Tractatus*, too, the will is associated with ethical categories—for example, when Wittgenstein speaks in 6.43 of "good or bad willing."

It is clear that in important respects Wittgenstein's ideas on these issues closely resemble those of Schopenhauer. This also holds for the special character of the relationship between world and will. In Schopenhauer's system the will is said to manifest itself in the phenomenal world. The world of knowing subjects and known objects in all its changing variety is but an expression of the will. It would be wrong, however, to read this as saying that the will creates the world, that the world springs forth from the will. For such concepts as creation and change have no meaning outside the sphere of the material world and the knowing subject. For they presuppose the notions of time and causality, which are essentially just epistemological categories of the knowing subject and hence do not apply to anything outside the sphere of the phenomenal world. In this sense the world is independent of the will. However, this is an independence according to the internal standards of the phenomenal world. Additionally, and more fundamentally, the world is dependent on the will inasmuch as both knowing subject and known objects, although entities that are separate in time and space, outside the spatio-temporal sphere are one and the same will. So the relationship between the world and the will viewed from an (epistemo)logical perspective is different from the way in which the two interact from an ethical point of view. It is important to note that the difference is categorical, and not gradual.[33]

The same apparent ambivalence can be found with Wittgenstein. On the one hand, we find Wittgenstein stating that "The world is independent of my will" (6.373) and, on the other hand, we read his claim that "my will pervades the world" (11/6/16). How are we to understand this? The key is already given in the passage from the *Notebooks* (4/11/16) cited above. There Wittgenstein makes a distinction between "will" and "wish," and this distinction reappears in the passage following 6.373, just quoted:

> Even if everything that we wish for were to happen, this would still be only a grace from fate, so to speak, for there is no *logical* connection between will and world that would guarantee this, and the assumed physical connection we could not will again, of course. (6.374)

This suggests the following. The wish is that which precedes our actions, and hence it is the wish that runs the risk of not being fulfilled. The act of wishing is located in space-time and enters into causal connections with other situations. The relationship between our wish that some situation be realized and the realization of that situation is not a logical one. And logical necessity is the only necessity that Wittgenstein acknowledges (6.37). Hence it follows that wish and wished for are separated by a gulf of contingency. This is one sense in which one may uphold that will and world are independent. It is in this independence that Wittgenstein locates the freedom of the will: since the wish and the act are separated in space and time, they are linked only by causal relationships, which from a logical point of view are contingent. This means that no strict inference is possible from the way in which the world (including its history) is at a given moment, to how it will be.[34]

Another sense in which Wittgenstein uses the term "will" appears in the following passage:

> If good or bad willing changes the world, it can only change the limits of the world, not the facts; not that which can be expressed by language. (6.43)

Unlike our wishes, our will does not precede our actions, but instead flows along with them, forms an intrinsic part of them. It is not something that results in something else being the case or not; it does not change the facts that make up the world, but it pervades the world, puts whatever facts that make up the world in a certain perspective. This is what is meant when it says in the *Notebooks* that "the will is an attitude of the subject to the world" (4/11/16). In one sense this expresses the transcendent nature of the will with regard to the world and the concomitant transcendent nature of ethics. It is important to bear in mind, however, that the will is an aspect of our acting and that therefore this transcendence is not ontological, but logical. All our acting takes place in the world and hence our will, our ethical attitudes, are immanent at the same time. To put it differently, the wish can be regarded as that aspect of the act of willing that belongs to the world as it is conceived of logically, that is, when it is treated as a complex of situations that can be grasped in thought and expressed in language. It is the intention, the decision that precedes the action; it is the psychologically real element, which can be detected empirically and analyzed logically. The will, in contrast, presents the ethical aspect of action. It is not definable in terms of situations preceding or following it; hence in that sense it is not part of the world as it appears in language and thought. This distinguishes wish and will, but not in an ontological sense. It is not that wish and will are different entities, which belong to different and separate realms of reality. Rather they are connected with two ways of viewing the world, with two ways of interacting with it.

This double aspect of willing, that is, the distinction between the contingent aspect of phenomenal wish and the necessary aspect of noumenal, ethical will, provides the key to Wittgenstein's solution of what apparently is a problem: if the world is ethically contingent, if all that happens in the world is accidental, yet ethical value is noncontingent, how can there be a relationship between ethics and the world, between values and our actions? The link is secured by the intrinsic relationship between action and will, the former being the "support" in the world for the latter.[35] In Schopenhauer's system, in which the phenomenal world is deterministic, we saw that a different, but analogous, problem arises. In what sense does such determinism leave room for ethical considerations? If the relationship between my actions and their causes and motives, on the one hand, and their consequences, on the other hand, are necessarily fixed, wherein then is my moral responsibility to be located? Again, the intrinsic relationship between will and action is meant to solve this problem.

However, if we inquire into the possibility of an ethics that is more substantial, the internal connection between will and action only provides the beginning of an answer, since it does not determine what ethics is all about. We now know that the will is the bearer of good and bad in an ethical sense and that it is a necessary aspect of our actions. But what is this good or bad will and how does it relate to ethics as we conceive of it ordinarily, that is, as a system of everyday moral precepts? Is the present view on ethics just an entirely abstract epiphenomenon of independent metaphysical and logical considerations or does it really have implications for our behavior, also in relation to others? To these questions we now turn.

THE NATURE OF THE GOOD

Ineffability

If we inquire how the nature of the good is viewed in the *Tractatus* and the *Notebooks*, it is important to realize at the outset that we are not investigating a philosophical ethical theory of the more common variety. For what we have called in Chapter 1 the "ethically contingent" character of the world directly implies that there can be no such theory. The most direct expression of this is to be found in 6.41 (which was already quoted in Chapter 1 but which we repeat here for the sake of convenience):

> The meaning of the world must lie outside of it. In the world everything is the way it is and everything happens the way it happens: *in* it, there is no value. If there is any value that has value, it must lie outside what happens and is the case. For everything that happens and is the case is accidental.
> What makes it nonaccidental cannot lie *in* the world; for if it did, then that in its turn would be accidental.
> It must lie outside the world. (6.41)

Given that anything that can be meaningfully expressed in language has to be located in the world and as such has to be contingent, it immediately follows that ethical values, being of a noncontingent nature, cannot be expressed:

> For that reason there can be no sentences of ethics. Sentences cannot express something higher. (6.42)

In the *Notebooks* this remark is immediately followed by a question:

But we could also say this: the happy life in some sense seems to be *more harmonious* than the unhappy life. But in what sense??

What is the objective feature of the happy, harmonious life? Here it is clear once more that there can be no such feature that can be *described*.
This feature cannot be a physical one, but only a metaphysical, transcendent one. (30/7/16)

That there are no meaningful sentences in ethics is not due to a lack of subject matter. Wittgenstein does acknowledge the objective status of values: there is an objective feature that distinguishes the happy life from the unhappy life. But this feature, being necessary, cannot be a physical, contingent, characteristic. Hence, it cannot be described.

The ineffability of value, of what ethics is about, is also the central theme in Wittgenstein's "Lecture on Ethics." In this lecture Wittgenstein begins by making a distinction between relative values and absolute values. Relative values enter into such determinations as "This is the right road to take," or "He is a bad tennis player." Such values are instrumental, goal-related, and cognitively assailable, but do not pertain to the ethical. Ethical values are absolute, and with regard to such, Wittgenstein says:

. . . at once I see clearly, as it were in a flash of light, not only that no description that I can think of would do to describe what I mean by absolute value, but that I would reject every significant description that anybody could possibly suggest, *ab initio*, on the grounds of its significance. That is to say: I see now that these nonsensical expressions were not nonsensical because I had not yet found the correct expressions, but that their nonsensicality was their very essence. For all I wanted to do with them was just *to go beyond* the world and that is to say beyond significant language. My whole tendency, and I believe the tendency of all men who ever tried to write or talk Ethics or Religion, was to run into the boundaries of language. This running into the walls of our cage is perfectly, absolutely hopeless. Ethics so far as it springs from the desire to say something about the ultimate meaning of life, the absolute good, the absolute valuable, can be no science. ("Lecture on Ethics," 11–12)

Ineffability is a necessary property of ethics: any theory, any single sentence even, that one could formulate about the nature of the Good would be wrong, ipso facto. Such a theory is a misguided though perhaps well-meant attempt to say what cannot be said, to escape what language is necessarily restricted to, namely, the contingencies that make up the world.

Similar claims can be found in the conversations Wittgenstein had with Waismann. For example, referring to theories about the nature of value Wittgenstein says:

Whatever people might say to me, I would reject it, and not because the explanation is false, but because it is an *explanation*.

If people would tell me that something was a *theory*, I would say: No, no! That does not interest me. Even if the theory were true, it would not interest me—it would never be *that* that I am looking for. (*Ludwig Wittgenstein and the Vienna Circle*, 17/12/30)

And the reason why such a theory, even if true, would be uninteresting is precisely that being true or false, that is, being meaningful, implies being connected with the contingent, not with the absolute. The world consists of contingent situations only, as language is made up of contingent sentences only. What can be the case coincides with what can be expressed, and so both value and its expression belong to another realm.

Will, Action, Value

But in what sense then can ethical value nevertheless be located in the world? Above we said that the key to answering this question lies in Wittgenstein's Schopenhauerean view that the will, being the bearer of good and evil, is an intrinsic aspect of action. Evidently, our actions are part of the world and in this way a link, and a noncontingent one at that, is secured between value and the world. But how, one may ask, do the good and the bad will affect the world? What difference does good or bad willing make in the world at large?

Of course, in view of the very ineffability of ethics that Wittgenstein upholds, we cannot expect him to be very informative about this. Since nothing meaningful can be said about it, what we can expect at most are hints, suggestive formulations that will enable us to find out for ourselves, in an essentially noncognitive manner, what is meant. One such lead is given by the metaphor Wittgenstein employs in 6.43, where he says the "good or bad willing" changes nothing in the world, but "the limits of the world." He continues:

In short, the world then must thereby become an altogether different one. It must, so to speak, decrease or increase as a whole.

The world of the happy person is a different one from that of the unhappy person. (6.43)

That it is not something in the world that is changed by the will is evident from the above. But how are we to understand the claim that the will changes the limits of the world? From the absolute character of logic it follows that we cannot interpret this as a change in the totality of possibilities, since that is fixed a priori by the principles of logic. The radical change that a certain ethical attitude can bring about rather has to do with the meaning of the world. In the *Notebooks* the waxing and waning of the world as a whole that 6.43 speaks of is related to its meaning: "As if by addition or loss of meaning" (5/7/16). So the good or bad will results in a fundamental change of our outlook on the world. It presents the world as a more or as a less meaningful whole. It is therefore that Wittgenstein calls the will an "attitude" of the subject toward the world (04/11/16).

Presumably it is only for those who have had an experience of the world as a meaningful whole that this metaphor is illuminating. However, although such an appeal to individual experience seems to be an important feature of Wittgenstein's treatment of the subject, it will perhaps prove worthwhile to try to find out whether a more informative and systematic account can be given of his views on ethics.

One way of doing so is by taking the intrinsic relationship between will and action seriously. If the will can be ethically good or bad and the will is an internal property of our actions, then our actions can be good or bad. In fact, this is implicit in 6.422 and connects what is said there with 6.43. In the former passage Wittgenstein acknowledges that ethical laws are real in this sense that acting in accordance with them or against them leads to "ethical reward" or "ethical punishment."[36] However, these "must reside in the action itself" since:

> [However] it is clear that ethics has nothing to do with punishment and reward in the usual sense. Hence this question after the *consequences* of an action must be inconsequential.—At least these consequences must not be events. (6.422)

Here Wittgenstein clearly dismisses any analysis of ethical value in terms of causes or consequences. The ethical quality of an action does not reside in its various relationships with other events or situations. What makes an act ethically justified or unjustified are neither its origins, that is, its motives and causes, nor its consequences. For both the relation that an action bears to its causes and the one it bears to its consequences are contingent. Hence, if the ethical quality of an action were to depend on such contingent relationships—it being ethically justified if preceded by such and such motives or if followed by such and such consequences—ethical value itself would be contingent as well.[37]

But it is not just past and future events or situations that are unable to provide ethical value. The action itself, too, as something that happens in the world, cannot per se be the locus of value. For any action is again a mere "coincidence," a contingent feature of the world, not necessary; transient, not permanent. So no action is in and of itself good or bad; it qualifies as such only in view of the ethical will that is connected with it. Thus the ethical dimension of an action is not connected with some particular aspect of the world, but with the world as a whole. Above we saw that Wittgenstein characterizes this in terms of the waxing and waning of the world, in the growing and diminishing of the meaning of the world, as a consequence of good and bad willing. This means that the ethical quality of an action is directly related to the meaning of the world.

Good Will

But what is the good will, what is an ethically correct action? From the above considerations we can immediately deduce a negative characterization, which we then might try to fill in more positively. *Ex negativo*, the good will is not directed at anything particular in the world. The good will is not willing this situation in contrast to that one, or willing that this will happen in opposition to that. That is, the good will is not related to anything in the future. Also, it is not connected with the past. The good will is not the willing that springs forth from a particular motive that we may have for an action or from a particular set of circumstances in which we perform it. This negative characterization of what the good will is directly follows from the ethically contingent character of the world. If ethical value does not reside, indeed cannot reside, in any particular situation in the world, be it present, past, or future, then the will cannot be ethically good by virtue of being directed at a particular situation. And likewise an action cannot be ethically right because it either springs forth from or results in a particular situation.

This negative characterization of the ethically good can also be viewed as follows. In terms of the distinction between will and wish we might say that the good will ipso facto is distinct from wishing. The wish is that aspect of the will that is manifested in the world, that is directed toward other situations, other objects. The will, by contrast, is the immanent aspect, the necessary, intrinsic aspect of our actions. In view of this the negative characterization just given reflects a categorical distinction between will and wish. The noumenal, ethical will is fundamentally distinct from the phenomenal, nonethical wish. Hence, the good will has no relations with wishing that are of ethical importance, since any relations that obtain between wish and will are contingent.

This observation suggests a way to arrive at a more positive characterization of what for Wittgenstein constitutes the good will. If the good will is not directed at anything in the world, then it follows that taking an ethically just stand must involve abolishing our attachments to particular aspects of the world. For remember that, although will and wish belong to different categories, they are related. The wish is the phenomenal "offspring," so to speak, of the noumenal will. In view of this, it seems that the good will is intimately tied to a denial of our wishes. Or to put it slightly differently, that the good will is to bring our wishes in accordance with the world. Given that no necessary connections exist between situations in the world this means that we must let our wishes be in accordance with whatever state of the world we find ourselves in. Our wishes should harmonize with the accidental way in which the world is, with "what happens and is the case" (6.41) and makes up the world. But this, of course, means that we must effectively put an end to our wishes, must stop our craving.

At this point it might be helpful to introduce another distinction, that between the absolute, or metaphysical, good and the individual good. This distinction is analogous to that between the metaphysical subject and the individual subject. The good is an attribute of the will. The absolute good then is an attribute of the metaphysical will, the "alien will" that Wittgenstein says we feel we depend on, and that he does not hesitate to call by the name that modern philosophy seems to have almost forgotten:

That is why we have the feeling that we are dependent on an alien will. *However this may be*, we *are* in any case dependent in a certain sense and that on which we depend we can call God. (8/7/16)

So the good in an absolute sense is an attribute of God's Will, and this is indeed the way in which Wittgenstein explains the matter to Waismann. Discussing Schlick's conception of ethics, Wittgenstein says:

Schlick says that in theological ethics there were two conceptions of the essence of the good: according to the more superficial interpretation the good is good because God wills it; according to the deeper interpretation God wills the good because it is good. I think that the first conception is the deeper one: good is what God orders. (*Ludwig Wittgenstein and the Vienna Circle*, 17/12/30)[38]

God's Will, which in effect can be equated with the absolute good, is not transcendent in an absolute sense. It is tied to the world, but in a particular way. A few weeks after Wittgenstein made the entry on the "alien will" he notes:

> How things stand, is God.
> God is, how things stand. (1/8/16)

How are we to understand this? In view of the identification of God's Will and the absolute good, we cannot interpret "how things stand" as a reference to some particular, actual state of the world. Rather, what is intended here is the world as the totality of logical possibilities, that is, "however things stand."[39] Given that much, it follows that the world, in the sense just indicated, is good. Not this particular world that we find ourselves in, or another one that we should strive to realize, or yet another one from which we fell by original sin, but the world as such, as the totality of all that is possible, is good. This can be connected with what Wittgenstein in the "Lecture on Ethics" describes as one of his paradigmatic ethical experiences, that there is a world at all:

> I believe the best way of describing it [that is, this experience, m.s.] is to say that when I have it *I wonder at the existence of the world.* And I am then inclined to use such phrases as "how extraordinary that anything should exist" or "how extraordinary that the world should exist." ("Lecture on Ethics," 8)[40]

The existence of the world, of any world at all, is considered to be an ethical "fact" and in view of the above we may venture to say that this is so because the world is the manifestation of the metaphysical will and that this being the Will of God it is intrinsically good. Similar thoughts are expressed in the *Tractatus*. In 6.432 Wittgenstein emphasizes that we are not speaking here of the world in the sense of some actual or possible realization:

> *How* the world is, is completely immaterial for what is higher. God does not reveal himself *in* the world. (6.432)

Rather, it is the existence of the world as such that is ethically relevant: "Not *how* the world is, is the mystical, but *that* it is" (6.44). So we must conclude that if we consider the will as the metaphysical will its ethical content is completely independent of the accidental way the world is or might be.

The Happy Life

Let us now return to the individual will. The ethically just individual will is one that is in harmony with the world, with whatever world it finds itself in. So the ethical task for the individual will is no other than to be in harmony with the metaphysical will, that is, with God's Will:

In order to live happily I must be in agreement with the world. And this is what "being happy" *means*. Then I am, so to speak, in agreement with that alien will on which I seem to depend. That means: "I am doing the Will of God." (8/7/16)

Being in harmony with the world is being happy: happiness is not a consequence thereof. But since the way the world is, is accidental, this implies that the happy life cannot depend on any particular feature of it. And that means that:

The only life that is happy is the life that can do without the comforts of the world.
    To it the comforts of the world are just so many graces of fate. (13/8/16)

This last remark should not be misunderstood: Wittgenstein is not advertising some kind of fatalism or pessimism.[41] He is not admonishing us to be content with whatever circumstances we find ourselves in, even though these leave a lot to be desired. What Wittgenstein is saying here goes much further. The point is not that we should accept that what we wish for cannot always be realized, but that we should wish no more, that we should abandon all our craving that is directed to something particular in the world. It is not just the sorrows of the world but also its amenities that bind us, and both kinds of bonds should be abandoned. Wittgenstein's message here is no other than the biblical "Not my will, but Thine." Of course, there are also important differences between Wittgenstein's views and those of orthodox Christianity, the most relevant in the present context being that whereas according to the orthodox conception God's Will is directed at a certain situation, God's Will as Wittgenstein views it, namely, as the totality of all that is possible, never takes on any particular situation as its aim.

    The individual will and its ethical task, and the metaphysical will and its ethical relevance, are thus clearly connected. The metaphysical will manifests itself in the world, but in any world, not in some world or aspect thereof in particular. In what world an individual finds himself is not relevant. It is simply the bare fact of this manifestation, that is, that there is a world at all, that is considered to be ethically good. Why should this be so? Why should the fact that there is a world be ethically significant, especially since nothing in the world, whatever way it is, inherits this significance? The answer lies in the fact that the existence of the world sets a task for the individual willing subject. That there is a world offers the individual the opportunity to take on and realize his ethical task, that of harmonizing with the world, that is, that of abandoning all individual wishing, all craving for external objects, situations or events.[42] It is with this idea of life itself as the penultimate ethical task that we should view Wittgenstein's rejection of suicide as what he calls "the elementary sin" (10/1/17). Committing suicide is committing the elementary sin because it constitutes an absolute rejection of the very task that life presents us with. It is a refusal to accept our fate:

> In this sense God would simply be fate, or, what is the same thing: the world, which is independent of our will. (8/7/16)

God, fate, the world, or, as 6.4321, has it: "the problem." The facts that surround us and that we ourselves constitute as well are our task. They are what we should come to grips with, what we should accept and be in harmony with. The fulfillment of this task is exactly the harmonizing of the individual will with the metaphysical will, of the individual will and the world. Whoever is able to live in this way, leads what Wittgenstein calls "the happy life," or, with a Schopenhauerean phrase, "the life of knowledge" (see 13/8/16).[43] Such a life is not a fact in the world in and of itself:

> The solution of the problem of life one can tell by the vanishing of the problem. (Is this not the reason why people to whom the meaning of life after a long period of doubt became clear, why these people then could not say what this meaning consisted in?) (6.521)

The solution of the problem of life is an intrinsic aspect of the way in which we are in the world, of the way we act. It shows itself in the way in which we view the world, that is, in our will, which is an attitude toward the world.

In the conversation with Waismann from which we already quoted above, Wittgenstein expresses the same point somewhat differently. To Waismann's question whether the existence of the world is connected with the ethical, Wittgenstein answers:

> People have felt that there is a connection here and they have expressed it as follows: the Father has created the world, the Son (or the Word emanating from God) is the ethical. That the Godhead is conceived of as divided and, again, as one, indicates that there is a connection here. (*Ludwig Wittgenstein and the Vienna Circle*, 17/12/30)

This echoes the following passage from the *Notebooks*:

The meaning of life, that is, the meaning of the world, we can call God. And connect with this the image of God as a father. (11/6/16)

That this expresses the same point as the passages from the *Tractatus* quoted above is evident if we observe, with John Moran, that the Son has come into the world.[44] In this way the world, that is, the contingent whole of situations and events that constitutes our life, and the ethical, that is, the necessity of value, are joined, without identification but in an intrinsic manner nonetheless. As the Father and the Son are distinct yet the same, so are the ethical and the factual.

This brings us somewhat closer to a positive view of what the good will according to Wittgenstein is. In the *Notebooks* Wittgenstein uses the phrase "the happy life" for the life of a person who harmonizes with the world. It should by now be clear that a hedonistic interpretation of this expression is way off the mark.[45] Also it is clear that this state of harmonizing with the world is not something that can be described; it is not a situation that can be identified with a particular set of facts in the world. Ethics is ineffable, not just in the sense that all attempts to formulate ethical principles necessarily result in meaningless sentences, but also in the stronger sense that the ethical ideal itself, the state that is the fulfillment of the ethical assignment, cannot be described (30/7/16). Given that in the ontology of the *Tractatus* everything that is or can be the case is describable, this means that the happy life cannot be identified with something in the world. Since the happy life is the life that results when the will of the individual harmonizes with the metaphysical will that manifests itself in the existence of the world (any world, not this or that world in particular), it is not something over and above our actions, nor can it be equated with some particular (kind of) action. The happy life, like the will, is an intrinsic aspect of our actions, an attitude of the subject to the world. Ethically speaking we face a choice between trying to mold the world according to our desires and detaching ourselves from it, refraining from wishing and craving.

It is in this sense that Wittgenstein's conception of the ultimate ethical goal is comparable to that of Schopenhauer. For the latter it all turns around the negation of the will. The will, which as the noumenal will is blind and undirected, by manifesting itself in the world reaches in the human mind a state of self-consciousness that enables it to see through itself. According to Schopenhauer this results in the insight that the ultimate task is self-denial. This aspect of Schopenhauer's theory has met with little sympathy. Some have disregarded it altogether; others have argued that this aspect of Schopenhauer's philosophy is germane to its core.[46] And it is true, of course, that it is not a logical consequence of Schopenhauer's theory of the will and its relationship to the world that the ultimate spiritual goal should be the negation of the will. But the relation is also not completely accidental.

In the case of Schopenhauer the connection is that the world as representation is the objectification of the will. In the multiplicity of phenomena, the one noumenon manifests itself and thereby gains self-consciousness. This self-consciousness is an awareness, a knowledge of a struggle, of pain and suffering, caused by the constant battle of separated individuals unaware of their fundamental unseparatedness. Awareness of the illusory nature of separated phenomena leads to renouncement of this strife for manifestation, to renouncement of the will.

For Wittgenstein, it seems, it is the logical contingency of the world that is the key factor. The fact that no necessary relationship can exist between me, that is, my will, and the way the world is, implies that nothing in the world that I can bring about (and, of course, there is a lot that I can and do bring about) can have any intrinsic significance. Ethical contingency and atomism, the logical analogue of separatedness, in Wittgenstein's vision are two sides of the same coin. Hence, this world, which is the world of language and thought, has to be renounced, not literally, but in the sense that as a view of reality it has to be balanced, if not superseded, by another view, the ethical view, which is that of the world as—limited—whole. Wittgenstein's spiritual ideal of harmonizing with the world in the end comes down to much the same thing as Schopenhauer's negation of the will. The individual will, confronted with the world in which it finds itself, by harmonizing with it neutralizes itself, silences its urge and directedness.

Living in the Present

The happy life is also described by Wittgenstein as "life in the present." This living in the present, which is a familiar way of describing the kind of existential condition that Wittgenstein is after, is characterized by the absence of both fear and hope: "Whoever lives in the present lives without fear and hope" (14/7/16).[47] This living without fear or hope is the result of living without desires. If our will does not attach itself to any future situation, there is nothing to fear about the future and neither is there any hope to be entertained. It thus involves abstaining from both positive and negative expectations. However, it would be wrong to conclude that there would be no joy in such a life. After all, Wittgenstein describes it as the "happy" life. But what makes it happy does not lie in either the future or the past, but in the present itself, in the way we exist and act now.

The mirror image of living without fear and hope is living without guilt. If we do not attach any intrinsic ethical significance to any contingent situations or relations between them, this holds for the past as much as it holds for the future. That means that living in the present we need not feel guilty about our actions in the past. Of course, this immediately raises the question whether such a position is consistent with the idea of personal moral obligations and responsibilities. To this problem we turn below.

Guilt and repentance do play an important role in Wittgenstein's biographical background. And the characterization of the happy life as life in the present certainly is connected with this. Wittgenstein once said that the concept of God as a judge is one that he could relate to, in contrast to the concept of God as creator.[48] In the literature there has been some discussion about the relationship between various biographical facts, in particular Wittgenstein's homosexuality, and his conception of ethics.[49] It is clear that Wittgenstein's homosexuality presented a problem for him. And the problem was not merely one of being homosexual in a society that was quite repressive in this respect, and of being brought up in a way that left no room for it. For Wittgenstein, his homosexuality, like almost every other aspect of his personal life, was basically an ethical problem. In this sense there is a clear and direct relationship between this aspect of his personal life and his ethical views. However, there is no reason to think that it was only, or even primarily, his homosexuality that shaped Wittgenstein's ethical views. For, with his characteristic single-mindedness and seriousness, Wittgenstein treated every aspect of his personal daily life as belonging to the sphere of the ethical. And that being so, there is no reason to attach a special importance to this aspect of Wittgenstein's life. Moreover, from a systematic point of view Wittgenstein's ethics is quite universal and the particular facts about his life that no doubt were of the greatest importance psychologically speaking nevertheless seem to have left hardly any systematic traces.[50]

It may be useful to make a terminological distinction between "ethics" and "morality."[51] The former is concerned with values that are intrinsic to our actions; the latter is occupied with value in an external sense, that is, with value in terms of consequences and causes. The moral point of view is the one in which our actions are viewed in time, connected with the future by their consequences and with the past by their motives. By taking the moral point of view we locate ourselves in time, view ourselves as caught in the web of temporal and causal relationships between events, which ends with our death. The ethical point of view, by contrast, recognizes just the present of the action itself, judging its intrinsic ethical character. Consequently, someone who is able to live according to the ethical point of view and who makes the intrinsic value of his actions his primary concern, becomes detached from the bonds of time and in that sense becomes "immortal":

> If one understands by eternity not infinite temporal duration but timelessness, then he who lives in the present lives eternally. (6.4311)

The association between ethical value and "timelessness" [*Unzeitlichkeit*] is familiar from the tradition and it comes up at several places in Wittgenstein's earlier work.

First of all, it permeates Wittgenstein's description of one of his paradigmatic ethical experiences, namely, his "wondering at the existence of the world" ("Lecture on Ethics," 8). This way of looking at the world, or rather of experiencing it, is what in 6.45 is called "The view of the world sub specie aeterni." This should be understood in line with what is said in 6.4311. It is not looking at the world in terms of infinite duration, as we do if we embrace the perspective of the eternity of an afterlife in an orthodox Christian sense. For that point of view, Wittgenstein remarks, is not ethically relevant at all:

> Not only is the temporal immortality of the human soul, that is, its eternal survival after death, in no way guaranteed, but this assumption moreover does not achieve at all what one wants to accomplish with it. Or is some mystery solved by my eternal survival? Is not this eternal life as mysterious as the present one? (6.4312)

Eternity in the sense of an actual infinite duration does not solve "the mystery of life," as the latter does not turn around the actual finiteness of our individual existence. Nothing in the temporal world, being of necessity a contingent whole of contingent situations, can provide this answer; hence Wittgenstein concludes that:

> The solution of the mystery of life in space and time lies *outside* space and time. (6.4312)

Unlike temporal immortality, timelessness does not signal a horizontal movement, but rather a vertical one. It means that we look at the world not merely as a contingent whole of temporally and causally connected situations, events, and actions, but as something of which the existence as such has an intrinsic ethical significance. However, it does not involve a negation or a disregard of the temporal nature of our existence. This is shown by what Wittgenstein says about death:

> Death is not an event of life. Death one does not experience. . . . Our life is as endless as our field of vision is limitless. (6.4311)

As an event in the world of facts, our death is an event like any other. But viewed from within the subject, it is not an event at all: I cannot experience my death, though others can. Again we hit on something that has essentially a dual nature, like the will that can be known as manifestation in others, but also as manifesting itself in myself. Likewise, death, my death, although I cannot experience it, is nevertheless very real. Its necessity forms the temporal dimension of my existence, as a limit, never to be reached, but a defining characteristic nonetheless. From a logical point of view, my possibilities are infinite, but my actualities are finite. Viewed in that way, my death is the limit of my existence, and it is in this limit that the ethical dimension of my life becomes acute. The infinitude of logical possibilities would render the ethical task that the world constitutes meaningless; it would turn it into a merely theoretical insight. The limit of death is what makes it concrete, inescapable, a task that I have to confront.

Again we see that ethics and logic constitute two different perspectives, two ways of interacting with reality. In the *Notebooks* these two ways of looking at the world occur at several places, for example in the following entry:

> If I have been contemplating the stove and one says to me: but now all you know is the stove, then my result does indeed seem petty. For it represents the matter as if I had studied the stove as one amongst the many, many things of the world. But when I was contemplating the stove, *it* was my world, and everything else pales in comparison.
>
> (In general many good points, but bad in details.) (8/10/16)

This passage contrasts two ways of looking at an object in the world. First of all, there is the ordinary way that an object can be perceived and studied. Here it appears as one among a multitude of others, that is, as something that is located in space and time, something that has certain connections with certain objects, but not with others, and so on. This is the matter-of-fact way of looking at the world and what inhabits it that constitutes our daily life and that we employ in scientific and everyday discourse. It is the view of the discursive, that is, thinking and speaking, mind. But there is, according to Wittgenstein, also another way of being confronted with objects, in which they "represent" the world, or, as Wittgenstein put it on 7/10/16, a way of confronting them "in such a way that they have the whole world as background." Here spatial and temporal connections and divisions no longer constitute the glasses through which we look at the world. It is a point of view that no longer focuses on the contingent and the temporal, but that fastens onto the necessary and, in ethical terms, the eternal.

The second of the experiences, which Wittgenstein in his "Lecture on Ethics" associates with absolute value, is also related to the atemporal:

I will mention another experience straightaway that I also know and that others of you might be acquainted with: it is, what one might call, the experience of feeling *absolutely* safe. I mean the state of mind in which one is inclined to say "I am safe, nothing can injure me, whatever happens." ("Lecture on Ethics," 8)

This experience turns around the detachment from all possible consequences of one's actions and therewith around the complete disappearance of all contingent and temporal relations between situations. The feeling of safety that Wittgenstein seems to refer to should not be understood in an everyday sense. Of course, anything can happen to me, and much of it will hurt me (and some of it might do me good, also), but not in an ethical sense. If I feel absolutely safe it is not because, considering contingencies, I think that nothing will happen to me, but because, ethically speaking, nothing of what will in fact happen to me will make a difference. In that sense I can feel (and be) safe from the future and hence live in the present.

In the foregoing we have indicated in some detail what Wittgenstein's views on the ethically good life amount to. The resulting picture raises at least two questions. First of all, it remains quite unclear what has become of more conventional morality in this lofty, "un-worldly" (but not "other-worldly") picture. Ethics deals with the atemporal, ethical dimension of action and not with contingent causal connections between situations. But most of our ordinary everyday moral prescriptions and regulations are concerned precisely with such relationships. Does this mean that there is no place for morality in Wittgenstein's ethics?

The second question is the one that we started out with: What is the relation between ethics and the world? It can be cast in the form of the question after the notion of transcendence that Wittgenstein uses to characterize ethics in 6.421: "It is clear that ethics cannot be put into words. Ethics is transcendental." In what sense is ethics transcendental? Does Wittgenstein make a tacit appeal to a notion of a transcendent ethical reality, as is suggested by *Notebooks* 30/7/16, cited above? Or should "transcendental" in 6.421 be understood in a more or less Kantian sense?[52]

To these two questions we turn in the following two sections.

ETHICS AND MORALITY

The main problem to be discussed in this section concerns the relationship between morality and ethics. Morality refers to our everyday moral prescriptions and regulations; ethics is concerned with absolute values intrinsic to our actions. Morality hence deals with the relationships between our actions and other events and typically treats them as located in time and space. Ethics, by contrast, views our actions *sub specie aeterni*, as disentangled from the web of causal relationships. The problem is that there seems to be a fundamental, unbridgeable gulf between the two. No ethical considerations, it seems, can be made to have any bearing in the sphere of the moral. And that seems to imply that whatever Wittgenstein's ethics is concerned with it, it is not with how we should behave in an ordinary, moral sense of the word.

Compassion and the Other

More specifically, we may ask whether Wittgenstein's ethical views can have any consequences for how we should behave toward our fellow men. In the *Notebooks* we find an entry on precisely this issue that states the following:

Can there be an ethics if, apart from me, there is no living creature? If ethics is to be something fundamental: yes! (2/8/16)

This seems to give us Wittgenstein's answer to our question. If there is a relationship between ethics and morality, then it is not an intrinsic, that is, a necessary relationship. There is no sense in which ethics presupposes the existence of others or even a concept of the other, and hence it cannot be a necessary characteristic of ethics that it is concerned with how we should interact with others. But notice that this does not imply that there is no relationship between ethics and morality at all. The only thing that follows is that such a connection cannot be a necessary one. In one sense this is easy to see. Like that of myself, the existence of others, any others, is contingent. Hence absolute values cannot be intrinsically related to others. In a sense this observation implies in a straightforward way the complete detachment of ethics from any subject whatsoever. However, this should not be misinterpreted and be taken to mean that therefore subjects are not ethically responsible. The fact that there is no intrinsic relationship between contingent subjects and absolute ethical values, because there are situations without subjects in which nevertheless the values are still present, does not imply that in situations in which there are subjects, they and these values are also unrelated. The relationship may be a contingent one, but it is a real one nevertheless, if it exists.

So let us inquire whether such a relationship does in fact exist and if so, what its nature is. There is in Wittgenstein's thinking on these matters a kind of ambiguity, which is clearly manifested in the *Notebooks*, though not so much in the *Tractatus*. Despite the drastic separation of ethics and subjects that speaks from the passage quoted above, the *Notebooks* contain quite a number of other remarks that show that Wittgenstein was painfully aware of the fact that for so many people life constitutes a continuous source of suffering. And the admonition "Live happily!" (29/7/16) should not be taken as an exhortation to make oneself insensitive to the suffering in the world. As Wittgenstein remarks:

Suppose man could not exercise his will, but had to suffer all the misery of this world, then what could make him happy?

How can man be happy at all, since he cannot fend off the misery of this world?

Precisely through the life of knowledge.

. . .

The life of knowledge is the life that is happy despite the misery of the world. (13/8/16)

This life of knowledge is the life that results from harmonizing one's individual will with the metaphysical will, that is, with whatever state of the world one finds oneself in. This remark bespeaks a clear awareness of the misery and pain that life causes. And it is important to bear in mind here that for Wittgenstein "the world" here means the totality of all that is possible, not just the accidental and contingent jumble of situations that we actually find ourselves in. No matter how the world is, it is also a source of continuous suffering.

Another relevant observation to make here is that in the *Notebooks* Wittgenstein repeatedly speaks of others in a way that shows compassion, even in a quite literal sense: for example, when he speaks of there being in reality only one world soul (23/5/15) or when he recognizes the spirit of the snake and the lion as his own (15/10/16). The idea of a fundamental unity that embraces all living beings and even includes nonanimate nature is mentioned a little later:

Is this the solution of the puzzle why men have always believed that *one* spirit is common to the whole world?

And then it would be common also to the inanimate things.
(15/10/16)

This sentiment is clearly related to the ethical view of the world, to the view *sub specie aeterni*. It bears an obvious resemblance to Schopenhauer's position that compassion, based on the insight that each individual is but a manifestation of the noumenal will, is the basis for all morality. And it seems to imply that after all there is something that connects ethics and other human beings. But if that is so, how do these remarks relate to the one we cited above, which says that ethics is not intrinsically related to our attitude toward our fellow beings? This calls for a closer investigation of the distinction between necessary and accidental relationships in this realm.

Moral Consequences

We start from what constitutes the core of Wittgenstein's conception of the ethical, namely, the idea that the ethically good will is the one that is in harmony with the world and that the ethical goal therefore is to bring about this harmony by bringing one's individual will in line with the metaphysical will. This has important consequences. In effect, it means giving up our everyday individual selves, which after all consist in large part of our individual desires that are directed at particular objects and situations in the world.

The pattern that evolves is this. Being in the world, a person has to act. That is part and parcel of his existence.[53] Every act is good that is in harmony with the world and every act is bad that goes against how the world is. This means that every act of desire, of wishing some situation to be realized that is not actual, is intrinsically bad, since it is not in harmony with how the world is. Such an act of desire does not accept the world as given and a life that is lived according to such desires is not a happy one "despite the misery of the world."

It seems that some of the more obvious and fundamental moral strictures follow from this. To give just one simple, but rather fundamental example: the willful taking of a life in order to satisfy an individual need for bloodshed obviously is an act of desire that is disharmonious, which goes against what is given and which is hence intrinsically bad. But notice that the ethically negative character of such an act derives neither from its consequence nor from the motive per se. It is the act itself, or rather the will that manifests itself in that act, that is ethically at fault. Hence, it may happen that the "same" act—same, that is, with regard to its contingently describable aspects—is not ethically condemnable.

So the status of morality with regard to ethics appears to be an instrumental one and it may be helpful to indicate at this point some analogies with an entirely different tradition, namely, that of Buddhist thought.[54] Buddhist tradition starts from the Four Noble Truths: that life is suffering; that the cause of suffering is craving; that suffering can be put to an end by the stopping of craving; that craving can be stopped by walking the Eightfold Noble Path. Notice that this is reminiscent of Wittgenstein's views at least in the following sense. First of all, there is the idea that all of life is suffering and unavoidably so. Suffering is the inevitable outcome of life since it always ends in loss, sickness, death. No happiness is permanent and grief is always the final outcome. This sentiment is prominently present in Wittgenstein's thinking as well. Not just the *Tractatus* and the many remarks in the *Notebooks* bear witness to this, but also the reports from his private life are completely in line.[55] Secondly, the Buddhist view that craving is the root of all suffering and that hence it is craving that must be stopped if suffering is to come to an end, has an analogue in Wittgenstein's view of the harmonizing of the individual will with the world as the ultimate ethical goal. This implies that all one's individual desires have to be given up. Finally, there is even an analogy on the ontological level. The Buddhist philosophy of "dependent arising," which is concomitant with the spiritual insights expressed above, the view of the world as being in a constant state of flux without any enduring elements, is reflected in Wittgenstein's view of the world as a contingent whole of contingent situations.[56] And a similar analogy exists between the Buddhist *anātman* doctrine of the subject and Wittgenstein's Humean view of the self.

So there are some, admittedly general, similarities in the fundamental starting points. Let us now see whether such also exist when it comes to the relation with ordinary, everyday action. The Eightfold Noble Path, which must be followed for craving and hence suffering to stop, consists of what are called the "eight perfections": right views; right intentions; right speaking; right conduct; right livelihood; right effort; right mindfulness; right concentration.[57] Of these eight, it seems that only the last two can be justifiedly called spiritual or ethical in Wittgenstein's sense. The other six are moral and are properly viewed as instrumental with regard to attaining the final goal, the state of liberation, *Nirvāna*. The perfections of these moral virtues are necessary steps in the process that leads to the ultimate goal, but it would be mistaken to view them as constituting part of this goal. Attaining the final state of *Arahant*-ship, that is, the state of one who has attained *Nirvāna*, is something that these virtues lead up to, but that itself goes beyond them in a fundamental way. It should be noted, however, that calling the relationship between the perfections of the Path and the final state of liberation instrumental can be interpreted in various ways. One strong interpretation would be that moral virtues can be and should be cast away once the final goal is reached. This is a view that ultimately regards morality as a hindrance rather than as a help. A less radical interpretation would be content with stating the categorical difference between the moral perfections and true liberation, but would stress that even when the final goal is reached, the perfection of morality goes on, necessarily so since not complying with these precepts would be irreconcilable with having attained the final state of *Arahant*-ship.[58]

The parallels with Wittgenstein are striking. For him, too, attaining the final ethical goal, that is, being in harmony with the metaphysical will, is like an escape, a liberation from the world in time and space by living in the eternal present. And the same view can be found in Schopenhauer: the

230   *Ethics*

only salvation is to be found in the renunciation of the will, in the abolishment of the personal noumenon.[59] And the relationship between "ordinary" conventional morality and the supreme ethical goal is an instrumental one, just like the relation between the perfection of virtues and the final liberation in Buddhism. Viewed from a different angle, one might regard observation of the ordinary moral precepts as a practical consequence of the nature of the ethical goal. Morally wrong acts are typically the result of desires that spring forth from our individual selves. They are directed toward the realization of certain contingent situations, often at the cost of the well-being of others. Thus, they are fundamentally disharmonious and present obstacles on our way toward attaining the state of harmony with the world. Again, the abolishing of individual desires is not ethically correct because of its consequences or motives, which are after all merely contingently related to it, but because it is the ethical goal itself.

Notice that this is not in conflict with what Wittgenstein claims in the "Lecture on Ethics," when he states that:

If, for instance, in our world-book [that is, a description of the world given by an omniscient being, *m.s.*] we read the description of a murder with all its details physical and psychological, the mere description of these facts will contain nothing that we could call an *ethical* proposition. ("Lecture on Ethics," 6)

Every description consists of meaningful sentences. And meaningful sentences are contingent sentences, depicting contingent situations. So whatever evaluative sentences were contained in this "world-book," they would, of necessity, be descriptions of relative values. Relative value is indeed to be found in the world and can be described in the world-book, since it is as contingent as the facts that make it up and the sentences that describe it:

. . . so far as facts and propositions are concerned there is only relative value and relative good, right, and so on. ("Lecture on Ethics," 7)

However, in no way does it follow that what is described in this contingent way for that reason is ethically neutral. Whether something that is described in a meaningful way is ethically speaking right or wrong, is a harmonious or a disharmonious act, is not itself again something that can be described or that follows from this meaningful description. But that does not mean that it does not have an absolute ethical value. In fact every act we undertake has this ethical dimension. It is just that this absolute dimension cannot be expressed in language. It is in this sense that Wittgenstein maintains that a description of all the details of a murder does not contain anything ethical at all. But this should certainly not be taken to imply that the act described, the murder, does not have an ethical status. It does, but what that status is cannot be derived from the description of it. It seems that we can conclude that absolute ethics in the Wittgensteinian sense is inherently in the world, conceived as a conglomerate of contingent facts. Absolute ethical values do not consist of contingent relations between contingent situations, nor do they lie in certain situations being the case or not. But every situation, every act has an intrinsic ethical value. By so permeating the world, drenching its constituents with absolute value, ethics is also related to conventional morality. Not in the more commonsense way that morally right behavior is ethically right behavior, but rather in the way that a destination is connected with the path or perhaps the many different paths that lead up to it.

Let us now turn to the more specific question of how Wittgenstein's views on ethics are related to our moral attitudes toward others. As was already remarked above, there seems to be a certain tension in Wittgenstein's thinking here, a tension that we can also detect in Schopenhauer and in Buddhist thought. On the one hand, we have seen that ethics is not intrinsically connected with the existence of others. This follows in fact from the unsubstantiality of the self, the Humean view on the subject, according to which this is a mere bundle of contingent experiences, feelings, perceptions, and desires. The nature of the ethical ideal, harmonizing the individual will with the metaphysical, world-will, also does not place the individual subject in the center. And it is, at least on the face of it, not an "activist" ideal. It emphatically denies that ethical values can be brought into existence in the world by actively pursuing certain goals. On the other hand, there is also an underlying notion of a fundamental unity of what appear as separate individuals, the idea of one spirit, one world-soul, which also can be said to have its roots in the specific view on the self that Wittgenstein subscribes to, and this idea naturally leads to compassion with others.

A similar tension can be found in Schopenhauer. Morality, according to Schopenhauer, is based on compassion, on the ability to correlate the suffering of others, of which we can have only indirect knowledge, with our own suffering, which we experience firsthand. Such a view, which appears to involve an active participation with others and hence with the world, seems at odds with what according to Schopenhauer constitutes the ultimate goal: the renunciation of the will. For how can we, on the one hand, renounce our individual will, and yet on the other, act on the basis of our compassion for others?

The Buddhist tradition, too, seems to bear witness to a similar problem. One of the main differences between the *Theravāda* and *Mahāyāna* traditions in Buddhist thinking is reflected in the difference between their respective ideals: the *Arahant* versus the *Bodhisattva*. The *Arahant* is the person who has reached the final goal, who by walking the Eightfold Noble Path has cast off the world and has entered the final state of *Nirvāna*. He has attained the highest knowledge and is perfect in wisdom. The *Bodhisattva* is characterized not just by having attained this state of knowledge and wisdom, but also by compassion. Although he is entitled, so to speak, to enter *Nirvāna*, he does not do so, out of compassion for others who are still struggling. He has vowed not to enter *Nirvāna* until the last sentient being has reached the state of ultimate liberation. The difference between these two ideals reflects a tension between, on the one hand, the insight into the illusory character of the self, which is part of the perfect knowledge, and on the other hand, the compassion for others, which seems to presuppose the reality, the hardness, of the other as a subject. In a certain sense the conflict is irreconcilable and in much of the *Mahāyāna*-literature, especially in the *Mādhyamika*-tradition, which started with *Nāgārjuna*, the contradiction is accepted as a starting point for reaching a higher form of insight.[60]

It is the tension described above that lies at the root of an objection that has been brought against Wittgenstein's view on ethics, namely, that it leads to a passive, fatalistic attitude that leaves no room for an active moral involvement with others.[61] One suggestion is that this follows from Wittgenstein's ontology, more in particular from the nature of the situations that he acknowledges.[62] Situations, the argument goes, are essentially physical entities, parts of a physical world (in a broad sense, including biology). But what would be needed for ethics to be concerned with morality, especially in relationship to others, is a notion of a social situation, that is, a social world involving subjects that are psychologically and socially real.

That this charge of fatalism is unfounded should be clear by now.[63] For, as we have argued above, ethics is connected with morality, albeit not in the usual sense. And the ethical ideal of the *Tractatus*, when practiced in the world, has concrete practical consequences for our being in the world, some of which are of a moral nature. And certainly quite a number of these moral consequences concern our interaction with others. Furthermore, the idea that the ontology of the *Tractatus* is one of physical objects and situations has to be rejected for several reasons. For one thing, the quotation from the "Lecture on Ethics" given above, in which Wittgenstein speaks of the "description of a murder with all its details physical *and psychological*" (emphasis added), makes clear that Wittgenstein himself did not consider facts to be just physical. Furthermore, the states of affairs that all situations are built from cannot be physical facts, on pain of contradiction with their logical independence. For physical facts are, by their very nature, located in space and time and hence not logically independent.

But there is also a more fundamental reason for rejecting the charge of moral passivity or fatalism. The fundamental opposition that lies at the heart of the *Tractatus* and that is also present in many remarks in the *Notebooks* is not that between physical facts and social facts, between a physical self and a social self. Rather, it is the opposition between two ways of viewing the world, two ways of placing oneself in the world and of interacting with it. This distinction, which is crucial for a proper understanding of how in Wittgenstein's view ethics and the world are related, is that between viewing the world from amidst the world, as a complex consisting of distinct objects and facts, and viewing the world from its ethical limit, *sub specie aeterni* as a *whole* (6.45). On the level of the subject this distinction reappears as that between the world from the point of view of the individual, psychological subject, which is in the world as a subject among other subjects, and the world viewed by the metaphysical subject, which is not in the world, but constitutes its limit.

The ethical dimension of this distinction is the following. The ethical ideal involves the dissolving of the individual subject as will in the metaphysical subject as will. In other words, part of the ethical goal is the replacement of the point of view of the individual, that is, the view of the world as a collection of distinct individuals, by the view of the world as a whole. Or to phrase it in yet another way: the ethical goal implies that in an ethical sense, in the ethical dimension, the distinction between my own individual self and others as individual selves should be abandoned. But this means that my attainment of the ultimate state, my liberation from the world, is necessarily tied to the liberation of others, in the sense that my liberation cannot be complete if it does not involve that of others. This consequence is reminiscent of the *Bodhisattva* ideal of the *Mahāyāna* tradition. But that being so, it follows directly that the desire-less, noncraving attitude toward the acts that I have to perform in order to stay alive, which after all is a necessary condition for my attainment of the ultimate state, extends to others in this sense that the life of others, being the presupposition of their liberation, is directly related to that of myself.

Summing up, we have seen that certain moral instructions and regulations are related to the ethical ideal of the *Tractatus*; that they are instrumental with regard to that ideal in the sense that following them is not the same as fulfilling this ideal; but that at the same time they are necessary in an ethical sense and can be followed in a desire-less, noncraving manner when they are performed from the point of view of the world *sub specie aeterni*.

Thus we conclude that ethics and morality are strongly connected after all, at least when the scope of morality is not extended too far. The connection rests on the possibility of viewing the world also in a different way than as a world of distinct objects and situations located in space and time and interconnected by contingent relationships, that is, different from the way in which the world appears to us in language and thought. And Wittgenstein's starting point is that this other way of viewing the world, and hence of interacting with is, exists, is at least as much real as the more common one. For after all:

> The unsayable, however, does exist. This *shows* itself; it is the mystical. (6.522)

"WORLD AND LIFE AS ONE"

Let us now, finally, turn to our initial question concerning the relationship between the ethics of the *Tractatus* and its ontology. To what extent does the ethical theory determine what is the proper interpretation of the ontology?

It will be evident from the above that the interpretation we have offered of the ethical views that Wittgenstein endorses in the *Tractatus*-period presupposes a strong relationship between ethics and the world. The liberation from the world that is the ultimate ethical goal is not a liberation in a spatio-temporal sense. This is evident once we realize that such a liberation would be the realization of a contingent situation and hence could have no intrinsic value. Recall also Wittgenstein's remark that suicide is the ultimate sin. Hence the idea that the ethics of the *Tractatus* is a form of escapism or fatalism is completely unfounded. The liberation from the world must be brought about while being in the world, yet does not consist in bringing about any particular situation in the world. To liberate oneself is to adopt a particular attitude toward the world: the view of the world *sub specie aeterni*, the view of the metaphysical subject. And appearances notwithstanding, this ethical goal has practical consequences of a moral nature.

The question to address now is how this interpretation can be reconciled with the ethically contingent character of the world, that is, with the transcendental status of ethics. Evidently, this can be done only given a specific interpretation of the ontology. Here we see how the interpretation of the ethics offered in this chapter may be connected with the interpretation of the ontology as it was discussed in Chapters 2 and 3.

The Linguistic Nature of Transcendence

Above we claimed that in the *Tractatus* the possibility of ethics presupposes the possibility of viewing the world from two different perspectives, namely, that of the individual, psychological subject and that of the metaphysical subject. In the latter the world shows its ethical dimension; in the former the world appears as it can be described in language and hence may appear in thought. Given that the ethical view is connected with our being in the world in a very concrete and practical sense, this distinction is not one between two separate ontological domains, one that of empirical reality and the other "other-worldly" and transcendent. Rather what is at stake here are two different ways of viewing what is the same in some fundamental but not cognitively explicable sense. In other words, the notion of transcendence that the *Tractatus* appeals to is not an ontological one. And neither is it epistemological, at least not in the traditional, Kantian sense of the word. As was argued in Chapter 2, the *Tractatus* gives the Kantian program a linguistic turn. Consequently, the very notion of transcendence changes as well. So, ethics is transcendental not because values are outside the world, in some otherworldly, platonic realm, nor because they cannot be grasped in thought, but because ethics "cannot be said." There are values and they are in the world, but not in the same way as contingent objects and situations are. And they are accessible, also for the individual subject, albeit not by means of its discursive powers of language and thought.

It is worth noting that Wittgenstein sometimes explicitly refers to the linguistically transcendent character of ethics when he motivates what he is doing. One example can be found in the letter to Ficker, which was cited in Chapter 1, where he states that ". . . everything of which *many* nowadays are blethering, I have defined in my book by being silent about it." And ten years later, at about the time he delivered the "Lecture on Ethics," he says to Waismann:

I think it is definitely important that all the prattle about ethics—whether there is insight, whether value exists, whether the good can be defined—be put to an end. (*Ludwig Wittgenstein and the Vienna Circle*, 30/12/29)

By placing ethics outside the realm of the meaningful, Wittgenstein tries to safeguard it from argumentation and disputes, dogmatism and feuds. There is absolute value, but it is not accessible for the discursive mind and the corresponding linguistic ways of interacting with the world. This presupposes a linguistic interpretation of the ontology, which implies that such notions as "transcendence," "immanence," and "transcendentality" need to be reinterpreted in a similar way.

From a critical Kantian perspective, the transcendental in the *Tractatus* is logic. This is clear from the discussion in 5.6 and following about the metaphysical subject and from the many passages concerning logic, logical space, and substance. The metaphysical subject is explicitly characterized as a limit of the world in 5.632. The same term is used in connection with logic in 5.61, which identifies the limits of logic with the limits of the world. That logical space is the totality of all that is possible is evident among others from 2.11, 3.4, 3.42, and 4.463. And substance is characterized is an analogous way. Being the totality of objects (2.021), it is what all worlds have in common (2.022); hence it contains all the possibilities that logical space contains. Clearly, logic, logical space, substance, and metaphysical subject are notions on the same level, namely, that of the transcendental in the Kantian sense of the term but with a distinct linguistic, logical twist. In effect, 5.6 and following can also be read as Wittgenstein's attempt to make clear what remains of the traditional epistemological content of the notion of a subject once this linguistic turn has been taken.

Given that logic is the central transcendental notion of the tractarian system, what remains to be explained is why ethics is characterized as transcendental as well. In 6.421 this is stated in so many words ("Ethics is transcendental"), and in 6.43 we find the familiar association of transcendentality with the notion of limits ("If good or bad willing changes the world, it can only change the limits of the world"). Here the notion of the limits of the world occurs not in a logical setting, but in an ethical one.[64] Logic, being a limit of the world, determines what is possible, but not what is actual. Likewise ethics, a limit of the world as well, also is concerned only with the world as a totality. Hence 6.43 claims that the world of the happy person, the world of the one who fulfills the ultimate ethical task, is entirely different from that of the unhappy person, but not because it is a different world in a factual, or even in a logical sense. It is the same reality but a different world.

Here the distinction between the two ways of viewing the world becomes relevant. On the one hand, there is the world as the totality of all that is possible, the world viewed from the midst of things. The limits of this world are given by logic, or, using the vocabulary of ontology, by the substance of which every world is made. But there is also the world viewed *sub specie aeterni*, the world as a limited whole, of which the limits are determined by the ethical will. It is crucial that these are not two different worlds in an ontological sense, that is, two different realities, but rather two different ways of viewing the one thing that confronts us. It is two different ways of interacting with it, and, in an extended sense of "knowing," also two different ways of knowing it: discursive knowledge versus ethical knowledge.

With these two different ways of viewing the world are associated two different notions of transcendentality. The world viewed as a totality of contingent situations is logical space, the actualities and possibilities that we can talk, and hence think and reason, about. Everything that logical space contains can be expressed by a meaningful sentence, that is, can be thought, and every meaningful sentence, that is, every thought, depicts a situation in this space. It is of this linguistically, logically conceived world that logic constitutes the limit. The ethical view of the world is concerned with the intrinsic ethical values of our actions and hence its limit is the ethical will. For it is the character of our will, the way our will does or does not attach itself to situations in the world, that determines its ethical status, or as Wittgenstein also phrases it, its meaning.

The connection between ethics, logic, and reality is as follows. Ethical value is in the world. It is an intrinsic aspect of our actions and our actions are clearly part of the world. In this sense the world has an ethical dimension and value is immanent. But these intrinsic ethical properties cannot be expressed in language and hence in the world as it appears in our language, and hence in our thought, value is not to be found. In that sense value is transcendent. Immanence and transcendence are logical and not ontological categories, since the world and its limits is a logical and not an ontological notion.[65] Only in this way can the *Tractatus* be read as a coherent whole.

The way in which Wittgenstein analyzes the world of language and thought is not just negatively motivated by his wish to safeguard the ethical from discursive theorizing. It also plays a positive role with regard to his ethical views. Attaining the ultimate goal, liberation from the world, is furthered by various aspects of the ontological theory, in particular the illusory character of the individual self and the ethically contingent character of facts and the relations between them.[66] A "right view" (6.54) concerning their nature should lead someone who is nevertheless convinced of the existence of ethical values to look for them outside the realm of what can be said and thought, outside the realm of spatio-temporally located situations and the contingent relationships between them. Since the world is essentially a linguistic notion, this does not mean that he should look for values in an ontologically transcendent realm. Hence his attention should stay fixed on what confronts him here and now. At that point the Schopenhauerean heritage becomes an essential aspect of Wittgenstein's method. The notion of the will as an intrinsic aspect of our actions, as something that, without being located in the world as an independently identifiable thing or situation, nevertheless drenches whatever we can find there, and that is the bearer of absolute value, plays a crucial role at this juncture. And it is the combination of the dependency of the individual willing subject on the metaphysical willing subject with the ethically contingent character of the world, from which Wittgenstein's (and Schopenhauer's) interpretation of the ultimate ethical goal follows almost immediately: agreement of the individual will with the metaphysical will on which it is dependent, that is, the Will of God, with its concomitant detachment of the will from the world.

Ethical Experience

It should be noted that probably this picture will appeal only to someone who is convinced of the existence of absolute ethical values in the first place.[67] Neither the *Tractatus* nor the *Notebooks* contains any argument or reasoning to establish the existence of values or their absolute character. (Analogously, there is no argument for the absolute status of logic either.) In other words, the entire construction is based on a certain kind of experience. This is not experience of actual situations, but the kind of experience that Wittgenstein describes in his "Lecture on Ethics," that is, experience of the ethical dimension of the world. For the reality of the world viewed *sub specie aeterni* is not something that can be argued for, let alone proven, from within the view of the world from the midst of things. The gap between these two, even though not an ontological one, is categorical and cannot be bridged by any kind of experience or reasoning or argument that can be given on the discursive side of it. In this sense, one might say, the ontological and linguistic theory of the *Tractatus* is independent from its ethical views. One may very well share Wittgenstein's views on meaning, logic, and language without subscribing to his ethical convictions. This holds for Schopenhauer as well. Like Wittgenstein's remarks on ethics in the *Tractatus*, the last part of *Die Welt als Wille und Vorstellung*, about the renunciation of the will, quite often is neglected or dismissed as not of systematic interest, even by people who are in agreement with the other parts.[68] And this is certainly not due to a lack of logical acumen or consistency on the part of those who do not agree. That the renunciation of the will is the ultimate ethical goal simply does not follow from anything that Schopenhauer says before. This remarkable dual nature of their work, which Wittgenstein and Schopenhauer share, deserves some closer attention.

In a certain sense, both Wittgenstein and Schopenhauer are "defensive" thinkers. Wittgenstein, and the same holds for Schopenhauer, puts forward his views with his back turned to the ethical, facing the discursive as an enemy. He defends a borderline that should not be transgressed and wants to confine the discursive to a clearly circumscribed realm. He is not describing a frontier that can and should be pushed further and further, ever increasing the domain in which language and thought reign. The *Tractatus* is meant to state once and for all what language and thought can do and, equally importantly, what they cannot touch on. And it is here that Wittgenstein's absolutism with regard to logic gets to play an ethical role. A definition of the realm of thinking and speaking in terms of an absolute logic characterizes it as a priori and necessary. And the same holds for its counterpart, the realm of the ethical.

The fact that their analyses of the world as it can be accessed in language and thought do not strictly imply their views on the ethical is first of all simply a logical consequence of the way in which Wittgenstein and Schopenhauer view the relationship between the two. For both maintain that the gap between the discursive and the ethical is unbridgeable in principle from within the sphere of the discursive. Secondly, both Schopenhauer and Wittgenstein seem to have come to their views on the nature of the ethical through what might be called "firsthand" experience. The reality, the hardness one might say, of the ethical is neither the conclusion of a logical, discursive process, nor is it a merely speculative ornament that satisfies some deep emotional need. Both seem to have had experiences, in the wider sense of that term, in which the ethical dimension of the world has proved itself real to them. For Schopenhauer this is what he calls his "better consciousness" [*bessere Bewußtsein*], an experience of detachment from the world and the self, which far antedates his doctrine of the will.[69] Although in his younger years Wittgenstein already clearly shows a concern for ethical and moral questions, the decisive turning point occurs while he was serving in the Austrian-Hungarian Army in World War I. The precise circumstances of Wittgenstein's experiences are not very clear, but it is obvious that they resulted in a decisive, fundamental change.[70] Various biographical facts testify to that. For example, the renunciation of his inheritance and his leaving philosophy and wanting to do "something useful" with his life are in clear contrast to the almost casual way in which he made use of his wealth beforehand.[71] There is also the testimony of Russell, who met with Wittgenstein after the war to discuss the *Tractatus* with him and found him completely changed.[72] It is concrete, firsthand experiences of the ethical that Schopenhauer and Wittgenstein start from. Their ethical views are not the speculative or logical outcome of their work, but the starting point. And a large part of their enterprise, though certainly not all of it, aims at securing a safe haven for the experiences on which these views are based.

These observations partly explain why their work failed to have the impact they might have hoped it would have. In the case of Schopenhauer, positive response to his main work only came after almost thirty-five years. Although most of it did not show great awareness of or affinity with the ultimate ethical views that Schopenhauer developed, that nevertheless did not prevent Schopenhauer from enjoying the success of his work when it came. Wittgenstein's case was different. When the *Tractatus* appeared it was immediately recognized as an important work. In this sense it was a success, but Wittgenstein was not too pleased with this success. His disappointment and anger about the way the *Tractatus* was received cannot have been motivated only by the fact that various people misunderstood various rather technical aspects of the book (although this, too, was a source of frustration for Wittgenstein, and for the other people involved). It is clear that the Vienna Circle, whose members more or less adopted the *Tractatus* as their manifesto, understood the technical parts quite well and apparently simply did not agree in every respect. But, it is equally clear that many of them had hardly any affinity with the ethical views proposed in the book, which must have been a sure sign for Wittgenstein that at least as far as its ethical aims are concerned, the *Tractatus* was a failure.[73]

The Proper Interpretation of Ontology

Let us now return to our main issue, the relationship between the ontology of the *Tractatus* and its ethics. We have argued above that the only way in which the *Tractatus* can be interpreted as a coherent whole is by interpreting the ontological theory that it starts out with, not as a straightforward exercise in ontology, that is, as a theory of the ultimate categories and structures of reality per se, but as a logical (re)construction thereof. The world and the way it is built up, as it is described in 1–2.063, is the world as language and thought present it. It is the way the world is presupposed to be by our discursive minds, or, to put it differently, it is the world insofar as we can know it and talk about it. It is only given this interpretation that we can reconcile the nature of the ontology with the ethical part of the *Tractatus*. From the ontology and Wittgenstein's absolutism with regard to ethical value, the ethically contingent character of the world immediately follows. Hence, given that Wittgenstein does presuppose that there is such a thing as ethical value and that it is linked to what we do, to the way we act, the ontology of the *Tractatus* cannot be a theory about the world per se, but must be interpreted as an exposition of the structure of the world that language and thought presuppose.

There are many more arguments that speak in favor of this interpretation, some of which we discussed in Chapter 3. Our main purpose in this chapter has been to argue that a proper and detailed interpretation of the remarks on ethics provide us with yet another one. Conversely, the interpretation of Wittgenstein's views on ethics also puts the various positions about the ontology that we discussed in Chapter 3 in a different perspective. Let us therefore by way of conclusion briefly review them in the light of the above considerations. The linguistic relativism that characterizes Maslow's (and to a certain extent, Stenius's) interpretation of the *Tractatus* is hard to reconcile with Wittgenstein's absolutism. We already noted this tension in our discussion of Maslow with reference to the tractarian concepts of logic and language. The discussion of the ethical part of the *Tractatus* only strengthens this point. Ethical values are absolute and ineffable. But on a reading like that of Maslow there simply is no reason why this should be so. On such an approach ineffability, just like necessity and contingency and hence meaningfulness, are relative notions, relative that is to the choice of a framework. But such relativism is lacking in the *Tractatus*, emphatically also with respect to ethics. Thus the present interpretation of the ethical part of the *Tractatus* can be regarded as an additional argument for rejecting the relativistic interpretation of its ontology that Maslow and Stenius propose.

The type of realistic interpretation exemplified by Malcolm, Pears, and others faces other, equally serious problems. If the tractarian ontology is a theory about reality as it is in and of itself, the only interpretation of the ethical part that makes any sense is one in which ethical values are considered to be ontologically transcendent. But that leaves a lot, in fact, too much, unaccounted for. The intrinsic relationship between actions and values, which is a necessary prerequisite for a connection between ethics and everyday life, proves to be a blind alley. Even if one construed ethical values as not just transcendent, but rather as constituting an ontologically separate domain by themselves, the nonaccidental relationship between such a domain and the world would seem to remain a mystery. And even if one construed some kind of "revelatory" link between the two, this would hardly do justice to the hardness and urgency of ethical matters that is so apparent from Wittgenstein's way of writing about them.

It is, of course, no coincidence that authors who have proposed these kinds of interpretations of the tractarian ontology have hardly commented on the ethics at all. Inspired, perhaps, by Wittgenstein's own declaration of its ineffability, but disregarding at the same time that on the tractarian premises the same holds for logic, meaning, and ontology, they have been satisfied with observing that Wittgenstein did not have much to say about ethics. But the real problem thereby remains unnoticed and unresolved. Their interpretations do not leave room for an account of ethical value that does justice to the few, but essential, characteristics that Wittgenstein does offer, and hence they fail to provide a really coherent account of the *Tractatus* as a whole.

For the kind of structuralist interpretation of the *Tractatus* proposed by Ishiguro and McGuinness, things are slightly different. Their "linguistification" of the ontology does not run into the difficulties that beset a realistic interpretation, since it makes no presumptions regarding the features of reality anyway. And, being faithful to Wittgenstein's absolutism, they do not encounter the problems that relativists like Maslow and Stenius run into. But, as was already remarked in the discussion in Chapter 3, the interpretation of Ishiguro and McGuinness does seem to take things too far and this also has repercussions for the place that is assigned to ethics. The exposition given above has emphasized that although Wittgenstein's discussion of ethics is abstract, it nevertheless holds that ethics deals with the way we act in the world in which we find ourselves. Our assumption has been that the picture that the *Tractatus* offers, of the world, of language and logic, and of ethics, is intended as a coherent whole. However, on the Ishiguro–McGuinness interpretation it is precisely this coherence that is hard to account for. If, as Wittgenstein claims, "the will must have an object" (4/11/16), then the *Tractatus* has to be interpreted as providing this object, that is, as giving an account of the world as something real. To be sure, the picture of the world is not a realistic one in the sense of, for example, Malcolm or Pears. It is an account of the way in which the world appears in language and thought; still, it *is* an account of the world. Thus, although we agree with Ishiguro and McGuinness on the predominance of language

244   *Ethics*

vis-à-vis ontology, their purely structural account seems to be one step too far, depriving ethics of the "support in the world" that it needs.

In view of this it is not surprising that McGuinness comes up with an interpretation of the ethics that is rather different from the one outlined in this chapter, a view that ties it much more closely to logic. In his paper on ethics in the *Tractatus*, McGuinness introduces the term "logical mysticism" and tries to establish a link between the grounding logical "experience" that Wittgenstein refers to in 5.552, the experience that there is anything at all, and ethical experience, of the world as a—limited—whole.[74] Although the two cannot be identified, the difference between them is, according to McGuinness, only gradual. But, as was already noted above, this fails to do justice to the categorical nature of the distinction that Wittgenstein makes here.[75] The world as such is ethically contingent; in it no value is to be found. Yet, ethics deals with values and in doing so assumes them to be very real. Thus, both right and wrong, good and evil, are considered to be realities, realities that we need to deal with. In no sense of the word are they illusory, as McGuinness would have it.

What the *Tractatus* offers us is neither a real world and a transcendent domain of values, nor no world and a description of mystical experience, but instead two ways of dealing with the one solid reality that confronts us. We can interact with this reality in a discursive way, in language and thought, and then we are bound by the laws of logic and the fundamental principles of meaning. But we also must cope with it in an ethical way, realizing the hardness of values and of the task that reality constitutes. Thus we arrive at what we have been after: an interpretation of the *Tractatus* as a coherent whole.

CONCLUDING REMARKS

Our reconstruction of the status and content of Wittgenstein's views on ethics provides an additional argument, we have claimed, for a logical, linguistic interpretation of the ontological theory that the *Tractatus* contains. This interpretation can be argued for also along other lines, some of which have been studied in detail in Chapter 3, and the argument from ethics constitutes just an additional one. The key observation in this argument was that ethics, being necessarily concerned with the way in which we act, in which we live our everyday lives, requires "a support in the world." And we saw that the only way in which Wittgenstein can secure such a support without delivering ethics to the "prattle" of ethical theorizing is through a strict and absolute separation, by logical means, of the world as it appears in language and thought—that is, the world of contingencies, of phenomena—from the noumenal world—that is, the world of ethical and aesthetical values.

By way of conclusion, we want to speculate a bit about the question whether the linguistic turn, of which the *Tractatus* is a classical example, has an additional value over traditional views when it comes to a characterization of the place and contents of ethics within a wider philosophical framework.

There is one distinctive feature inherent in the linguistic, logical way of looking at things that we already briefly touched on earlier and that one might regard as constituting a major advantage in this respect. It is that the linguistic perspective enables us to sidestep traditional ontological and epistemological frameworks and that it thereby provides us with another notion of transcendence, according to which the transcendent nature of some subject or domain is not a matter of it belonging to a distinct ontological plane or of it being inaccessible for any of our intellectual powers.[76] Thus it allows us to account for the ineffability and the essentially noncontingent character of ethics without committing us to some kind of otherworldliness in the traditional sense of the word. Thereby, it makes it possible to deal with the relationship between absolute, necessary values and relative, contingent actions in a direct way, without creating new ontological or epistemological puzzles.

It is important to observe that far from being highly abstract and remote from our everyday concerns, this way of viewing ethics in effect creates the possibility of a very concrete and almost pragmatic approach to questions of morality. By keeping ethics free from the primarily discursive and rationalizing aspects of our human intelligence, it paves the way for a practical, more down-to-earth way of coping with moral problems.[77] Closely connected with this feature is another one, namely, that the *Tractatus* does not contain an ethical theory in the more common sense of the word. It does not present us with general ethical principles, nor with a method for deciding what in a given situation is the ethically most justified way to act.[78] The ineffability of ethics is one of its essential features, and every speculative expression of it is therefore doomed to fail. Ethics is concerned with action, with the practical questions of how to act in concrete circumstances, not with speculations about the metaphysical nature of the good or with highly abstract theorizing about fictitious cases. Wittgenstein's main concern is to prevent just that: that the concrete question of how we are to live our daily lives become the subject of speculative thought, something that leads to brilliant arguments, but not automatically also to ethically just actions. For many a reader of the *Tractatus* this will be disappointing. Is this a theory of ethics? No, and it is not intended as one. But what then, one might ask, is its practical value? We have tried to provide something of an answer to this question above, pointing out that the characteristics of ethically just actions that Wittgenstein provides indicate a particular view of the world, of ourselves and others, which does have concrete, practical moral consequences.

But this way of trying to share ethical insights admittedly has a weak spot, namely, that it presupposes some particular kind of experience and a concomitant understanding on the part of the reader. Wittgenstein starts, as did Schopenhauer, not from theoretical insights or postulates, but from a concrete experience, a particular way of viewing the world, namely, the mystical experience of the world as a limited whole. For someone who does not share this experience, the entire procedure fails, or at least it might do so if no similar experience of the ultimate unity and connectedness of what one experiences in everyday life can take its place.

A natural question to ask then is what the value of an enterprise such as Wittgenstein's is in the first place. If what it wants to communicate about ethics presupposes some particular kind of experience, one that not everyone can be assumed to have had, what good, literally, does it do to treat of ethics in this way? How and to what extent can Wittgenstein's views really influence people? Taking our lead from the last question, we may observe that, in effect, the ethical part of the *Tractatus*, for Wittgenstein personally no doubt the most important one, has met with little sympathy, certainly in the earlier years. We have already mentioned the way in which many members of the Vienna Circle reacted to this part of a book that they hailed as the most important philosophical work to have appeared since Kant.[79] Russell, too, although certainly someone who did have a keen interest in ethical and moral problems, did not value the *Tractatus* in this respect. More generally, the bulk of the secondary literature on Wittgenstein's work does not treat of the ethics extensively. And the few works that do, tend to concentrate, not on Wittgenstein's own views, but on the possible consequences that in particular his later work might have for questions of ethics and theology.[80] In the ethical literature Wittgenstein by and large is lacking. In conclusion, one might say that at least so far as academic philosophy is concerned the influence of Wittgenstein's views on ethics is negligible and that this is no mere coincidence but as much a direct consequence of the very contents of these views as of the way in which these are presented.

In the altogether different context of personal relationships, however, Wittgenstein's views on how to live did exercise a considerable influence. When one reads the recollections of his former pupils, such as Malcolm, Rhees, and Drury, when one considers how Wittgenstein influenced the life of his nephew Arvind Strømberg and that of his friend Francis Skinner, it is clear that the ideas Wittgenstein had formed about the good life, the decent life that he wanted to live, not only were a constant and predominant factor in his own life, but also in that of others who were close to him.[81] As a matter of fact, the fascination and adoration that some of his students displayed borders on the unsound. For many apparently it was as if Wittgenstein had cast a spell on them. No doubt, Wittgenstein did not want this, but it is a matter of fact that he did. In more than a few cases the effect was decidedly negative, and Wittgenstein was well aware of this.[82]

This naturally leads to the following question: To what extent did Wittgenstein himself succeed in living up to his ethical ideals? Was he one of the "great men" whom Schopenhauer points out to us as exemplary when he discusses the ultimate ethical goal, the denial of the will? Certainly, Wittgenstein was no saint, unlike perhaps some of the people Schopenhauer refers to. This much is clear from what is known about his life and he most certainly did not regard himself as one. On the contrary, his self-esteem in these matters, as in others, is low. Nevertheless, it must be said that Wittgenstein is one of the rare examples of a philosopher who proposes certain ethical ideals and really tries to live up to them. No matter how much he failed, he was "out there trying"; at least that much must be granted to him. For example, the way in which after the war Wittgenstein accepted the consequences of his ideas, denounced his heritage, and tried to do something that he could regard as decent with his life, whatever the actual outcome, deserves admiration. In this respect, if not in others,

Wittgenstein may yet serve as an example for all those professional philosophers who leave out the trying and stick with the speculating.

The influence of Wittgenstein's views seems to be have been confined to the sphere of personal relationships. But that goes for the contents of his views, and not for the linguistic turn as such. The latter did exercise a considerable influence on philosophical ethics, at least for a certain period. It is ironic, but not illogical, that the *Tractatus*, with its strong emphasis on the relationship between contingency and meaningfulness and its concomitant dismissal of the possibility of genuine philosophical knowledge, fostered a way of dealing with ethics that is almost the opposite of what Wittgenstein himself had in mind. The positivistic interpretation of speculative philosophy as the mere expression of a "Lebensgefühl," comparable to poetry or music, and the ideal of a "scientific worldview," in which all questions concerning life would be subjected to investigation with scientific methods or be dismissed as mere gibberish, have been influential for quite some time and to some extent this is due to the *Tractatus*.[83] There is no doubt that Wittgenstein loathed the way in which the book was used, but it is a fact that it did lend itself to this purpose, at least for a while. And this seems to be integral to the linguistic view as such that the *Tractatus* exemplifies. Given the way in which ordinary descriptive sentences acquire their meaning, it leads quite naturally, though not unavoidably, to the idea that there is a categorical distinction between the cognitive and the noncognitive that coincides with that between the scientific and the speculative. With the ethical thus being placed outside the sphere of the cognitive, the result may give rise to a negative evaluation of ethics as such, along with other activities and concerns that fall outside the scope of "respectable," that is, rational, scientific methods.

In view of these considerations, how are we to evaluate what Wittgenstein says about ethics and the way he says it? Again, it seems that the key to a proper understanding lies in the appeal he makes to our own experience. Ethics starts with experience, not with theory. The source of our moral attitudes is the same as the medium in which they find their expression: our acting, our experiencing, our being in the world. Thus, expressing his views on ethics the way he does, Wittgenstein first and foremost appeals to our own authentic ethical experiences, which spawn an urgent need to find a morally just attitude toward life. Such experiences, of course, differ from individual to individual. No doubt the world provides ever so many ways for people to be morally aroused, to be awakened to fundamental ethical questions. But these experiences are a starting point, not an end in themselves. Ultimately, our ethical considerations should converge on an objective ethical view, that of the world as a whole, as one interconnected being, from which our fundamental moral obligations and strictures can be derived.[84] The entire framework of the *Tractatus* is in a sense subsidiary to this goal. It is Wittgenstein's way of explaining what this objective view is and how it relates to our other way of looking at the world, the rational, discursive one.

From this point of view, it seems that the best way to look at what Wittgenstein has to say about ethics in the *Tractatus* is to take it as an appeal, an urgent invitation to consider the world from an ethical perspective and, most importantly, to act accordingly. And the value of the book lies herein, in the extent to which it actually arouses its readers toward such a fundamentally ethical way of leading the life of every day.

REFERENCE MATTER

Notes

CHAPTER I

1. Among the most important sources of this kind are Malcolm 1958; Rhees 1965; Pascal 1979; Drury 1984; and Rhees 1984a.

2. Some authors who emphasized the continuity in Wittgenstein's thinking early on are Stenius 1960 (see also Stenius 1984); Ishiguro 1969; and Kenny 1973. The work of Ishiguro will be discussed in some detail in Chapter 2.

3. Thus Black claims that "some of the concluding remarks on ethics and the will may have been composed still earlier [than 1913, *m.s.*]" (1964, 1). This is surprising in view of the fact that most of the remarks alluded to appear almost verbatim in entries in the *Notebooks* that date from July 1916 and later.

4. The recognition of this fact is due to a large extent to the work of Janik and Toulmin (1973), whose extensive studies of the cultural and political backdrop against which the *Tractatus* was written did much to foster at least an awareness, especially among Anglo-Saxon philosophers, that Wittgenstein was as much an Austrian, continental philosopher as an English, analytical one.

5. See, for example, the work of Pears (1987), already referred to in the Preface. Another example is that of Carruthers, who, although he acknowledges that "it seems likely that Wittgenstein himself believed in a connection between his work on logic and his views on value," nevertheless maintains that it is "clearly unnecessary to take any particular stance on [Wittgenstein's] doctrine of the Ethical in order to interpret and assess [his] semantic and metaphysical doctrines" (1990, xii). See also McDonough 1986 for a similar position.

In more recent research, among others by Diamond (2000), the ethics is recognized as an intrinsic part of the *Tractatus*. However, this research fails to address head on the most important question that one faces if one wants to read the book in this way, namely, how to construe the relation between ontology and language from within the tractarian system itself.

6. That such connections between ontology and ethics exist often goes unnoticed. Not only are there analyses of the ontology of the *Tractatus* that do not take into account the ethics, but also there are treatments of the ethics that are not con-

cerned at all with its repercussions for the status of the ontology. See, for example, Edwards 1985; Shields 1993; and Gmür 2000.

7. At the time Wittgenstein was trying to get Ficker to publish the *Tractatus* in the latter's periodical "Der Brenner." For more information on the publication history of the *Tractatus*, see McGuinness 1988, chapter 9; for more on the relationship between Wittgenstein and Ficker, see Janik 1979.

8. Several facts, some of them of a biographical nature, can be adduced to support this point. We will come back to them briefly in Chapter 4.

9. Throughout, a reference by number is to a passage from the *Tractatus*.

10. Thus Black, commenting on 6.41, says: "This is irredeemable nonsense, not the nonsense that arises through the attempt to say what can only be shown" (1964, 370).

11. Examples of analyses that fall under the first heading are those of Malcolm 1986; Hacker 1984a, 1996; Hintikka and Hintikka 1986; and Pears 1987. With some qualifications, McDonough 1986 and Peterson 1990 can be included here as well.

Some examples of interpretations that fall within the second class are those of Stenius 1960; Maslow 1961; Ishiguro 1969; Moran 1973; McGuinness 1984; and Watzka 2000. Carruthers (1990) also belongs in this broad class, although his analysis is not as radically "linguistic" as that of Ishiguro, for example.

12. The modern reader will miss a reference to conceptual necessity. The *Tractatus* offers no treatment of this, except for the famous remark on the "color exclusion problem," which, Wittgenstein claims, is at bottom a case of logical exclusion.

13. A good example of this type of reception of the *Tractatus* is the early study by Maslow (1961), which dates from 1933 and which will be treated in Chapter 3. There we will also discuss the relation between Wittgenstein's ideas and those of the logical empiricists in some more detail.

14. See, for example, the recollections of Carnap, which are discussed below in Chapter 3.

15. In particular the ineffability of ethics does not appeal to Russell: "It leaves me with a sense of intellectual discomfort" (1921, xxi).

16. See, for example, Mounce 1981; Hintikka and Hintikka 1986; Fogelin 1987; Pears 1987; and Carruthers 1990, to mention just a few.

17. One example is John Moran, who as early as 1973 wrote an intriguing introduction to the *Tractatus* that centers around these issues.

18. See Janik and Toulmin 1973, chapter 6.

19. See Russell 1975, 330.

20. That Frege thought of himself as a (neo-)Kantian philosopher and that he was heavily influenced by developments in mainstream nineteenth-century German philosophy has been argued convincingly by, among others, Hans Sluga (1980). The ensuing dispute between him and Dummett (see, for example, the lat-

ter's 1985) seems in a certain sense misdirected. Dummett's "canonical" interpretation of Frege as the founding father of twentieth-century linguistic philosophy (see Dummett 1973) is correct in a systematic sense: Frege did develop notions and ideas that formed the essential ingredients of much of linguistic philosophy. But historically Frege was as much a German, neo-Kantian philosopher. It seems that this is another instance of the "official" history of a discipline, which is almost always approached from a systematic point of view, being at odds with actual historical fact.

21. Contrary to what Kant had claimed. Geometry Frege regarded, with Kant, as synthetic a priori.

22. As was just noticed, the history of a systematic discipline tends to survive in a streamlined and idealized form. Of course, Frege's work did not appear out of the blue; others had been working on the same problems. For example, Peirce developed his theory of quantification at more or less the same time as Frege. However, it is quite certain that Wittgenstein was only familiar with Frege's work, besides that of Russell, of course.

23. See Sainsbury 1979, chapter 8, section 7, for extensive discussion. Nevertheless, Frege's system of the *Grundgesetze* continues to inspire logicians, for example, Aczel and Boolos, to develop other ways of dealing with self-reference and truth.

24. It may strike a modern reader as odd that precisely at a time when with hindsight enormous progress was being made there should be such confusion about what logic is. First of all, it must be remembered that the time of fundamental advances usually is a time of fundamental questions. And secondly, we may do well to keep in mind that the questions that Russell, Frege, and Wittgenstein were wrestling with have not been solved. The technical developments in logic may have pushed these questions into the background and it may very well be true that for the average working logician or semanticist they are not particularly relevant, but this does not mean that they are not still there. To give one simple example, we know that we do not need an ontology of facts to do propositional logic, that we can also make do with truth tables. But what are truth tables that we can do logic with them? An ontology of facts is an attempt to answer that question, and perhaps the truth of the matter is that at present it is not so much the case that we do not need an answer (this one, or another one) but that we do not raise the question in the first place.

25. At some point Russell favored the viewpoint that logical laws and principles are the most general and most valid kind of empirical laws. He regarded the axiom of infinity as an empirical sentence, one which may be true in some situations, but not in others. See Russell 1919, 141. But that view seems to be tied too intimately to empiricism to be really attractive for Wittgenstein. At no stage of his philosophical development did he feel attracted to empiricism. His interests were always

ontological and logical, not epistemological. "Not empiricism and yet realism in philosophy, that is the hardest thing," he was to remark later on (*Remarks on the Foundations of Mathematics*, VI-23).

26. The phrase "logical sentences" [*Sätze der Logik*] here refers to logically valid sentences.

27. Another passage that illustrates Wittgenstein's position vis-à-vis the classical interpretation of the axiomatic approach is 6.1233, where he claims that Russell's axiom of reducibility (which states that for every property P there is a corresponding predicative property P', an axiom that Russell needed in order to soften the consequences of his ramified theory of types) cannot be fundamental since "one can imagine a world in which the axiom of reducibility does not hold. But it is clear that logic has nothing to do with the question whether our world really is like that or not."

28. Throughout, references to passages from the *Notebooks* are given by date.

29. Again this is historically inaccurate, but systematically correct. For instance, already in the work of Bolzano one may find traces of the distinction, though of course not formally worked out. See van Benthem 1985.

30. See Hodges 1986.

31. Here there seems to be a connection with the more immanent logical tradition, with its emphasis on decidability.

32. And in this respect he differs fundamentally, not only from Russell and Frege but also from the formalists.

33. Although not in the sense of logicism. What the *Tractatus* says about mathematics does not fit in with logicism as conceived by Frege and Russell and in many ways is closer to Hilbert's formalism. See Frascolla 1994, 39ff.

34. This is another source of misunderstanding between Wittgenstein and the logical empiricists.

35. Thus he was to claim later (Russell 1944, 693–94) that:

> I have never intended to urge seriously that such a [logically perfect] language should be created, except in certain fields and for certain problems. The language of mathematical logic is the logical part of such a language, and I am persuaded that it is a help toward correct thinking in logic.

This sounds reasonably pragmatic, but Russell continues as follows:

> We ought [not], in our attempts at serious thinking, to be content with ordinary language, with its ambiguities and its abominable syntax. I remain convinced that obstinate addiction to ordinary language in our private thoughts is one of the main obstacles to progress in philosophy.

Language reform, then, certainly figured on Russell's agenda.

36. See Russell 1905.

37. In a sense, this foreshadows Wittgenstein's attitude toward language and

philosophical confusion in his later work. Both in the *Tractatus*-period as well as in the later work Wittgenstein holds natural language in high regard and has no use for any kind of reform: natural language is in order as it is. The difference is that in the *Tractatus* Wittgenstein is of the opinion that the true, that is, logical nature, of language may be hidden from us, whereas in his later work he claims that everything that is of interest philosophically is surveyable at the surface and lies open to view.

38. See, for example, Hacker 1984a and Fogelin 1987, chapter 6, for more detailed expositions.

39. As for the nonreferring nature of logical constants, compare:

> Logical indefinables cannot be predicates or relations, because propositions, owing to sense, cannot have predicates or relations. Nor are "not" and "or," like judgments, *analogous* to predicates or relations, because they do not introduce anything new. ("Notes on Logic," 99)

> It's obvious that the dots and brackets are symbols, and obvious that they haven't any *independent* meaning. You must, therefore, in order to introduce so-called "logical constants" properly, introduce the general notion of *all possible* combinations of them = the general form of a proposition. ("Notes Dictated to Moore," 117)

As for the occurrence of the saying–showing distinction in Wittgenstein's earliest work, we give just one example:

> Logical so-called propositions *shew* [the] logical properties of language and therefore of [the] Universe, but *say* nothing. ("Notes Dictated to Moore," 108)

40. As does Black. See n. 3, above.

41. See McGuinness 1988, chapter 2. McGuinness's judgment that Wittgenstein was not "particularly impressed by the work of Schopenhauer" (39–40) seems odd, in view of the almost verbatim way in which some of the latter's views appear in the *Notebooks*. More on this below.

42. See the biographies of McGuinness (1988) and Monk (1990), and the recollections of Engelmann (1967).

43. That nevertheless a case can be made for the existence of important parallels between Wittgenstein's views on language and quite definitely modernist authors such as Gertrude Stein and Samuel Beckett, as has been argued by Marjorie Perloff (1996), is remarkable, but does not contradict this fact. It just illustrates one of the ways in which a work can surpass its maker.

44. See Wijdeveld's study (1994) for an extensive account of both the building and its history. Wijdeveld tries to trace some of the architectural ideas to the *Tractatus*, but, as in the case of Janik and Toulmin, the results he comes up with

are more of an "atmospheric" than of a concrete nature. See also Gmür 2000, chapter 5.

45. See Janik and Toulmin 1973, chapter 5.

46. From Mauthner's *Beiträge zu einer Kritik der Sprache* (1901–1903), quoted from Janik and Toulmin 1973, 126. See also Mauthner 1986.

47. See Weiler 1970 for extensive discussion. According to Weiler, Mauthner's work in many respects anticipates what has become known as "linguistic philosophy." See, Mauthner 1970, chapter 9. See also Haller 1988.

48. Thus Mauthner charges Schopenhauer with being misled by language in his unwarranted reification of the will, for example.

49. Quoted from Janik and Toulmin 1973, 131.

50. And even that idea has its forebears, as it goes back at least to Boole and Leibniz.

51. See von Wright 1958, 20. See also, Chapter 2, n. 3, below.

52. See Magee 1983, appendix 3, for more details. For the influence of Schopenhauer on Wittgenstein's early thinking, see also Janik 1966 and Brockhaus 1991.

53. See von Wright 1958, 5.

54. See also his remarks on Schopenhauer reported by Drury 1984, 158.

55. See also the discussion below.

56. According to some, for instance Clegg (1978), in writing the *Tractatus* Wittgenstein was actually concerned with assigning the logician the place that the musician occupies in Schopenhauer's vision: that of an artist who is in closest contact with the will. McGuinness's (1966) view of Wittgenstein's ethics as a kind of "logical mysticism" is in line.

57. Nietzsche, for example, although very much *en accord* with Schopenhauer's idea of the will as the driving force of the world of appearances, thought this an unmotivated consequence and was of the opinion that, on the contrary, the full development and "living out" of the will was what was required.

58. See Russell's letter to Lady Ottoline Morrell of 20/12/19, included in the *Letters to Russell, Keynes and Moore*, 82.

59. One of Wittgenstein's favorite novels by Tolstoy was *Hadji Murat*, which provides a good example of the kind of detached attitude toward life that Wittgenstein seems to have favored. Once he recommended reading this work to Russell (see McGuinness 1988, 33).

60. In a letter to Ficker of 24/07/15. See also: "I carry Tolstoy's 'Comments on the Gospels' *always* with me, like a talisman" (*Geheime Tagebücher*, 11/10/14).

61. Thus he is reported to have said, referring to Smythies and others: "I could not possibly bring myself to believe all the things they believe" (Monk 1990, 463).

62. See McGuinness 1988, chapter 7, and Monk 1990, chapter I.6–7, for details. See also the recollections of Engelmann (1967), who got to know Wittgenstein quite well during the war. Wittgenstein's struggle during those years is also testified to by

the notes he made during those years, which were only quite recently published as the so-called *Secret Notebooks*. In these notes we can see Wittgenstein struggle to the utmost to live up to his own ethical and moral precepts. Locked up in an environment that was utterly strange and repugnant to him, he tries to adapt himself to it, but often finds himself unable to do so. Several times he considers suicide. He fears death and most of all he fears that he will behave in a cowardly fashion. Consolation comes, in the end, from what can only be described as a strongly religious impulse.

63. See Levi 1978, 1979; Bartley 1985.

64. Compare the rather secretive allusion to Wittgenstein's homosexuality to the fierce debate instigated by Bartley 1985 on page 294 of McGuinness 1988. It is ironic and unjustified that this element in Bartley's book is the only one that is regularly referred to in the literature. (See Bartley 1985, afterword, section I, for an account of the upheaval the book caused when it first appeared in 1973.) In fact, only a few pages are devoted to this topic. The larger part of it is concerned with Wittgenstein's activities in what Bartley calls his "lost period," that is, the years between the end of the war and Wittgenstein's return to Cambridge. In particular, it clarifies the motives Wittgenstein had in embarking on a career as a school-teacher, placing this decision in the context of the *Schulreform* movement in Austria and, more in general, that of the political and social activities of the Wittgenstein family.

65. This is illustrated by the way in which the *Notebooks* were edited. All his life Wittgenstein kept notes. These concern not just the "technical" philosophical and logical problems he was working on, but also thoughts on music, literature, general issues concerning religion and culture, and remarks of a more personal nature. Wittgenstein intended to destroy the set of *Notebooks* he kept during the years 1914–16, but some of these have survived. They contain notes that are of eminent importance to understanding the emergence and subsequent development of his views on logic and language, as they finally found their form in the *Tractatus*. As such we will make ample use of them. But besides these, there are also remarks of a strictly personal nature, most of them written in a simple cipher, dealing with events of everyday life and his thoughts and feelings about them. The editors decided that these should not be published, presumably because they were of the opinion that they have no bearing on the contents of the *Tractatus* as such. The rationality of that decision is subject to some debate, since these remarks do shed more light on what Wittgenstein thought about ethical and spiritual matters, and as such they are not without relevance for understanding the *Tractatus* as a whole. But the main objection is that the editors never revealed the existence of the *Secret Notebooks*, as they have now come to be known, and actively tried to prevent their publication. See Baum's editorial comments on the German edition (1991a). Excerpts of the later notebooks, too, have been published (as *Culture and Value*), but doubts concerning the selection remain.

66. See Janik 1985. Compare also the following passage of a letter of 23/08/31 which Wittgenstein wrote to Moore (*Letters to Russell, Keynes and Moore*, 159):

> I can quite imagine that you don't admire Weininger very much. . . . It is true that he is fantastic but he is *great* and fantastic. It isn't necessary or rather not possible to agree with him but the greatness lies in that with which we disagree. It is his enormous mistake which is great. That is, roughly speaking, if you just add a ~ to the whole book it says an important truth.

67. According to some, Weininger's feelings about his homosexuality played a decisive role in shaping his views on sexuality, masculinity, and femininity.

68. See also Schwarzschild 1979.

69. See Gudmunsen 1973,; Canfield 1975; Gudmunsen 1977; Tominaga 1982; and Tominaga 1983. For a dissenting opinion, see Kalupahana 1977, of whom we may note, by the way, that elsewhere (in Kalupahana 1976) he presents Wittgenstein's views on the matter too crudely. We will come back to this issue in Chapter 4.

70. It should be pointed out that Schopenhauer's knowledge of the Indian philosophical tradition was limited. In fact, for a modern reader it is quite amazing how little of the vast Indian and Chinese philosophical literature was known in Europe at that time and how little of what was known was available to a non-specialist like Schopenhauer.

71. See Mauthner 1913.

72. For some discussion of the parallels and some speculations about the historical connections, see Conze 1967.

CHAPTER 2

1. Although we will sometimes quote extensively from the *Tractatus*, we nevertheless assume that the reader will read this overview with the text itself close at hand, so as to be able to fill in the many details that we will have to ignore.

2. It is interesting to note that in the German text the verb "müssen" is used and not the verb "sollen." The latter has only a normative meaning, whereas the former's primary meaning is that of necessity. This suggests that Wittgenstein is drawing a logical conclusion here rather than giving an ethical prescription. The observation is important because it reveals something about the intentions Wittgenstein apparently had with the analysis that leads to up this conclusion.

3. To what extent Wittgenstein can be considered a Kantian philosopher in the stricter sense of the word is a matter of debate. Many authors have noted a critical, Kantian twist in Wittgenstein's work, and not just in the *Tractatus*. Early examples are Stenius 1960; Maslow 1961; and Black 1964. However, almost all of the familiar Kantian conceptual apparatus (of transcendental deductions, categories,

and so on) is lacking and in that sense Wittgenstein certainly stands in a different tradition. See, for example, Johannessen and Nordenstam 1981, and Ferber 1983 for more elaborate discussion. It is known that Wittgenstein read Kant's first *Critique* after the war, while being held captive as a prisoner of war in Monte Cassino. There Ludwig Hänsel gave courses in logic, and Wittgenstein is reported to have read the *Critique* with Hänsel. That seems to have been the first occasion on which Wittgenstein studied Kant directly and this was only after the *Tractatus* was finished. (At the time the manuscript was with Russell.) Of course, indirectly, both through Frege's and in particular through Schopenhauer's work, Wittgenstein was familiar with the Kantian tradition.

4. Describing this change as a radical and epoch-making one does not imply that one thinks of it in terms of progress or something like that. Surely one may at the same time acknowledge that the linguistic turn has changed the face of philosophy in our time and be of the opinion that philosophy is in none the better shape for it.

5. Here it needs to be pointed out that the term "world" [*Welt*] is used in different senses in different contexts. In the passages under discussion, 1–1.21, the term clearly refers to that which actually is the case. More frequently, however, it is used in a wider sense, more or less like "possible world" (for example, in 2.022). And the term is also used to refer to what at other points is called "logical space," that is, the totality of all that is possible and of which what is actual in some world or other is always a subset. This extended use of the term "world" is prominent in the later parts of the *Tractatus*, for example, in 5.6.ff., 6.124, and 6.22.

6. It should be noted that in 2.06 Wittgenstein uses the term "fact" [*Tatsache*] in a different but related sense. There he calls the existence (that is, the being realized, the obtaining) of states of affairs a "positive fact" and their nonexistence a "negative fact." This is an extension of the main use of the term. Connected with this is the confusing use of the term "reality" [*Wirklichkeit*]. In 2.04 the totality of existing states of affairs is called the world. In 2.06 Wittgenstein introduces the term "reality" to refer to the existence and nonexistence of states of affairs, a term that has a wider coverage. (It should be noted, by the way, that it does not refer to the same thing as the term "logical space": reality is logical space with the actual world, that is, the totality of existing states of affairs, identified. So, "reality" is a relative term, "logical space" an absolute one.) But then in 2.063 we read that "All of reality is the world" [*Die gesammte Wirklichkeit ist die Welt*]. This seems incorrect at first sight, but the reason that this identification does hold is given a little earlier, in 2.05: "The totality of existing states of affairs also determines which states of affairs do not exist." The point is important because it concerns a central feature of Wittgenstein's atomism: from the totality of existing states of affairs we can deduce what the totality of nonexisting ones is, precisely because the totality of all possible states of affairs is given a priori. (The same point is made in 1.12.) Here

Wittgenstein's absolutism with respect to logic surfaces again: there is, and can be, one and only one totality of logical possibilities. Given that, the identification of reality and world in 2.062 presents no further problems.

7. Thus, the absolute character of logic provides us with a route from the contingent to the necessary, from the a posteriori to the a priori:

> And it is like that in philosophy in general: the individual case always turns out to be unimportant, but the possibility of each individual case gives us information about the essence of the world. (3.421)

Philosophy is not interested in the particular and the individual ("das Einzelne"), in the contingent. But it can use (observations concerning) the contingent to come to grips with the necessary, because everything contingent is determined by the necessary and shows the features of the latter through its form.

8. The maximality requirement follows, it would seem, from a silent appeal to the law of the excluded middle. Every state of affairs not just has the possibility to obtain and the possibility not to obtain, but, given the excluded middle, in every world it must either obtain or not.

9. This point reappears in the context of the discussion of language (see 3.4–3.42) and of logic (see 6.124). See below for more discussion. This feature of the ontology is intimately related to Wittgenstein's contention that logical constants do not refer and his rejection of the ideas of Russell and Frege on the nature of logical objects and of their use of the axiomatic method in logic.

10. Compare also:

> Either a thing has properties that no other thing has, in which case one can immediately single it out among the others by means of a description and refer to it; or, on the other hand, there are several things that have all of their properties in common, in which case it is impossible to point at one of them at all. For if a thing is not singled out by anything, I cannot single it out, since otherwise it is singled out after all. (2.02331)

Like 2.0233, cited in the text, this passage clearly indicates that objects come in different varieties and that there may be more than one object of the same variety. (For the question how many objects there are, see n. 14, below.) Finally, notice that objects are remarkably like variables in a type-theoretic or sortal framework in this respect.

11. A similar kind of argument can be constructed as follows. Suppose we wanted to view the tractarian objects as material entities. According to our ordinary conception of matter and material objects, such objects are necessarily located in space and time. The property of being spatio-temporally located at a certain position, however, is not a simple property of an object, in the sense that being located at such and such a position in space-time is not a state of affairs. For it lacks the property of logical independence, which is characteristic for states of affairs:

being located at a certain position excludes being located at others. So spatio-temporal location is logically complex; it is a complex situation, not an atomic state of affairs. But then this means that if we were to take an object as a spatio-temporally located material thing, no structure involving an object could constitute a state of affairs, for it would never be logically independent of other ones involving the same object located at a different point in space-time.

12. There is a remarkable analogy with names and sentences, which are likewise mutually dependent, as is formally expressed in the context principle, which states that only in the context of a sentence does a name have meaning, and the compositionality principle, which expresses that the meaning of a sentence is determined by the meanings of the names that make it up. Remark also that 2.0122, the passage in which it is claimed that objects are dependent on their occurrence in states of affairs, contains a parenthetical reference to the context principle: "(It is impossible that words occur in two different ways: by themselves and in sentences.)"

13. Notice that the context principle and the principle of compositionality, according to which the internal properties of a complex are determined by those of its constituents (see, for example, 2.032 and 2.034), tend to work in opposite directions. More on this below, n. 63, and Chapter 3.

14. In Fogelin (1987, 12), the following argument is given that there must be an infinite number of objects. Suppose that the numbers of objects of two types that combine to form a state of affairs is finite, say m and k. Then, the argument runs, if we ask ourselves whether a certain object of the second type is combined with some object of the first type and we establish that it is not so combined with $m-1$ objects of this first type, we would be able to infer that it is combined with the last, m-th object of this type, which would contradict the logical independence of states of affairs. However, the argument seems to rest on the mistaken identification of the realization of a state of affairs with the combination of certain objects. The point to bear in mind is that the latter constitutes only a possible state of affairs, not an actual one. Notice also that the postulate of an infinite number of objects does not really help; it only shifts the problem. For according to this line of reasoning there should always be realized at least one combination determined by the forms of objects in the actual world. But then it cannot really be said that states of affairs are independent in the sense that each one of them can be realized and not-realized without consequences for the realization of the others. For surely that allows that none of them are realized in some world, even when they are infinite in number.

15. It may be more natural for us to call this its structure, but, alas, Wittgenstein's choice of terminology is different.

16. That Wittgenstein speaks of facts, that is, existing situations, and not of situations *tout court* should not be taken to imply that a picture and what it depicts always have to be realized. For what a picture depicts, this is clear from 2.11, where

it is said that a picture presents a situation in logical space. As for the pictures themselves, there seems to be no reason why we could not speak of possible pictures. Presumably, Wittgenstein uses the term "fact" mainly to stress the difference with "thing." A similar use can be found in 3.14, with regard to sentential signs. Compare also the context: "We make ourselves pictures of the facts." A picture we make ipso facto is a fact. Note further that this suggests ("*We make* ourselves pictures [. . .]") that the distinction between a situation and a thing is a relative distinction, not an absolute one. An entity is not inherently either a thing, or a situation, but it can be viewed as both, depending on the circumstances. Consider again the map. In certain circumstances it may be used purely as a material object, say to chase away an irritating insect. More naturally, but not exclusively, it will be viewed as a structured whole, when we use it to find our way about. This reinforces the view of facts and objects in the tractarian sense as logical concepts. See also the remarks on sentential signs and sentences below.

17. This is the ideal situation, in a sense. When the picture theory is applied to language, we must reckon with the fact that sometimes the mapping may be many-to-one. In that case two elements in the picture represent one and the same element in the situation depicted, which may occur with synonymous expressions. However, Wittgenstein is of the opinion that such deviations are merely superficial and can be eliminated at the level of complete analysis.

18. In algebraic terms, the pictorial relationship can be thought of as generating an isomorphism between two situations: a one-to-one correspondence between their respective elements that respects the types, that is, the logical form, thereof.

19. This provides a clue as to how to understand the following passage:

> Not: "The complex sign 'aRb' says that a stands to b in the relation R," but: *That* "a" stands to "b" in a certain relation says *that aRb*. (3.1432)

The interpretation of this passage is controversial. According to some, it shows that the ontology of the *Tractatus* is nominalistic, that is, contains only particulars and no universals. However, this view is clearly untenable, as the extensive research of Maury (1977) has shown. We will come back to this issue below. So the meaning of this passage has to be another one. If we consider the passage immediately preceding, it becomes clear what that is:

> The essence of a sentential sign becomes very clear if we imagine it being composed of spatial objects (such as tables, chairs, books) instead of written signs.
>
> Then the spatial arrangement of these things among each other will express the meaning of the sentence. (3.1431)

This fits the example given in the text nicely. The nature of the sentential sign that Wittgenstein refers to here is that it is articulate (3.141), that is, that the sign has a form. The spatial relationship is as much part of the picture as the visible things.

20. This convention is almost universally adopted, which makes it hard to recognize it as such. But certain types of maps, for example those showing certain features of coasts and entries to harbors, make clear that other conventions are possible (and useful) as well. Such maps are not oriented toward the north, but in the direction in which someone using them is likely to travel.

21. An even more abstract example is the following. Recall the first and third diagram given above, representing two states of affairs. The first can be seen to picture the second by establishing two things. To begin with we notice that the two share a form: both are instantiations of the same underlying form, represented by the second diagram. However, this is not enough. There should also be a relationship between their respective elements. By pairing a with c, R with S, and b with d, we establish the required pictorial relationship.

22. That logical form is described as "the form of reality" is remarkable: it shows that the notion of reality itself is highly abstract one. Actually, this is already indicated by the way in which the notion is introduced in 2.06 (see n. 6 above). Being the totality of existing and nonexisting states of affairs, reality deals with what is logically possible, abstracting away from all the nonlogical, contingent features that a world may have.

23. See Russell's discussion of the matter in Lecture III of *The Philosophy of Logical Atomism* (1918–19, 211ff.). It should be noted that Wittgenstein, too, at one time availed himself of "negative facts talk," in his early "Notes on Logic," which date from 1913. However, according to Wittgenstein negative facts are not false, that is, untrue facts. A negative fact is what justifies a negative sentence.

24. As Demos did, against Russell. This is not to say that the doctrine has not survived, in one way or another. For example, modern situation theory (see Barwise and Etchemendy 1987; Barwise and Perry 1983) seems to endorse this view, albeit in a more sophisticated form.

25. We can turn this into a theory of the meaning of negative sentences in general by using the familiar truth-table definition of negation.

26. Compare also:

> In any ordinary proposition, for example, "Moore is good," this *shews* and does not say that "*Moore*" is to the left of "good"; and *here what* is shewn can be *said* by another proposition. But this only applies to that *part* of what is shewn which is arbitrary. The *logical* properties which it shews are not arbitrary, and that it has these cannot be said in any proposition. ("Notes Dictated to Moore," 111)

27. It already occurs in the "Notes Dictated to Moore," which date from 1914.

28. Thus Wittgenstein says in 4.1121 that "epistemology is the philosophy of psychology" and that "psychology is no more closely related to philosophy than any other natural science." There is indeed a relation between the study of language and that of thoughts and thought processes, but Wittgenstein warns that this should not

entangle us in "irrelevant psychological investigations" (4.1121). Traditional epistemological concerns have no place in the tractarian conception of philosophy.

29. Compare what Wittgenstein says about tautologies and contradictions:

> Tautologies and contradictions are not pictures of reality. They do not depict a possible situation. (4.462)

This means that they do not express a thought either.

30. Of course, this continues to be a moot point. In fact, the analysis of propositional attitudes, especially that of belief, is so intimately tied up with the analysis of meaning that it seems virtually impossible to argue for a particular view while remaining neutral with respect to a semantic framework. In the light of that, we are satisfied to note that this particular analysis of Wittgenstein's does indeed square with his semantic presuppositions.

31. Recall what was said above, that no thing is intrinsically a picture, nor an object, for that matter. Rather, such qualifications as "picture" and "object" mark the way in which something is used.

32. See also:

> We can indeed spatially depict a state of affairs that runs counter to the laws of physics, but not one that goes against the laws of geometry. (3.0321)

33. Compare also:

> To depict something that "contradicts logic" in language is as impossible as it is to specify in geometry a figure that contradicts the laws of space through its coordinates; or to give the coordinates of a point that does not exist. (3.032)

34. Another relevant observation is that the requirement of identity of form between picture and depicted situation is also meant to do away with a "third man": the relationship between picture and depicted is not brought about by anything else than picture and depicted themselves. For postulating such a third element leads to obvious difficulties (such as the threat of an infinite regress), which have plagued traditional theories of the proposition.

35. Again, this suggests that the distinction between situations and things is a relative one, not a categorical ontological distinction. See what was said in n. 16, above.

36. This may seem to lead to a rather relativistic conception of how sentences depict. However, in the end Wittgenstein abstracts away from concrete signs to symbols and in the abstraction process—which is basically a logical process in which we abstract over all signs with the same meaning, that is, over all "meaning bestowing" acts—he secures the absolute character of the outcome.

37. And given that the meaning is a thought, the terminology is not as strange as it may seem at first sight.

38. In connection with this, it should be noted that Wittgenstein uses the term "Satz" in various ways, not just to refer to sentences in the strict sense just given, but also to meaningful sentences (for example, in 4.01) and to logically valid sentences (6.1).

39. The example is Wittgenstein's, who uses it in 4.032 to make the same point.

40. See also the remark on 3.1432 in n. 19, above.

41. That the latter is itself grammatically complex is not relevant for the point that we want to make here, so we leave that out of consideration.

42. See Frege 1892b.

43. Again, this seems more a matter of how we look at things than something that is inherent to them. For example, in certain circumstances it seems most natural to look at the city of Amsterdam as a thing in itself, that is, as a saturated object, in Frege's terminology. But in other circumstances, for example from the perspective of relative geographical locations, it must be taken to be unsaturated, since when considered in such a way, it has to bear certain relationships to other objects that are similarly conceived. Thus, in his analysis of language, too, Wittgenstein seeks to avoid an appeal to a "third man," to some element or operation that ties various expressions together. Presumably the reason is that such an account would lead to an infinite regress. If we assume that some predication relation connects predicate and argument(s), we may well be led to ask what it is that connects it to the expressions it operates on. (A similar observation can be made with respect to the structure of situations. See also n. 34, above.) For modern theories that work around this problem, see, for example, Bealer 1982.

44. From this perspective, it seems, something like the so-called redundancy view of truth follows quite naturally. Although Wittgenstein does not go into this issue explicitly in the *Tractatus*, he does discuss such a view in connection with the idea of a "general form of sentences" in his later work. See, for example, *Philosophical Investigations*, 136.

45. Pure categorical syntax comes closest to this ideal, but actual grammars for substantial segments of natural language usually make a distinction between a lexical and a structural component.

46. Wittgenstein mostly uses "Ausdruck," which translates as "expression." But his use of the term here is a technical one, which we will cover by the term "symbol" [*Symbol*].

47. The examples are rather traditional and not altogether convincing for a modern reader, who may be familiar with the use of higher-order logic to give an analysis of the verb *to be* that encompasses both its use as a copula and its use as an expression of identity. See Montague 1973.

48. This seems not to apply to names, which, as we shall see shortly, are considered only to have reference (*Bedeutung*), but not meaning (*Sinn*). However, the discrepancy is only apparent. First of all, it is clear that Wittgenstein intends

the notions of "symbol" and "essential symbol" (3.341) also to apply to names. In 3.3411 names are explicitly mentioned in an illustration of what is intended with the latter notion. Secondly, the distinction between *Sinn* and *Bedeutung* in a sense is a technical distinction that distinguishes two aspects of what in a more loose and intuitive sense is considered as one phenomenon, namely, meaning. That we use the term "meaning" to refer to what Wittgenstein calls *Sinn*, and "reference" to refer to his notion of *Bedeutung*, should not confuse us here. Reference in the technical sense contributes as much to meaning in the intuitive sense as does meaning in the technical sense. The distinction is important, nevertheless. The *Sinn* of an expression denotes its descriptive content, that is, the qualitative characteristics it contributes to the meaning of a larger expression. And with *Bedeutung* we mean the entity or entities referred to, which also contributes to the overall meaning of an expression, be it in a different way. Both *Sinn* and *Bedeutung*, then, are relevant for the determination of the meaning of a complex expression, such as the situation that is the meaning of a sentence. Analogously, we can say that an expression, such as a name that has only *Bedeutung* but no *Sinn*, still has meaning, albeit not a descriptive, qualitative meaning. In this sense the semantic contribution of names to larger expressions is the same as that of rigid designators in the style of Kripke, Donnellan, and Putnam.

49. Wittgenstein uses the terms "constant" and "variable" in a more extended sense than is common today. A "constant" is what contains no variables (in the strict sense), a "variable" is what contains at least one variable (in the strict sense). Remark further that the range of sentence forms of which a symbol represents a characteristic feature does not include sentential constructions involving logical constants. This is connected with Wittgenstein's view on the status of logical constants (more on this below).

50. Compare also 5.513, where it is said that "... what is common to all symbols that affirm both p and q is the sentence $p \wedge q$." This, by the way, indicates that the logical symbolism that Wittgenstein uses in the *Tractatus* should not be interpreted as one particular logical symbolism.

51. According to Wittgenstein, Russell's theory of types is guilty of doing just that, which is why he rejects it :

> Russell's mistake shows itself herein, that, when establishing the rules for signs, he had to mention their reference. (3.331)

In the theory of types rules are formulated that limit the combinatorial possibilities of expressions. These rules explicitly mention the types of entities that expressions refer to.

52. Notice that because form and structure are distinguished there can be two sentences that have the same logical form, yet differ in meaning. The same form can be "embodied" by different structures, in this case by sentences composed of different expressions, which stand in different pictorial relationships to elements of

different situations. Also two sentences may have a different form, yet convey the same meaning. But this may happen only when the sentences are not completely analyzed. At the level of complete analysis a difference in form implies a difference in meaning.

53. One immediate consequence is that, having uncovered a set of principles that uniformly govern any symbolic system, all such systems, at that basic level, are "the same," that is, have the same expressive power and, hence, are intertranslatable. This feature Wittgenstein illustrates in 4.014ff. by drawing on examples that have radically different physical dimensions. For example:

> The grammophone record, the musical idea, the musical score, and the sound waves all stand to one another in the internal relation of depicting that holds between language and the world.
> They all have the logical construction in common. (4.014)

And the common logic construction is the logic of depiction:

> The possibility of all images, of the entire pictorial character of our way of expression, rests in the logic of depiction. (4.015)

54. From now on we will use the term "sentence" and cognate terms such as "discourse" and "expression" to mean "meaningful sentence," and so on, unless explicitly stated otherwise.

55. Wittgenstein subscribes to Russell's theory of descriptions, according to which a description of an entity can be analyzed in terms of sentences describing its properties. See 2.0201, 3.24, and 4.0031.

56. The former position has been defended by, among others, Copi 1958 and Anscombe 1963. Ishiguro, whose interpretation will be discussed at length below in Chapter 3, also seems to defend this position when she claims: "It seems to me to be a central thesis of the *Tractatus* that subject-predicate propositions, that is propositions in which properties are ascribed to objects, can be expressed as a function of the objects" (1969, 28). However, in other places this view appears qualified. Thus on 26–27 she stresses that what is to count as an object is a logical matter and may vary from context to context. To be an object is to be the value of a variable, she states, referring to 4.1272, or to be the argument of a function. In view of the possibility of higher-order predication and quantification, this does not exclude entities which "in isolation" we would classify as properties and relations. The latter view is taken by for example Stenius 1960; Hintikka and Hintikka 1986; and Maury 1977, who investigated the issue in considerable detail.

57. This passage was already referred to above, in n. 19.

58. We only mention some of them and refer the reader to Maury 1977 for more extensive discussion.

59. To prevent misunderstanding, note that Wittgenstein does not claim that Socrates and Mortality are simple objects in an absolute sense. They are (merely)

to be considered as such in the context of application. The relevant point for the present discussion is that he does not differentiate between the particular Socrates and the universal Mortality.

60. Compare also the following passages from the *Notebooks* (22/6/15): "If a name signifies an object, it thereby stands to it in a relation which is completely determined by the logical nature of the object. . . ." What purpose would it serve to notice this if objects came only in one kind?

61. Again, this occurs also in the *Notebooks*, the "Notes on Logic," the "Notes Dictated to Moore," and in Wittgenstein's correspondence of 1919 with Russell. Finally, we note that Wittgenstein, in his exposition of the *Tractatus* to Desmond Lee, claimed: "'Objects' include also relations: a proposition is not two things connected by a relation. 'Thing' and 'relation' are on the same level. The objects hang as it were in a chain" (*Wittgenstein's Lectures, Cambridge 1930–32*, 120). Such statements must be treated with care; after all the comment is made some sixteen years after Wittgenstein completed the *Tractatus*. However, in combination with the evidence from the *Notebooks* it means that *if* Wittgenstein did not include universals among the objects in the *Tractatus*, he must have changed his mind twice, which seems quite unlikely.

62. A slightly different, more general expression of it can be found in 3.314: "An expression has reference only in a sentence." The context principle is also what is alluded to by the parenthetical remark in 2.0122, an early passage that deals with the dependent nature of objects: "(It is impossible for words to appear in two different ways: by themselves and in sentences.)"

63. To what extent this interpretation does justice to Frege's intentions in formulating the principle in the *Grundlagen* is a matter of debate, but one we need not go into here. Likewise we will ignore the much-discussed issue of how to interpret the role of the context principle and that of the principle of compositionality in Frege's thought. However, the same issues also arise in the *Tractatus* and according to some are crucial for a proper interpretation.

64. The only point at which the intensional character of the ontology is used is in Wittgenstein's account of how false sentences can be meaningful, something which is quite difficult to account for in purely extensional approaches, such as Russell's.

65. Here, too, Frege led the way with his dismissal, in the *Begriffsschrift*, of the modalities as being only of grammatical significance. See Frege 1879, 13.

66. The notation in 5.5 and its relation to the familiar truth tables is explained in 4.442. It is curious to note that whereas usually joint denial is denoted by $\downarrow$ and alternative denial by | (the so-called Sheffer stroke), Wittgenstein used the stroke notation in 5.1311 to denote joint denial.

67. Of course, this paraphrase only covers quantified sentences with an elementary body. But the generalization to arbitrary quantified sentences is straightforward.

68. This difficulty is one that does not seem to disturb Wittgenstein: although infinity is discussed at several points in the *Tractatus*, it is not in connection with this problem.

69. Actually, it would be in line with other aspects of the tractarian system, to strengthen this assumption to the requirement that the relation between names and objects (in the tractarian sense) be one-to-one.

70. Here "$[c/x]$" denotes the operation of replacing all free occurrences of x in the argument by c.

71. Or, to make the same point in a different way, with regard to a logical language we are not interested in any specific interpretation of the descriptive expressions (including the individual constants) and therefore we abstract away from them. Hence, when we ascribe semantic competence to a user of such a language, we are actually not claiming much knowledge on his part, certainly not knowledge of what constitutes the domain. With natural languages, however, things are different. Here we do have one specific interpretation in mind (the "intended interpretation," as it is often called) and hence in this context the problem does arise. Of course, this is not to suggest that this problem arises also in the context of the *Tractatus*. Objects in the tractarian sense are surely not what we quantify over in natural language and, analogously, names in Wittgenstein's sense are not to be confused with ordinary names.

72. The other remarks Wittgenstein makes about generality should not lead us astray here. More in particular, we should not confuse generality with universality; that is, we should not interpret what is said about generality as pertaining to universally quantified sentences only. The remarks in question are clearly intended to pertain to all forms of quantification. For example, when Wittgenstein says, in 5.523, that "the indication of generality occurs as an argument," what he means to say is that quantification uses the device of the sentential function as an argument of the basic truth-functional operation. It is through the variable(s) occurring in such functions that we get at all the elementary sentences, and through them at all the objects in the domain of quantification (see also 5.522). Compare in this connection the common, albeit for a novice often misleading, name of the rule that allows us to derive, $\exists x\, fx$ from fa: "existential *generalization*."

73. Actually, this way of deriving quantified sentences from a base that consists of atomic sentences and their negations is not so strange: recall the notion of literals in resolution logic, elementary sentences with polarities in situation theory, tokens in Scott's domain theory, and so on.

74. There still are, however, other problems with Wittgenstein's approach. Fogelin has argued (1987, chapter 6; see also Geach 1981; Soames 1983) that Wittgenstein's scheme does not allow for the derivation of sentences with "mixed" quantifier prefixes, such as $\forall x \exists y\, Rxy$. We will not go into these more technical matters here.

75. The terminology used, "*propositional* attitude verbs," is *sensu strictu* not neutral, since it seems to claim that such verbs operate on an intensional entity, namely, a proposition. However, since the phrase has become so familiar, it will be used in the sequel, in as neutral a way as possible.

76. Which is not to say that no problems are left in this area. For example, a fully satisfactory treatment of such propositional attitudes as *believe* and *know* still remains to be given. However, the problems here seem to involve not so much the intensional aspect per se, but rather the particular properties of the concepts in question themselves.

77. In proper Quinean fashion, Davidson curtly dismisses an appeal to intensional entities:

> There is even a danger that the know-nothings and the experts will join forces. The former, hearing mutterings of possible worlds, transworld heirlines, and the like, are apt to think *now* semantics is getting somewhere—out of this world, anyway. (Davidson 1973, 68)

78. And neither could Frege: after all, his notion of "Sinn" is an intensional one, and it is this notion that is formalized in modern-day intensional type-theoretical semantics.

79. See Cook 1985, and Hintikka and Hintikka 1986 for contrary opinions. According to Hintikka and Hintikka, tractarian objects are Russellian objects of acquaintance.

80. Again, Wittgenstein's absolutism, or monism, with regard to logic speaks up here. Above, we noted that if we were to acknowledge other logical systems, such as minimal or intuitionistic logic, on a par with classical logic, this would not necessarily go through.

81. This is another instance of what was noted in n. 7, above, about the relation between the contingent, a posteriori, and the necessary, a priori.

82. For more or less the same reasons, Wittgenstein rejects an axiomatic approach to logic: axioms and theorems are basically on the same level, showing the properties of logical space. Thus there can be no fundamental difference between the two.

83. This view of philosophy as a therapeutic activity is one of the continuous elements in Wittgenstein's thinking. His views on the means that philosophy has at its disposal and, consequently, on the end results, did change over time. Thus he says in *Philosophical Investigations*, 128:

> Should one want to formulate *theses* in philosophy, there could never be any discussion about them, since everyone would agree with them.

So there is a change in Wittgenstein's view on philosophy. In the *Tractatus* it is a subject in which no theses can be advanced, in the *Philosophical Investigations* one in which one could formulate only theses about which there cannot be disagreement. And this is related to a change in Wittgenstein's view on meaning and the meaningful. However, the conception of philosophy as a subject without a domain of inquiry of its own remains.

84. See also the preface, where it is said of philosophical problems that "the way in which these problems are formulated rests on a misunderstanding of the logic of our language."

85. A similar instrumental outlook is expressed at several other places, for example, in 6.1261: "In logic process and result are equivalent."

86. At least in the sense in which the truth table is commonly used, as a model-theoretic way of defining the semantics of propositional logic.

87. Or "tautology" in the case of propositional logic. Wittgenstein uses the term "tautology" in an extended sense, to denote all logically valid sentences. See, for example, 6.1 and 6.12. Note that the German noun *Satz* can mean both "sentence" and "theorem."

88. In effect, since 1936 we know from Church's famous result that no effective method for testing validity of the quantificational calculus exists.

89. Compare also:

> Identity of reference of two expressions cannot be asserted. For in order to assert something about their reference, I must know their reference: and by knowing their reference, I know whether they refer to the same or to something different. (6.2322)

An identity sentence cannot have content in the sense that it asserts something that we hold to be true but also know to be contingent. For if we know what the expressions involved refer to we know that this is either the same, or not. In both cases what we know is not contingent, but necessary. The point can also be made in a different way, namely, by pointing out that the question $?(a = b)$ cannot be raised significantly. For in order to understand the question, we must know what a and b mean, which in the case of a and b being names, means that we must know what they refer to. Hence, if we assume that we know what $?(a = b)$ means, we must also assume that we know the answer. Hence the query $?(a = b)$ can never be used significantly, which implies that both the positive answer, $a = b$, and its negative counterpart, $a \neq b$, are not meaningful either. This consequence, that identity sentences are necessary, is turned from vice into virtue in Kripke's influential work on names and identity. See Kripke 1980. Of course, other options are also available, one being an analysis in terms of individual concepts, along the lines of Frege's analysis in "Über Sinn und Bedeutung" (1892a). For Wittgenstein this option is not available when it comes to names. For Frege's analysis only works when the individual concepts in question are "contingent," that is, do not rigidly fix a value. But transposing this solution to names in the tractarian sense would not work, since it would assign to them a contingent, descriptive content. But this they cannot have on pain of not being able to fulfill the role they are assigned.

90. For the connection between logical form and Wittgenstein's conception of a "protopicture" [*Urbild*], see 3.315.

91. Perhaps it could be applied to a copy of itself, which is the way in which domain theory, one way of providing a semantics for the untyped lambda-calculus, mimics self-reference. See Scott 1980.

92. Compare also:

> If there were mathematical objects—logical constants—then the sentence "I am eating five plums" would be a sentence of mathematics. And it is also not a sentence of applied mathematics. (14/2/15)

93. The extensionality of language that the *Tractatus* assumes plays an important role here, of course.

94. But it does contain a densely formulated theory of the fundamental principles of arithmetic, including the concept of infinity. See Frascolla 1994, chapter 1, for extensive discussion.

95. Most of the literature that deals with Wittgenstein's views on mathematics is restricted to his work of the later period, mainly to the *Remarks on the Foundation of Mathematics*. Shanker 1987 devotes much attention to Wittgenstein's views in the transitional period. Frascolla 1994 contains a chapter that is devoted exclusively to the *Tractatus*.

96. Thus we are presented with an entirely different perspective on the age-old problem of the possibility of *futura contingentia* sentences. Notice that the propositional example given above does not obviously fit this case. This is due to the occurrence of the intensional *know*, which, presumably, Wittgenstein would want to analyze away in the same way as the intensional *think*.

97. Compare also the following passage in the *Notebooks*:

> It is clear that the logical product of two elementary sentences can never be a tautology.
> If the logical product of two sentences is a contradiction, and the sentences appear to be elementary sentences, then we can see that in such cases appearances are deceptive. (For example: A is red and A is green.) (8/1/17)

98. This is the only work of Wittgenstein's, besides the *Tractatus*, that was published during his lifetime. It is the text of a lecture that Wittgenstein was supposed to give at a meeting of the Aristotelian Society in 1929. But Wittgenstein grew dissatisfied with it even beforehand and in the end lectured on a different topic. See Monk 1990, chapter III.11.

99. According to Magee (1983, 311), Wittgenstein may have borrowed the metaphor of the ladder from Schopenhauer.

100. In the light of the ultimate, ethical aim of the *Tractatus*, this terminology may after all not be inappropriate.

101. A different interpretation of the status of the tractarian sentences them-

selves has recently been proposed by, among others, Diamond 1988, 2000; Conant 2000; and Ricketts 1996. These authors hold that Wittgenstein intended his own remarks, the very sentences and phrases of which the *Tractatus* consists, as "real nonsense," "plain nonsense," and that hence they need to be discarded altogether. This is a controversial view, which some claim brings us a "new Wittgenstein" (see Crary and Read 2000). But being controversial is not necessarily a mark of being right. Let me briefly point out why I think this view is seriously misguided. (Similar criticisms can be found in Hacker 2000.)

First of all, if Wittgenstein really meant that the sentences of *Tractatus* are literal nonsense, that is, do not convey anything (either by saying or by showing) about meaning, logic, language, thought, then why did he continue working on the very problems and claims of the *Tractatus*? (For example, on color exclusion in "Some Remarks of Logical Form"; on simplicity and related topics in the *Philosophical Remarks*.) And why did he later repudiate some of the things "the author of the *Tractatus*" had said? (For example, in the *Philosophical Investigations* about simplicity, names, the general form of the proposition, the unified nature of language.) And even more remarkably, why did he later vindicate (in a way) various of the tractarian concepts, for example, the saying–showing distinction? (As he did in *On Certainty*, but also in the *Philosophical Investigations*, where the notion of "grammar" plays a role that in important respects is quite similar to the one played in *Tractatus* by "form.") And what about the remark that "this running up against the limit of language is *ethics*" (*Ludwig Wittgenstein and the Vienna Circle*, 30/12/29)? It shows that Wittgenstein was well aware of the fact that sentences about ethics are nonsense, but that yet one somehow cannot avoid making them, in order to convey something. Many more instances of Wittgenstein taking up tractarian themes could be quoted and all of them would remain complete mysteries on the view of Diamond *cum suis*.

Secondly and more generally, this view does not do justice to Wittgenstein's objections to philosophy. These are not directed against philosophy (that is, "nonsense") as such, but against a misrepresentation of its status. Philosophy should not present itself as if it were some kind of (super)science, capable of verification, aiming at stating (very general) truths. And moreover, do note that the *Tractatus* is a tightly structured whole and that it contains lots of arguments. But how could it present arguments, if all its sentences are simple and literal nonsense? Note further that in the preface Wittgenstein explicitly says that the "thoughts announced" in the *Tractatus* are true. Compare also the following passage from the letter to Ficker: "And therefore, if I am not altogether mistaken, the book will say many things you want to say yourself, although perhaps you will not see that it is said there." Wittgenstein apparently does feel that the *Tractatus* has something to say and something of importance at that. It does solve certain philosophical problems and its value is not restricted to exposing all of philosophy as utter and literal nonsense.

It also makes a certain positive contribution. To put it differently: If all of philosophy were literal nonsense, why would Wittgenstein take the trouble to criticize certain views of Russell and Frege by arguing against them? Or, for that matter, how could he say that at some points he agrees with them and at others present a detailed alternative? If all of philosophy is literal nonsense, it would be sufficient to point that out (and perhaps argue for that), but there certainly would be no reason to argue against some specific philosophical positions. But he does. And that presupposes that both the positions and the arguments of the *Tractatus* do have a content.

Of course the sentences of the *Tractatus*, by its own standards, have a peculiar, indeed impossible, status. Actually, the book is a good example of the kind of aporia that any radically absolutistic attempt to give a completely general picture of language, thought, and the world is bound to end up in. And 6.54, among others, shows that Wittgenstein was well aware of this, that he knew that he could not avoid it and yet believed that what he somehow succeeded in saying was right.

102. This role of elucidations will be discussed in greater detail in Chapter 3, below. See also n. 7, above.

CHAPTER 3

1. See, for example, the early (1963) paper on realism, published in Dummett 1978.

2. Dummett traces the origins of this criterion back to Frege. See 1973, chapter 19. Herein, Dummett argues, lies Frege's major contribution to philosophy.

3. See Nieuwendijk 1997, for a recent overview of the literature and for a penetrating discussion of the various difficulties involved in the application of Dummett's ideas.

4. See also Chapter 2, above, and n. 122, below.

5. The point can be made more concretely in terms of the following observation. Often a certain fragment of natural language can be described in radically different ways. Usually, a model-theoretic semantics would start from a domain of individuals, characterizing such higher-order entities as properties and relations, or events and situations, in terms of set-theoretic constructions from this domain. But one may also proceed in a different way: for example, by taking properties as basic and defining individuals in terms of these, in what is basically a Leibnizian fashion, as maximally consistent sets. The point is not that there might not be empirical arguments for preferring one approach over the other, but that one and the same set of empirical phenomena can be described in ways that differ radically as to their ontological presuppositions. In that sense, we might say, a semantics of a language, even one that gives a definition of truth, always underdetermines the ontology the language presupposes. Consequently, we need additional arguments, of an essentially nonsemantic nature, to pinpoint one particular set of ontological

presuppositions. This point has been argued in the recent literature by various authors, notably by Putnam in his attack on metaphysical realism. See, for example, Putnam 1978, 1983. The relationship with the issue of ontological relativity familiar from the work of Quine and Davidson is also to be noted.

6. Note the subjunctive in: "Then it would be impossible. . . ." Obviously, Wittgenstein assumes that it is possible to picture the world. Compare also 2.1: "We make ourselves pictures of the facts."

7. The contingent nature of the existence of a complex follows, in effect, from what is said in 2.0201: since it can be described, the composition must be a contingent situation. Compare also 3.24: "A complex can be given only by its description and this will be correct or not." Notice that this implies that complexity of entities and logical multiplicity (*logische Mannigfaltigkeit*) are categorially different, the former being contingent, the latter necessary.

8. Another instance of this we already encountered above, where we noted that in 2.0122, where it is argued that objects are not independent in the sense that they cannot occur on their own but only as constituents of situations, Wittgenstein makes the following parenthetical remark:

> (It is impossible that words occur in two different ways: by themselves and in sentences.) (2.0122)

The upshot of this passage is clear; in fact it is an allusion to the context principle, which is stated explicitly in 3.3. The argumentative status is more doubtful. It could be interpreted as an illustration, as a remark that says that the point made about objects also applies to words. However, the remarks on language that we are concerned with in 2.0211–2.0212 are clearly meant as an argument, not as a mere analogy.

9. The same point is expressed, conditionally, in the *Notebooks*:

> If there is a finite meaning and a sentence expressing it completely, then there are also names for simple objects. (18/6/15)

Why finiteness is an issue here, will be discussed later on.

10. Compare also the following passage from the *Notebooks*, which addresses the same issue in a slightly different context:

> For if in a sentence possibilities *are left open, exactly this* must be *determined: what* is left open. . . . What I do not know I do not know, but the sentence must show me WHAT I know. (17/6/15)

11. The connection with simplicity is made immediately in the *Notebooks* passage just quoted, as it continues as follows:

> And then is not this *determined* thing, which I *must* arrive at, just simple in the sense that I always had in mind? (17/6/15)

12. Compare also the following passage from the *Notebooks*:

> One could also require determinateness thus!: If a sentence is to have a meaning, then first of all the syntactic use of every part must be determined.—One could not, for example, *only afterward find out* that a sentence follows from it. But, for example, which sentences follow from a sentence must be completely settled before this sentence can have a meaning! (18/6/15)

As for the a priori character of logical relationships hinted at in this passage, compare the ontological analogue in 2.0123: "If I know an object I also know all its possibilities to occur in states of affairs.... A new possibility cannot be discovered afterwards." Compare also 5.5563: " All the sentences of our everyday language are actually, the way they are, logically well ordered." In both cases the same point is made, namely, that in logic there are no surprises (6.1251).

13. That is, the *Tractatus* should not be interpreted as stating that the picture theory of meaning only applies at the level of completely analyzed sentences.

14. But not their actual meaning; compare the discussion of expressions and symbols in Chapter 2, above.

15. It is this feature of language, its ability to talk about the nontrue, the hypothetical, the conditional, that according to George Steiner is its most essential property (1975, 215). It is curious to note that the all-pervading indexicality of natural languages seems at odds with this view and hence with the nature of meaning as explicated by Wittgenstein, Frege, and many others. Frege's problems with the incorporation of indexicality into his platonic view on "Sinn" are well known. Of course, contextuality becomes a central issue in Wittgenstein's later work.

16. The first entry stating the picture theory can be found in the *Notebooks* in September of the same year.

17. This is what in Hintikka and Hintikka 1986, chapter 1, is called "the ineffability of semantics." In Wittgenstein's later work this continues to be an important theme, to which he frequently returns. Compare, for example, the following passage from the *Philosophical Remarks*:

> But this means that every way to make a language understandable already presupposes a language. And [that] the use of language in a certain sense cannot be thought. That is, [it can]not be taught through language, the way one can for example learn to play the piano through language.—And that means nothing else but: I cannot escape from language by means of language. (6)

In the *Philosophical Investigations* the point is made in various ways, most clearly perhaps in Wittgenstein's rejection of ostension as a way to found meaning, using observations that are already foreshadowed in the *Philosophical Remarks*.

18. Recall what Wittgenstein says on the impossibility of depicting logical form: "In order to be able to depict logical form, we would have to be able to position ourselves with sentences outside logic, that is to say outside the world" (4.12).

19. The analogies with the choices one faces when setting up a truth theory are intriguing, but will not be pursued here.

20. See what was said above, Chapter 2, n. 48, about the meaning and reference of names.

21. Compare also the quotation from *Philosophical Remarks*, 36, discussed above.

22. Notice that the argument makes essential use of the feature that the lack of reference of a name makes the sentences in which the name occurs meaningless, not just false. This is what 2.0211 means, given that names are the expressions that refer to substance, that is, objects. Since names do not have meaning but only reference, this is as it should be.

Apparently, there is a conflict with what Wittgenstein says later on in the *Tractatus*, in 3.24:

> A complex can be given only by its description, and this will be correct or not. A sentence that says something about a complex will not be nonsensical if the complex does not exist, but is simply false. (3.24)

This passage seems a clear reference to a Russellian analysis of descriptions. If a description describes a complex entity, then the existence of this complex is contingent, on the fulfillment of the descriptive conditions contained in the description. If these conditions are not met, the result is a false sentence, not a meaningless one. The key to understanding that the conflict is only apparent, lies in the thesis of determinateness of meaning. Every description of a complex in the end has to be analyzed away in a truth-functional combination of elementary sentences, in which only names occur. This is what determinateness of meaning requires. But at this level, that of names referring to something in the world, lack of reference results in meaninglessness and not just in falsehood. Hence the conclusion must be that at the level of complete analysis the references consist of objects, which are simple and which therefore cannot fail to exist.

We can reconstruct this as follows. Let S be of the form $P(\imath x\, Dx)$, that is, a sentence that ascribes some property P to a complex entity $\overline{C}$ uniquely satisfying the description $\imath x\, Dx$. Using Russell's contextual definition of descriptions (which seems licensed by 4.0031), we can analyze S as S', which is of the form $\exists x\,(\forall y\,(Dy \to x = y) \wedge Px)$. Clearly S' is false if $\overline{C}$ does not exist. However, determinateness of meaning implies that S' can be analyzed further, ultimately in terms of some (infinite) disjunction of (infinite) conjunctions of (negations of) elementary sentences, containing only names. That is, in the end S can be completely analyzed into S'' of the form: $((\neg)P^1 a_1 \wedge \ldots \wedge (\neg)P^n a_1 \wedge \ldots) \vee \ldots \vee ((\neg)\, P^1 a_n \wedge \ldots \wedge (\neg)P^n a_n \wedge \ldots) \vee \ldots$. Here, the P^i and a_i are names, which means that if one of them lacks reference, then S'' is meaningless. See Chapter 2, above, for a more detailed exposition of the relationship between quantified expressions and elementary sentences. Whether ultimately the analysis needs to take recourse to "literals," that is, to both atomic sentences and their negations, is a point we can leave out of consideration here.

23. Compare 5.135–5.1361.

24. Compare also:

> If two sentences contradict one another, then this shows their structure; similarly if one follows from the other, and so on. (4.1211)

25. In fact, we do have to reckon seriously with the possibility that there is no "right" interpretation of the *Tractatus* on this point. It may simply have not been clear to Wittgenstein himself at the time of writing what objects "really" are. Compare the remark Wittgenstein made years later in a conversation with Malcolm that "it was not his business, as a logician, to try to decide whether this thing or that was a simple thing or a complex thing, that being a purely *empirical* matter" (Malcolm 1958, 86). However, in order to remain faithful to our starting point, that we will try to interpret the *Tractatus* as a consistent whole, we will not pursue this possibility any further, at least not before we have tried the alternatives.

26. Throughout, "logical" and "linguistic" are used as basically synonymous qualifications, since for Wittgenstein analysis of language, including everyday language, is a logical enterprise.

27. Compare also the following passage from the *Tractatus*:

> Even if the world is infinitely complex, so that every fact consists of infinitely many states of affairs and each state of affair is composed of infinitely many objects, there would still have to be objects and states of affairs. (4.2211)

This remark occurs in a slightly different context. The point here is not that there are no simples, but that the process of analysis leading up to them might be infinite (and thus certainly not practically executable). The interesting thing to note is that this passage, which is stated in purely ontological terms, is a comment on an observation concerning language:

> It is obvious that in the analysis of sentences we must hit upon elementary sentences, which consist of names in immediate connection.
>
> The question here is how the sentential connection comes about. (4.221)

Again, the starting point is language, not ontology, and it is remarkable that Wittgenstein seems to appeal, not to a conceptual argument, but to a kind of intuition ("It is obvious [. . .]"). Such appeals, which seem rather out of place in a text that has such a tight argumentative structure, also occur elsewhere. For example, when discussing the relation between elementary sentences and complex ones, Wittgenstein states:

> Indeed the understanding of general sentences *palpably* depends on that of elementary sentences. (4.411)

But such appeals to intuition should come as no surprise. In the end the basic structure of logic cannot be established by deductive or conceptual argument: "Logic must take care of itself" (5.473) and ultimately it rests on a kind of understanding, or experience, that is noncontingent (5.552).

28. Parts of this passage were already quoted above, where we argued that Wittgenstein endorses an essentially linguistic approach to simplicity. Here we use it to illustrate Wittgenstein's views on the relation between simple and complex.

29. See also the passage of 18/6/15, which we also quoted already, about the linguistic relativity of simplicity.

30. We will discuss two of these in somewhat more detail below.

31. See Malcolm 1986, chapter 1.

32. See Malcolm 1986, 39.

33. Compare also the following passage from the *Notebooks*:

> The decomposition of bodies into *material points*, as we have them in physics, is nothing more than an analysis into *simple components*. (20/6/15)

This may seem a straightforward identification of simple objects with material objects, but appearances are misleading here. The point that Wittgenstein makes is a different one, namely, that within a physical description of reality (at a certain macroscopic level) we make use of a notion of material object that *in the context of that description* is simple. This is the same point as is made in the passage quoted above (of 18/6/15) about the "relativity" of simplicity to what a sentence expresses, that is, the determinateness of its meaning. This interpretation is borne out by the fact that immediately following the passage in question it is precisely the issue of determinateness of meaning that comes up again:

> But could it be possible that the sentences we normally use have, as it were, only an incomplete meaning (quite irrespective of their truth or falsity) and that the sentences of physics, so to speak, approach the stage in which a sentence really has a complete meaning? (20/6/15)

However, the idea that there is a distinction between ordinary language and the language of physics in this respect, which would turn logical analysis into a kind of physicalistic reductionism, is immediately rejected:

> When I say "The book is lying on the table," does this really have a completely clear meaning? (An EXTREMELY important question!)
> But the meaning must be clear, for after all we do mean *something* with the sentence, and as much as we *certainly* mean must surely be clear. (20/6/15)

Once more, it seems, we must conclude that Wittgenstein is not so much occupied with the question of what simplicity is, but with the problem of how it functions, that is, how it applies, as it evidently does, to ordinary sentences.

34. Some additional, though admittedly circumstantial, evidence for the sec-

ond interpretation comes from the *Philosophical Remarks*. Here Wittgenstein develops a new view on what elementary sentences are, and it is important to note that on this new view they are no longer supposed to be logically independent. Then he notices:

> In my old conception of elementary sentences there was no determination of the value of a coordinate; although my remark that a colored body lies within a color space, and so forth, could have brought me there directly. (83)

This refers, of course, to 2.0131 and clearly suggests that the *Tractatus* sentence is not about objects in the technical, tractarian sense of the word. For what Wittgenstein seems to say here is that his new view on elementary sentences is only one step away from what he says in the *Tractatus* about visual, auditory, and tactile entities. In other words, if in the *Tractatus* Wittgenstein would have regarded these phenomenal entities as examples of objects, he would have drawn the conclusion that elementary sentences are not logically independent, and indeed cannot be, right away. But he did not. On the contrary, the logical independence of elementary sentences is a cornerstone in the tractarian construction.

35. See also the discussion in n. 33, above.

36. See the references cited in Chapter 2, n. 3.

37. Through Schlick, who had regular meetings with Wittgenstein, Maslow may have learned something about Wittgenstein's ideas as they were developing at the time. But this information must have been little and no mention is made of it Maslow's book, nor does it show up in any other form.

38. Or, alternatively, that of a logical positivist. The two denominators are used in the literature more or less interchangeably, one stressing the connection with empiricism, the other that with positivism, two philosophical traditions on which logical empiricism draws. Our choice of terminology should not be interpreted as taking a stand on the issue of which tradition logical empiricism owes most to.

39. Maslow 1931, 1. Interestingly, Maslow supports this with a reference to 5.6: "*The limits of my language* mean the limits of my world."

40. Maslow 1931, 2–3.

41. Ibid., 7.

42. Ibid., 20. See also 19 and 31–32.

43. See Blackwell 1984, 11.

44. Russell said to Wittgenstein's sister Hermine, who was visiting him in Cambridge in the summer of 1912, "We expect the next big step in logic is to be taken by your brother" (H. Wittgenstein 1984, 2).

45. See Blackwell 1984 for a detailed account. Probably this is what *Tractatus* 5.5422 refers to. See also Russell, who in a letter to Lady Ottoline Morrell of 1916 recalls:

> [Wittgenstein's] criticism . . . was an event of first-rate importance in my life, and affected everything I have done since. I saw he was right, and I saw that I could not hope ever again to do fundamental work in philosophy. (Russell 1975, 282)

The irony of Russell, who destroyed Frege's life work, in his turn being shattered by Wittgenstein's criticism is remarkable.

46. See above, Chapter 2.

47. See Sluga 1980, chapter 1, for Frege's motives.

48. Recall Hume's (in)famous exclamation in his *An Enquiry Concerning Human Understanding*: "When we run over libraries . . . what havoc must we make? If we take in our hand any volume; of divinity or school metaphysics, for instance; let us ask, 'Does it contain any abstract reasoning concerning quantity or number?' No. 'Does it contain any experimental reasoning concerning matter of fact and existence?' No. Commit it then to the flames: for it can contain nothing but sophistry and illusion."

49. See Chapter 2, above, where this point is treated in some detail.

50. Like so many restrictive views on what philosophy (or knowledge, or value, or meaning) is, the empiricist conception fails to meet its own criterion of meaningfulness. Such radical views presume the existence of an archimedean point that enables the formulation of a universal claim or characterization that does not apply to the view itself. The very existence of such a point is what may legitimately be called into question.

51. His work in the "middle period," of the late 1920s and early 1930s, such as the *Philosophical Remarks* and the *Philosophical Grammar*, does show a concern with "verifiability," but arguably construes this notion in a much more extended sense than that of the logical empiricists.

52. See above, Chapter 2, n. 7.

53. Although Wittgenstein did meet with Frank Ramsey in 1923 and 1924 and discussed the *Tractatus* with him, at the time he thought himself unable to do any creative research. See McGuinness's introduction to *Ludwig Wittgenstein and the Vienna Circle*, section II.

54. See *Ludwig Wittgenstein and the Vienna Circle* for detailed records of these conversations over the years 1929–32. The meetings with the circle started in 1927.

55. Carnap 1963, 26–27.

56. See von Wright 1958.

57. See Monk 1990, 243.

58. The poem is from Tagore's 1916 collection *Stray Birds*.

59. This is very well appreciated by Paul Engelmann, who writes:

> A whole generation of disciples was able to take Wittgenstein as a positivist because he has something of enormous importance in common with

> the positivists: he draws the line between what we can speak about and what we must be silent about just as they do. The difference is only that they have nothing to be silent about. Positivism holds—and this is its essence—that what we can speak about is all that matters in life. Whereas Wittgenstein passionately believes that all that really matters in human life is precisely what, in his view, we must be silent about. (Engelmann 1967, 97)

In view of Schlick's interest in ethics and Neurath's political and social engagement (see Hilmy 1987, 307–16) this judgment is perhaps a little too harsh. But it does capture the gulf between Wittgenstein's ethical and spiritual concerns and the main objectives of the logical empiricists.

60. Maslow 1931, introduction, xiii, emphasis added.
61. Maslow 1931, 11–12.
62. Ibid., 19, emphasis added.
63. Ibid., 19–20.
64. Ibid., 2.
65. Ibid., 20.
66. Ibid., 16.
67. At least in this sense that he says the existence of reality in this sense cannot be denied: "... to say that it is nonsensical to discuss reality if it does not conform to the prerequisites of language is not the same as to deny any reality" (ibid., 16).
68. Compare:

> We cannot discuss a reality that does not conform to the necessary prerequisites of all symbolism, because we cannot have any discussion (and therefore knowledge) without the medium of symbolism. (16)

Yet it cannot be denied either, and Maslow notices that Wittgenstein acknowledges its existence in some way:

> That reality is not confined to the describable is admitted by Wittgenstein in his "mystical." (16)

69. Ibid., 12.
70. Thus Maslow says that "the term 'object' ... will stand indiscriminately for the elements which are simple in relation to our language in actual use" (12).
71. Recall that in Wittgenstein's symbolism different variables stand for different objects.
72. See also the letter to Russell of 19/8/19 (*Notebooks*, 131). Here the notion of an expression showing a property that cannot be expressed comes rather close to the notion of "characterization" in possible-world semantics for modal logic, where, for example, a formula such as $\Box \phi \rightarrow \phi$ is said to characterize the property of reflexivity of the accessibility relation, by virtue of being valid on all and only those models in which this relation is reflexive. The point is that the language (of

modal propositional logic) as such does not have the means to express this feature directly—that is, it cannot be said—yet does have the means to characterize it—that is, it can be shown.

73. Maslow 1931, 13.

74. Also, it presumably assumes that an infinite analysis, one without a terminus, is not conceivable, a possibility that Wittgenstein explicitly leaves open (see 4.2211).

75. Maslow 1931, 24.

76. Also remarkable is one of the examples that Maslow gives to illustrate this point. Referring to the conventional establishment of the length of one foot, he writes ". . . thus [a] foot was not of the length of one foot before the original decision" (28). This reminds one, of course, of Wittgenstein's discussion in *Philosophical Investigations* of the standard meter in Paris, where Wittgenstein says: "There is *one* thing of which one cannot assert either that it is 1 meter long or that it is not 1 meter long, and that is the standard meter in Paris" (50). Other remarkable anticipations of themes from Wittgenstein's later work that can be found in Maslow's book concern the comparison of language with games, notably chess (30), a concept that Wittgenstein employed to great extent in his middle period, and Maslow's use (29–30) of the phenomenon of reading to explain the distinction between rules and causal connections, a phenomenon that Wittgenstein also discusses extensively in his rule-following considerations in *Philosophical Investigations*.

77. That this is perhaps not the most likely interpretation of 6.3751 is not relevant here. See Chapter 2, above, for another interpretation.

78. Maslow 1931, 35.

79. Ibid., 36.

80. Ibid., 20.

81. Ibid., 38.

82. Ibid., 39.

83. See Carnap's notion of a "linguistic framework" (1950), which is quite like Maslow's choice of a language.

84. Another, more contemporary way of expressing what the difference comes down to is the following. Consider the model-theoretic interpretation of some language of intensional predicate logic. Usually, the meaning (interpretation) of the descriptive constants is stated relative to a model, but that of the logical constants is not. Their interpretation is fixed by the definition of what an acceptable model for the language is in the first place. Thus, such a semantics is absolutistic with respect to the underlying logic. At the same it may allow for nonlogical necessities in the following sense. There may be formulae ϕ and classes of models Γ such that $\Gamma \vDash \phi$ while at the same time $\nvDash \phi$, that is, formulae that hold in a certain class of models, but not in all, and that hence are not logically necessary. Actually, it is on

the possibility of this distinction that the entire semantical approach to intensional logic rests. Alternatively, the semantics of nonlogical expressions may abstract over all models, thus in effect giving no theory of meaning for the descriptive constants at all. Notice that both alternatives are not in line with what Wittgenstein wants. He is an absolutist not just with respect to logic but also with respect to descriptive meaning. By that we mean the following. Given that a set of descriptive expressions has meaning at all, all semantic relationships between them are fixed, and hence are logical relationships: there is only logical necessity. Thus phrased, the connection with what was called "determinateness of meaning" earlier on should be obvious. Put in model-theoretic terms, what Wittgenstein sees as the (theoretical) goal of a semantic theory is that it fix, not a class of acceptable models, but the one, "true" model. But that is what a relativistic approach such as that of Maslow will not give us.

85. Stenius 1960, 79.

86. In model-theoretic vocabulary: a frame, that is, a domain together with an interpretation function.

87. Nor does Wittgenstein want to resort to a special logical intuition in the manner of Frege, although this possibility is not discussed explicitly in the passages at hand.

88. The present discussion is mainly based on Ishiguro 1969 and McGuinness 1984.

89. McGuinness 1984, 62.

90. Ishiguro 1969, 40.

91. See what was said at the beginning of this chapter, about the distinction between metaphysics proper and "natural language metaphysics."

92. McGuinness 1984, 72. But notice that, since the structure of a state of affairs or a situation is determined by that of the objects constituting it (2.032, 2.034), it follows that we do learn something about the latter by grasping the former.

93. The generalization from names to all subsentential expressions is implicit in 3.314: "An expression has reference only in a sentence."

94. What follows is based only partly on Ishiguro's paper. In other respects it is a rational reconstruction of a particular type of argument that I think is exemplified in her paper.

95. See, in particular, "Über Sinn un Bedeutung" (1892a) and "Über Begriff und Gegenstand" (1892b).

96. Which for Frege comprise any individual denoting expression, including proper names ("Aristotle"), descriptions ("The teacher of Alexander the Great"), functional expressions applied to an argument ("The square root of 9"). See "Über Sinn und Bedeutung." Frege applies the meaning–reference scheme also to sentences and to predicative expressions, but we restrict ourselves to the case of individual-denoting expressions here.

97. Consider for example "the first person to set foot on Mars," which clearly has a meaning, as is apparent from the meaningfulness of a sentence such as "The first person to set foot on Mars will be a woman." Frege's own example (in "Über Sinn und Bedeutung") is even more striking: "the least convergent series" is a name that has a meaning, but necessarily lacks a reference. The applicability of the meaning–reference distinction to all categories of expressions is imperative here, as is the functional relationship between them, that is, the compositionality principle.

98. The former because "Sinn" follows a cognitive notion and the latter since "Sinn" is also a semantic concept. This conflation of functions is one of the sources of problems with Frege's theory, which has led to the development of alternatives such as the rigid designator view on names of Kripke (1980). See Salmon 1982, chapter 1, for extensive discussion.

99. See "Über Sinn und Bedeutung," n. 2.

100. Which is why many people have assumed that Frege at a certain point traded in the context principle for that of compositionality. Such an assumption seems compulsory if one interprets the context principle in the strong way outlined above (on pain of ascribing inconsistency to Frege on this point). Alternatively, one may give a weaker interpretation to the context principle, on which it is consistent with compositionality. For one such account, see Dummett 1973, chapter 6. Roughly speaking, Dummett argues that compositionality and contextuality are not at odds, but serve to highlight different aspects of meaning. Compositionality is what explains our ability to use and understand language, ever-new sentences being built up from a fixed set of words that have independent meaning and hence are basic for the meanings of larger expressions. Contextuality serves to stress that the sentence, and not the word, is the primary unit when it comes to explaining the function of language.

101. Russell 1905, 1918 are the main sources. See also Russell 1918–19.

102. Here Ishiguro refers to Wittgenstein's argumentation in *Philosophical Investigations*, 28–36, against the foundational use of ostension, which immediately precedes his treatment of the name–object relation. Of course if, unlike Ishiguro, one assumes that in these sections of the *Philosophical Investigations* Wittgenstein is criticizing his former views, one might regard these passages as proof that Wittgenstein did hold this view of ostension at the time he wrote the *Tractatus*.

103. See McGuinness 1984, 72–73.

104. The relationship between a name and the object it represents is not a contingent relationship mediated by a descriptive content, which names lack by definition.

105. That a formal concept and its instantiations in a certain sense cannot be distinguished is clear from the following passage:

A formal concept is already given with one object that falls under it. So one cannot introduce both the objects of a formal concept *and* the formal concept itself as basic concepts. (4.12721)

106. See McGuinness 1984, 72.

107. The weak interpretation is by Dummett. See n. 100, above.

108. This notion of a formal object is quite a common one in current information-based theories in formal semantics, witness the so-called discourse referents of discourse representation theory and similar notions in other theories of dynamic semantics. See, for example, Groenendijk, Stokhof, and Veltman (1996).

109. Compare also the following passage, in which having a reference is equated with having a use, and having the same use is tied to equivalence:

Signs that serve *one* purpose are logically equivalent; signs that serve *no* purpose are logically meaningless. (5.47321)

110. This way of speaking gets some support from Wittgenstein's interpretation of mathematical expressions, which in 6.2 are characterized as equations (*Gleichungen*), hence "pseudosentences" [*Scheinsätze*], but which are declared to be not without use, since they show the logic of the world (6.22). See Frascolla 1994, chapter 1.

111. Of course, meaningful identity sentences involving complex denoting expressions are not excluded. And being meaningful, they are contingent. But notice that such identities are dismantled at the level of complete analysis, by the use of Russell's analysis of ordinary names and descriptions.

112. In 5.53–5.5352 Wittgenstein discusses the subject of identity sentences more extensively. He claims that identity is not a relation between entities ("By the way: to say of *two* things that they are identical is a non-sense, and to say of *one* thing that it is identical with itself is to say nothing at all," 5.5303) and that, hence, identity as a linguistic expression is superfluous ("The identity-sign therefore is not an essential constituent of the conceptual notation," 5.533). Wittgenstein's particular way of using names and variables is an important factor here. Both names and variables are assumed to distinguish their reference, in the sense that different names, and different variables, refer to different objects:

Identity of object I express by identity of sign, and not by means of an identity sign. Difference of objects by difference of signs. (5.53)

Thus, $f(a,b)$ implies that $a \neq b$, and $f(x,y)$ that $x \neq y$. This is, of course, completely in line with the view that identity sentences are a grammatical device.

113. The reader may wonder why Wittgenstein expressed himself the way he did. But notice that the *Tractatus* contains more examples of one and the same term used in different ways. For example, "world" [*Welt*] sometimes refers to a concrete (possible or actual) world, sometimes to all of logical space, and sometimes even to something that is neither of the foregoing (compare 6.45). Apparently,

Wittgenstein relied on the context to prevent any misunderstanding. And so did his translators, by the way: the Pears and McGuinness translation gives "meaning" for both occurrences of "Bedeutung" in 4.241 and 4.242, trading on the same ambiguity as the German. In Dutch, however, one would be forced to give two distinct translations.

Actually, Wittgenstein also uses "Bedeutung" sometimes in the ordinary, intuitive sense, of "semantical content." Compare 4.243, 2d para., where he speaks of "gleichbedeutend," obviously meaning "synonymous."

114. One should note, by the way, that McGuinness gives a weaker interpretation of 3.263 and of the notion of an elucidation. According to him, the upshot of 3.263 is simply that only complete sentences are able to carry information about objects and about the world. That is, the use of a mere name, outside the context of a sentence, will not tell us anything. This in effect is quite like the weak, Dummettian interpretation of the context principle (see n. 100, above), according to which it expresses the priority of sentences over names when it comes to carrying information.

115. Here there is a difference with names as rigid designators as conceived of by Kripke. On Kripke's analysis they may be assigned a reference by contextual stipulation ("fixing the reference" in an act of "initial baptism"), but may lose the properties that have been used in this stipulation later on, or even may turn out not to have had them in the first place. See Kripke 1980, Lecture II.

116. Recall what was noted above (see Chapter 2, n. 72) concerning Wittgenstein's use of "general" and "generality."

117. Likewise, given Wittgenstein's particular convention regarding variables and given the fact that different names stand for different objects (compare 5.531: "And [I do not write] '$f(a,b) \land a \neq b$', but '$f(a,b)$.'"), $fa \land fb$ comes to the same as $\exists x \exists y \, (fx \land fy)$.

118. Ishiguro 1969, 43.

119. Compare also the following claim in the early (1913) "Notes on Logic": "It is *a priori* likely that the introduction of atomic propositions is fundamental for the understanding of all other kinds of propositions. In fact the understanding of general propositions obviously depends on that of atomic propositions" (106). In the *Tractatus* this remark occurs, slightly differently phrased (with "obviously" replaced by "*palpably*"), in 4.411.

120. We slightly deviate from 5.526, which talks about a sentence that claims that there is a unique x such that.... The difference is not relevant here.

121. In fact, it is quite unclear in what sense we could talk of a "description" of logical space in the first place.

122. See Genesereth and Nillson 1987, chapter 4, for an overview. Skolem-constants are used for occurrences that are not in the scope of an occurrence of a universal quantifier. Otherwise we use Skolem-functions: functional constants applied

to the variable bound by the universal quantifier, in order to account for the dependency. Since our toy example, $\exists x\, fx$, falls within the easier, first class, we can limit our discussion to Skolem-constants.

123. Recall the remark made in Chapter 2, n. 73.

124. Another example of this kind of use of individual constants is provided by the familiar Henkin-construction, used in completeness proofs for quantificational languages, where constants are introduced as witnesses to build representations of (sets of) quantified formulae.

125. Malcolm 1986, viii.

126. Ibid.

127. Ibid., 14.

128. Ibid., 30.

129. Ibid., 52.

130. And which constitutes a feature that seems to be contradicted in 2.0122, where it is said that objects cannot appear independently of states of affairs.

131. Consider, for example, states of affairs that involve a specific spatio-temporal location of an object they contain.

132. Malcolm 1986, 30.

133. Ibid., 33.

134. Ibid., 34.

135. See also above, n. 25. And then, the evidence from later years is not unambiguous. Thus Wittgenstein said in a conversation with Waismann in 1931:

> Thus I used to believe, for example, that it is the task of *logical* analysis to discover the elementary sentences. (*Ludwig Wittgenstein and the Vienna Circle*, 9/12/31, emphasis added)

Given the isomorphic relationship between language and the world, it seems hard to believe that finding out the ultimate structure of the latter is an empirical matter, while the same task with regard to the former is a logical one.

136. The German terms are *vertreten* and *Vertretung*; compare, for example, 3.22 and 4.0312.

137. This seems to be corroborated by the exchange between Wittgenstein and Ogden about the English translation. Concerning the translation of the German *kennen* Wittgenstein writes: ". . . to know here just means: I know *it* but I needn't know anything *about* it" (*Letters to Ogden*, 59).

138. See also 5.524, where the same phrase is used.

139. A similar objection can be raised against the analogy that Malcolm construes between Russell and Wittgenstein at this point. Both Russell and Wittgenstein, Malcolm claims, are involved in a reductionist enterprise, that of reducing knowledge by description to knowledge by acquaintance. But the parallel breaks down, essentially for the reason just outlined. From Wittgenstein's point of view, knowledge of external properties cannot be reduced to that of internal prop-

erties, since the former belong to the realm of the contingent, the latter to that of the necessary, and these two are strictly and absolutely separated. (Compare 2.223–2.225.) Of course, with Russell things are different. For him, knowledge by acquaintance, being concerned with sense data, which are "ordinary" empirical objects, is contingent, empirical knowledge, albeit of a special kind. See Russell 1914.

140. As Malcolm does; see 1986, 76.

141. See the various passages from the *Notebooks* that were analyzed above.

142. Malcolm 1986, 39. Likewise, 2.0211 and the argument discussed in *Philosophical Investigations* (55) are characterized as "arguments from the possibility of language" (Malcolm 1986, 48).

143. Ibid., 40.

144. See Pears 1987, vol. I, chapter 5. See Hintikka and Hintikka 1986, chapter 3. See also the additional references in Chapter 1, n. 11, above.

145. Stenius's analysis also makes clear that even with respect to the picture theory there is more room for continuity in Wittgenstein's thinking than is sometimes supposed. He notes that the picture theory is independent from the logical atomism of the *Tractatus* in the sense that the two coincide only given a specific interpretation of the notion of logical form. (Compare the reconstruction of 2.02–2.0212 above, where the key notion of the atomistic theory, the logical independence of states of affairs, was seen to depend on both the picture theory and the ineffability of meaning conditions, which in its turn rests upon a certain idea about logical form.) Consequently, one could argue that "picturing" may be one way of expressions having meaning that has a place in the gamut of language games that Wittgenstein discerns in his later work. It no longer occupies a privileged position, but there is also no need to assume that along with his original atomism it has been abandoned by Wittgenstein as a possible way of having meaning. See Stenius 1984 for more details; and Hacker 1984b for a dissenting opinion.

146. As for example David Pears seems to do. See Pears 1987, vol. I, 100.

147. See also Carruthers, who acknowledges the pivotal role of language, yet insists that this does not lead to some kind of linguistic idealism and consequently takes Ishiguro and McGuinness to task for thinking it does; see Carruthers 1990, 24–27, 171–72.

148. See also Garver 1994, chapter 6, for a discussion of Malcolm's and Pears's views, which is akin in spirit to the one presented here.

149. This conception of substance as a logical construction seems also what Wittgenstein is hinting at in the following passage from his remarks on Frazer:

> The picture in terms of which one conceives of reality here is that beauty, death, and so on, are the pure (concentrated) substances, while they are present as an admixture in a beautiful object.—And do I not recognize here my own observations concerning "object" and "complex"? (*Remarks on Frazer's Golden Bough*, 10)

One way to read this, admittedly cryptic, passage is as follows. The notion of an object, of the absolutely simple, is like that of a pure substance: an abstraction underlying, or present in, as an "admixture," real, complex things. This is a picture of reality, a particular, significant way of viewing it. In this case, it is a picture that is suggested by the way in which our language seems to work.

CHAPTER 4

1. This theme of "saying by not saying" constitutes in a sense the very essence of Wittgenstein's view on ethics, as we shall see in more detail later on. In a letter to Engelmann, dated 09/04/17, Wittgenstein expresses it as follows:

> And it is like that: if one does not strain oneself to say the unsayable, *nothing* gets lost. Rather the unsayable is—unsayably—*contained* in what is said! (Engelmann 1967, 6)

2. See Wittgenstein's own notes from this period, published as the so-called *Secret Notebooks*. See also the recollections of Paul Engelmann (1967), who was in close contact with Wittgenstein during these years.

3. See, for example, the recollections of Norman Malcolm (1958); Paul Engelmann (1967); and Fania Pascal (1979). See also the extensive discussion in Monk 1990.

4. Compare the following remark he once made to his former student, Drury: "I am not a religious man but I cannot help seeing every problem from a religious point of view" (Drury 1984, 94).

5. Wittgenstein's attitude toward suicide clearly also has a biographical background. Three of his brothers committed suicide, and in the period he was working on the *Tractatus*, the thought of killing himself was never far from his own mind.

6. According to some the influence of Schopenhauer is not restricted to the *Tractatus*-period but extends to the later work. See Magee 1983, appendix 3, for some discussion. We will leave this matter out of consideration here. Below we will argue that already in the *Tractatus* period there are, besides remarkable analogies, some important differences between Wittgenstein and Schopenhauer. See further Janik 1966; Phillips Griffiths 1974; Clegg 1978; and Brockhaus 1991.

7. For example, Maslow 1961; Kenny 1973; Hintikka and Hintikka 1986; Malcolm 1986; Peterson 1990; Carruthers 1990; and Garver 1994 do not mention Schopenhauer at all. Stenius 1960; Anscombe 1963; Black 1964; Edwards 1985; and Bearn 1997 refer to him only passing.

8. A typical example is Hacker's treatment of the matter in Hacker 1984a, as will be made clear below. Similar objections can be raised to Pears 1987.

9. See Chapter 3, above, where we discussed Wittgenstein's attitude toward traditional epistemological issues in the context of his relationship with logical empiricism.

10. Interestingly, this is one of the points discussed extensively in Russell's introduction to the *Tractatus* (see Russell 1921, xviii–xx). Although Russell's analysis focuses on different issues, his (implicit) conclusion is in line with the one reached here, namely, that the subject, being a complex, does not have any privileged status, metaphysically speaking.

11. Such a conception of the subject, that is, of an individual, may very well be counterintuitive, yet, on closer reflection turns out to be certainly not inconsistent. The relation between a set and its elements in set theory may provide a partial model.

12. This view on intensional constructions, which actually analyses them away and thus holds on to the extensional point of view that all sentences are truth-functional, is one of the points at which Wittgenstein strongly influenced Russell. See the introduction to the second edition of the *Principia* (xiii–xlvi), in which Russell and Whitehead (1912–13) acknowledge this influence of Wittgenstein's explicitly. See also n. 10 above.

Another point worth noticing here is that there is an interesting parallel between Wittgenstein's analysis and the one proposed by Davidson of sentences expressing certain attitudes, for example, in Davidson 1968. Davidson, too, is motivated by the wish to remain within the confines of an extensional theory. It should be pointed out, though, that in the context of the *Tractatus* the extensionality regards just the semantics, not the ontology. (See also Chapter 2, above.)

13. This analysis of 5.542ff. is corroborated by the "Notes Dictated to Moore" of 1914, where at the very end we read the following:

> The relation of "I believe p" to "p" can be compared to the relation of "'p' says [*besagt*] p" to p: it is just as impossible that I should be a simple as that "p" should be.

14. Schopenhauer 1844. We follow the text as given in Schopenhauer 1986, volumes I and II.

15. Note that in 6.34 Wittgenstein characterizes this principle, along with some others, as "an a priori insight into the possible design of the sentences of science."

16. Schopenhauer 1844, part II, book 1, chapter 1.

17. That experience is always experience of something that is the case, that is, of situations, not of things, follows from Wittgenstein's logical atomism, in the same way as it does in his treatment of picturing, meaning, knowledge, thinking.

18. See the illuminating discussion in Apel 1973 of the parallels between Wittgenstein and Heidegger in this respect. See also Fay 1991.

19. In the original German: "(der Sprache, die allein Ich verstehe)". This phrase has caused much confusion, as some authors—for example, Anscombe in the first edition of her introduction—have interpreted it as referring to a private language, thus reinforcing a solipsistic interpretation of these passages. See Hintikka 1958, for

some relevant criticism; and Anscombe 1963, 167, n. 1, for the correction of her former view.

20. See above, Chapter 2, n. 53.

21. The corollaries with certain (*Mahāyāna-*)Buddhist views on the self are too obvious not to notice. Compare the following quotation from the *Heart Sutra*:

> Avalokita, The Holy Lord and Bodhisattva, was moving in the deep course of the Wisdom which has gone beyond. He looked down from on high, he beheld but five heaps, and he saw that in their own-being they were empty. (Conze 1958, 99–100)

The five heaps are the five constituents of the personality: (bodily) form, feelings, perceptions, impulses, and consciousness. ". . . in their own-being they were empty" means that they have no substance, no underlying bearer distinct from them, and hence are impermanent and changing. See Conze 1958, 104, for more details. Of course, one must be careful not to draw unwarranted conclusions from the mere observation of the existence of parallels such as these. See below, n. 54.

22. In this sense the *Tractatus* can be viewed as embodying a kind of linguistic idealism: logic and the world are mutually dependent on each other. Without logic there is no world; without the world there is no logic. See 5.552, in which it is said that the fundamental experience underlying logic is that something is, that is, that there is the world, a world, any world at all. However, in the end Wittgenstein's position is more akin to realism than to idealism. For the world that is dependent on logic, that is, the world that can be thought of in an idealistic fashion vis-à-vis logic, in the end turns out to be not the world as such but the realization of one aspect of what also has other dimensions. The other dimension is that of ethics, which shows itself not in language or in logic, but in our actions. This indicates that that of which language (logic) and ethics are distinct dimensions, must be distinguished from both language and ethics. And that suggests a realistic perspective.

23. See the discussion in 6.32–6.342 of causality and the principle of sufficient reason. Is this what Wittgenstein meant when he said about Schopenhauer that "where real depth starts his stops" (*Culture and Value*, 1939–40)? This remark could perhaps (also) be interpreted as suggesting that Wittgenstein's own logical analysis digs deeper than the epistemological analysis of Schopenhauer. According to Magee (1983, 298), this is indeed the right interpretation.

24. But recall what was said in Chapter 1, n. 54, about the historical justification of this claim.

25. See, for example, Hacker 1984a; Pears 1987.

26. In particular, see Frege's "Über Sinn und Bedeutung" (1892a) and "Der Gedanke" (1918).

27. Another element of the standard interpretation as proposed, for example, by Hacker, is the suggestion that Wittgenstein was concerned with solipsism as a real problem, not just in the *Tractatus*, but also in his later work. However, that

view seems not quite correct, as it can be argued that the problem that really occupied Wittgenstein was not solipsism in the traditional, epistemological sense, but rather the constitution and status of the subject. Especially in the later work on psychology, but also in the *Philosophical Investigations*, this is a recurrent theme.

28. As was noted above, the principle of sufficient reason is said to be an "a priori insight" (6.34) and in 6.3211 it is said that: "Here, as always, what is a priori certain proves to be something purely logical." Thus this principle (along with some others, such as that of continuity) is classified as logical, not empirical. It should be noted, however, that the term "logical" is used in an extended sense here. It is not implied that such principles are tautologies. Rather, they seem to have the same kind of status as that of the sentences of the *Tractatus* itself.

29. So Schopenhauer's appeal to platonic forms serves both an epistemological and an ethical goal. See also his references to the Platonism of Pseudo-Dionysios. It is interesting to speculate whether Schopenhauer's esteem for early Christian thought is based in part on the Neoplatonist, gnostic elements therein.

30. This idea has certain Spinozistic overtones. Schopenhauer's attitude here could be characterized as a Spinozistic pantheism without God. For Spinozistic elements in Wittgenstein, see Garver 1994, chapter 8.

31. Recall Russell's remark in his introduction to the *Tractatus*: ". . . it leaves me with a sense of intellectual discomfort" (Russell 1921, xxi).

32. Schopenhauer 1851, II. We follow the text as given in Schopenhauer 1986, volume V.

33. As McGuinness's interpretation of the ethics of the *Tractatus* as a kind of "logical mysticism" would have it. See McGuinness 1966. According to McGuinness the basic logical "experience," namely, that something is, which Wittgenstein alludes to in 5.552, "has the same object as the mystical feeling," both being "an attitude towards the existence of the world" (313). There is no doubt that there are some striking parallels in the ways in which Wittgenstein speaks of mystical experience and of logic, the foregoing being just one example. Compare also:

> Ethics is not about the world. Ethics must be a condition of the world, like logic. (24/7/16)

Here Wittgenstein explicitly observes that there exists a similarity between ethics and logic vis-à-vis the world. But notice that he does not equate the two. Both ethics and logic are not in the world, but rather are constitutive of it. But in being such, logic and ethics function in radically different ways and they are correlated with two fundamentally different ways of viewing the world.

34. Of course, it does not follow that Wittgenstein does not acknowledge all kinds of other constraints, of a physical or psychological nature, on the relation between our wishing and our actions.

35. Compare also:

If the will must have an object in the world, then this can also be the intended object.

And the will must have an object.

Otherwise we would not have a support and could not know what we willed. (4/11/16)

36. Parenthetically, he adds: "(And this is clear too, that the reward must be something pleasant, the punishment something unpleasant.)" (6.422). This throws serious doubt on the interpretation of Wittgenstein's ethics as some kind of hedonism.

37. The idea that ethical value does not depend on causes or consequences and that hence ethical reward and ethical punishment are intrinsic to the action itself seems to be a constant in Wittgenstein's thinking. He once said to Malcolm (see 1958, 70–71) that whereas the concept of God as creator had no appeal for him, the concept of God as judge did. Then in the "Lectures on Religious Belief" he says:

If I do so-and-so, then someone will put me in fires in a thousand years. I wouldn't budge. The best scientific evidence is just nothing. (56)

Evidently this cannot mean that Wittgenstein rejects the concept of divine judgment as such. Rather, this passage should be read in line with the *Tractatus*: God as a judge is not an external instrument of punishment, someone who exercises his powers of judgment after the act. Rather, punishment and reward, good and bad, must be viewed as intrinsic to the action itself. One is punished for performing an ethically bad action not because of it, but by it, that is, by it being an ethically unjust thing in itself.

38. In this Wittgenstein is, of course, not alone, but stands in a tradition. To give just one example, in *Das Buch der Göttlichen Tröstung* Meister Eckehart writes that "man if he is good, wills everything God wills" (136).

39. See 6.432 cited below.

40. Wittgenstein says that this is an entirely personal matter, but we take it that in calling it "personal" he refers to the fact that he has it, and others may not, but not that the content of the experience as such is personal. The idea of existence as such being the primary impetus for philosophical reflection, is quite common and can be found also in entirely different traditions. An example is Heidegger's emphasis on the question of Being as the first question, the one which should be at the root of all philosophy. In Wittgenstein's case, this experience, which in tractarian terms is not a proper experience at all, has a distinctly ethical meaning. For him the very existence of the world constitutes the primordial ethical task.

41. As seems to be the interpretation by Phillips Griffiths (1974, 111).

42. This spiritual ideal is, of course, familiar from various traditions. Compare, for example, the following formulation from Meister Eckehart (also from *Das Buch der Göttlichen Tröstung*):

So when man loves him and all things and performs his works not for reward, for honor, or for comfort, but only for God and God's honor, that is a sign that he is God's son. (121)

Later in this chapter we will point out some parallels with a non-Christian tradition, namely, that of Buddhism.

43. Describing the ethical life as a life of knowledge is not uncommon and can be found in some form or other in various traditions. For example, in the mystical writings of Meister Eckehart emphasis is placed on a certain type of knowledge (*Vernunft*) that is a prerequisite for the ultimate *unio mystica*. Similar notions play a role in various Platonist and Neoplatonist traditions. Compare also the role of *gnosis* in early Christian gnosticism (which was influenced by Neoplatonism) and that of *prajñā* in *Mahāyāna* Buddhism. This knowledge, which has nothing to do with knowledge of facts, constitutes the basis of the ultimate liberation. And conversely, in both traditions ignorance is considered to be the primary source of delusion and suffering. In both traditions there is a concomitant notion of wisdom (*sophia, prajñāpāramitā*), which is often personified. So what Wittgenstein is referring to here is a kind of noncognitive knowledge that forms the basis of the ethical and that is familiar from various traditions.

44. See Moran 1973, 46.

45. And the same holds for the interpretation of Hintikka and Hintikka, who ascribe to Wittgenstein some kind of Bloomsburean aestheticism (1986, 67–68).

46. See, for example, Magee 1983, 242ff.

47. Again, we quote, as just one example, from the work of Eckehart (*Erste Predigt* ["Intravit Jesus"]):

To live ... without before or after and without hindrance by all the works and all the images of which he ever becomes conscious, receiving anew, unattached and free, the divine gift in this now.

48. See, above, n. 37.

49. See Levi 1978, 1979; Rudebush and Berg 1979; and Bartley 1985.

50. Levi's account of the influence of Wittgenstein's homosexuality on the *Tractatus*, although on the right track in certain respects, actually leads to a misrepresentation of some of its main features. For example, according to Levi, Wittgenstein proposes a kind of "two worlds" hypothesis, in which the world of values is completely distinct from that of facts. In other words, on Levi's interpretation, ethics is transcendent, not transcendental. But this completely misses the crucial point that Wittgenstein makes, namely, that ethical values and actions are intrinsically related.

Unlike Levi, Bartley does not draw any conclusions from Wittgenstein's homosexuality with regard to the interpretation of the *Tractatus*. In the afterword to the second edition (1985, afterword, section II) Bartley discusses and rejects the idea that "a man's work, whether of art or of philosophy, is an expression of his inner state, of his emotions, of his personality" (171) as general principle of interpretation. Acknowledging that, nevertheless, sometimes personal circumstances do play a decisive role in shaping someone's philosophical views, he then discusses Levi's account in some detail and criticizes it, mainly for not allowing any room for the religious aspects of Wittgenstein's views on ethics.

51. See Dilman 1974, who makes a similar distinction.

52. Note that Anscombe translates the German "transcendent" as "transcendental," though Wittgenstein's own use of "transcendental" in 6.421 could be adduced in support.

53. This, incidentally, is another reason why the facts of the world constitute a "problem," as 6.4321 has it.

54. The remarks that follow are made solely with an eye toward getting a better grip on what Wittgenstein's views on this matter are. Although some have tried to make more of them (see Goodman 1976; Tominaga 1982, 1983 on Wittgenstein and Taoism; Hudson 1973, Canfield 1975 on the relationship with (Zen) Buddhism; and for critical discussion, see Phillips 1977; Gudmunsen 1973, 1977; and Kalupahana 1977), in my opinion the analogies that do exist between some of Wittgenstein's ideas and certain views in the Buddhist and Taoist traditions are historically and systematically by and large accidental.

55. A warning is in order here. The idea of suffering does not have to be interpreted in a nihilistic or even a pessimistic way. Although it is not uncommon to read Buddhist doctrine thus, other perspectives are possible as well. On the one extreme, some hold that Buddhism teaches that it is life itself, quite independently of us, that is suffering. But others argue that the right interpretation of the Buddha's teaching is that suffering essentially arises from the fact that we view life in a certain way and live it accordingly. The impermanent character of life gives rise to suffering because of our craving for permanence, our inability to accept the ever-changing nature of life. On such a view, it is not life itself that causes suffering, but our ordinary, unreflective way of interacting with it. For a clear exposition along these lines, see Kalupahana 1976, 1977. Obviously the term "Buddhism" does not refer to one single, well-defined body of doctrine, but rather denotes a wide variety of views and opinions.

Analogously, Wittgenstein's views on this issue can also be interpreted in such a way that the suffering of life is located in our way of interacting with the world rather than in the world as such. In the same way as philosophical problems arise from our misunderstanding of the logic of our language, which as such is perfectly in order (see the preface of the *Tractatus* and 5.5563), our problems in life are caused by a similar misunderstanding of the fundamental traits of the latter.

56. We will come back to the question of whether the relationship between such an ontological view and these spiritual, ethical insights is accidental or not.

57. As given in Conze 1951.

58. See Keown 1992, for extensive discussion. The tension between morality and ethics (in the present sense of that term) has a curious ontological analogue, namely, in the tension between immanence and transcendence. See the discussion below, for some further remarks.

59. Thus we disagree with Phillips Griffiths (1974, 108ff.), who sees a difference between Schopenhauer and Wittgenstein here.

60. Similar observations play a role in the discussion about the relationship between Buddhism and human rights. Whereas other religious traditions seem to offer a well-defined philosophical foundation for the concept of universal human rights, the matter is less clear as far as Buddhist philosophy (but not actual practice) is concerned. This is connected with Buddhist philosophy's view on the subject, in particular its *anātman* doctrine. For some relevant discussion, see Inada 1995; Keown 1995.

61. See, for example, Moran 1973; Dilman 1974; and Phillips Griffiths 1974. Thus, Phillips Griffith states that according to the tractarian picture "[ethics] is not in any way about how we should act" (97). For, he argues, if the willing subject is a mere limit of the world, it cannot constitute any a priori ethical laws. This is true in one sense, namely, that ethical laws are not concerned with contingent situations and relationships between them. But this does not warrant the conclusion in a strict sense, for it assumes that the world as a contingent set of contingent situations is all there is to reality. But ethics is concerned with reality in a totally different way.

62. See Moran 1973, 69ff.; Phillips Griffiths 1974, 113ff.

63. See the following quote, admittedly of a later date, from a letter to Drury:

> As to religious thoughts I do not think that the craving for placidity is religious; I think a religious person regards placidity or peace as a gift from heaven, not as something one ought to hunt after. (Drury 1984, 39)

64. Hence it is rather natural to think that there is a more than incidental link between ethics and logic. See, for example, McGuinness 1966. Such a view, however, does not do justice to the completely different roles that logic and ethics play in the tractarian system. Compare, above, n. 33.

65. The following passage illustrates that at other times, in other places, transcendence and immanence have been viewed in a remarkably similar manner:

> There is no difference whatever between *Nirvāna* and *Samsāra* [that is, the everyday world of appearances, *m.s.*]; Noumenon and Phenomena are not two separate sets of entities, nor are they two states of the same thing. The absolute looked at through the thought-forms of constructive imagination is the empirical world; and conversely, the absolute is the world *sub specie aeterni*, without the distorting media of Thought. (Murti 1955, 274, quoted from Conze 1958, 106)

But for the linguistic turn, this description of the kernel of *Mahāyāna* Buddhism could serve very well as a summary of Wittgenstein's views on the matter.

66. Again, there is an analogy with Buddhist doctrine. There, insight into the illusory character of the self and the impermanence of the world plays a similar role, forming part of the "right views," which are a step on the Eightfold Noble Path.

67. Perhaps it was also because he was aware of this aspect of his thinking that Wittgenstein started the preface of the *Tractatus* as follows:

> Perhaps this book will be understood only by someone who already has thought the thoughts expressed in it—or at least similar thoughts, himself. (Preface, first para.)

68. See above, n. 46.

69. See Safranski 1987, chapter 9, for extensive discussion and fragments of Schopenhauer's Nachlass.

70. The most detailed account is given in Baum 1991b. See also McGuinness 1988, chapter 7.

71. That Wittgenstein had no problems with his being wealthy is perhaps best illustrated by the following often related anecdote (see Monk 1990, chapter I.2): When studying in Manchester, Wittgenstein wanted to go to Blackpool on a Sunday afternoon. Upon discovering that there was no suitable train connection, Wittgenstein suggested to his companion Eccles that he hire one.

72. In a letter to Lady Ottoline Morrell of 20/12/19 Russell says:

> I had felt in his book a flavor of mysticism, but was astonished when I found that he has become a complete mystic. He reads people like Kierkegaard and Angelus Silesius, and he seriously contemplates becoming a monk. . . . He has penetrated deep into mystical ways of thought and feeling, but I think (though he wouldn't agree) that what he likes best in mysticism is its power to make him stop thinking. (*Letters to Russell, Keynes and Moore*, 82)

73. Recall what was related about the interaction between Wittgenstein and some members of the Vienna Circle in Chapter 3, above.

74. McGuinness 1966.

75. See, above, n. 33.

76. Of course, when the latter are taken to coincide with our rational, discursive mind, the inaccessibility would follow in the tractarian system. But notice that such a stand is not a necessary outcome of the linguistic turn as such, and that Wittgenstein clearly leaves room for some kind of nondiscursive access to this "other realm." See above, n. 43.

77. In this respect the tractarian framework seems eminently suited for a philosophical reconstruction of the empiricistic and pragmatic views of early Buddhism.

See Kalupahana 1987, for an analysis and an interesting comparison with the views of William James, whose *The Varieties of Religious Experience* also exercised a considerable influence on Wittgenstein. According to Kalupahana, this pragmatic character of early Buddhism has had to give way in later stages of the development of Buddhist thought to a more metaphysically oriented approach, with which Buddhism is now commonly associated.

78. It is also in this sense that the *Tractatus* is not a "textbook" (preface, first para.).

79. See also the discussion in Chapter 3, above.

80. Among others Hudson 1981; Kerr 1986; Johnston 1989; and Phillips 1970, 1981, and 1993.

81. See Monk 1990, chapter 17, for a detailed account.

82. As Malcolm reports, "[Wittgenstein] believed that his influence as a teacher was largely harmful" (1958, 62).

83. And speculative philosophy was bad poetry in many cases, at least to the taste of Rudolf Carnap; see Carnap 1932.

84. Here we need to keep in mind what was said above in n. 40.

Works Cited

PRIMARY SOURCES

Notes on Logic. 1913. In *Notebooks 1914–1916*, appendix I.
Notes Dictated to Moore. 1914. In *Notebooks 1914–1916*, appendix II.
Tractatus Logico-Philosophicus. 1921. English trans. David Pears and Brian McGuinness. 1961. London: Routledge and Kegan Paul.
Wittgenstein's Lectures, Cambridge 1930–32. 1980. Ed. D. Lee. Oxford: Blackwell.
Philosophical Investigations. 1958. Ed. G. E. M. Anscombe, R. Rhees, and G. H. von Wright. 2d ed. Oxford: Blackwell.
Letters to C. K. Ogden. 1973. Ed. G. H. von Wright. Oxford: Blackwell; London: Routledge.
Letters to Russell, Keynes and Moore. 1974. Ed. G. H. von Wright. Oxford: Blackwell.
Philosophical Grammar. 1974. Ed. R. Rhees. Oxford: Blackwell.
Philosophical Remarks. 1975. Ed. R. Rhees. Oxford: Blackwell.
Lectures on Religious Belief. 1978. In *Lectures and Conversations on Aesthetics, Psychology and Religious Belief*, ed. C. Barrett. Oxford: Blackwell.
Remarks on the Foundations of Mathematics. 1978. Ed. G. E. M. Anscombe, R. Rhees, and G. H. von Wright. 3d ed. Oxford: Blackwell.
Letters to Ludwig von Ficker. 1979. In *Wittgenstein: Sources and Perspectives*, ed. C. G. Luckhardt. Ithaca, N.Y.: Cornell University Press.
Ludwig Wittgenstein and the Vienna Circle. 1979. Conversations recorded by Friedrich Waismann, ed. B. McGuinness. Oxford: Blackwell.
Notebooks 1914–1916. 1979. Ed. G. H. von Wright and G. E. M. Anscombe. 2d ed. Oxford: Blackwell.
On Certainty. 1979. Ed. G. E. M. Anscombe and G. H. von Wright. Oxford: Blackwell.
Remarks on Frazer's Golden Bough. 1979. Ed. R. Rhees. Denton, UK: Brynmill Press.
Geheime Tagebücher 1914–1916. 1991. Ed. Wilhelm Baum. Wien: Turia and Kant.
Lecture on Ethics. [1929] 1993. In *Philosophical Occasions 1912–1951*, ed. J. Klagge and A. Nordmann. Indianapolis, Ind.: Hackett.

Some Remarks on Logical Form. [1929] 1993. In *Philosophical Occasions 1912–1951*, ed. J. Klagge and A. Nordmann. Indianapolis, Ind.: Hackett.

Culture and Value. 1998. Ed. G. H. von Wright. 2d ed. Oxford: Blackwell.

SECONDARY SOURCES

Anscombe, G. E. M. 1963. *An introduction to Wittgenstein's 'Tractatus.'* 2d ed. London: Hutchinson.

Apel, Karl-Otto. 1973. Wittgenstein und Heidegger. In *Transformation der Philosophie*. Band I. Frankfurt a/M.: Suhrkamp.

Bartley, William Warren III. 1985. *Wittgenstein*. 2d ed. LaSalle, Ill.: Open Court.

Barwise, Jon, and John Etchemendy. 1987. *The liar: An essay in truth and circularity*. Oxford: Oxford University Press.

Barwise, Jon, and John Perry. 1983. *Situations and attitudes*. Cambridge, Mass.: MIT Press.

Baum, Wilhelm. 1991a. Nachwort zur Edition. In *Ludwig Wittgenstein: Geheime Tagebücher 1914–1916*. Wien: Turia and Kant.

Baum, Wilhelm. 1991b. Wittgensteins Kriegsdienst im Ersten Weltkrieg. In *Ludwig Wittgenstein: Geheime Tagebücher 1914–1916*. Wien: Turia and Kant.

Bealer, George. 1982. *Quality and concept*. Oxford: Clarendon Press.

Bearn, Gordon C. 1997. *Waking to wonder: Wittgenstein's existential investigations*. Albany: State University of New York Press.

Benthem, Johan van. 1985. The variety of consequence according to Bolzano. *Studia Logica* 44:389–403.

Black, Max. 1964. *A companion to Wittgenstein's 'Tractatus.'* Ithaca, N.Y.: Cornell University Press.

Blackwell, Kenneth. 1984. Early Wittgenstein and middle Russell. In *Perspectives on the philosophy of Wittgenstein*, ed. Irving Block. Oxford: Blackwell.

Boltzmann, Ludwig. 1905. *Populäre Schriften*. Leipzig: Barth.

Brockhaus, Richard R. 1991. *Pulling up the ladder*. LaSalle, Ill.: Open Court.

Canfield, John V. 1975. Wittgenstein and Zen. *Philosophy* 50:383–408.

Carnap, Rudolf. 1932. Überwindung der Metaphysik durch Logische Analyse der Sprache. *Erkenntniss* 2. English trans. in Alfred J. Ayer, ed. 1959. *Logical positivism*. Glencoe, N.Y.: Free Press.

Carnap, Rudolf. 1950. Empiricism, semantics and ontology. *Revue International de Philosophie* 4:20–40.

Carnap, Rudolf. 1963. Intellectual autobiography. In *The philosophy of Rudolf Carnap*, ed. Paul A. Schilp. LaSalle, Ill.: Open Court.

Carruthers, Peter. 1990. *The metaphysics of the 'Tractatus.'* Cambridge: Cambridge University Press.

Clegg, James. 1978. Logical mysticism and the cultural setting of Wittgenstein's Tractatus. *Schopenhauer Jahrbuch* 59:29–47.

Conant, James. 2000. Elucidation and nonsense in Frege and early Wittgenstein. In *The new Wittgenstein*, ed. Alice Crary and Rupert Read. London: Routledge.
Conze, Edward. 1951. *Buddhism: Its essence and development*. Oxford: Cassirer.
Conze, Edward. 1958. *Buddhist wisdom books*. London: Allen and Unwin.
Conze, Edward. 1967. Buddhism and gnosis. In *The origins of gnosticism*, ed. Ugo Bianchi. Leiden: Brill.
Cook, John W. 1985. The metaphysics of Wittgenstein's On Certainty. *Philosophical Investigations* 8:81–119.
Copi, I. M. 1958. Objects, properties and relations in the *Tractatus*. *Mind* 67:145–65.
Crary, Alice, and Rupert Read, eds. 2000. *The new Wittgenstein*. London: Routledge.
Davidson, Donald. 1968. On saying that. *Synthese* 19:130–46.
Davidson, Donald. 1973. In defense of convention T. In *Truth, syntax and modality*, ed. Hugues Leblanc. Amsterdam: North-Holland.
Diamond, Cora. 1988. Throwing away the ladder. *Philosophy* 63:5–27.
Diamond, Cora. 2000. Ethics, imagination and the method of Wittgenstein's *Tractatus*. In *The new Wittgenstein*, ed. Alice Crary and Rupert Read. London: Routledge.
Dilman, İlham. 1974. Wittgenstein on the soul. In *Understanding Wittgenstein*, ed. G. Vesey. London: MacMillan.
Drury, M. O' C. 1984. Conversations with Wittgenstein. In *Recollections of Wittgenstein*, ed. Rush Rhees. Oxford: Oxford University Press.
Dummett, Michael. 1973. *Frege: Philosophy of language*. London: Duckworth.
Dummett, Michael. 1978. Realism. In *Truth and other enigmas*. London: Duckworth.
Dummett, Michael. 1985. *The interpretation of Frege's philosophy*. London: Duckworth.
Meister Eckehart. 1979. Das Buch der göttlichen Tröstung. In *Deutsche Predigte und Traktate*, ed. Josef Quint. Zürich: Diogenes.
Edwards, James C. 1985. *Ethics without philosophy: Wittgenstein and the moral life*. Tampa: University Presses of Florida.
Engelmann, Paul. 1967. *Letters from Wittgenstein: With a memoir*. Oxford: Blackwell.
Fay, Thomas. 1991. The ontological difference in early Heidegger and Wittgenstein. *Kantstudien* 82:319–28.
Ferber, G. 1983. Der Grundgedanke des *Tractatus* als Metamorphose des obersten Grundsatzes der Kritik der reinen Vernunft. *Kantstudien* 74:460–68.
Fogelin, Robert J. 1987. *Wittgenstein*. 2d ed. London: Routledge and Kegan Paul.
Frascolla, Pasquale. 1994. *Wittgenstein's philosophy of mathematics*. London: Routledge.

Frege, Gottlob. 1879. *Begriffsschrift. Eine der arithmetischen nachgebildete Formelsprache des reinen Denkens*. Halle a.S.: Louis Nebert. English translation in van Heijenoort, ed. 1970.
Frege, Gottlob. 1884. *Die Grundlagen der Arithmetik*. Breslau: Wilhelm Koebner. English trans. J. L. Austin. 1950. *The foundations of arithmetic*. Oxford: Blackwell.
Frege, Gottlob, 1891. Funktion und Begriff. *Jenaischen Gesellschaft für Medizin und Natuurwisschenschaft*. English trans. in Geach and Black, eds. 1980.
Frege, Gottlob. 1892a. Über Sinn und Bedeutung. *Zeitschrift für Philosophie und philosophische Kritik* 100:25–50. English trans. in Geach and Black, eds. 1980.
Frege, Gottlob. 1892b. Über Begriff und Gegenstand. *Vierteljahrschrift für wissenschaftliche Philosophie* 16:192–205. English trans. in Geach and Black, eds. 1980.
Frege, Gottlob. 1895. *Grundgesetze der Arithmetik*. Band I. Jena: Pohle. English trans. of section 1–27 by M. Furth. 1967. *The basic laws of arithmetic*. Berkeley and Los Angeles: University of California Press.
Frege, Gottlob. 1918. Der Gedanke: eine logische Untersuchung. *Beiträge zur Philosophie des deutschen Idealismus* 2:58–77. English trans. in Geach, ed. 1977.
Garver, Newton. 1994. *This complicated form of life*. LaSalle, Ill.: Open Court.
Geach, Peter, ed. 1977. *Gottlob Frege: Logical investigations*. Oxford: Blackwell.
Geach, Peter. 1981. Wittgenstein's Operator N. *Analysis* 41:168–71.
Geach, Peter, and Max Black, eds. 1980. *Translations from the philosophical writings of Gottlob Frege*. Oxford: Blackwell.
Genesereth, Michael R., and Nils J. Nillson. 1987. *Logical foundations of artificial intelligence*. Los Altos, Calif.: Morgan Kaufmann.
Gmür, Felix, 2000, *Ästhetik bei Wittgenstein*. Freiburg: Alber.
Goodman, Russell. 1976. Style, dialectic, and the aim of philosophy in Wittgenstein and the Taoists. *Journal of Chinese Philosophy* 3:145–57.
Groenendijk, Jeroen, Martin Stokhof, and Frank Veltman. 1996. Coreference and modality. In *The handbook of contemporary semantic theory*, ed. Shalom Lappin. Cambridge: Blackwell.
Gudmunsen, Chris. 1973. *Wittgenstein and Buddhism*. London: Macmillan.
Gudmunsen, Chris. 1977. The "empty mind" of Professor Canfield. *Philosophy* 52:482–5.
Hacker, P. M. S. 1984a. *Insight and illusion*. 2d ed. Oxford: Clarendon.
Hacker, P. M. S. 1984b. The rise and fall of the picture theory. In *Perspectives on the philosophy of Wittgenstein*, ed. Irving Block. Oxford: Blackwell.
Hacker, P. M. S. 1996. *Wittgenstein's place in twentieth-century analytic philosophy*. Oxford: Blackwell.
Hacker, P. M. S. 2000. Was he trying to whistle it? In *The new Wittgenstein*, ed. Alice Crary and Rupert Read. London: Routledge.
Haller, Rudolf. 1988. Philosophy and the critique of language: Wittgenstein and Mauthner. In *Questions on Wittgenstein*. London: Routledge.

Heijenoort, Jean van, ed. 1970. *Frege and Gödel: Two fundamental texts in mathematical logic.* Cambridge, Mass.: Harvard University Press.
Hertz, Heinrich. 1899. *Principles of mechanics.* London: MacMillan.
Hilmy, Stephen. 1987. *The later Wittgenstein: The emergence of a new philosophical method.* Oxford: Blackwell.
Hintikka, Jaakko. 1958. On Wittgenstein's solipsism. *Mind* 67:88–91.
Hintikka, Merryll, and Jaakko Hintikka. 1986. *Investigating Wittgenstein.* Oxford.
Hodges, Wilfrid. 1986. Truth in a structure. *Proceedings of the Aristotelian Society* 86:135–51.
Hudson, W. D. 1973. Wittgenstein and Zen Buddhism *Philosophy East and West* 23:471–81.
Hudson, W. D. 1981. The light Wittgenstein sheds on religion. *Midwest Studies in Philosophy* 6:275–92.
Inada, Kenneth. 1995. A Buddhist response to the nature of human rights. *Journal of Buddhist Ethics* 2:55–66.
Ishiguro, Hide. 1969. Use and reference of names. In *Studies in the philosophy of Wittgenstein,* ed. Peter Winch. London: Routledge and Kegan Paul.
Janik, Allan S. 1966. Schopenhauer and early Wittgenstein. *Philosophical Studies* 15:76–95.
Janik, Allan S. 1979. Wittenstein, Ficker, and Der Brenner. In *Wittgenstein: Sources and perspectives,* ed. C. G. Luckhardt. Ithaca, N.Y.: Cornell University Press.
Janik, Allan S. 1985. *Essays on Wittgenstein and Weininger.* Amsterdam: Rodopi.
Janik, Allan S., and Stephen Toulmin. 1973. *Wittgenstein's Vienna.* New York: Simon and Schuster.
Johannessen, K. S., and T. Nordenstam. 1981. Wittgenstein, aesthetics and transcendental philosophy. In *Ethics: Foundations, problems and applications,* ed. Edgar Morscher and Rudolf Stranzinger. Wien: Hölder-Pichler-Tempsky.
Johnston, Paul. 1989. *Wittgenstein as a moral philosopher.* London: Routledge and Kegan Paul.
Kalupahana, David. 1976. *Buddhist philosophy: A historical analysis.* Honolulu: University of Hawaii Press.
Kalupahana, David. 1977. The notion of suffering in early Buddhism, compared with some reflections on early Wittgenstein. *Philosophy East and West* 27:423–31.
Kalupahana, David. 1987. *The principles of Buddhist Psychology.* Albany: State University of New York Press.
Kenny, Anthony. 1973. *Wittgenstein.* Harmondsworth, UK: Penguin Press.
Keown, Damien. 1992. *The nature of Buddhist ethics.* London: MacMillan.
Keown, Damien. 1995. Are there 'human rights' in Buddhism? *Journal of Buddhist Ethics* 2:3–27.
Kerr, Fergus. 1986. *Theology after Wittgenstein.* Oxford: Blackwell.
Kripke, S. A. 1980. *Naming and necessity.* Oxford: Blackwell.

Levi, Albert W. 1978. The biographical sources of Wittgenstein's ethics. *Telos* 38:63–77.
Levi, Albert W. 1979. Wittgenstein once more: A response to critics. *Telos* 40:165–73.
Luckhardt, C. G., ed. 1979. *Wittgenstein: Sources and perspectives.* Ithaca, N.Y.: Cornell University Press.
Magee, Bryan. 1983. *The philosophy of Schopenhauer.* Oxford: Clarendon Press.
Malcolm, Norman. 1958. *Ludwig Wittgenstein: A memoir.* With a biographical sketch by G. H. von Wright. Oxford: Oxford University Press.
Malcolm, Norman. 1986. *Nothing is hidden: Wittgenstein's criticism of his earlier thought.* Oxford: Blackwell.
Maslow, A. 1961. *A study in Wittgenstein's 'Tractatus.'* Berkeley and Los Angeles: University of California Press.
Maury, Anders. 1977. *The concepts of 'Sinn' and 'Gegenstand' in Wittgenstein's 'Tractatus.'* Amsterdam: North-Holland.
Mauthner, Fritz. 1901–1903. *Beiträge zu einer Kritik der Sprache.* 3 vols. Stuttgart: Cotta Verlag.
Mauthner, Fritz. 1913. *Der Letzte Tod des Gautama Buddha.* München: Georg Müller.
Mauthner, Fritz. 1986. Sprache und Leben. In *Ausgewählte Texte aus dem philosophischen Werk,* ed. Gershon Weiler. Salzburg/Wien: Residenz Verlag.
McDonough, Richard M. 1986. *The argument of the 'Tractatus.'* Albany: State University of New York Press.
McGuinness, Brian F. 1966. The mysticism of the *Tractatus*. *The Philosophical Review* 75:305–28.
McGuinness, Brian F. 1984. The so-called realism of the *Tractatus*. In *Perspectives on the philosophy of Wittgenstein,* ed. Irving Block. Oxford: Blackwell.
McGuinness, Brian F. 1988. *Wittgenstein: A life. Young Ludwig, 1889–1921.* London: Duckworth.
Monk, Ray. 1990. *Ludwig Wittgenstein: The duty of genius.* London: Jonathan Cape.
Montague, Richard M. 1973. The proper treatment of quantification in ordinary English. In *Approaches to natural language,* ed. J. Hintikka, J. Moravcsik, and P. Suppes. Dordrecht: Reidel.
Moran, John D. 1973. *Toward the world and wisdom of Wittgenstein's 'Tractatus.'* The Hague: Mouton.
Mounce, H. O. 1981. *Wittgenstein's 'Tractatus:' An introduction.* Oxford: Blackwell.
Murti, T. R. V. 1955. *The central philosophy of Buddhism.* London: Allen and Unwin.
Nieuwendijk, Arthur. 1997. *On logic.* Amsterdam: ILLC.
Pascal, Fania. 1979. Wittgenstein: A personal memoir. In *Wittgenstein: Sources and perspectives,* ed. C. G. Luckhardt. Ithaca, N.Y.: Cornell University Press.

Pears, David F. 1987. *The false prison.* 2 vols. Oxford: Blackwell.
Perloff, Marjorie. 1996. *Wittgenstein's ladder.* Chicago: University of Chicago Press.
Peterson, Donald. 1990. *Wittgenstein's early philosophy.* New York: Harvester Wheatsheaf.
Phillips, D. Z. 1970. Religious beliefs and language-games. *Ratio* 12:26–46.
Phillips, D. Z. 1977. On wanting to compare Wittgenstein and Zen. *Philosophy* 52:338–43.
Phillips, D. Z. 1981. Wittgenstein's full stop. In *Perspectives on the philosophy of Wittgenstein*, ed. Irving Block. Oxford: Blackwell.
Phillips, D. Z. 1993. *Wittgenstein and religion.* New York: St. Martin's Press.
Phillips Griffiths, A. 1974. Wittgenstein, Schopenhauer and ethics. In *Understanding Wittgenstein*, ed. G. Vesey. London: MacMillan.
Putnam, Hilary. 1978. Realism and reason. In *Meaning and the moral sciences.* London: Routledge and Kegan Paul.
Putnam, Hilary. 1983. Models and reality. In *Realism and reason.* Cambridge: Cambridge University Press.
Rhees, Rush. 1965. Some developments in Wittgenstein's view of ethics. *The Philosophical Review* 74:17–26.
Rhees, Rush. 1984a. Postscript. In *Recollections of Wittgenstein.* Oxford: Oxford University Press.
Rhees, Rush, ed. 1984b. *Recollections of Wittgenstein.* Oxford: Oxford University Press.
Ricketts, Thomas. 1996. Pictures, logic and the limits of sense in Wittgenstein's *Tractatus.* In *The Cambridge companion to Wittgenstein*, ed. Hans Sluga and D. G. Stern. Cambridge: Cambridge University Press.
Rudebush, Thomas, and William M. Berg. 1979. On Wittgenstein and ethics: A reply to Levi. *Telos* 40:150–60.
Russell, Bertrand. 1903. *The principles of mathematics.* London: Unwin.
Russell, Bertrand. 1905. On denoting. *Mind* 14:479–93. Reprinted in *Logic and knowledge* 1956.
Russell, Bertrand. 1908. Mathematical logic as based on the theory of types. *American Journal of Mathematics* 30. Reprinted in *Logic and knowledge* 1956.
Russell, Bertrand. 1914. On the nature of acquaintance. Reprinted in *Logic and knowledge* 1956.
Russell, Bertrand. 1918–19. The philosophy of logical atomism. *The Monist* 28–29:495–527, 32–63, 190–222, 345–80. Reprinted in *Logic and knowledge* 1956.
Russell, Bertrand. 1919. *Introduction to mathematical philosophy.* London: Allen and Unwin.
Russell, Bertrand. 1921. Introduction. In *Tractatus Logico-Philosophicus.* London: Routledge and Kegan Paul.
Russell, Bertrand. 1944. Reply to criticisms. In *The philosophy of Bertrand Russell*, ed. Paul A. Schilp. LaSalle, Ill.: Open Court.

Russell, Bertrand. 1956. *Logic and knowledge: Essays 1901–1950*, ed. R. C. Marsh. London: Allen and Unwin.

Russell, Bertrand. 1975. *The autobiography of Bertrand Russell*. London: Allen and Unwin.

Russell, Bertrand, and Alfred North Whitehead. [1912–13] 1925–27. *Principia mathematica*. 2d rev. ed. Cambridge: Cambridge University Press.

Safranski, Rüdiger. 1987. *Schopenhauer und die wilden Jahre der Philosophie*. München/Wien: Carl Hanser Verlag.

Sainsbury, R. 1979. *Russell*. London: Routledge and Kegan Paul.

Salmon, Nathan. 1982. *Reference and essence*. Oxford: Blackwell.

Schopenhauer, Arthur. 1844. *Die Welt als Wille und Vorstellung*. Leipzig: Brockhaus. English trans. E. F. J. Payne. 1966. *The World as will and representation*. New York: Dover.

Schopenhauer, Arthur. 1851. *Parerga und Paralipomena*. Leipzig: Brockhaus. English trans. E. F. J. Payne. 1974. *Parerga and Paralipomena*. Oxford: Clarendon.

Schopenhauer, Arthur. 1986. *Sämtliche Werke*, ed. Wolfgang Frhr. Von Löhneysen. 5 vols. Frankfurt a/M.: Suhrkamp.

Schwarzschild, Steven S. 1979. Wittgenstein as an alienated Jew. *Telos* 40:160–65.

Scott, Dana. 1980. Lambda calculus: Some models, some philosophy. In *The Kleene symposium*, ed. J. Barwise, G. Kreisler, and H. Kunen. Amsterdam: North Holland.

Shanker, Stuart G. 1987. *Wittgenstein and the turning point in mathematics*. London: Croom Helm.

Shields, Philip R. 1993. *Logic and sin in the writings of Ludwig Wittgenstein*. Chicago: University of Chicago Press.

Sluga, Hans. 1980. *Frege*. London: Routledge and Kegan Paul.

Soames, Scott. 1983. Generality, truth functions, and expressive capacity in the Tractatus. *The Philosophical Review* 92:573–89.

Steiner, George. 1975. *After Babel: Aspects of language and translation*. Oxford: Oxford University Press.

Stenius, Eric. 1960. *Wittgenstein's 'Tractatus': A critical exposition of its main lines of thought*. Oxford: Blackwell.

Stenius, Eric. 1984. The picture theory and Wittgenstein's later attitude to it. In *Perspectives on the philosophy of Wittgenstein*, ed. Irving Block. Oxford: Blackwell.

Tominaga, Thomas T. 1982. Taoist and Wittgensteinian mysticism. *Journal of Chinese Philosophy* 9:269–89.

Tominaga, Thomas T. 1983. Ch'an, Taoism, and Wittgenstein. *Journal of Chinese Philosophy* 10:127–45.

Watzka, Heinrich. 2000. *Sagen und Zeigen*. Stuttgart: Kohlhammer.

Weiler, Gershon. 1970. *Mauthner's critique of language*. Cambridge: Cambridge University Press.

Weininger, Otto. 1903. *Geschlecht und Character*. München: Matthes and Seitz.
Wijdeveld, Paul. 1994. *Ludwig Wittgenstein: Architect*. London: Thames and Hudson.
Wittgenstein, Hermine. 1984. My brother Ludwig. In *Recollections of Wittgenstein*, ed. R. Rhees. Oxford: Oxford University Press.
Wright, G. H. von. 1958. Biographical sketch. In *Ludwig Wittgenstein: A memoir*. Oxford: Oxford University Press.

Index

Action: ethical quality of, 213–14; ethics as concerned with, 2, 246; future, 100; reward and punishment as internal to, 7, 213, 296n37; and values, 7, 187, 189, 209, 213–14, 297n50; willing and, 195, 203, 206–7, 208–9, 212, 213–14; as in the world, 212
Aesthetics, 9, 26, 245
Afterlife, 222–23
Analysis: conceptual, 101–2. *See also* Logical analysis
Anātman, 229
Angelus Silesius, 30, 300n72
Anscombe, Elisabeth, 11, 31, 189, 293n19
A priori principles, 101
Arahant, 229, 232
Aristotle, 16
Arithmetic, 13, 164
Art, in Schopenhauer's hierarchy, 205
Atomism: in Malcolm's interpretation of *Tractatus*, 173. *See also* Logical atomism
Augustine, Saint, 30
Axiom of infinity, 14, 95, 255n25
Axiom of reducibility, 256n27
Axioms, 14–15, 17, 114, 119–20, 272n82

Bartley, William Warren, III, 31, 259n64, 297n50
Beckett, Samuel, 257n43

Begriffsschrift (Frege), 13, 86, 94, 165
Belief, 61, 84, 266n30
Bipolarity, 179
Bivalence, 86, 104, 112, 178–79
Black, Max, 11, 253n3, 254n10
Bodhisattva, 232, 234
Böhme, Jakob, 30, 34
Boltzmann, Ludwig, 21–22
Bolzano, Bernhard, 13, 139, 256n29
Boole, George, 13, 139
Buddhism: *anātman*, 229; *Arahant* versus *Bodhisattva*, 232; Eightfold Noble Path, 228, 229, 232, 300n66; Four Noble Truths, 228; and human rights, 299n60; on life as suffering, 228–29, 298n55; *Nirvāna*, 229, 232, 299n65; pragmatic character of early, 300n77; on the self, 294n21, 300n66; Wittgenstein's views compared with, 33–34, 298n54

Carnap, Rudolf, 142, 301n83
Carruthers, Peter, 253n5, 254n11, 291n147
Causality: as contingent, 100, 119, 200, 201; as external relation, 99–100; Schopenhauer's derivation of, 194; willing contrasted with, 195–96, 204
Change, 173, 207
Christianity, 30–31, 33, 217
Church, Alonzo, 273n88

Clegg, James, 258n56
Color exclusion problem, 101–2, 120, 151, 254n12, 275n
Comments on the Gospels (Tolstoy), 30
Commonsense realism, 131
Compassion, 28, 205, 227, 231–32
Complex sentences, 80–85, 99
Composition: compositionality principle, 79, 164, 270n63, 287n100; of facts, 42; reality and language as compositional, 70
Comte, Auguste, 137
Conceptual analysis, 101–2
Conceptual necessity, 254n12
Conjunction, 80, 81–84
Constants: logical constants as not referring, 15, 17, 22, 43, 92, 257n39, 262n9; in Wittgenstein's system, 73, 268n49
Context principle, 78–79; allusion in *Tractatus* 2.0122, 270n62, 277n8; and compositionality, 270n63, 287n100; Dummett on, 287n100, 289n114; Frege and, 79, 157, 270n63, 287n100; Ishiguro on, 157, 160–71, 176–77, 270n63; and mutual dependence of names and sentences, 263n12
Contingency: in Buddhist view of the world, 229; of causal relationships, 100, 119, 200, 201; for coming to grips with the necessary, 262n7; complexity and, 48, 111, 277n7; and the empirical, 93; ethically contingent character of the world, 9, 187, 209, 210, 214, 220, 239, 242; of external properties, 46; of language, 38, 137; logic delineating sphere of, 88; of meaning, 38, 106, 140, 179, 210, 248; of pictures, 62; of reality in *Tractatus*, 8; and saying-showing distinction, 18; Schopenhauer's determinism versus Wittgensteinian, 200, 201; of science, 139; of thoughts, 38, 61–62

Contradictions, 21, 61–62, 93–94, 266n29, 280n24
Conventionalism, 18, 26, 27, 28, 144, 146
Craving, 215, 217, 218, 219, 228, 229
Creativity, 69–70
Critical realism, 8, 9
Culture and Value (Wittgenstein), 3, 29, 32, 259n65

Davidson, Donald, 85, 272n77, 277n5, 293n12
Death, 223
Deduction, 99, 136
Demos, Raphael, 265n24
Derivability, 16
Desire, 221, 228, 229, 230
Determinism, 200, 201, 209
Diamond, Cora, 253n5, 274n101
Discourse representation theory, 288n8
Disjunction, 80, 81–84
Donnellan, Keith, 77
Dostoevsky, Fyodor, 30
Double negation, 104
Drury, Maurice O'Connor, 247, 292n4, 299n63
Dummett, Michael: on contextuality and compositionality, 287n100, 289n114; on Frege and Kant, 254n20; semantic criterion for realism, 104–8, 156

Eastern philosophy, 33–34. *See also* Buddhism
Eckehart, Meister, 296n38, 296n42, 297n43, 297n47
Eightfold Noble Path, 228, 229, 232, 300n66
Elementary sentences, 75–76; and completely analyzed sentences, 117, 280n27; complex sentences as truth functions of, 80, 82, 83–84, 90, 91, 279n22; as consisting of names, 76,

168–69, 184; logical independence of, 99, 119, 120, 131, 274n97, 281n34; Maslow on, 150; and quantified sentences, 83–84, 94; Stenius on, 154; truth of, 91

Elucidation: as aim of sentences of *Tractatus*, 102, 107; of names, 103, 163, 164, 165, 166, 167, 289n114

Engelmann, Paul, 3, 186, 283n59, 292n1

Entailment, 16

Epistemology: logical empiricism and, 134; of Mauthner, 26; metaphysical subject's epistemological role, 202–3; Russell concerned with, 134–35; *Tractatus* and, 61, 85, 135–37, 139; Wittgenstein and, 12, 65, 134–37, 265n27

Equations, mathematical, 98, 288n110

Eternity, 222–23, 224

Ethics: as absolute, 211; action as concern of, 2, 246; background of *Tractatus* views on, 24–34; and contingency of reality, 8–9; delimiting from the inside, 6, 187; ethically contingent character of the world, 9, 187, 209, 210, 214, 220, 239, 242; ethical view of the world, 238, 249; and everyday life, 187, 189–90; ideal as harmony of individual and metaphysical wills, 227–31, 233–34; ineffability of, 36, 211–12, 219, 236, 242, 243, 245–46; influences on Wittgenstein's, 28–34; Kraus identifying aesthetics and, 26; life of knowledge as ethical life, 218, 297n43; as limit of the world, 237; logical versus ethical aspects of *Tractatus*, 4–9, 234–44; Maslow on tractarian, 132; Mauthner on critique of language and, 27–28; McGuinness on logic and, 295n33, 299n64; morality distinguished from, 222, 224–34, 299n58; the necessary as concern of, 38; as negatively characterized in *Tractatus*, 5; in *Notebooks*, 23, 186, 253n3; and others, 225, 231; as outside realm of meaningful, 236; as point of *Tractatus*, 5–6, 35, 39, 187; positive interpretation of *Tractatus* on, 5, 7; and "saying by not saying," 292n1; and scientific worldview, 10, 248; as starting with experience, 239–41, 248–49; and timelessness, 222–23; *Tractatus* as not an ethical theory, 245–46; *Tractatus* on, 186–249; as transcendental, 102, 225, 235–39; the will associated with ethical categories, 207, 209; the world as limited whole for, 89, 197, 220, 237, 246; the world's relation to, 186–87, 205–6, 209, 225, 233, 235. *See also* Good, the; Values

Existential quantifier, 81–84, 170, 271n72, 271n74

Experience: ethics as starting with, 239–41, 248–49; limits of possible, 197–98; and logic, 196–97; Maslow on, 147, 148, 150, 151, 152; as of situations, 196, 197, 293n17; will as outside sphere of, 206. *See also* Sense-data

External properties, 45, 46, 77, 167, 290n139

Facts: atomic, 43; as composite, 42; negative, 58, 265n24; as not just physical, 233; as obtaining, 42–43; pictures as, 52–53, 263n16; positive and negative, 261n6; sentential signs as, 66; as situations that obtain, 43; structure of, 50–52; values distinguished from, 25, 139, 183, 297n50; the world as totality of, 40–41, 109; "the world is everything that is the case," 40. *See also* States of affairs

False sentences, meaning of, 69, 85
Fatalism, 217, 232–33, 235
Feigl, Herbert, 142
Fichte, Johann Gottlieb, 194, 202

Ficker, Ludwig, 5–6, 35, 187, 236, 254n7, 275n
Fogelin, Robert J., 263n14
Form: of logical space, 52; of objects, 45, 46, 49–50; pictorial relation and pictorial form, 53–55; as possibility, 45, 56; of sentences, 66–67; as shown not said, 74; of situations, 52; of states of affairs, 49–51; of symbols, 72–73; of the world, 45, 48, 52. *See also* Logical form
Formalism, 98, 256n32
Formal languages, 16, 18, 21, 65, 256n35
Formal objects, 164, 288n8
Four Noble Truths, 228
Frazer, James George, 291n149
Freedom of the will, 100, 201, 208
Frege, Gottlob: antipsychologism of, 136; arithmetic reduced to logic by, 13; *Begriffsschrift*, 13, 86, 94, 165; on context principle, 79, 157, 270n63, 287n100; "Funktion und Begriff," 92; *Grundgesetze der Arithmetik*, 12, 13–14, 255n23; *Grundlagen der Arithmetik*, 13, 79; on identity, 165–66; on indexicality, 278n15; intensional ontology of, 272n78; as Kantian, 13, 36, 254n20; linguistic turn in, 37; on logical and grammatical form, 16; logical empiricists influenced by, 139; on logical objects, 15–16; on logicism, 14, 98; meaning-reference distinction, 158–59, 160, 166, 286n96, 287n97; on modalities, 84, 270n65; on natural language, 18–19, 159; in the "new logic," 13; platonism of, 16, 19, 92, 145, 278n15; Schopenhauerean idealism versus conceptual realism of, 201–2; on self-evidence, 15; and semantic criterion for realism, 276n2; "Über Sinn und Bedeutung," 18, 165, 273n89; Wittgenstein advised to go to Cambridge by, 12

"Funktion und Begriff" (Frege), 92
Future: future actions, 100, 274n95; inferences about the, 99–100, 208; moral point of view and, 222

Geschlecht und Character (Weininger), 32
Gnosis, 297n43
God, 215–16, 217, 218–19, 221, 296n37, 296n38
Good, the: the good will, 214–16, 219, 227, 296n38; the happy life, 216–25; metaphysical versus individual, 215; nature of, 210–25; the world as good, 216
Grammar: logical syntax, 69, 72–74; logical versus grammatical form, 16, 20–21, 55, 90–91, 113–14; Maslow on, 150–51, 152
Griffiths, A. P., 296n41, 299n59, 299n61
Grundgesetze der Arithmetik (Frege), 12, 13–14, 255n23
Grundlagen der Arithmetik (Frege), 13, 79
Guilt, 221

Hacker, Peter, 254n11, 294n27
Hadji Murat (Tolstoy), 258n59
Hänsel, Ludwig, 261n3
Happiness: as attitude toward the world, 219; as being in harmony with the world, 217–20; the happy life, 216–25; as indescribable, 210–11; as living in the present, 220–25; and suffering, 226; worlds of the happy and unhappy person, 237
Hedonism, 219
Hegel, Georg Wilhelm Friedrich, 194
Heidegger, Martin, 293n18, 296n40
Henkin-construction, 290n124
Hertz, Heinrich, 21, 22
Hintikka, Jaakko, 180, 254n11, 278n17, 297n45

Hintikka, Merryll, 180, 254n11, 278n17, 297n45
Homonyms, 72
Human rights, 299n60
Hume, David, 193, 198, 229, 231, 283n48
Identity: with complex denoting expressions, 288n111; criteria for objects, 45, 46, 163, 167–68, 184; identity sentences as without content, 273n89; as inessential for Wittgenstein, 95, 288n112; mathematical equations as identity sentences, 98; as not relating objects, 95, 288n112; and substitution principle, 164–66

Immortality, 222–23
Indexicality, 278n15
Induction, 13, 100–101
Internal properties: defined, 45; identity depending on, 45–46, 166, 167, 174; logical form and, 153, 167; as necessary, 45, 77, 290n139; sentences as unable to express, 77; will as internal property of actions, 213
Intuition, 15
Ishiguro, Hide: Malcolm on, 176–77; motive of interpretation of, 156, 157–58; on ontology of *Tractatus*, 154–71, 181–82, 243–44; on Wittgenstein on properties as objects, 269n56

James, William, 30, 301n77
Janik, Allan S., 11, 24–25, 26, 253n4
Joint denial, 81, 270n66

Kalupahana, David, 260n69, 301n77
Kant, Immanuel: Frege and, 13, 36, 254n20; on metaphysics, 137; Schopenhauer's notions of subject and object compared with, 200; on transcendence, 235, 236–37; Wittgenstein and, 29, 130, 134, 181, 184, 191, 260n3

Kierkegaard, Søren, 30, 300n72
Knowledge: by description and by acquaintance, 160, 290n139; discursive versus ethical, 237, 240, 245; life of knowledge as ethical life, 218, 297n43; of objects, 164, 174–75, 184; willing versus knowing subject, 191, 194–96. *See also* Epistemology
Kraus, Karl, 25–26
Kripke, Saul, 77, 273n89, 287n98, 289n115

Language: ability to talk about the untrue, 115, 278n15; Austrian critique of, 25–28; capacity to understand, 69–70; as compositional, 70; as contingent, 38, 137; drawing limits of expression of thought, 37, 38, 200; formal languages, 16, 18, 21, 65, 256n35; form of, 45; as key to logical questions, 15; "the language that I alone understand," 198, 293n19; "the limits of my language mean the limits of my world," 147, 197–98; linguistic nature of transcendence, 235–39; logical necessity as embedded in, 18; logic as prior to, 137; logic as ultimate foundation of, 88, 152–53; Maslow on, 146, 147–48; and ontology, 7–8, 108–9, 121, 125, 129, 130–32, 172, 174, 183–85; pictorial relationship in, 55; and reality, 4, 89, 131, 155–56, 182; and simplicity of objects, 110–20; in structure of experience, 147; and thought, 37–38, 63, 89, 135–36, 192–93, 202; *Tractatus* on, 63–85; translation, 69, 198; two-valued logical form of, 105; what can be said and what can be thought as the same, 37–38; and the world, 197. *See also* Grammar; Linguistic turn; Meaning; Names; Natural language; Saying-showing distinction; Sentences

"Lecture on Ethics" (Wittgenstein): on absolute and relative values, 211; on description of a murder, 230, 233; on experience of absolute safety, 224; on experiencing ethical dimension of the world, 239; on formulating ethics in meaningful sentences, 188; as source for Wittgenstein's views on ethics, 3, 186; on wondering at existence of the world, 216

"Lectures on Religious Belief" (Wittgenstein), 3, 296n37

Lee, Desmond, 270n61

Levi, Albert W., 31, 297n50

Life: the happy life, 216–25; living in the present, 220–25, 297n47; meaning of, 219; solution to problem of, 218–19, 223; suffering in, 226–27, 228, 298n55; suicide, 189–90, 218, 235, 292n5; "world and life as one," 234–44

Linguistic turn, 37–38; as giving ethics wider philosophical framework, 245, 300n76; as not necessarily an improvement, 261n4; *Tractatus* giving to Kantian program, 134, 201, 235

Logic: axiomatic approach to, 14–15, 17, 114, 119–20, 272n82; background of *Tractatus* views on, 10–24; and contingency of reality, 9; empirical versus the logical, 93; and experience, 196–97; as foundation, 85–89, 152–53; Frege reducing arithmetic to, 13; as independent of ontology, 17; intuition for, 286n87; limits of the world as limits of, 200, 236, 237, 238, 294n22; logical versus ethical aspects of *Tractatus*, 4–9, 234–44; McGuinness on ethics and, 295n33, 299n64; no theory of, 95–97; as outside sphere of meaningful, 39, 93–94; as prior to language and thought, 137; problems at beginning of twentieth century, 13; scope of term, 12; status of logical laws, 14, 255n25; structure of the meaningful explicated in, 37; and substance as two sides of same coin, 202; syntactical approach to, 16–17, 21, 114, 118, 119; in *Tractatus*, 85–97; as transcendental, 236–37; two-valued, 86, 104, 105–6, 112, 178–79, 183; as ultimate foundation of language, 88; Wittgenstein becoming interested in, 12; Wittgenstein's absolutism regarding, 39, 46, 63, 86, 105, 119–20, 152–53, 179, 181, 183, 184, 199–200, 212, 240, 272n80, 285n84. *See also* Logical analysis; Logical form; Logical necessity

Logical analysis, 89–91; as clarification, 21, 113–14; complete, 113, 117, 123, 124, 125, 163; infinite analyzability, 123, 280n27, 285n74; logical empiricists' use of, 139–40; Malcolm on, 177; Schopenhauerean epistemological analysis versus Wittgensteinian, 294n23; and simplicity of objects, 122–26, 290n135; therapeutic value of, 20; and traditional epistemology, 136; ultimate results of, 90, 184

Logical atomism: picture theory of meaning and, 153, 291n145; of the *Tractatus*, 40–44; Wittgenstein abandons, 102, 120

Logical concepts, 15

Logical constants, as not referring, 15, 17, 22, 43, 92, 257n39, 262n9

Logical empiricism: conventionalism of, 18, 144; elements of, 133; ethics of *Tractatus* ignored by, 4–5; and logical positivism, 282n38; Maslow and, 132, 133, 144, 147, 181; on metaphysics, 137–40; on science, 138; Wittgenstein and, 10, 132, 134–44, 283n59

Logical form, 55–57; analysis for explicating, 113; depicting as impossible,

58–59, 86, 115, 265n26, 278n18; as form of reality, 56–57, 265n22; versus grammatical form, 16, 20–21, 90–91, 113–14; and internal properties, 153; interplay of variables and constants and, 73; knowledge of objects and, 175; logical relationships to be made evident by, 17, 21, 118, 119; as most general form, 45, 62; of natural language, 89, 91, 108; Russell on apparent versus real, 27; saying-showing distinction and, 18, 22; and semantic ineffability, 115, 291n145; and simplicity of objects, 179

Logical necessity: as embedded in language, 18; and logical concepts, 15; as the only necessity, 9, 22, 48, 86, 93, 97, 99, 119, 120, 203; problem of source of, 14

Logical objects, 15–16, 17, 262n9

Logical positivism, *see* Logical empiricism

Logical space: and complete description of the world, 169; forms of, 52; knowledge of objects and, 175; logical form as form of, 57; logical truths reflecting properties of, 17; physical space compared with, 43–44; and reality in *Tractatus*, 261n6; situations in, 43–44; tautologies showing properties of, 93–94; as totality of possibilities, 43, 261n5; as transcendental, 236–37; uniqueness of, 86; in world viewed as totality, 237–38

Logical syntax, 69, 72–74

Logical truths, 17

Logicism, 13, 14, 98, 256n33

Loos, Adolf, 25

McDonough, Richard M., 254n11

McGuinness, Brian F.: "Bedeutung" as translated by, 289n113; motive of interpretation of, 156–57; on ontology of *Tractatus*, 154–71, 181–82, 243–44; on Schopenhauer's influence on Wittgenstein, 257n41; on Wittgenstein's ethics as logical mysticism, 244, 258n56, 295n33; on Wittgenstein's homosexuality, 31; on Wittgenstein's interest in logic, 12

Malcolm, Norman: on ontology of *Tractatus*, 171–80, 182–83, 242–43; on tractarian objects as material, 127, 173, 182–83; on Wittgenstein's personal ethical influence, 247, 301n82

Maps, 52–53, 265n20

Maslow, Alexander: anticipations of Wittgenstein's later work in, 285n76; antimetaphysical attitude of, 145; as logical empiricist, 132, 133, 144, 147, 181; on ontology of *Tractatus*, 132–34, 144–53, 181, 242; relativism of, 149, 151, 180, 181, 242; and Schlick, 132, 282n37; Stenius compared with, 154; on *Tractatus* as logical enterprise, 11, 254n13; two strains of thought in interpretation of, 146, 149; on Wittgenstein and Kant, 34

Material implication, 91, 92

Mathematics: arithmetic, 13, 164; and contingency of reality, 9; formalism, 98, 256n32; logicism, 13, 14, 98, 256n33; necessity of sentences of, 97–99, 288n110; "new logic" stimulated by, 13; non-Euclidean geometries, 13, 14; as outside sphere of meaningful, 39; Wittgenstein studying, 12

Maury, Anders, 264n19

Mauthner, Fritz, 25, 26–28, 33, 258n47

Meaning: completeness of, 112; context principle on meaning of names, 79, 157, 160, 263n12; as contingent, 38, 106, 140, 179, 210, 248; determinateness of, 111–15, 118, 119, 150, 179, 279n22, 286n84; drawing the limits

Meaning *(continued)*
of, 37, 70–71; Dummett's semantic criterion for realism, 104–8, 156; of elementary sentences, 75–76; ethics as outside realm of, 236; extensional semantics of *Tractatus*, 80, 84–85; Frege distinguishing reference from, 158–59, 160, 166, 286n96, 287n97; ineffability of conditions of, 115–17, 291n145; of language as such, 116; of life, 219; logical empiricists' criterion for, 139–40, 144, 283n50; logical sentences as meaningless, 39, 93–94; logic as ultimate foundation of, 88, 152–53; in natural languages, 18, 19–20, 22, 65; realm of the meaningful, 75–85; of sentences, 64–69; situation as meaning of sentence, 64, 69; structure of the meaningful, 37; substance as prerequisite for, 49; of symbols, 72, 267n48; "a thought is a meaningful sentence," 38; of the world, 7, 210, 212–13, 214, 238. *See also* Picture theory of meaning

Metaphysics: Hume on, 283n48; logical empiricists on, 137–40; Malcolm on tractarian ontology as, 173; of natural language, 107, 121; *Tractatus* on, 88, 137–40, 145–46

Mill, John Stuart, 77

Modalities, 84, 270n65

Monk, Ray, 12, 31

Morality: contingency and determinism as incompatible with responsibility, 201; ethics distinguished from, 222, 224–34, 299n58; living without guilt and responsibility, 221. *See also* Ethics

Moran, John D., 219, 254n11, 254n17

Murder, 228, 230, 231, 233

Murti, T. R. V., 299n65

Music, in Schopenhauer's hierarchy, 205

Mystical, the, 36, 216, 234, 246, 257n39, 295n33

Naive realism, 8, 9

Names: in completely analyzed sentences, 117, 125, 163; context principle on meaning of, 78–79, 157, 160, 170, 263n12, 270n62; elementary sentences consisting of, 76, 168–69, 184; elucidation of, 103, 163, 164, 165, 166, 167, 289n114; Frege on, 158–59; as having reference not meaning, 76, 117, 267n48, 279n22; as logical constructions, 77; and Malcolm's interpretation of logical analysis, 177; Maslow on, 150; nominalistic interpretation of, 77–78, 264n19; in pictorial relationship, 55; proper names, 77, 159, 167, 170; as protosigns, 76, 163; as referring to objects, 76–80, 155, 157–71, 173–74; rigid designator view of, 77, 167, 170, 287n98, 289n115; Russell on, 159–60; as simple, 76, 86, 111; in ultimate analysis of a sentence, 90, 184; unanalyzable, 131

Natural language: contingency of, 137; conventional assignment of meaning in, 65; Frege and Russell's criticism of, 18–21, 159; indexicality of, 278n15; logical form underlying, 89, 91, 108; Mauthner on, 27; metaphysics of, 107, 121; philosophy arising from ambiguities of, 39, 89, 273n84; quantificational expressions in, 83, 271n71; simplicity and, 126; symbolic systems compared with, 74; Wittgenstein on well-orderedness of, 20–21, 22, 89, 113, 256n37, 278n12

Natural laws, 99–101, 138

Necessity: conceptual, 254n12; contingency of reality and necessary truths, 8–9; the contingent for coming to grips with, 262n7; ethics as concerned with, 38; as grammatical for Maslow, 151; of internal properties, 45, 46; nonlogical, 97–103; and saying-showing distinction, 18. *See also* Logical necessity

Negative sentences, truth of, 58, 265n24

Neurath, Otto, 284n59

Nietzsche, Friedrich, 258n57

Nirvana, 229, 232, 299n65

Nominalism, 77–78, 107, 264n19

Non-Euclidean geometries, 13, 14

Nonlogical necessity, 97–103

Notation, 16, 17, 18, 22, 72, 87–88

Notebooks (Wittgenstein): on determinateness of meaning, 111–12, 277n9, 277n10, 277n11, 277n12; on ethics, 23, 186, 253n3; on happiness, 210, 219; human experience as central to, 1–2; on intuition, 15; logical insights prior to ontological issues in, 125, 178, 182; on logical relationships as shown, 21; "logic must take care of itself," 87; on meaning in natural languages, 19; on meaning of life as God, 219; on one world soul, 199, 206, 227; on others and ethics, 225; personal material in, 31, 259n65; picture theory of meaning in, 22–23; on relations and properties as objects, 78, 270n50; on Russell's theory of types, 96; Schopenhauer's ideas in, 28; *Secret Notebooks*, 258n62, 259n65, 292n2; on self-sufficiency of logic, 17; on simplicity of objects, 118, 122–26, 127, 128, 177–79, 281n33; on solipsism, 199; on suffering and happiness, 226; on suicide, 189; on two ways of viewing the world, 223–24; on waxing and waning of the world, 213; on Wittgenstein's work under Russell, 12

"Notes Dictated to Moore" (Wittgenstein), 12, 22, 78, 115–16, 257n39, 265n27, 293n13

"Notes on Logic" (Wittgenstein), 12, 22, 78, 257n39, 289n119

Numbers, 98, 274n92

Objects: essence of, 46; external properties of, 45, 46, 77; formal objects, 164, 288n8; forms of, 45, 46, 49–50; identity as not relation between, 95, 288n112; identity conditions for, 45, 46, 163, 167–68, 184, 262n10; infinite number postulated, 263n14; internal properties of, 45–46, 77; Ishiguro on identity of, 160–61; knowing, 164, 174–75, 184; as logical entities, 47, 121–26, 129, 162–63, 164; Malcolm and physical interpretation of, 127, 173, 182–83; Maslow on tractarian, 145, 149–52; as material, 47, 127, 131, 170–71, 182–83, 262n11, 281n33; names as referring to, 76–80, 155, 157–71, 173–74; nature of, 120–29; other views of tractarian, 126–28; in pictorial relationship, 54; pictures as not depicting, 52; as sense-data, 127–28, 131, 145, 149, 170–71; simplicity of, 48–49, 86, 109–26, 151–52, 154–55, 172, 173, 177–79, 280n25; situations distinguished from, 264n16; states of affairs as composed of, 44–45, 49–50, 184, 277n8; and states of affairs as mutually dependent, 46–48; as "substance of the world," 47, 48, 110, 160, 172; in traditional ontology, 40–41; two ways of looking at, 224; use determining what are, 266n31; varieties of types of, 45, 262n10

Ogden, C. K., 290n137

On Certainty (Wittgenstein), 1–2, 4, 275n

Ontology: characteristics of tractarian, 109; ethics and proper interpretation

322 Index

Ontology *(continued)*
of, 241–44; extrinsic motivation of Wittgenstein's, 38; Frege's platonism, 16, 19, 92, 145, 278n15; Ishiguro and McGuinness on tractarian, 154–71, 181–82, 243–44; language and, 7–8, 108–9, 121, 125, 129, 130–32, 172, 174, 183–85; as logical construction, 2, 108–9, 121, 129, 148, 185, 236, 242, 244–45; logic as independent of, 17; Malcolm on tractarian, 171–80, 242–43; Maslow on tractarian, 132–34, 144–53, 181, 242; order of components of *Tractatus*, 23; other views on tractarian, 129–80; picture theory requiring, 38; Russell's empiricism and, 16, 19, 92; Stenius on tractarian, 153–54, 181, 242; in *Tractatus*, 7–9, 40–52, 80, 85, 104–85, 270n64; traditional approach to, 40–41. *See also* Objects
Ostension, 161, 287n102
Others, 225–27, 231–32
Otherworldliness, 245

Paradoxes of self-reference, 13–14, 17, 95–96
Particulars, names applying to, 77–78, 264n19
Peano axioms, 164
Pears, David F., 180, 242–43, 253n5, 254n11, 289n113
Peirce, Charles Sanders, 13, 81, 139, 255n22
Perloff, Marjorie, 257n43
Peterson, Donald, 254n11
Philosophical Investigations
(Wittgenstein): as antirealist, 2, 3; human experience as central to, 1–2; Malcolm on *Tractatus* and, 172, 176; on ostension, 287n102; on philosophical theses, 272n83; on semantic ineffability, 278n17; on simples, 171; on solipsism, 295n27; on standard meter, 285n76; tractarian themes in, 275n; on use, 162
Philosophical Remarks (Wittgenstein), 114, 278n17, 281n34
Philosophy: change in Wittgenstein's view of, 272n83; clarification as aim of, 10, 144; elucidation as aim of, 103; as method not subject, 88–89, 102, 138, 275n; necessary inferred from contingent in, 262n7; as outside sphere of meaningful, 39; positivism on, 137, 248; problems resting on misunderstandings of language, 39, 89, 273n84; as therapeutic, 272n83; wonder at existence as impetus for, 296n40. *See also* Epistemology; Linguistic turn; Metaphysics
Picture theory of meaning, 52–63; in compositional interpretation process, 181; as consequence of Wittgenstein's earlier insights, 22–23; contingency of pictures, 62; and creativity, 69–70; language and ontology related by, 8; and language's extralinguistic significance, 155; and logical atomism, 153, 291n145; as logical basis of symbolic representation, 108; logical form and pictorial form, 55–57; logically impossible pictures, 62–63; and meaning-as-use view, 157; ontological theory implied by, 38, 184; order of components of *Tractatus*, 23; pictorial form and pictorial relation, 53–55; pictorial form as shown not depicted, 58–59, 86, 114; pictures as facts, 52–53, 263n16; and semantic ineffability, 115, 116; sentences as pictures, 63–69; theory of types and, 18; "third man" in picturing relationship, 266n34; thoughts as pictures, 60–63, 70; truth and falsity in, 57–58; use determining what is a picture, 53, 266n31

Pitcher, George, 11
Platonic forms, 204–5, 295n29
Populäre Schriften (Boltzmann), 21
Positivism: on science and philosophy, 137, 247. *See also* Logical empiricism
Possible worlds, 43, 110, 261n5
Prajñā, 297n43
Principles of Mathematics, The (Russell), 12, 13, 14
Principles of Mechanics (Hertz), 21, 22
Proper names, 77, 159, 167, 170
Properties: external, 45, 46, 77, 167, 290n139; names applying to, 77–78. *See also* Internal properties
Propositional attitudes, 84, 266n30
Propositions: unity of, 67. *See also* Sentences
Punishment, 7, 213, 296n36, 296n37
Putnam, Hilary, 277n5

Quantification, 13, 81–84, 86, 94–95, 255n22
Quine, W. V. O., 277n5

Ramified theory of types, 14, 256n27
Ramsey, Frank, 142, 283n53
Realism: commonsense, 8, 131; critical, 8, 9; Dummett's semantic criterion for, 104–8, 156; Fregean conceptual, 201–2; naive, 8, 9; and objectivity of values, 4; *Philosophical Investigations* seen as source of antirealism, 2, 3; reading the *Tractatus* nonrealistically, 2, 184–85; and reference of names, 157; solipsism coinciding, 198–200; of *Tractatus*, 2, 3, 104–9, 121, 129, 146, 155, 156, 174, 177, 180–85, 202, 242–43, 294n22
Reality: as compositional, 70; contingency of, 8; and language, 4, 89, 131, 155–56, 182; logical form as form of, 56–57, 265n22; logic establishing fundamental traits of, 88; in Maslow's interpretation of Wittgenstein, 148, 284n68; scientific theories as models of, 22; sentences as attempting to determine, 68–69; two-valued logical form of, 105; and the world in *Tractatus*, 261n6. *See also* World, the
Reductio ad absurdum, 104
Reference: Frege distinguishing meaning from, 158–59, 160, 166, 286n96, 287n97; logical constants as not referring, 15, 17, 22, 43, 92, 257n39, 262n9; names as referring to objects, 76–80, 155, 157–71, 173–74; names having only, 76, 117, 267n48, 279n22
Relations, names applying to, 77–78, 270n61
Relativism: antirealism and ethical, 4; of Maslow, 149, 151, 180, 181, 242; of Mauthner, 26; of Stenius, 153, 180, 181, 242; in Wittgenstein's later work, 2, 3
Remarks on the Foundations of Mathematics (Wittgenstein), 1–2, 274n95
Repentance, 221
Rewards, 7, 213, 296n36, 296n37
Rhees, Rush, 31, 247
Rigid designators, 77, 167, 170, 287n98, 289n115
Russell, Bertrand: axiom of infinity of, 14, 95; axiom of reducibility of, 256n27; empiricism of, 16, 19, 92; epistemology as concern of, 134–35; on intensional constructions, 293n12; on knowledge by description and by acquaintance, 160, 290n139; on logical and grammatical form, 16, 21, 27; on logical laws, 255n25; on logical objects, 15–16; on logic as subject of *Tractatus*, 11, 246; on logicism, 14, 98; on names, 159–60; on natural language, 18, 19, 159, 256n35; on

324   Index

Russell, Bertrand *(continued)*
negative facts, 58; and nonlogical necessity, 120; on paradox in Frege, 13–14; *The Principles of Mathematics*, 12, 13, 14; on the subject, 293n10; theory of descriptions of, 16, 19, 90, 91, 159–60, 269n55, 279n22; theory of types of, 14, 17–18, 95–96, 268n51; on Wittgenstein after the war, 239, 300n72; on Wittgenstein on logic and sin, 11; Wittgenstein's criticism of, 135, 282n45; on Wittgenstein's ethics, 254n15, 295n31; Wittgenstein studies with, 12, 134

Safety, 224
Saint-Simon, Claude-Henri de Rouvroy, comte de, 137
Saying-showing distinction: "about what one cannot speak, one must remain silent," 36; and absolutist view of logic, 153, 183; and contingent-necessary distinction, 18, 60; ethics as not sayable, 236; and impossibility of depicting pictorial form, 58–60; and logical empiricism, 144; and logical necessity as linguistic, 22; and the mystical, 36, 234, 257n39; *Tractatus* as showing not describing, 103, 141; as true dichotomy, 60; in Wittgenstein's earliest work, 257n39, 265n27
Schlick, Moritz: and Maslow, 132, 282n37; as source for Wittgenstein's ethical views, 3, 186, 284n59; Wittgenstein on ethical views of, 215; Wittgenstein on Vienna Circle and, 143; Wittgenstein's conversations with, 3, 10, 141–42
Schopenhauer, Arthur: on compassion, 28, 205, 227, 231–32; as defensive thinker, 239–40; dual nature of work of, 239; on early Christianity, 31, 33; on Eastern philosophy, 33, 260n70;

on exemplary great men, 247; Fregean conceptual realism versus idealism of, 201–2; on individual versus metaphysical subject, 191, 192–94, 199; on knowing versus willing subject, 191, 194–96; on life of knowledge, 218; platonic forms in system of, 204–5, 295n29; on renunciation of the will, 205, 219–20, 229–30, 232; response to work of, 239, 241; on the subject, 191, 200, 202; "where real depth starts his stops," 294n23; on the will, 28, 30, 191, 258n56, 258n57; on will and action, 203–6; Wittgenstein as influenced by, 23–24, 28–30, 190, 191, 257n41, 292n6; on the world as representation, 194, 200, 220
Science: necessity of sentences of, 99–101; parts as outside sphere of meaningful, 39; philosophy distinguished from, 88, 138; positivism on, 137, 138; in Schopenhauer's hierarchy, 205; scientific worldview, 10, 248; the speculative contrasted with, 248; Wittgenstein on, 138–39
Scientific Conception of the World, The (Vienna Circle manifesto), 143
Secret Notebooks (Wittgenstein), 258n62, 259n65, 292n2
Self-reference, paradoxes of, 13–14, 17, 95–96
Sense-data: and knowledge by acquaintance, 290n139; objects as, 47, 127–28, 131, 145, 149, 170–71; and Russell's theory of descriptions, 19, 159
Sentences: accidental and essential features of, 71, 74; completely analyzed, 113, 117, 123, 124, 125, 163; complex, 80–85, 99; context principle on meaning of names in, 78–79, 157, 160, 170, 263n12, 270n62; essence of, 69; form of, 66–67; logical form of reality shown by, 60; meaning of, 64–

69; pictorial relationship in, 55; as pictures, 63–69; potentially infinite number of, 69–70; as showing their meanings, 68; situations as meanings of, 64, 69; structure and form distinguished, 268n52; as structured wholes, 68; as tableaux vivants, 68; "a thought is a meaningful sentence," 38; as thoughts in perceptible form, 63, 70. See also Elementary sentences
Sentence system, 120
Sentential functions, 83, 271n72
Sentential signs, 64–66, 264n19
Sheffer, H. M., 81, 270n66
Signs, 72; and logical syntax, 73; as meaningful ipso facto, 87; sentential, 64–66, 264n19. See also Symbols
Situations: constituents of, 44; disjoint, 200–201; experience as of, 196, 197, 293n17; facts as situations that obtain, 43; forms of, 52; intensional nature of, 58; in logical space, 43–44; as meaning of sentences, 64, 69; pictures and the depicted as, 53, 55, 56, 57, 61, 263n16; sentential signs and, 64; things distinguished from, 264n16
Skinner, Francis, 247
Skolemization, 170, 289n122
Sluga, Hans, 254n20
Smythies, Yorick, 31, 189, 258n61
Solipsism, 198–200, 294n27
"Some Remarks on Logical Form" (Wittgenstein), 102, 132, 274n98
Spinoza, Benedict, 295n30
Sraffa, Piero, 142
States of affairs: as atoms, 41–42, 49; as composed of objects, 44–45, 49–50, 184; forms of, 49–51; intensional nature of, 58; as logically independent, 42, 49, 109, 118, 120, 129, 131, 146, 233, 291n145; Malcolm and physical interpretation of, 173; and objects as mutually dependent, 46–48; as

obtaining or not, 43, 262n8; and spatio-temporal location, 262n11; structure of, 49–52
Stein, Gertrude, 257n43
Steiner, George, 278n15
Stenius, Eric: on ontology of Tractatus, 153–54, 181, 242; on picture theory of meaning, 153, 181, 291n145; relativism of, 153, 180, 181, 242; on Tractatus as logical enterprise, 11
Strømberg, Arvind, 247
Structure: of facts, 50–52; pictorial relation defined in terms of, 53–54; of states of affairs, 49–52
Subject: Humean view of, 193, 198, 229, 231; idealist notion of, 194, 195; as limit of the world, 202, 233, 236; materialist notion of, 195; metaphysical versus individual, 191, 192–94, 198–200, 202, 215, 235, 238–39; as not belonging to the world, 199; Schopenhauer on, 191, 200, 202; the will and the willing, 203–10; willing versus knowing, 191, 194–96
Substance: as logical construction, 184, 200, 291n149; and logic as two sides of same coin, 202; "objects as substance of the world," 47, 48, 110, 160, 172; as prerequisite for meaningfulness of language, 49, 184; Stenius's relativist interpretation of, 154; as transcendental, 236–37
Substitution interpretation of first-order logic, 82–83
Substitution principle, 164–66
Suffering, 226–27, 228, 229, 231–32, 298n55
Sufficient reason, principle of, 100, 101, 194, 295n28
Suicide, 189–90, 218, 235, 292n5
Symbols, 71–75; all systems as essentially the same, 269n53; content of, 72; defined, 71; essential, 74; form

Symbols *(continued)*
  of, 72–73; legitimacy of, 87–88; and logical syntax, 73–74; meaning of, 72, 267n48; picture theory as basis of symbolic systems, 108; and signs, 72
Synonyms, 72
Syntax, logical, 69, 72–74

Tagore, Rabindranath, 142
Taoism, 33, 298n54
Tarski, Alfred, 16
Tautologies: logically valid sentences as, 93–94, 119, 120; logicism seeing mathematical sentences as, 98; as showing that they're tautologies, 21, 280n24; tautological pictures as impossible, 61–62, 266n29; Wittgenstein's extended sense of, 273n87
Theory of descriptions, 16, 19, 90, 91, 159–60, 269n55, 279n22
Theory of types, 14, 17–18, 95–96, 268n51
Things, *see* Objects
Thought: as contingent, 38, 61–62; drawing the limits of, 36–37, 60–61, 63, 70, 89–90, 136, 200; everyday language as "dressing up," 113; and language, 37–38, 63, 89, 135–36, 192–93, 202; logic as prior to, 137; logic as ultimate foundation of, 88, 152–53; Malcolm on ontology and, 172, 174, 175; as pictures, 60–63, 70, 175; sentence and situation related by thinking, 64–66; sentences as thoughts in perceptible form, 63, 70; "a thought is a meaningful sentence," 38; two-valued logical form of, 105; what can be said and what can be thought as the same, 37–38
Time: contingency of events separated in, 201; death as temporal dimension of our existence, 223; moral point of view and, 222. *See also* Future

Timelessness, 222–23
Tolstoy, Leo, 30, 258n59
Toulmin, Stephen, 11, 24–25, 26, 253n4
Tractatus (Wittgenstein): aims of, 35–37; antimetaphysical trend of, 10; on axioms, 14–15; background of ethical views of, 24–34; background of logical views of, 10–24; characteristics of ontology of, 109; on contingency of reality, 8; and epistemology, 61, 85, 135–37; on ethics, 186–249; extensional semantics of, 80, 84–85; ground-plan of, 38–39; human experience as central to, 1–2; ideal of transparent notation motivating, 17, 22; on impossibility of stepping out of frame of reference, 59; intensional ontology of, 80, 85, 270n64; Ishiguro and McGuinness on ontology of, 154–71, 181–82, 243–44; Kantian spirit of, 130, 181, 184; on knowledge by description and by acquaintance, 290n139; on language, 63–85; as linguistic idealism, 294n22; on logical and grammatical form, 21; on logical constants not referring, 17, 22, 43, 92, 257n39, 262n9; logical versus ethical aspects of, 4–9, 234–44; logic in, 85–97; main themes of, 35–103; Malcolm on ontology of, 171–80, 242–43; Malcolm on *Philosophical Investigations* and, 172, 176; Maslow on ontology of, 132–34, 144–53, 181, 242; on Mauthner, 26, 27; and metaphysics, 88, 137–40, 145–46; as monistic and absolutistic, 2, 183; more than one interpretation possible for, 183; nominalistic interpretation of, 77–78, 264n19; on nonlogical necessity, 97–103; nonrealistic reading of, 2, 184–85; as not an ethical theory, 245–46; ontology of, 7–9, 40–52, 104–85; order of components of, 23; other views on ontology

of, 129–80; on philosophical problems, 39; point of book as ethical, 5–6, 35, 39, 187; positive part of, 38; reading as coherent whole, 1, 6, 11, 238, 241, 243–44; as realist, 2, 3, 104–9, 121, 129, 146, 155, 156, 174, 177, 180–85, 202, 242–43, 294n22; reception of, 241; response to ethical views of, 10–11, 246–47; saying-showing distinction as central to, 18; Schopenhauer's ideas in, 28, 29, 258n56; on scientific worldview, 10; status of sentences of, 102–3, 106–7, 141, 274n101; Stenius on ontology of, 153–54, 181, 242; on tautologies as showing themselves, 21, 280n24; on throwing away the ladder, 102; two-valued logic of, 86, 104, 105–6, 112, 178–79, 183; as understood only by those who have already thought the thoughts, 239, 300n67; on use, 161–62, 166
Transcendental, the: ethics as transcendental, 102, 225, 235–39; limits associated with, 237; linguistic turn providing new notion of, 245; logic as transcendental, 236–37; two notions of, 237–38
Translation, 69, 198
Truth: determinateness of meaning and, 112; of elementary sentences, 91; of logically valid sentences, 93; logical truths, 17; pictures staking claim to, 62; redundancy view of, 267n44; Tarski on, 16; *Tractatus* theory of, 57–58; uniform substitution preserving, 167
Truth functions, 80–85, 90, 91, 92, 108
Truth tables, 80, 81, 91–92, 255n24
Two-valued logic, 86, 104, 105–6, 112, 178–79, 183

"Über Sinn und Bedeutung" (Frege), 18, 165, 273n89

Universal quantifier, 81–84, 271n72, 271n74
Universals, 77–78, 264n19, 270n61
Unsaturated concepts, 67, 267n43

Values: absolute and relative, 211, 226, 230–31, 236, 242; as accessible, 236; action and, 7, 187, 189, 209, 213–14, 297n50; ethical versus moral, 222; facts distinguished from, 25, 139, 183, 297n50; ineffability of, 210–12; as in the world, 236, 238; as not contingent, 9, 102, 183, 209, 210; objectivity of, 4, 211; as outside the world, 7, 9, 187, 210, 236; reality of, 189; as transcendent, 238; will as bearer of, 201, 238–39. *See also* Good, the
Variables, 73, 268n49
Verifiability, 140, 283n51
Vienna, Wittgenstein influenced by culture of, 24–25
Vienna Circle: Boltzmann and Hertz influencing, 21; on *Tractatus* as logical enterprise, 10, 132, 241, 246; Wittgenstein and, 132, 141–44. *See also* Logical empiricism

Waismann, Friedrich: as source for Wittgenstein's ethical views, 3, 186; Wittgenstein's conversations with, 3, 10, 142, 186, 211, 215, 218, 290n135
Watzka, Heinrich, 254n11
Weiler, Gershon, 258n47
Weininger, Otto, 30, 32, 260n66, 260n67
Wijdeveld, Paul, 257n44
Will: and action, 195, 203, 206–7, 208–9, 212, 213–14; as attitude toward the world, 213; as bearer of ethical values, 201, 238–39; double aspect of, 209; ethical categories associated with, 207, 209; ethical ideal as harmony of individual and metaphysical wills,

Will *(continued)*
  227–31, 233–34; experiencing ourselves as, 195–96, 204–5; freedom of the, 100, 201, 208; of God, 215–16, 217, 296n38; the good will, 214–16, 219, 227, 296n38; knowing versus willing subject, 191, 194–96; meaning of the world determined by, 238; as outside experience, 206; renunciation of, 205, 219–20, 229–30, 232, 239; Schopenhauer on, 28, 30, 191, 258n56, 258n57; as thing-in-itself, 195, 196, 203–4; and the willing subject, 203–10; wishing contrasted with, 206–7, 208–9, 214–15; the world's relation to, 207–8, 212–13
Winch, Peter G., 176, 177
Wishing, 206–7, 208–9, 214–15
Wittgenstein, Ludwig: antipsychologism of, 64–65, 136; architectural taste of, 25, 257n44; Christianity's influence on, 30–31, 33; continuity in work of, 3–4, 157, 171, 172, 175–76; *Culture and Value*, 3, 29, 32, 259n65; as defensive thinker, 239–40; and Eastern philosophy, 33–34; and empiricism, 255n25; and epistemology, 12, 65, 134–37, 265n27; ethical concerns of, 188–89; ethical experience of, 239–41; Hertz and Boltzmann influencing, 21–22; homosexuality of, 31–32, 188, 221, 297n50; influences on ethics of, 28–34; interest in logic, 12; Jewishness of, 32; and Kant, 29, 130, 134, 181, 184, 191, 260n3; and Kraus, 26; "Lectures on Religious Belief," 3, 296n37; literary and musical tastes of, 25, 257n43; on logical analysis, 20, 21; and the logical empiricists, 10, 132, 134–44, 283n59; and Mauthner, 26–28, 33; on money, 188, 300n71; on natural language, 18–21, 256n37; "Notes Dictated to Moore," 12, 22, 78, 115–16, 257n39, 265n27, 293n13; "Notes on Logic," 12, 22, 78, 257n39, 289n119; on objectivity of values, 4; *On Certainty*, 1–2, 4, 275n; personal ethical influence of, 247–48, 301n82; in personal relationships, 188; *Philosophical Remarks*, 114, 278n17, 281n34; *Remarks on the Foundations of Mathematics*, 1–2, 274n95; Schopenhauer influencing, 23–24, 28–30, 190, 191, 257n41, 292n6; "Some Remarks on Logical Form," 102, 132, 274n98; sources of ethical views of, 3, 186; studies with Russell, 12, 134; transition from monism to pluralism, 2–3; as trying to live up to his ideals, 247–48; vanity and low esteem as tension in, 30; and Vienna Circle, 132, 141–44; Viennese culture influencing, 24–25; wartime experiences of, 31, 188, 240, 258n62. *See also* "Lecture on Ethics"; *Notebooks*; *Philosophical Investigations*; *Tractatus*
Wittgenstein's Vienna (Janik and Toulmin), 24–25
World, the: action as in, 212; describing completely, 169; different senses of term, 261n5; ethically contingent character of, 9, 187, 209, 210, 214, 220, 239, 242; ethical view of, 238, 249; ethics as limit of, 237; ethics' relation to, 186–87, 205–6, 209, 225, 233, 235; as everything that is the case, 40; explanations of as going beyond, 138; forms of, 45, 48, 52; as good, 216; happiness as being in harmony with, 217–20; holistic approach to, 41; how it is versus that it is, 197, 216; and language, 197; liberation from, 232, 234, 235, 238, 239; as limited whole, 89, 197, 220, 237, 246; limits of as limits of logic, 200, 236, 237, 238, 294n22; "the limits of my language mean the

limits of my world," 147, 197–98; meaning of, 7, 210, 212–13, 214, 238; objects as substance of, 47, 48, 110, 160, 172; as part of logical space, 43; possible worlds, 43, 110, 261n5; and reality in *Tractatus*, 261n6; as representation for Schopenhauer, 194, 200, 220; sentences as attempting to determine, 68–69; states of affairs composing, 43; subject as limit of, 202, 233, 236; the subject as not belonging to, 199; sub specie aeterni, 197, 222, 227, 235, 237, 239; suffering in, 227; as totality of facts, 40–41, 109; two ways of viewing, 89, 223–24, 233, 235, 237; values as in, 236, 238; values as outside of, 7, 9, 187, 210, 236; waxing and waning of, 213, 214; the will's relation to, 207–8, 212–13; wonder at existence of, 216, 222, 296n40; "world and life as one," 234–44

Wright, Georg Henrik von, 29, 31

Cultural Memory in the Present

Michael Naas, *Taking on the Tradition: Jacques Derrida and the Legacies of Deconstruction*

Herlinde Pauer-Studer, ed., *Constructions of Practical Reason: Interviews on Moral and Political Philosophy*

Jean-Luc Marion, *Being Given That: Toward a Phenomenology of Givenness*

Theodor W. Adorno and Max Horkheimer, *Dialectic of Enlightenment*

Ian Balfour, *The Rhetoric of Romantic Prophecy*

Martin Stokhof, *World and Life as One: Ethics and Ontology in Wittgenstein's Early Thought*

Gianni Vattimo, *Nietzsche: An Introduction*

Jacques Derrida, *Negotiations: Interventions and Interviews, 1971-1998*, ed. Elizabeth Rottenberg

Brett Levinson, *The Ends of Literature: Post-transition and Neoliberalism in the Wake of the "Boom"*

Timothy J. Reiss, *Against Autonomy: Global Dialectics of Cultural Exchange*

Hent de Vries and Samuel Weber, eds., *Religion and Media*

Niklas Luhmann, *Theories of Distinction: Re-Describing the Descriptions of Modernity*, ed. and introd. William Rasch

Johannes Fabian, *Anthropology with an Attitude: Critical Essays*

Michel Henry, *I am the Truth: Toward a Philosophy of Christianity*

Gil Anidjar, *"Our Place in Al-Andalus": Kabbalah, Philosophy, Literature in Arab-Jewish Letters*

Hélène Cixous and Jacques Derrida, *Veils*

F. R. Ankersmit, *Historical Representation*

F. R. Ankersmit, *Political Representation*

Elissa Marder, *Dead Time: Temporal Disorders in the Wake of Modernity (Baudelaire and Flaubert)*

Reinhart Koselleck, *The Practice of Conceptual History: Timing History, Spacing Concepts*

Niklas Luhmann, *The Reality of the Mass Media*

Hubert Damisch, *A Childhood Memory by Piero della Francesca*

Hubert Damisch, *A Theory of /Cloud/: Toward a History of Painting*

Jean-Luc Nancy, *The Speculative Remark (One of Hegel's bon mots)*

Jean-François Lyotard, *Soundproof Room: Malraux's Anti-Aesthetics*

Jan Patočka, *Plato and Europe*

Hubert Damisch, *Skyline: The Narcissistic City*

Isabel Hoving, *In Praise of New Travelers: Reading Caribbean Migrant Women Writers*

Richard Rand, ed., *Futures: Of Derrida*

William Rasch, *Niklas Luhmann's Modernity: The Paradox of System Differentiation*

Jacques Derrida and Anne Dufourmantelle, *Of Hospitality*

Jean-François Lyotard, *The Confession of Augustine*

Kaja Silverman, *World Spectators*

Samuel Weber, *Institution and Interpretation: Expanded Edition*

Jeffrey S. Librett, *The Rhetoric of Cultural Dialogue: Jews and Germans in the Epoch of Emancipation*

Ulrich Baer, *Remnants of Song: Trauma and the Experience of Modernity in Charles Baudelaire and Paul Celan*

Samuel C. Wheeler III, *Deconstruction as Analytic Philosophy*

David S. Ferris, *Silent Urns: Romanticism, Hellenism, Modernity*

Rodolphe Gasché, *Of Minimal Things: Studies on the Notion of Relation*

Sarah Winter, *Freud and the Institution of Psychoanalytic Knowledge*

Samuel Weber, *The Legend of Freud: Expanded Edition*

Aris Fioretos, ed., *The Solid Letter: Readings of Friedrich Hölderlin*

J. Hillis Miller / Manuel Asensi, *Black Holes / J. Hillis Miller; or, Boustrophedonic Reading*

Miryam Sas, *Fault Lines: Cultural Memory and Japanese Surrealism*

Peter Schwenger, *Fantasm and Fiction: On Textual Envisioning*

Didier Maleuvre, *Museum Memories: History, Technology, Art*

Jacques Derrida, *Monolingualism of the Other; or, The Prosthesis of Origin*

Andrew Baruch Wachtel, *Making a Nation, Breaking a Nation: Literature and Cultural Politics in Yugoslavia*

Niklas Luhmann, *Love as Passion: The Codification of Intimacy*

Mieke Bal, ed., *The Practice of Cultural Analysis: Exposing Interdisciplinary Interpretation*

Jacques Derrida and Gianni Vattimo, eds., *Religion*

The authorized representative in the EU for product safety and compliance is:
Mare Nostrum Group
B.V Doelen 72
4831 GR Breda
The Netherlands